Post-Soviet Power

Post-Soviet Power tells the story of the Russian electricity system and examines the politics of its transformation from a ministry to a market. Susanne A. Wengle shifts our focus away from what has been at the center of post-Soviet political economy – corruption and the lack of structural reforms – to draw attention to political struggles to establish a state with the ability to govern the economy. She highlights the importance of hands-on economic planning by authorities – post-Soviet developmentalism – and details the market mechanisms that have been created. This book argues that these observations urge us to think of economies and political authority as mutually constitutive, in Russia and beyond. Whereas the political arena often thinks of market arrangements resulting from political institutions, Russia's marketization demonstrates that the political arena is also produced by the market arrangements that actors create. Taking this reflexivity seriously suggests a view of economies and markets as constructed and contingent entities.

Susanne A. Wengle is a Research Fellow and lecturer in the political science department at the University of Chicago. Her research has appeared in *Studies in Comparative International Development, Economy and Society, Europe-Asia Studies, Russian Analytical Digest*, and *Chicago Policy Review* and is forthcoming in *Regulation & Governance*. She is currently working on a project on the political economy of agriculture and food systems in Russia and the United States.

T0384533

Post-Soviet Power

State-Led Development and Russia's Marketization

SUSANNE A. WENGLE
University of Chicago

CAMBRIDGE
UNIVERSITY PRESS

32 Avenue of the Americas, New York NY 10013-2473, USA

Cambridge University Press is part of the University of Cambridge.

It furthers the University's mission by disseminating knowledge in the pursuit of education, learning and research at the highest international levels of excellence.

www.cambridge.org
Information on this title: www.cambridge.org/9781107420922

First published 2015
First paperback edition 2015

A catalogue record for this publication is available from the British Library

Library of Congress Cataloguing in Publication data
Wengle, Susanne A., 1977–
Post-Soviet power: state-led development and Russia's marketization /
Susanne A. Wengle, University of Chicago Lecturer
Department of Political Science, University of Chicago.
    pages   cm
Includes bibliographical references and index.
ISBN 978-1-107-07248-0 (hardback)
1. Russia (Federation) – Economic policy – 1991–   2. Post-communism –
Russia (Federation)   I. Title.
HC340.12.W46   2014
337.47–dc23   2014020954

ISBN 978-1-107-07248-0 Hardback
ISBN 978-1-107-42092-2 Paperback

For Jay, Oren, Artur, Aino, and Alex, the light of my day.

Contents

Tables

Figures

Acknowledgments

I incurred many debts while researching and writing this book; the following is a partial accounting that can hardly do justice to the support I feel so privileged to have received.

First I would like to thank my dissertation committee at UC Berkeley, Steven Vogel, Kiren Chaudhry, Jason Wittenberg, and Yuri Slezkine, who taught me to value history but to keep looking for lessons beyond a particular time and place. I am grateful for the many conversations that molded and enriched my understanding of political economy and Russia, and for advice in matters ranging from academic to practical. My dissertation would not have shape-shifted into this book at the University of Chicago without the critical support by Gary Herrigel. His intellectual energy and generosity are unparalleled, and I am truly fortunate to have been able to benefit from them. Wendy Brown, Ruth Collier, Stephen Collier, Julie Cooper, Andrew Janos, Stan Markus, Bob Orttung, Douglas Rogers, Peter Rutland, Alberto Simpers, Dan Slater, Edward Walker, Yves Winter, David Woodruff, and Alexei Yurchak also provided thoughtful input, invaluable support, and criticism at different stages of the project. Ivan Ascher, Jennifer Brass, Jennifer Dixon, Jonathan Hassid, Elif Kale, Jody LaPorte, Jay Rehm, Regine Spector, Rachel Stern, and Zhivka Valiavicharska read many early drafts of this work. I owe them a great deal for their friendship and for countless comments on my work. I also would like to thank the anonymous reviewers enlisted by Cambridge University Press for close readings of the manuscript when it was in a much rougher shape and for their suggestions how to improve it. I want to acknowledge the generous financial support by the Swiss National

Science Foundation, IREX, the William Davidson Institute, the Janggen Poehn Stiftung, and – at UC Berkeley – the Institute for East European and Eurasian Studies, the Institute for International Studies, and the Department of Political Science. I thank Robert Dreesen for shepherding my work through the publication process with great care and professionalism, and Kostya Dyakonov and Natalia Forrat for expert research assistance. All remaining errors are entirely my own.

In Russia, I have benefited greatly from critical support of friends, colleagues, and strangers, who volunteered their time and shared their experience of a difficult period in Russian history. I am truly grateful for the people who agreed to be interviewed for this project. Often on weekends and in their spare time, and usually over tea, they shared their views and experiences and told me about their role in the transformation of the electricity system. With every detail they added an invaluable puzzle piece to my understanding of the matter. I am particularly indebted to Margarita Mezonshnik and Alexey Klaptsov, who opened countless doors, behind which I learned more about the electricity sector's transformation than anywhere else. I also thank the people who have generously opened their personal archives, that is, their collection of newspaper articles that seemed particularly important to them, often stretching back years. In three different cities, three such personal archives produced gems that I would not have been able to locate by myself.

Select elements of the book were originally published as "Post-Soviet Developmentalism and the Political Economy of Russia's Electricity Sector Liberalization" in *Studies in Comparative International Development* 47, no. 1 (2012); they are reprinted here with the permission of Springer Science and Business Media. Taylor and Francis agreed to the reproduction of Chapter 6, an earlier version of which appeared as "Engineers versus Managers: Experts, Market-Making and State-Building in Putin's Russia" in *Economy and Society* 41, no. 3 (2012).

Last but not least, I would like to thank my parents, who have always supported me and my travels, no matter how outlandish the project or how far-flung the destination. The book is dedicated to Jay, Oren, Artur, Aino, and Alexandra Rehm. Their contributions defy words on paper for they are the light of my day.

Note on Transliteration and Translation

I preserved the original Russian Cyrillic for important concepts and for Russian-language sources. I transliterated Russian words that are frequently used in English-speaking media and academic discourse (such as *perestroika* and *siloviki)*. For these transliterations I used the ALA transliteration schemes. Following established conventions, I departed from the ALA transliterations for a few names and words that are well known in English (Anatoly rather than Anatolii, and Yeltsin rather than El'tsin). All translations from Russian are my own.

Introduction: Russia's Political Marketization

"Chubais wants electricity to be a purely commercial good. Well, it never was and it never will be."[1]

Post-Soviet Power and Politics

The Russian winter of 2005–2006 was the coldest in a generation. Electricity consumption nationwide had increased steadily during the economic recovery after 1998. When radiators and lights were turned on all over the country in January 2006, consumption levels reached their peak since the collapse of the Soviet Union.[2] The electricity infrastructure strained to keep up with demand, and the media was full of reports of imminent blackouts, emergency measures, and unfortunate provincial towns left in the cold dark, without power and heat for hours and days.

The physical pressures on electricity grids in post-Soviet Russia became a metaphor for the political forces fighting for influence on the transformation of the Soviet-era electricity system. All eyes turned to UES (United Energy Systems, or *Единые Энергетические Системы*), the state-owned electricity monopoly that had been the guarantor of heat and power since

---

[1] Interview #43 with electricity sector economist, Khabarovsk, 20071010.

[2] *Энергия России*, No. 212, January 2006, available at http://www.rao-ees.ru/ru/news/gazeta/ show.cgi?arh_2006.html. Also reported by *Associated Press*, AP Press Release, January 19, 2008. Unlike in the United States, heat in Russia is produced centrally, usually in the same plants as electricity, rather than in individual apartments and houses.

the early days of Soviet Union. For much of the 1990s, Russia's electricity sector looked like a ministry, struggling to reliably provide heat and power. Electricity production was still organized as a vertically integrated, predominantly state-owned monopoly, administered by a bureaucracy that made most production and investment decisions. Despite the apparent lack of change, UES was in the midst of a far-reaching transformation, subject to an ambitious liberalization project. It was a monopoly that was undoing itself. Partly it was unraveling in an unpredictable, ad hoc manner. But the end of UES was mostly an orchestrated dissolution brought about by the sector's liberalization. Liberal reforms unbundled vertically integrated production systems, privatized power plants, created markets for electricity, and ended state control over the price of power. This transformation, pushed ahead by a group of liberal reformers centering around Anatoly Chubais, was as controversial as it was ambitious. Liberalization entailed the reorganization of a vast number of economic relationships. For most of the first two post-Soviet decades, the future of electricity production and of exceptionally valuable power plants was subject to fierce political battles, pitting shifting alliances against the reformers and their vision of private actors trading power on competitive markets.

The threat of blackouts and surging demand for electricity in that cold winter of 2006, and in the years since 1998 more generally, served as a powerful argument *for* liberalization and privatization. It was the "only way," argued liberal reformers, to raise vast amount of capital needed for technological updates and capacity increases.[3] Many parts of Soviet-era infrastructure were fatigued; others had long reached the end of their working life. Some regions had to deal with acute capacity shortfalls. And even while generation capacity in other regions was redundant owing to the economic collapse in the 1990s, nobody disputed that Russia's electricity system needed large-scale investments. But who should pay for the capital upgrades? Who should own the most and the least valuable power plants? How was the system to be modernized and what should happen to users that for years had relied on heavily subsidized

---

[3] Estimates of the overall investment needs in the sector skyrocketed over the years that GOELRO-II was discussed, and eventually reached as much 400–500 billion rubles for the period until 2030. This is according to Anatoly Chubais, who mentioned this sum at a conference "*Энергетика: тормоз или локомотив развития экономики?*" Moscow, February 13, 2007. It was widely noted that this is a very large sum – more than Gazprom, one of the world's largest companies, planned to invest over the same period. The comparison with Gazprom is mentioned in news reports following this conference in *Коммерсантъ*, "РАО ЕЭС пересчитало источники финансирования," February 28, 2007.

electricity? These were critical political questions that underpinned Russia's marketization.

This book tells the story of Russia's electricity system and the politics of its post-Soviet transformation to help us understand the making of Russian capitalism in a new way. Electricity is a basic infrastructure and an energy sector. In Russia, electricity was also an index for Soviet modernity and industrialization. The political battles surrounding the unbundling of monopolies, the privatization of power companies, and the liberalization of tariffs were materially important and symbolically charged in this country with cold and long winters. The story that unfolds, then, is about the marketization of Russia's economy in the wake of Soviet communism.[4] Russia's marketization is also an opportunity to rethink how we theorize economic development elsewhere. I will outline the argument specific to the Russian context first, before turning to the more general claims.

Post-Soviet Developmentalism

My focus shifts away from what has been at the center of the discussion on post-Soviet political economy – the country's corrupt bureaucrats and its authoritarian government – to offer what I hope is a new and useful lens to understand this tumultuous period in Russian history. This book draws attention to the struggles to establish a state with the ability to govern the economy. This ability was elusive during the 1990s, especially during the first few years after the unraveling of the planned economy, but it had been a challenge even prior to that, as successive Soviet leaders sought to compel powerful ministries and factories to comply with their reform plans.[5] Corruption was, and is, indeed absolutely endemic in post-

---

[4] Michel Callon and Koray Calışkan called for attention to processes of economization, stressing that the Economy is "an achievement rather than a starting point or a pre-existing reality that can simply be revealed." Although I started this project well before Callon and Calışkan called for a research program that examine processes of economization, the story of the marketization of Russia's electricity sector in many ways fits the research they call for. Koray Çalışkan and Michel Callon, "Economization, Part 1: Shifting Attention from the Economy towards Processes of Economization," *Economy and Society* 38, no. 3 (2009): 369–398; and Koray Çalışkan and Michel Callon, "Economization, Part 2: A Research Programme for the Study of Markets," *Economy and Society* 39, no. 1 (2010): 1–32.

[5] John Padgett's comparison of the politics of communist economic reforms in the Soviet Union and China presents an argument and overview of these difficulties. See chapter 9 in John Frederick Padgett and Walter W Powell, *The Emergence of Organizations and Markets* (Princeton, NJ: Princeton University Press, 2012), 267.

Soviet Russia, and the political regime has become more authoritarian and chauvinistic and less accountable and tolerant under Vladimir Putin.[6] Albeit important, these attributes neglect another aspect of state power. The reassertion of sovereign authority during Putin's first two terms as president and the elimination of challengers to the central government – the establishment of the famous "power vertical" *(вертикаль власти)* – was also about efforts to rebuild a state with the ability and legitimacy to govern and plan, efforts to return to (or to realize) the modern axiom that the state provides for economic prosperity. Putin wanted to bring back a state that takes charge of progress through hands-on planning, rather than rely on the invisible hand. And years before he became president, this kind of hands-on marketization characterized the approach to economic policy of many regional governments. They opposed the laissez-faire approach advocated by Boris Yeltsin's team of liberal reformers and pursued their own paths toward post-Soviet economic policy. What I argue in this book is that we should take seriously these efforts and the agenda to forge the state's role in post-Soviet marketization – which I call post-Soviet developmentalism – and to analyze their impact on the way market institutions took shape.

Post-Soviet developmentalism is a form of hands-on economic planning that charts the market integration of regional economies as they responded to myriad challenges following the collapse of the Soviet planned economy. The end of Soviet planning meant the collapse of a vast state procurement system and the need for each and every actor to recreate new economic relationships. Economic strategies of political authorities varied greatly across regions and over time, and various tiers of the government came up with different solutions to these challenges. Despite variation, Russian authorities tended to want to create strong domestic economic actors through state support, who could compete internationally and employ Russians domestically. Many regional developmental strategies sought to prevent deindustrialization, unemployment, and labor migration that would turn provincial cities into ghost towns. These strategies continued a long tradition of the Russian state's push for economic development through ambitious, top-down modernization projects, precisely what successive Soviet leaders had attempted, no less than the earlier schemes designed by Sergey Witte, Pyotr Stolypin, and Peter the Great. In most respects, however, post-Soviet developmentalism bore

---

[6] Documented for example by Masha Geesen, *The Man Without a Face: The Unlikely Rise of Vladimir Putin* (New York: Riverhead Books, 2012).

only faint resemblance to Soviet-era planning: cost and prices mattered in a way they did not under Soviet planning, and all actors were acutely aware of domestic and international markets, of competitiveness and arbitrage. Post-Soviet developmentalism embraced market forces and had to wrestle with new economic actors, first and foremost Russia's notorious oligarchs, closely tied to these markets. In fact – and this is important for the marketization of the Russian economy – the post-Soviet developmental agenda depended ultimately on the government's ability to *enlist* oligarchs for broad social aims. These efforts failed as often as they were successful. The developmental strategies that I am describing were often the strategies of a relatively weak state, whose authority and legitimacy were acutely in question. Yet the negotiated relationships between the Russian state and the oligarchs rested on mutual dependence; neither side could determine the outcome a priori. The complex patterns of Russia's marketization then, I argue, were shaped in such evolving pacts between the government and newly emerging economic actors.

Russia's electricity sector reforms were both remarkably market-liberal and strikingly étatist. By 2008, liberal reformers largely succeeded in transforming the electricity sector from a ministry to a market, with de novo institutions that regulated a profit-seeking private sector. At the same time, the state kept control of key levers of the sector, and new market institutions varied greatly across Russia's regions. These complex combinations of apparently liberal and illiberal elements that characterize the reorganization of power provision are puzzling for analysts that view corruption and rent seeking as the driving force of post-Soviet institutional reform. Nor can they be adequately explained with omnibus traits such as free/liberal versus regulated/coordinated that dominate public and much of academic discourse.[7] A political economy approach that can better understand and theorize such patterns is important for a number of reasons. For one, new market arrangements translated into very real ruble amounts on every electricity bill, small and large, which was the element of power reforms Russians typically cared about.[8] The

---

[7] Work by Gary Herrigel (2000) and Monica Prasad (2013), for example, undo these categories and distinctions. Gary Herrigel, *Industrial Constructions: The Sources of German Industrial Power* (Cambridge: Cambridge University Press, 2000); and Monica Prasad, *The Land of Too Much: American Abundance and the Paradox of Poverty* (Cambridge, MA: Harvard University Press, 2013).

[8] See Chapter 5 for results from survey by FOM (*Фонд Общественное Мнение*) concerning public opinion on electricity sector reforms. Excerpts also published in Susanne Wengle, "Power Politics Electricity Sector Reforms in Post-Soviet Russia," *Russian Analytical Digest*, no. 27, Center for Security Studies ETH Zurich (2007): 6–10.

cost of power played a role in everyday lives and affected cost and incentive structures across the economy. They were crucial aspects of Russia's post-Soviet transition. Complex combinations of various types of market institutions are also characteristic of late modern capitalism elsewhere. They are precisely what define heterogonous economies; classifying them as distortions or aberrations from a stylized norm is ultimately not conducive to a better understanding of their origin and how they function. Finally, they reflect an image of markets that are political and contingent constructs, rather than the result of interacting private interests that are exogenous to the political arena.

This book will detail the patterns of liberal and illiberal elements that characterize Russia's new electricity markets. I will demonstrate that they result from regionally specific developmental bargains or pacts, in which different tiers of the government shaped electricity sector institutions in the interests of conglomerates, while also enlisting them for regional developmental strategies. Based on a close observation of how these development bargains and development strategies function, the book then suggests an approach to the political economy of development that draws attention to economic and political institutions evolving in reflexive processes.

Post-Soviet developmentalism has gone largely unnoticed and remains under-theorized.[9] Dominant theories of state-market relations regard the Russian state as captured by either oligarchs or corrupt bureaucrats. In the capture framework, emerging market institutions are deemed flawed and distorted by concessions the state makes to these rent seekers. The trajectory and outcome of electricity reforms traced in this book confirm that emerging market institutions did indeed reflect the interest of emerging oligarchic conglomerates. But they also demonstrate very clearly the limits of the capture approach. If we look more closely at emerging institutions and how they align with the interests of different types of conglomerates, the regionally patterned adaptation of market institutions appears to be more than a mere reflection of short-term rent seeking. Concessions to conglomerates addressed their long-term international competitiveness and their ability to employ Russians in towns across this

---

[9] Exceptions to this trend are sociological studies of the post-Soviet transition, discussed in Chapter 1. Many Western accounts of the transition have focused primarily on the predatory nature of the Russian state, but the kind of strategies that I highlight have not gone unnoticed. In Russian political discourse, strategies to "modernize" the Russian economy were widely discussed. Regional development strategies, their effectiveness, and their challenges were also intensely debated in the Russian academia and media; see Chapter 2.

vast country. Oligarchic conglomerates, while often represented as rapacious individuals, were in fact industries, paying real salaries to people all over Russia. Rather than buying off oligarchs, the government adapted market reforms in the electricity sector in exchange for these conglomerates' contributions to regionally specific development strategies. These regional bargains wound up shaping the electricity sector's transformation from a ministry to a market.

The difference between enlisting and capture logics rests on a distinct understanding of the motivation of public officials vis-à-vis Russia's oligarchic conglomerates. Underlying the former is a conceptualization of a state seeking to promote competitive national champions (regardless of success), and more broadly, a state continuously involved in creating market institutions and actors.[10] The capture logic, by contrast, imagines the state as an exogenous actor. A liberal faction (weaker or stronger, depending on the period) struggles to advance reforms in the face of an opposition that needs to be co-opted to implement reforms. In this view, liberal reforms and liberal market institutions are a set of stable rules put in place during reforms that then frame the market. Competitiveness is inherent in market participants; it is not created by or dependent on the state. This book demonstrates what can be gained from seeing Russian authorities reform the former type of state, rather than assessing its distance from the latter.

Interests and Ideas in Developmental Strategies

In January 2006, at the height of that cold winter, the liberal reform team led by Anatoly Chubais announced an ambitious modernization plan to upgrade the ailing Soviet-era infrastructure. It was named "*GOELRO-2*," after Lenin's 1920 *GOELRO* initiative to bring electricity to the newly created Soviet Union.[11] As every Russian schoolchild knew, Lenin conceived of electricity as the basis for the spread of modern industry and technology, as captured by the slogan "Communism = Soviet Power + Electrification of the whole country."[12] During the decades

---

[10] See Herrigel, *Industrial Constructions*.

[11] GOELRO stands for *Государственная комиссия по электрификации России*/State Commission for the Electrification of Russia.

[12] See, for example, a 1920 letter by Lenin to the engineer in charge of electrification, Gleb Maximilianovich Krzhizhanovsky, in В. И. Ленин, *О Развитии Тяжелой Промышленности И Электрификации Страны*, 1956, 45. See also Р. Я. Бриль and И. М. Хейстер, *Экономика Социалистической Энергетики: Допущено В Качестве Учебника Для Инженерно-Экономических Вузов И Факультетов* (Высшая школа, 1966).

of Soviet planning that followed, electric power was a potent symbol of progress and development.[13] Contemporary reformers similarly stressed that electricity was a key infrastructure and an absolutely essential part of economic life. Literally they referred to it as "the backbone" of the economy, the basis for future economic prosperity, and the miracle that turns night into day, darkness into light.[14] The strategic use of resonant norms is evident in Chubais's reliance on Lenin's electrification to justify privatization. What is even more poignant is that opponents of liberal reforms mobilized the very same memory of the Soviet-era electrification project for their rejection of liberal reforms. They argued that the state should remain firmly in control of the "master switch" in the sector.[15] Ironically, but perhaps typical for post-Soviet politics, both liberal reformers and their opponents mobilized Lenin's legacy, relying on the symbolic capital imbued in turbines, grids, and wires since the earliest days of the Soviet Union.

How can we make sense of the way interests and ideas were mobilized during reforms? On a conceptual level, post-Soviet developmentalism is best understood as a set of ideas that was strategically and pragmatically deployed by various actors.[16] Political and private actors relied on inherited and shared ideas, while also adapting and mobilizing them in political arguments, thereby forging new meaning. The reasoning why and how the electricity sector and the economy were to be modernized routinely reflected particularistic interests as well as resonant narratives about how a region was to benefit from these arrangements. Broadly, historically situated rationales about regional prosperity and development legitimated particular interests embedded within these rationales, thereby making their realization possible. I should clarify here that by emphasizing ideas I do not mean to downplay the importance of oligarchic interests. This is not a story of how lofty ideals won out over base interests; in fact, the way narratives were deployed helps us overcome the dichotomy of interests versus ideas, which pervades much

---

[13] See discussion in Chapter 3.

[14] Chubais cited by Колесников, А. В. *Неизвестный Чубайс: Страницы из Биографии.* Москва: Захаров, (2003): 133.

[15] Moscow's Mayor Yuri Luzhkov, one of the most prominent opponents of liberal reforms, frequently emphasized the need for "state control of the master switch" ("госконтроль над рубильником"); cited by Vitalii Tseplyaev in "Чубайс – Лужков – боевая ничья," *Аргументы и факты,* October 16, 2002.

[16] On strategic constructivism, see Nicolas Jabko, *Playing the Market: A Political Strategy for Uniting Europe, 1985–2005* (Ithaca, NY: Cornell University Press, 2006).

of political economy.[17] Subsequent chapters emphasize that a decontextualized, stylized notion of interests is insufficient to explain how
a particular "capturer" shaped electricity reforms. Different types of
conglomerates had very different interests vis-à-vis the electricity sector. To understand the shape of marketization, we need to understand
the way the government selectively accommodated these interests during the electricity sector reforms, and how these interests were legitimized through development strategies that charted the region's market
integration.

Development strategies were ubiquitous reference points in regional
imaginations of future well-being. As such they served important political functions, justifying a particular reform trajectory as efficient and
necessary for a region. Development strategies provided resonant and
coherent narratives to legitimize one set of views or interests while dis-
crediting others.[18] For political actors, these narratives were critical to
realizing their vision of a region's future. For conglomerates, they were a
way to write themselves into the future of a region. Could it mean that,
by legitimizing special interests in this way, development strategies were
no more than fig leaves that detracted attention from corrupt behavior by bureaucrats and oligarchs? If that were the case, developmental
strategies would be hypocritical documents, designed to conceal what
is really going on. As mentioned at the outset of this chapter, there is
no doubt that rent seeking was pervasive, and ambitious super-projects
were indeed effective siphons of state money into select private hands.
This does not mean, however, that we need to look no further than such
arrangements to explain Russia's marketization, or that they provide a
sufficient explanation of how markets evolved. Development strategies
played a significant role: they made particular market arrangements possible. Providing continuity between a region's past, present, and future,
they legitimated an emerging conglomerate's role in that story and governing authorities' decisions to promote particular economic actors. In
fact, they could only legitimize particular interests if they managed to
project an image of future prosperity rooted in credible notions of a
region's comparative advantage. So, even if development strategies were

---

[17] Constructivist political economy has started to undo this dichotomy; see discussion in
Chapter 1.

[18] My interest in development strategies as legitimating narratives draws on the work
of Timothy Mitchell, *Rule of Experts: Egypt, Techno-Politics, Modernity* (Berkeley:
University of California Press, 2002), 41.

often vague, overly ambitious, and only partially realized, they were in the literal sense of the word, meaningful.

Developmental strategies were particularly visible in the marketization of Russian electricity, precisely because UES was more than a collection of turbines and grids. As "one of the big achievements of the Soviet Union,"[19] it embodied key norms and standards of the Soviet order. The Soviet Union's first electrification-plan, Plan-GOELRO was also the first legendary Five-Year Plan, the pulse of planning for the rest of the Soviet era. The symbolic power imbued in electric light tightly linked electricity to the legitimacy of the state. It meant that the sector was too important for the state to neglect. Power failures in the 1990s both symbolized economic collapse and exposed the state's absolute weakness, its inability to provide the most basic prerequisite for a "civilized," modern life.[20] A state that failed to provide heat and light was a failed state. "Power failures" then literally assumed a dual meaning, and Russian politicians at all levels of government could not afford to ignore problems in electricity provision. Conversely, the modernization of electricity infrastructure, in reality and in rhetorical references, projected an image of a strong state with clear plans for future prosperity. Hence the claim by an electricity sector economist, whom I interviewed on a brisk fall day in Khabarovsk in a well-heated office of the city's public university: "[Electricity]... never was, and never will be a purely commercial good."[21]

Economic Development and Political Authority as Reflexive Processes

The Russian version of state-led development is a central aspect of the way the Russian economy marketized. It is also an interesting case to

---

[19] Interview #39 with electrical engineer/electricity sector expert, Vladivostok, 20071004.

[20] Reports of outages in regional newspapers were often accompanied with a statement that civilized life is only possible with electricity; for example, "В ногу с цивилизацией," *Красноярский рабочий*, June 9, 1992. Reports of outages were described as causing unbearable inconveniences; for example, "Острый Сигнал: Прошли выборы – отключили батареи," *Утро России*, January 15, 1994. See also Stephanie Platz, "The Shape of National Time: Daily Life, History and Identity during Armenia's Transition to Independence 1991–1994," in *Altering States: Ethnographies of Transition in Eastern Europe and the Former Soviet Union*, ed. Daphne Berdahl, Matti Bunzl, and Martha Lampland (Ann Arbor: University of Michigan Press, 2000), 114–138.

[21] See epigraph of this chapter.

reflect on economic development and developmental states elsewhere. Above all, the Russian experience urges us to take seriously the reflexivity inherent in economic and political development.[22] By reflexivity I am referring to the dynamic reciprocity in the relationships between emerging markets and political authority – we will see that markets and political arenas were fundamentally intertwined and mutually constitutive. In David Woodruff's prescient analysis, the construction of state power and economic order in the post-Soviet space were inextricably related – "twin projects" and twin challenges that authorities had to confront.[23] The post-Soviet period was an exceptionally dynamic institutional setting; new market institutions were constructed in a very short time. The novelty and fluidity of markets and political authority had an extraordinary effect: they made apparent and observable how each step in either process reshaped the conditions for the other. Political science often examines how market arrangements are premised on certain political structures – the political conditions of liberal reform, for example. Yet, Russia's marketization demonstrates clearly that actors' political and social status is also produced and maintained by the markets they create. A preoccupation with distilling a unidirectional causal relationship, often through cross-national comparisons, has diverted attention away from empirical studies that explore how market reforms and polities evolved in relation to each other. *Post-Soviet Power* is a study of economic development and political authority as mutually constitutive social constructs.

On the one hand, politics shaped market institutions. Despite the increasingly authoritarian tendencies of Russian politics, there were always competing interpretations of what Russia's marketization should look like; post-Soviet developmentalism was often a highly contested policy agenda. Liberal and more statist views were variously represented in Moscow and in different regions, each at times successful in influencing the electricity sector's post-Soviet transformation. The solutions that

---

[22] This formulation draws on Kiren Chaudhry's argument that "state and market building are mutually dependent and potentially conflictual processes" in K. A. Chaudhry, "The Myths of the Market and the Common History of Late Developers," *Politics & Society* 21, no. 3 (1993): 247. I use the term reflexivity instead of mutual dependence, because it allows for a more dynamic and mutually transformative relationship between the two. Reflexivity refers to a circular relationship between cause and effects. Reflexive relationships then can also be described as mutually constitutive. See Chapter 1 for a more detailed discussion.

[23] David Woodruff, *Money Unmade: Barter and the Fate of Russian Capitalism* (Ithaca, NY: Cornell University Press, 1999), 1.

actors agreed on evolved over the two decades of Russia's transition, along with the centralization of political authority and the turnover of political elites under Putin. While Putin allowed liberal reformers to restructure the sector along market lines, and to sell off the state's assets, the liberal vision was adapted in ongoing conflicts over the architecture of market institutions. For example, Chubais initially wanted to create hundreds of private electricity generation companies across Russia, modeled on the U.S. electricity system. Even as he succeeded in privatizing generation assets, he wound up creating only twenty-two new power companies. More generally, answers to a myriad of questions that came up during the day-to-day progression of electricity reform – on concrete issues such as who should control a particular asset, what systems of asset valuation should be used, how to reform tariff regulations for particular consumers, and so on – were all essentially contingent on the outcomes of political battles about the appropriate role of the state in newly created markets.

At the same time, we will see that reforms and development projects also affected political power and authority, as actors' status was either strengthened or undermined by the markets that were created. One of the most intriguing aspects of the marketization of the electricity sector was that it solidified Putin's centralization of political power. Chubais's reforms intentionally and effectively eliminated the influence of a set of political actors in the electricity sector, who had seriously threatened the sovereign authority of the federal government in the 1990s – regional administrations and their allies in the electricity sector. The centralization of political authority made the reorganization of electricity possible as it sidelined the opposition to reforms by various stakeholders. But at the same time, liberal reforms also consolidated the federal center's position as the ultimate arena for politics as they undercut regional authorities' role in power provision and institutionalized supra-regional decision making. For example, we will see that de-territorialized holding companies replaced the vertically integrated regional monopolies as the main form of ownership in power generation, and incumbent electricity executives with ties of regional governors were replaced with new managers loyal to Moscow's reformers. In other words, economic reforms and political centralization were mutually reinforcing. And it was precisely because marketization contributed to political goals that the new market institutions in the sector were coveted prizes in ongoing political struggles. Again, in highlighting that actors' motivations in Russia's economic transformation were highly political, the book demonstrates that their goals were broader than rent seeking and capture explanations would suggest.[24]

Dynamic Contexts and Evolving Markets

The book's key theoretical suggestion, then, is a critical revision of our thinking about state-led development based on the recognition that the relationship between authority and markets is reflexive, dynamic, and contingent. Unlike in much of the literature on the developmental state, foundational market institutions in this book are not conceptualized as static national types that result from particular structural conditions. Nor are they a stable set of rules put in place when a powerful coalition of reformers deems this to be in their best interest. Instead, they are provisional, elusive, but highly prized outcomes in ongoing political struggles about what form development should take. Ownership regimes, subsidy regimes, and regimes of expertise are such high-stake outcomes examined in detail in the chapters to come. Economic development itself is something quite different as well. It is a historically situated collective project – polities forging, negotiating, and implementing visions of future well-being – rather than a set of recipes for growth.

Situating markets and economic development in political contexts is hardly a novel suggestion.[25] At least since Karl Polanyi's *Great Transformation*, an established tradition in political economy treats markets as historically specific and politically contingent phenomena. I draw on this tradition, but I use the fluidity of the post-Soviet context as an opportunity to explore the possibility of a highly dynamic notion of embeddedness and context.[26] The case of post-Soviet power specifically

[24] This is a point that Andrew Barnes has also stressed in his exceptional analysis of Russia's privatization struggles: Andrew Scott Barnes, *Owning Russia: The Struggle over Factories, Farms, and Power* (Ithaca, NY: Cornell University Press, 2006).
[25] This intellectual tradition is based on Karl Polanyi's and Alexander Gerschenkron's work; see Karl Polanyi, *The Great Transformation: The Political and Economic Origins of Our Time* (Boston, MA: Beacon Press, 1944); and Alexander Gerschenkron, *Economic Backwardness in Historical Perspective, a Book of Essays* (Cambridge, MA: Belknap Press, 1962). Also in this tradition is Andrew C. Janos, *The Politics of Backwardness in Hungary, 1825–1945* (Princeton, NJ: Princeton University Press, 2012).
[26] This possibility is a central aspect of theoretical approaches to institutional change that examine the mutual constitution of action and context; see most recently, Gerald Berk, Dennis C. Galvan, and Victoria C. Hattam, eds., *Political Creativity: Reconfiguring Institutional Order and Change*, 1st ed. (Philadelphia: University of Pennsylvania Press, 2013); and Gary Herrigel, *Manufacturing Possibilities: Creative Action and Industrial Recomposition in the United States, Germany, and Japan* (Oxford: Oxford University

brings into focus the complex role of industrial and post-industrial geography that Russia inherited from the Soviet planned economy. Soviet-era industrial policy spread populations and industries thinly across vast and distant territories. We will see that the remnants of the inherited material structures mattered for the marketization of Russia's electricity sector. Depending on the industrial geography of a region, either energy-led conglomerates or industry-led conglomerates – the input providers and the main customers of power plants – had strong physical ties and relationships to the electricity sector across Russia. These material ties profoundly shaped economic actors' interests and views.

But we will also see that actors' embeddedness in particular geographies was not necessarily a force of continuity. As introduced earlier, the purpose of post-Soviet developmental strategies was to rescue regions and towns from decline. What was to become of each locality, its inherited factories, and its economic relationships in the new post-Soviet era – hence its industrial geography? These were pressing, but essentially open questions that developmental strategies and reform policies needed to address, often pitting central-government liberals against regional leaders who fought for their towns and industries in remote areas. Russian liberals and their Western advisors were generally not in favor of preserving existing industrial structures that had been built in accordance with Soviet-era planning priorities deemed incompatible with market principles. Post-Soviet economic turmoil and liberal reforms idled many aspects of Soviet-era industry. Some elements of the inherited industrial structures withered and did not shape post-Soviet outcomes, but others survived because they were kept alive and even updated despite the insistence of liberal observers that the economic costs of doing so were too high.[27] As Stephen Collier observed, some material structures proved resilient during post-Soviet reforms, as liberal reforms "*selectively* reconfigure[d] inherited material structures, demographic patterns and social norms."[28]

Press, 2010). See also Mustafa Emirbayer and Anne Mische's insightful discussion of the various ways structure and agency relate: Mustafa Emirbayer and Ann Mische, "What Is Agency?" *American Journal of Sociology* 103, no. 4 (January 1, 1998): 962–1023.

[27] For the logic of the liberal argument about the cost of maintaining industrial production in the North, see Fiona Hill and Clifford G. Gaddy, *The Siberian Curse: How Communist Planners Left Russia out in the Cold* (Washington, DC: Brookings Institution Press, 2003).

[28] Stephen J. Collier, *Post-Soviet Social: Neoliberalism, Social Modernity, Biopolitics* (Princeton, NJ: Princeton University Press, 2011), 3, emphasis added.

Which ties and relationship were to be rescued and preserved in post-Soviet state-oligarch pacts, and which structures withered was not at all clear in the early stages of the country's economic transformation. What mattered was whether inherited industrial structures were mobilized in political struggles about economic reforms. A powerful aluminum conglomerate, for example, relied on the physical proximity of aluminum smelters and hydroelectric power plants as an argument why it should retain control of the valuable plant and why it should continue to have access to subsidized electricity. The "integrity" of the inherited industrial structures was thereby validated as a necessity for regional development, and hence became influential in the transformation of the electricity sector. In more general terms, inherited contexts – industrial geographies and relationships – situated and shaped interests but did not guarantee that interests were met. Materiality (the structuring context in our case) mattered not as a mechanistic structural determinant, but only if actors validated them in a political battles and visions about regional development. In this sense, embeddedness and material structures appeared not only, and not necessarily, as constraints, but also as tools and enabling forces for political actors. And economic development was not necessarily only path-dependent, it was also an open-ended, contingent transformation, collectively forged by Russia's powerful economic and political actors.

Beyond Success and Failure

The emphasis on developmental considerations might suggest that I view the Russian state as a successful, coherent developmental state, which seems odd given the country's sluggish growth performance, persisting oil dependency, and inability to reign in corruption. Many observers classify Russia as a laggard that has neither fostered robust economic development, nor created the kind of effective bureaucracy that is generally deemed a prerequisite for a successful developmental state. I should clarify then that the analytical framework I am suggesting here is not meant to vet development or the state's effectiveness in this way. Such assessments tend to be based on stylized version of institutional best practice and modeled on either the most successful Asian economies or the advanced industrialized West. They measure the distance between "dysfunctional" Russian and ideal-typical institutions, gauging and explaining progress (or lack thereof) toward a set of indicators such as degree of price liberalization, privatization, and the establishment of secure property rights.[29] Research in this vein remains the dominant framing device of studies of the political economy of transition and development. My research offers neither an account of how development works nor an assessment whether post-Soviet developmentalism was, or will be, ultimately successful. It is not a book about why the Russian Bear is not an Asian Tiger.

What it does suggest is an approach to studying state-led development as projects that simultaneously forge markets and generate authority; it does not take the coherent, effective state for granted. Instead, it investigates development as embattled construction projects, and suggests that this is a lens for political economy of development that can yield new and unexpected insights into what development means in different contexts. In our case, the evidence surfaces that contemporary Russia exceeds the rubrics of corrupt autocrats, greedy oligarchs and vanishing ghost towns. While many Russian towns were indeed suffering as residents migrate or emigrate, and analysts that decry a failing state make valid points, few observers have addressed the strategies that tried to stem the tide of post-industrial decay. My focus here is on the plans that were devised to keep electricity flowing and factory doors open, and on how these influenced the market institutions that have taken shape. The chapters that follow demonstrate that developmental strategies mattered for towns and regions for a number of reasons (and regardless of their role in spurring overall national economic growth) – they shaped emerging market institutions, they legitimized oligarchic privilege and political authority, and they were intricately linked to post-Soviet state-building.

The suggestion to devote attention to studies of markets as continuously evolving social institutions links this work with that of development economists who are moving beyond a "good governance" agenda. Though a useful corrective to the Washington Consensus with its minimalist view of the state, the essence of good governance was the attempt to single out a set of institutions that promote economic prosperity across the world. Yet, a number of studies introduced in more depth in Chapter 1 have called into question the notion that it is one set of institutions, or

[29] See for example Barry Weingast and Rui De Figueiredo, "Russian Federalism: A Contradiction in Terms," *Hoover Digest*, no. 4 (2001), online at http://www.hoover.org/research/russian-federalism-contradiction-terms; and Barry Weingast and Rui De Figueiredo, "Pathologies of Federalism, Russian Style: Political Institutions and Economic Transition", April 2002, http://faculty.haas.berkeley.edu/rui/mpfrussia.pdf. Critiques of linear approaches to the post-Soviet transformation have been made since the late 1990s; see Chapter 1 for a discussion.

one set of critical factors that have most successfully furthered domestic economic opportunities. Instead this research suggests that development happens in a multiplicity of governance arrangements, and results from institutional innovation, experimentation, and learning rather than the application of one particular model of development. This notion of development confirms that local adaptations of global reform trends, qualitative parameters of market institutions, and the political processes in which they are forged deserve far more attention than they have received to date.

Overview and Organization

Post-Soviet Power is an account of who shaped post-Soviet markets, how, and why. The politics surrounding liberal reforms are key to understanding market outcomes, and the pages that follow try to make sense of post-Soviet power and politics in a new way. Based on these empirical observations, I develop three nested arguments, one specific to Russia's post-Soviet transformation while the other two are more general. First, the narrative of the electricity sector's transformation draws attention to post-Soviet developmentalism and to the government's negotiated agreements with oligarchic conglomerates, demonstrating how regionally differentiated market institutions in the electricity sector reflect such bargains. Second, *Post-Soviet Power* suggests that political authority and market reforms are essentially codependent, each shaping the other in mutually constitutive processes. Finally, it offers a framework to understand economic development and emerging markets as a set of politically embattled and continuously evolving social institutions.

Post-Soviet Power offers an original framework to study the political economy of development that broadens the parameters of the "political" and the "economy" in political economy. Markets are treated not as exogenous to politics, a set of relations governed by generalizable laws that govern the economy. There is more politics and contestation in these pages than might be expected from a book on an increasingly authoritarian country. We will see that competition over valuable assets and market institutions remained heated, even when formal channels of democratic accountability weakened.

The book is divided into two parts. Part I provides a number of basic building blocks for the analysis of how the electricity sector was transformed: what were post-Soviet developmental strategies? What were the aims of liberal reforms? What was "power politics" – the politics that shaped reforms?

Chapter 1 introduces defining features of post-Soviet developmentalism and discusses the theoretical implications of taking it seriously for three established debates in political science: for research on the post-Soviet transition, for debates on state-led development, and for constructivist political economy.

Chapter 2 focuses on the negotiations of electricity reforms among political actors. A key infrastructure and an energy sector, electricity became a focal point of power relations between federal and regional levels of government. The chapter lays out how liberal reformers intended to reorganize the sector along market lines, and then provides an analytical overview of the shifting alliances that supported and opposed liberalization.

Chapter 3 is devoted to an analysis of the regionally specific developmental bargains with Russia's conglomerates. The empirical focus turns to the three regions – European Russia, Siberia, and the Far East – detailing for each case how the electricity sector is tied into inherited material and human networks. The chapter also puts forth a theoretical argument about the role of industrial geography.

Part II then turns to three foundational market institutions – ownership regimes, subsidy regimes, and regimes of expertise – outlining how each was transformed during sector reforms in regionally specific bargains.

Chapter 4 focuses on property and ownership, detailing the battles to control power plants, turbines, and grids. The chapter examines the success and failure of ownership claims and establishes who emerged as new owners after repeated rounds of privatization in European Russia, Siberia, and the Russian Far East. The chapter makes the argument that ownership transfers helped sideline governors and empowered new owners of electricity assets, thus shifting the political arena in important ways.

Chapter 5 takes up the subject of tariff liberalization and the elimination of subsidies. The chapter demonstrates that despite tariff liberalization and political centralization under Putin, various subsidy regimes governed price regulation in the sector, empowering specific economic actors. Subsidy regimes in the electricity sector are arrangements, formal and informal, involving governments, regulators, utilities, and industrialists that enable the provision of electricity at below long-run average cost in an effort to achieve certain political, economic, and social goals.

Chapter 6 turns to the role of experts in electricity sector reforms. The chapter traces how Soviet-trained technical experts with ties to regional political authorities were gradually replaced by managerially trained experts without regional loyalties. This expert turnover was a constitutive element of market reforms as it allowed the introduction of new forms of asset valuation. It also consolidated federal efforts to centralize political power under Putin as it helped the government disempower regional governors.

Finally, the Conclusion explores the Russian electricity sector's transformation in cross-sectoral and cross-national perspective. I examine the relevance of a developmental logic in two other sectors of the Russian economy: gas and railways. I also compare the Russian experience with the politics of utility liberalization in the European Union and the United States. The chapter concludes with a restatement of the implications of the Russian experience for studying economic development elsewhere.

Part I

I

From Ministry to Market

*"The fate of the electricity and energy sector (энергокомплекс)
is directly and naturally connected to the preservation of the state,
and the political and economic sovereignty of Russia."*[1]

Regionally Fragmented Markets

Liberal reformers in post-Soviet Russia wanted to create a single national market for electricity, with one set of rules for all market participants. In contrast to political economy narratives that regard the Russian economy as either essentially unreformed or stuck in a "partial-reform equilibrium," *Post-Soviet Power* will make the case that a great deal of change *has* happened, and will document in detail the extent and type of marketization in the electricity sector. While liberals succeeded in undoing UES, the state-owned monopoly, the electricity sector's transformation did not follow a single trajectory across Russia's regions. In the 1990s, governors attained de facto authority to regulate economies. In pacts with regional economic actors, they defied federal directives in the electricity sector and beyond and made largely autonomous decisions about the electricity sectors' transformation. Partly in response to Yeltsin's inability to regulate the economy, Putin consolidated federal power after 2000: governors lost authority and policy leverage, and the pacts with Russia's oligarchs shifted to the federal level. Putin's political centralization is widely considered to

---

[1] Вероника Белоусова, "Под флагом борьбы с монополизмом," *Утро России*, January 14, 1997.

have been remarkably successful. So why did this not lead to a unified national electricity market, governed by one set of rules?

Theories that model the behavior of oligarchs and bureaucrats as rent seeking cannot account for the significant subnational variation in how electricity markets evolved and how they are regulated, as detailed in the second half of this chapter. I found that the sector's regionally patterned marketization aligned with development pacts between the state and newly emerging oligarchic conglomerates.[2] The sector was transformed over almost two decades in complex bargains between regional governments, Moscow's power elites, newly emerging oligarchs, and energy companies.[3] The chapters that follow trace these pacts through the 1990s and through the first eight years of Putin's presidency. The Russian government, first at the regional and later at the federal levels, shaped the electricity sector's marketization by making concessions to Russia's emerging oligarchs to *enlist* their assistance for broader social and developmental aims, rather than for the narrow goal of creating rent-seeking opportunities. Figure 1.1 provides a graphic of the relationship between regional development pacts and the institutional underpinnings of the electricity sector. (Part I of the book details how these pacts were contested and negotiated among political and economic elites – the left side of the figure. Part II is devoted to exploring the regionally patterned changes in ownership, subsidies, and expertise of electricity markets in detail – the right side of the figure).

The main aim of this chapter is to introduce post-Soviet developmentalism and to discuss how it contributes to theoretical debates in political economy. The last section explains the methodological choices that define this research. To facilitate the theoretical discussion in this chapter, I introduce the combinations of liberal and illiberal characteristics in a condensed form here. I use the terms "ownership regimes" and "subsidy regimes" as shorthand for the cross-regional variation in the electricity sector's institutions.

---

[2] A note on the terms "oligarch" and "oligarchic conglomerates:" Russia's new class of powerful magnates was initially known as the oligarchs. After two decades of ownership changes and power struggles within this group, only a few of the original oligarchs have remained in Russia and retain control of the economic empires they amassed. Also, many of the oligarchic empires were consolidated in the period after the 1998 collapse and during the elite turnover at the regional and federal levels. I am using the terms "oligarch" and "conglomerate" more or less interchangeably to refer to the economic empires that gained control of the Energos, although I tend to use "oligarchs" when referring to the 1990s and "conglomerates" when referring to later periods.

[3] David Woodruff first described these kinds of arrangements in the mid-1990s.

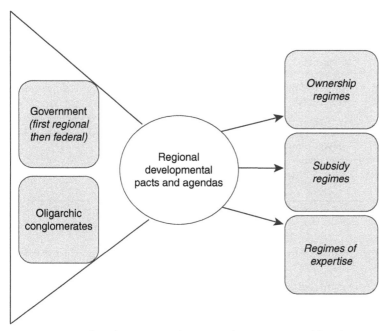

FIGURE 1.1. Political economy of Russia's electricity sector liberalization.

The most notable pattern evident in the electricity sector's transformation is a triptych. Three broad, geographically situated reform trajectories and outcomes define the sector's post-Soviet transformation, named after the three subnational, but supra-regional, zones in which they were most prevalent: European Russia, Siberia, and the Far East.[4] In these three regions, oligarchs with different interests vis-à-vis the electricity sector were selectively accommodated in the kind of pacts that I highlight. In a nutshell, cross-regional differences in Russia's new electricity sector have the following characteristics:

1. In European Russia, most generation assets were privatized and various types of electricity subsidies decreased. The energy behemoth Gazprom sought these ownership and subsidy regimes; it allowed the fuel provider control over income streams from domestic electricity production that relied on its gas. Gazprom could thereby recoup profits that it was losing by having to supply gas cheaply, below cost at times, to domestic industry and power plants.

[4] This triptych was first brought to my attention by a veteran electricity sector expert in interview #39 with electrical engineer/electricity sector expert, Vladivostok, 20071004.

TABLE 1.1. *Ownership and subsidy regimes*

	Ownership and Subsidy Regimes	Development Pacts
European Russia	power plants privatized / subsidies generally decrease	Government & Gazprom (upstream energy conglomerate)
Siberia	power plants privatized / industrial subsidies continue	Government & Rusal (downstream industrial conglomerate)
Russian Far East	no privatization / subsidies continue	Government & electricity companies

2. In Siberian regions, by contrast, where industrial oligarchs dominated as the new owners of privatized power plants, pricing mechanisms allowed for electricity to be sold below national market prices to industrial customers. Electricity-intensive industries, aluminum companies in particular, sought this outcome because it effectively maintained a separate low-cost zone that kept their production costs low, enhancing their international competitiveness.[5]
3. In Far Eastern regions, generation assets have not been privatized and electricity prices remained regulated. This outcome protected Far Eastern electricity companies from low-cost Siberian competition and allowed for the continuation of direct government subsidies on which these companies have relied for years.

Regionally distinct developmental pacts and strategies explain how market institutions evolved differently across Russia and why certain demands and claims were successful while others failed. Table 1.1 provides an overview of the cross-regional differences in subsidy and ownership regimes and how they align with regional developmental pacts. Note again that concessions to oligarchs in the electricity sector that are matched by contributions to regional development strategies appear

[5] For an overview the post-Soviet history of the gas sector, see, for example, Thane Gustafson, *Capitalism Russian-Style* (Cambridge; New York: Cambridge University Press, 1999); and Jonathan P. Stern, *The Future of Russian Gas and Gazprom* (Oxford: Oxford University Press, 2005). For a post-Soviet history of the aluminum sector, see Barnes, *Owning Russia*.

contradictory in a capture framework that relies on short-term rent seeking as the primary motive of private actors.

Post-Soviet Developmentalism: Consistent Goals, Evolving Bargains

Developmental pacts and developmental strategies are both premised on the existence of a long-term developmental perspective, which I refer to as post-Soviet developmentalism. Post-Soviet developmentalism manifested itself as a loosely coordinated economic policy agenda that many regional and federal authorities shared. This agenda was comprised of overlapping regional and supra-regional development strategies, formulated both by regional and federal governments, which relied on a variety of policy tools to create strong domestic actors to compete internationally and employ Russians domestically. And among many other things, regional development strategies addressed the modernization of the ailing electric power system. They thereby influenced how the sector evolved from a ministry to a market.

Post-Soviet developmentalism was at once dynamic and consistent. On the one hand, it had a number of persistent goals and defining characteristics. A set of ideas about regional development, a list of goals and even specific projects that had gained currency in the 1990s and earlier, were carried over to the Putin-era bargains. On the other hand, core tenets as well as their realization were always contested by different political factions and in struggles between regional and federal administrations. This meant that as a policy agenda, it evolved as it was implemented. I am emphasizing three defining elements here, as the remainder of Part I focuses on how goals were contested and varied across regions. Firstly, albeit a program for state-led economic development, post-Soviet developmentalism was always premised on enlisting Russia's newly emerging *private* owners – the oligarchs. Secondly, post-Soviet developmentalism was intricately linked to the project of state-building. Finally, developmental strategies included plans for the modernization of the electricity sector: as both an infrastructure and energy sector, it featured prominently in post-Soviet planning documents.

The realization of post-Soviet developmental programs relied on a type of pact or cooperation between the state and Russia's new economic actors – both the private oligarchs and the semi-statal conglomerates. Successive governments needed and relied on the private sector in multiple ways. No significant faction of the federal government wanted a return to full state ownership of factories and power plants, even if there has always been significant political disagreement over the degree and nature of state ownership in the post-Soviet economy. Conglomerates in turn relied on the state. This applied, in particular, to the period since Putin strengthened the federal government, but protection (*крыша*) or just "good relations" with regional governors were just as important during the 1990s. Under Putin, this relationship took the form of an explicit policy that promoted "national champions." Political factions that viewed state support of "champions" as essential were more influential than more liberal faction that sought a less activist state. Champions were endowed with state resources to help them compete in global markets, but they were also put in charge of keeping factory doors open in towns across Russia and asked to fulfill various "social functions" in these towns. These social functions, often bundled under the vague notion of corporate social responsibility, varied widely and depended largely on informal, paternalistic pacts between regional authorities and enterprises.[6] The term "corporate social responsibility" was a recent and post-Soviet import, but many of the relationships on which these agreements rested dated back to the Soviet period. Collaborations between authorities and enterprises attempted to adapt these relationships to the radically new environment of domestic markets and international integration.

Another important aspect of state-oligarch pacts was that they were based on fundamentally negotiated and hence political relationships. They were neither inherently arm's-length interactions nor entirely personalistic and corrupt. The relationships of Gazprom and Rusal with the

---

[6] There are interesting accounts of how these kinds of pacts and corporate social responsibility programs work at the local level, and how Russian and foreign companies interact with local authorities; see Douglas Rogers, "The Materiality of the Corporation: Oil, Gas, and Corporate Social Technologies in the Remaking of a Russian Region," *American Ethnologist* 39, no. 2 (2012): 284–296; Laura A. Henry, Soili Nysten-Haarala, Svetlana Tulaeva, and Maria Tysiachniouk, "Corporate Social Responsibility and the Oil Industry in the Russian Arctic: Global Norms and Neo-Paternalism" (unpublished manuscript under review) and Svetlana Tulaeva, "Transformation of Corporate Social Responsibility in the forest sector in the context of global processes: the case of forest certification" and other contributions in *Russia and Europe: From Mental Images to Business Practices* (Kotka, Finland: Kymenlaakso University of Applied Sciences, 2010). See also Niobe Thompson, *Settlers on the Edge: Identity and Modernization on Russia's Arctic Frontier* (Vancouver: University of British Columbia Press, 2009); and Yuko Adachi, *Building Big Business in Russia: The Impact of Informal Corporate Governance Practices* (London; New York: Routledge, 2010). Finally, Timothy Frye also writes about corporate social responsibility, although his account focuses on whether or not these programs redeem oligarchs's tainted image. Timothy Frye, "Original Sin, Good Works, and Property Rights in Russia," *World Politics* 58, no. 4 (2006): 479–504.

government illustrate this well. Whether Gazprom was an arm of the government or a "normal" enterprise interested in maximizing profits was subject to much debate in Russia.[7] During the 1990s, the government and Gazprom frequently disagreed over the volume and the price of gas to be delivered to Russian industry. During the second post-Soviet decade, the government increased its ownership in the company and staffed the board with high-level government officials. But even after the government thereby more formally gained control of the company, the Gazprom-government relationship remained a political issue, subject to negotiations between various Kremlin factions. No single political force, including President Putin, controlled the gas behemoth in the sense that it could unilaterally determine the role it played domestically and internationally. This mattered for electricity reforms, because for most of the reforms, there was much disagreement about just how much influence Gazprom should be allowed to gain in the sector.

This kind of political, evolving relationship with the state is not unique to Gazprom.[8] Nor is the relationship between a Russian company and the government necessarily determined by its status as either a private or public company. Rusal is a private company, yet it is far from independent. We will see in Chapter 3 that under Putin, the "loyal oligarchs" had to comply with the government's wishes in many different ways. The government had a number of legal tools at its disposal,[9] but its leverage also works in extralegal, unpredictable ways, as the government's crackdown of Mikhail Khodorkovsky's oligarchic empires amply demonstrated.

In the electricity sector, too, relationships between government and Russian companies were thus negotiated, evolving pacts based on mutual dependence. Electricity is a vital infrastructure, important for both private and public actors, and both wanted to influence the reorganization

---

[7] Many members of the Putin administration want Gazprom to serve as an arm of the government, for example, Igor Shuvalov, interview in *Russian Investment Review*, Vol. 3/3 (2004), p. 9.

[8] See, for example, the chapter by Peter Rutland in Stephen K. Wegren and Dale Herspring, eds., *After Putin's Russia: Past Imperfect, Future Uncertain* (Lanham, MD: Rowman & Littlefield, 2010).

[9] An example pertaining to the relationship between Rusal and the government is illustrative here: while Rusal owned and controlled the physical installations of the Irkutsk hydroelectric power plant – its turbines, grids, and switches – it only leased the actual dam from the federal government, as it had not been privatized along with the power plant attached to it. Rusal thus depended on the government to uphold and periodically renegotiate the terms of the lease agreement. Interview #53 with employee of electricity company, Irkutsk, 20071119; see also interview with Vladimir V. Kolmogorov, general director of Irkutskenergo, in *Свет негасимый: энергетике Приангарья 50 лет* (Иркутск: Восточно-Сибирская издательская компания, 2004), 10.

of power plants and grids.[10] For the government, electricity played an important role in post-Soviet developmentalism. For the new private sector, concessions in the provision of this crucial infrastructure provided a competitive advantage in domestic and international markets. At the same time, neither side was able to dictate the terms of their cooperation. Pauline Jones-Luong and Erika Weinthal argued along similar lines in their account of how Russian institutions were built, which stressed the role of mutually beneficial contracts between the government and a set of powerful economic actors.[11] Unlike Jones-Luong and Weinthal, however, the analytical framework I am suggesting does not rely on stylized notions of oligarchic behavior. What we gain from detailed empirical accounts of state-oligarch pacts is an understanding of how they shaped market outcomes differently across regions. Developmental pacts entailed agreements with conglomerates that had very different interests vis-à-vis the electricity sector. Energy-led conglomerates, industry-led conglomerates, and electricity companies each had distinct aims when it came to electricity sector reforms. Attention to post-Soviet developmental bargains thus helps us understand *how* conglomerates shaped new markets.

A second defining feature of post-Soviet developmentalism was its link to state-building. Governing requires a degree of sovereign control. The centrifugal forces unleashed with the collapse of the Soviet state and

---

[10] See epigraph and note 1 in this chapter.

[11] Jones-Luong and Weinthal argue that the creation of Russia's fiscal institutions "represents a negotiated settlement between the Russian government and the most powerful set of domestic economic actors – the Russian oil companies." Pauline Jones Luong and Erika Weinthal, "Contra Coercion: Russian Tax Reform, Exogenous Shocks, and Negotiated Institutional Change," *American Political Science Review* 98, no. 1 (2004): 139–152. Although Jones-Luong and Weinthal's research provides a richer account of state-oligarch bargains than the capture literature does, it relies on broad, stylized predictions of government's motivations: variation is shaped by the central government's needs to consolidate political control. See also Peter Rutland's work on state-business relationships; for example, Peter Rutland, "Business-State Relations in Russia" (presented at the World Congress of the International Council for Central and East European Studies, Berlin, 2005), accessed March 14, 2014, http://prutland.web.wesleyan.edu/Documents/berlin1.pdf; and, most recently, Peter Rutland, "The Business Sector in Post-Soviet Russia," in *Routledge Handbook of Russian Politics and Society*, ed. Graeme J. Gill and James Young (London: Routledge, 2012), 288–304. The most recent accounts of Russia's state-market relations have argued that the state has relatively more power, as it can easily revoke property rights. This reasoning underlies, for example, Gerald Easter's notion of "concession capitalism." Gerald M. Easter, "Revenue Imperatives: States over Markets in Postcommunist Russia," in *The Political Economy of Russia*, ed. Neil Robinson (Lanham, MD: Rowman & Littlefield, 2013), 51–68.

the subsequent attempts by the Russian federal government to re-center authority were one of the most salient political dynamics of the post-Soviet period.[12] For federal and regional authorities to implement their vision for a regional economy's future, they had to wrest control of key levers of the state's administration. Post-Soviet developmentalism was thus deeply implicated in the center-regional power struggles. Russian, and before that Soviet, politics have been characterized by ebbs and flows in the ability of the center to compel the regions. After a period of decentralization beginning with Gorbachev's reform and lasting through the economic crisis of the mid-1990s, the federal government succeeded in regaining control over the channels of power and bureaucratic authority in the decade that followed. The history of the electricity sector offers compelling evidence that one of the federal government's goals in strengthening the center was the reassertion of its ability to regulate the economy.[13] This interpretation of the state's motives contrasts with one that sees Putin's centralization as the strategy of an increasingly predatory state that seeks control to increase rent-seeking opportunities.

Since the late Soviet period, different tiers of the government competed for the authority to govern, regulate, and plan the economy. We see the outcome of this competition reflected in the way the locus and the authority to plan for the market shifted over the years. The Soviet model of economic development was squarely based on Moscow's planning *for* the regions, as centrally formulated plans took precedence over development strategies *by* the regions.[14] A characteristic feature of Soviet planning was that regional development strategies were designed to serve "All-Union" (*всесоюзные*) needs and goals, instead of serving parochial needs of regions. The economic development of Siberia, for example, was

[12] Nikolay Petrov, "How Have the Presidential Envoys Changed the Administrative-Political Balance of Putin's Regime?" in *The Dynamics of Russian Politics: Putin's Reform of Federal-Regional Relations*, ed. Peter Reddaway and Robert W. Orttung, vol. 2, 2 vols. (Lanham, MD: Rowman & Littlefield, 2005), 33–64. See also Daniel Treisman, *After the Deluge: Regional Crises and Political Consolidation in Russia* (Ann Arbor: University of Michigan Press, 1999).

[13] The state's loss and attempts to regain control over natural resources in particular was one of the core issues in comparisons of the Yeltsin and Putin years. The tug-of-war surrounding the oil sector is widely documented; see, for example, Richard Sakwa, *The Quality of Freedom: Khodorkovsky, Putin, and the Yukos Affair* (Oxford: Oxford University Press, 2009). This was often mentioned in interviews, for example, in interview #49 with an academic, Irkutsk, 20071114.

[14] Georgi Derlugian suggests that the Soviet Union was a developmental state. See Georgi M. Derluguian, *Bourdieu's Secret Admirer in the Caucasus: A World-System Biography* (Chicago: University of Chicago Press, 2005).

part of the GOSPLAN vision for building socialist modernity. Neither the
wartime eastward shift of factories beyond the Urals nor the postwar construction of Siberian mega-factories were designed as development strategies specifically for Siberian regions, but rather as puzzle pieces within
a larger program of Soviet modernization.[15] Even as they were hailed as
unprecedented achievements in Siberia's industrialization, regional well-
being was not the primary concern. This was more than an academic
distinction for Siberians, as the intensive push to industrialize was associated with significant social and ecological cost. Resettling entire villages,
damming rivers, and constructing huge, polluting industrial plants were
deeply unsettling events for affected populations. In the eyes of central
planners, these costs were outweighed by the goal of industrializing the
Hinterland (*Целина*) and extracting vast Siberian resources. In the post-
Soviet period, then, some regions tried to formulate development strategies as a direct response to perceived neglect of regional well-being by
Soviet planners.

Gorbachev's Perestroika (*перестройка*) promised to end the established
tradition of centralized development. In the late 1980s, the Soviet all-
union division of labor (*всесоюзное распределение труда*) mandated by
central planning (*госплан*) gave way to increasing regional autonomy; for
the first time in Soviet history regions were involved in developing plans
to promote economic development. Decentralization of economic decision making started as a policy to address the Soviet economy's shortage
problems. After 1991, decentralized economic policy rapidly became a de
facto reality, as Soviet-era chains of command lost force and the new command structures were often not able to contend with the regional power
centers that had emerged. Regional administrations were devising strategies for the future of their economies under market conditions – a task
actively embraced by some regions while studiously avoided by others.[16]

[15] Алексеев, В. В. *Электрификация Сибири*, Siberian Branch of the Russian Academy of
Sciences/*Наука*, Novosibirsk (1973).
[16] Some regions had extensive regional development goals, usually the more independent
regions. Interestingly, many Russian regional scholars turned to theories of agglomeration and industrial clusters as theoretical frameworks for framing development plans
for their regions. Note that the geographical scope of various development strategies
overlaps: strategies are simultaneously formulated as national-level documents (National
Energy Strategy, the "Putin Plan"), for large meta-regions (Federal Development Strategy
for the Transbaikal and Far East), and on the oblast', i. e., regional, level (Irkutsk Oblast'
Development Strategy). Further, each of the seven "federal *okrugs*" has a development
strategy, and there is also a national energy strategy.

Under Putin, the authority of regions to plan for their own development was once again curtailed. Unlike in the 1990s, under Putin, a newly strengthened Ministry of Regional Development oversaw the formulation and implementation of regional development strategies, initially in coordination with regional administrations.[17] An increase in the number of federal programs for regional development since the late 1990s – from seven in 1996, to fourteen in 1997, twenty-three in 1998, and "dozens" in 2005 – was dubbed "the rebirth of interest for regional programs as documents of strategic planning."[18]

A third important feature of post-Soviet developmentalism concerns the legitimization of authority. The drive to gain (or regain) control over regional economies, to regulate and to devise plans for regional economic development had much to do with the way post-Soviet officials perceived of legitimacy since Soviet times. Whereas the sources of legitimacy of authority are as diverse in post-Soviet Russia as they are elsewhere, "performance legitimacy" – namely the legitimation of authority not via the claim to represent the population, but via delivering economic prosperity – played an important role.[19] In part, this kind of legitimization of authority is a memory of Soviet political legitimacy premised on raising living standards. It is also the result of the traumatic crises of the 1990s. Aron notes that "instead of seeking to ground its legitimacy on broad-based, transpersonal institutions with character and integrity of their own, the regime has chosen to bank overwhelmingly on Vladimir Putin's popularity. This, in turn, seems to derive from the economic growth that he presided over between 2000 and the first half of 2008."[20] Similarly, Feklyunina and White find that, by 2008, "the claim to power by the Russian authorities had been increasingly based on performance

---

[17] In 2007, Dmitry Kozak became head of the Ministry of Regional Development. This was interpreted as a sign of the ministry's importance as Kozak was a close ally of Putin. An interesting detail is also that Putin kept control over the ministry during the four years as prime minister, from 2008 to 2012.

[18] Alexander Granberg, Alexander Pelyasov, and Ul Vavilova, "Programs of Regional Development Revisited: Case of the Russian Federation," in *ERSA Conference Papers* (Amsterdam: European Regional Science Association, 2005), accessed March 13, 2014, http://www-sre.wu.ac.at/ersa/ersaconfs/ersa05/papers/101.pdf.

[19] Huntington called this "performance legitimacy." Samuel P. Huntington, *The Third Wave: Democratization in the Late Twentieth Century* (Norman: University of Oklahoma Press, 1991), cited in Leon Aron, "The Merger of Power and Property," *Journal of Democracy* 20, no. 2 (2009): 66–68. See also Chapter 6 for a discussion of the link between performance legitimacy and technocratic governance.

[20] Ibid.

legitimacy."[21] Basing their conclusion on opinion surveys and elite discourse analysis, they show that the Putin government owed its support "to its apparent success in reversing years of economic failure in which GDP and living standards had fallen to not much more than half their level at the end of the Soviet period."[22]

Importantly, this kind of legitimation was predicated on a credible claim to regulate economic matters and to plan for prosperity, nationally as well region by region. Post-Soviet planning for economic development served as a manifestation of a government that is working toward future prosperity.[23] Infrastructure projects in general and electricity sector modernization in particular featured prominently in regional economic development plans, partly because of their ability to demonstrate a state that is engaged in planning for the future. Ambitious state-funded investment projects and modernization plans were not only materially a necessary prerequisite for economic growth; they also served as a symbolic down payment on future prosperity. During the Putin years, the Ministry of Regional Development designated infrastructure development a "highly important tool for the socio-economic development of Russia's regions."[24] The link between electricity and legitimacy was also evident in instances of breakdown and crises. Failure to provide power reliably quickly became a political problem for regional leaders and, ultimately, for the federal government when governors sought to shift blame and responsibility to the center. As we will see in later chapters, the Far East's energy shortages, or the catastrophic explosion at the Sayano-Shushenskaya dam, for example, prompted authorities at different tiers

---

[21] Feklyunina and White provide a nuanced account of the sources of legitimacy of the Putin regime at the end of eight years of his presidency. Valentina Feklyunina and Stephen White, "Discourses of 'Krizis': Economic Crisis in Russia and Regime Legitimacy," *Journal of Communist Studies and Transition Politics* 27, no. 3–4 (2011): 385–406. See also Aron, "The Merger of Power and Property."

[22] Feklyunina and White, "Discourses of 'Krizis.'"

[23] This link to legitimacy was evident in post-Soviet developmentalism's tendency to frame the state as a "provider" rather than as an enabler. The state's role in "providing a livelihood" (*жизнеобеспечение*) is sometimes cited as a goal of development strategies, expressing the notion of the state as a provider – for example, in "Ради социальной стабильности," *Утро России*, February 8, 1994. The state as the provider was also the concept used in Interview #59 with politician/former electricity executive, Irkutsk, 20071130 (see also Chapter 2).

[24] In Russian: "*Важнейшим инструментом влияния на социально-экономическое развитие субъектов Российской Федерации ... является размещение и развитие ... инфраструктуры*" in "Концепция совершенствования региональной политики в Российской Федерации" (*Концепция 2008*, in what follows), Ministry of Regional Development (2008), p. 3.

of the government to search immediately for solutions to restore power, lest these crises be seen as a reflection of the state's weakness.

The modernization of electricity infrastructure held an important place in development strategies. On one level, electricity sector reforms were just one part of a larger set of strategies to reform the Russian economy and push ahead the "transition" from plan to market. But electricity sector reforms – together with energy strategies and infrastructure modernization – were also a characteristic tool for the kind of planning that characterizes post-Soviet developmentalism. They feature prominently because assets that had been built or updated in the first few post–World War II decades were aging. Many power plants and parts of the grid were reaching the end of their life spans, although some regions were more affected than others, depending on their status in the Soviet hierarchy of needs. And while the economic crisis of the 1990s led to overcapacity in the system overall, an uneven recovery resulted in capacity bottlenecks and strained networks in Moscow, Saint Petersburg, and other urban areas. The inclusion of electricity into state-led modernization plans was also related to its particular status and resonance in Russia. "Infrastructure projects provide prospects," noted one observer.[25] The strong symbolism of electricity as the basis for future economic growth creates a link between electricity, prosperity and legitimacy: devising programs to update the former promised the latter. Regional and federal governments pursued infrastructure projects, and electricity modernization in particular, because they were useful symbols of a state that builds the foundations for future prosperity: "The fate of the electricity and energy sector (энергокомплекс) is directly and naturally connected to the preservation of the state, and the political and economic sovereignty of Russia."[26]

Finally, electricity transformation was linked particularly to *regional* development. The Soviet-era electricity system bequeathed each region with its own vertically integrated monopoly provider – the so-called Energo. The Energos were named after their region, Mosenergo for Moscow's Energo, Irkutskenergo for Irkutsk, for example.[27] The Soviet-era organization of the electricity sector had regional features: the Energos were administered via the regional branches of the Soviet Ministry of Energy

---

[25] The last term of this quote in Russian is "*перспективы,*" which entails the promise of opportunities in the future. "Сталин греет Красноярск," *Красноярский рабочий*, August 31, 1993.

[26] Вероника Белоусова, "Под флагом борьбы с монополизмом," *Утро России*, January 14, 1997.

[27] With some exceptions: Primorskii Krai's Energo is called Dal'energo.

and their physical assets were designed to serve regional economies.[28] During the early post-Soviet period, when regional governors were devising plans for their region's integration into domestic and international markets, control of "their" Energos was a logical starting point.[29]

Theorizing Post-Soviet Political Economy and State-Led Development

We can gain broader theoretical insights from a focus on these evolving pacts and agendas that shape Russia's marketization, because post-Soviet developmentalism challenges the way we understand and theorize the state and its relationship to the emerging private owners. The Russian state's project of market integration outlined here differs in a few important respects from how state-led development projects have been theorized elsewhere; at the most general level, it suggests a way to understand the developmental state and economic development as intertwined social constructions.

The Limits of Capture and Predatory State Approaches

Given the pace of change in Russia's political life, theories about the nature of the post-Soviet state have cycled through several revisions over the last fifteen years. In the early post-Soviet period, influenced by views of the Soviet government, the Russian state was regarded as a predatory Leviathan.[30] This characterization was revised as President Yeltsin's government failed to control a rising class of powerful oligarchs. For much

---

[28] This is noted in Kristine Petrosyan, *What Is the Current Status of Russian Electricity Sector in the Light of Restructuring Laws and RAO UES Breakup Strategy* (University of Dundee, UK: Centre for Energy, Petroleum and Mineral Law and Policy, 2004), http://www.dundee.ac.uk/cepmlp/gateway/files.php?file=car8_article23_863317730.pdf. On the structure of the Soviet electricity system, see Бриль and Хейстер, *Экономика Социалистической Энергетики*, 13; Лев Александрович Мелентьев, *Очерки Истории Отечественной Энергетики: Развитие Научно-Технической Мысли* (Наука, 1987), 140.

[29] These plans will be detailed in Chapter 2.

[30] The most prominent post-Soviet observer who places rent-seeking firms and bureaucrats center stage is Anders Åslund, *Building Capitalism: The Transformation of the Former Soviet Bloc* (Cambridge: Cambridge University Press, 2002); and *How Capitalism Was Built: The Transformation of Central and Eastern Europe, Russia, and Central Asia* (Cambridge: Cambridge University Press, 2007). See also Timothy Frye and Andrei Shleifer, *The Invisible Hand and the Grabbing Hand*, Working Paper (National Bureau of Economic Research, December 1996), accessed March 14, 2014, http://www.nber.org/papers/w5856; and Andrei Shleifer and Robert W. Vishny, *The Grabbing Hand: Government Pathologies and Their Cures* (Cambridge, MA: Harvard University Press, 1998).

of the second half of the 1990s, the Russian state was considered captured by these new business interests.[31] Under President Putin, however, capture approaches tend to underestimate the ability of the state to shape economic outcomes. After the reassertion of state authority under Putin, assessments again emphasized that the state is stronger vis-à-vis economic actors, observing that it is increasingly authoritarian, illiberal and invasive.[32] Since the 2004 "renationalization" of Yukos, Russia's largest oil company, and the imprisonment of its owner, the state is typically portrayed as corrupt and unaccountable, arbitrarily applying the rule of law for the personal enrichment of insider elites while pursuing great-power politics in international affairs.[33] While these observations account for salient developments, they miss as much as they grasp.

[31] For arguments about a weak and captured state, see Michael McFaul and Tova Perlmutter, eds., *Privatization, Conversion, and Enterprise Reform in Russia* (Boulder, CO: Westview Press, 1994); Joel S. Hellman, "Winners Take All: The Politics of Partial Reform in Postcommunist Transitions," *World Politics* 50, no. 2 (1998): 203–234; Joel S Hellman, Geraint Jones, and Daniel Kaufmann, "Seize the State, Seize the Day: State Capture and Influence in Transition Economies," *Journal of Comparative Economics* 31, no. 4 (December 2003): 751–773; Andrei Shleifer and Daniel Treisman, *Without a Map: Political Tactics and Economic Reform in Russia* (Cambridge, MA: MIT Press, 2000); and Richard E. Ericson, "Does Russia Have a 'Market Economy'?" *East European Politics & Societies* 15, no. 2 (March 1, 2001): 291–319. More recently, Richard Sakwa relied on the capture argument: "powerful elite groups have an interest in arresting the course of reform." Richard Sakwa, "Systemic Stalemate: *Reiderstvo* and the Dual State," in *The Political Economy of Russia*, ed. Neil Robinson (Lanham, MD: Rowman & Littlefield, 2013), 8. The capture argument is also a common chorus of the news media; see, for example, Georgy Bovt, "King of the Hill," *Moscow Times*, July 31, 2008.

[32] M. Steven Fish, *Democracy Derailed in Russia: The Failure of Open Politics*, Cambridge Studies in Comparative Politics (Cambridge: Cambridge University Press, 2005); and Michael McFaul and Kathryn Stoner-Weiss, "The Myth of the Authoritarian Model: How Putin's Crackdown Holds Russia Back," *Foreign Affairs* 87, no. 1 (2008): 68–84. On the rise of threats to property rights by state actors, see also Jordan Gans-Morse, "Threats to Property Rights in Russia: From Private Coercion to State Aggression," *Post-Soviet Affairs* 28, no. 3 (2012): 263–295.

[33] A recent assessment of the Russian state as an arbitrary predator can be found in McFaul and Stoner-Weiss, "The Myth of the Authoritarian Model." For an account of Russia's great-power ambitions, see James M. Goldgeier and Michael McFaul, "What to Do about Russia?" *Policy Review* 133 (2005): 45–62. Before the 2004 re-nationalization of Yukos, prominent observers credited Putin's government for setting in motion a "far-reaching process of market-friendly change" and for "improving the Russian business environment," praise that acknowledged fiscal reforms as exemplary, see Philip Hanson, "The Russian Economic Recovery: Do Four Years of Growth Tell Us That the Fundamentals Have Changed?" *Europe-Asia Studies* 55, no. 3 (2003): 365, 374. Andrei Yakovlev provides an interesting synopsis of capture before and after the Yukos affair: Andrei Yakovlev, "The Evolution of Business – State Interaction in Russia: From State Capture to Business Capture?" *Europe-Asia Studies* 58, no. 7 (2006): 1033–1056.

The analytical framework for understanding the post-Soviet transition was long dominated by what Collier and Way termed the "deficit model."[34] In the early 1990s, post-Soviet political economy was influenced by the then widespread belief that markets arise naturally, as functional solutions to transaction cost problems. As markets appeared to not develop equally well across post-socialist economies, research turned to measuring degrees of progress and identifying obstacles in the way of reforms.[35] Approaches that emphasized the predatory nature of the state looked to bureaucrats and state-sector employees to assess their ability to block reforms. As the influence on politics by these actors in the public sector turned out to be limited, the view that state actors were captured by powerful private actors came to dominate explanations for the lack of reforms in Russia. In this paradigm, economic development is narrowly conceived as the implementation of liberal reforms. The politics of liberal reform is then conceptualized as concessions made by liberalizing forces to opponents of reform in order to "buy" their approval "through a combination of expropriation and cooptation of stakeholders."[36] The course of reform is easily arrested, as powerful elites capture economic and political reform processes. Concessions are usually considered rents, or rent-seeking opportunities. Private influence on reforms is almost always treated as an obstacle to the creation of markets, and it is assumed that rents "inevitably create distortions."[37] Probably the most influential account of the influence of economic actors is Joel Hellman's argument of the "politics of partial reform."[38] In *Winners Take All*, Hellman argues that collusion between corrupt officials and powerful oligarchs resulted in failed or incomplete reforms. He showed that the "winners" of the early transition phase, a diverse group in which he included "enterprise managers, local officials and Mafiosi," benefiting from a "partial reform equilibrium," prevented the implementation of structural changes that would

[34] See Stephen J. Collier and Lucan Way, "Beyond the Deficit Model: Social Welfare in Post-Soviet Georgia," *Post-Soviet Affairs* 20, no. 3 (2004): 258–284. For similar critiques, see Michael Burawoy and Katherine Verdery, eds., *Uncertain Transition: Ethnographies of Change in the Postsocialist World* (Lanham, MD: Rowman & Littlefield, 1999); and Woodruff, *Money Unmade*.

[35] Studies that measure the degree of progress were often based on the transition scores published by the European Bank for Reconstruction and Development (EBRD). These cross-national measures, published annually, provided a convenient metric to compare how far a country had come in its transition from plan to market.

[36] Shleifer and Treisman, *Without a Map*, 18.

[37] Ibid., 19.

[38] Hellman, "Winners Take All."

have brought Russia closer to a market economy.[39] His account was a corrective to earlier conceptualizations of an overbearing state, whose "grabbing hand" prevented entrepreneurs from reaching their potential.[40] The concept of capture by powerful business interests remains the dominant framework to understand state-business interactions in Russia, although capture approaches adapted to the changing political and economic landscape after the 1998 economic crisis.[41]

Predictions for the trajectory and outcomes of market reforms based on the predatory state or capture approaches have shaped research on the post-Soviet transition. For the electricity sector, these predictions clearly do not explain the sector's historic transformation. The predatory state approach predicts that reforms are prevented by incumbent state actors, hence that the UES monopoly remained intact – serving as a vehicle for public sector employment and bureaucratic rent seeking. The liberal reforms that did happen over the years – most notably, the unbundling of the vertically integrated monopolies, the dissolution of UES, the quite radical reduction in staff numbers across the whole sector, the replacement of incumbent technical experts with new managers at the helm of newly created companies the creation of wholesale markets (processes that will be detailed in the remainder of this book) – are all developments that are fundamentally inconsistent with the predatory state approach.

The capture approach, at first glance, seems to hold more explanatory power. Russian oligarchs did gobble up the most valuable assets of the electricity sector. The argument that these were market-distorting concessions granted by liberal reformers seems plausible. Similarly, my findings seem compatible with the assumption that actors acted in their own interest. Controlling Moscow's profitable power company was no doubt in the interest of Gazprom, for example. The trouble with capture and rent-seeking and interest-based explanations is that they offer only very blunt analytical tools to understand the process of liberal reforms, tools that ignore critical aspects of the trajectory and outcomes of marketization and are eminently unsuitable to explain the complex patterns

---

[39] Ibid., 204.

[40] For the Russian state as the "grabbing hand," see Frye and Shleifer, *The Invisible Hand and the Grabbing Hand*; as well as Åslund, *Building Capitalism*.

[41] The relationship between the state and the oligarchs changed as the federal government strengthened its authority and succeeded in reigning in the oligarchs. The powerful business interests that were thought to have captured the reform process are now members of President Putin's inner circle, occupying dual seats as heads of state-owned and quasi-statal enterprises as well as Kremlin insider. These developments are discussed in detail in Chapter 2.

of liberal and illiberal elements that characterize markets in Russia and elsewhere. They are ultimately not persuasive because they rarely explain *what* conglomerates sought to achieve in different reform arenas, or *how* this lobbying actually affected institutions formed during the reform process.

A first problem of capture approaches is that actors are defined via a set of highly stylized, decontextualized notions of public and private interest that shape their behavior vis-à-vis each other.[42] These kinds of stylized, interest-based notions of state-business interaction are useful if one seeks to model causal factors at play across time and space. The assumption of uniform self-interest is less compelling for studies of marketization and economization. In particular, decontextualized models of interest cannot explain why actors have differentiated positions and shaped reforms differently across Russia's regions. How would a capture approach explain that Gazprom, the largest and undoubtedly most powerful of all Russian firms, supported liberal reforms, while Rusal, another powerful oligarchic conglomerate did not? And how would it explain that subsidies persisted in the Far East but were being gradually phased out in European Russia? As soon as we seek to understand the complex trajectories and outcomes of reforms, we need an explanation for how a particular "capturer" shaped reforms and what its interests were in the particular sector at stake. But to obtain such an explanation, we need to understand the conglomerate's ties to the electricity sector (Gazprom sought out gas-fired power plants, for example), the industrial geography of Russia's regions (Rusal's aluminum smelters were built adjacent to Siberia's valuable hydroelectric dams), and the development strategies of a particular region (the Far East's integration with East Asia relies on energy cooperation, for example). In more general terms, seeking to understand how various interests shaped reforms prompts us to contextualize interests in physical landscapes and ideational frameworks.

Finally, capture approaches rely on other notions that are not well suited to grasp the marketization and economization. Even if not explicitly prescriptive, research often ends up assessing or measuring the distance between Russian and ideal-typical institutions.[43] The very

---

[42] The assumptions of rational choice institutionalism underlie much of post-Soviet political economy; they are explicitly endorsed, for example, by Li-Chen Sim, *The Rise and Fall of Privatization in the Russian Oil Industry* (New York: Palgrave Macmillan, 2008), 9.

[43] See, for example, Weingast and De Figueiredo, "Russian Federalism: A Contradiction in Terms"; Weingast and De Figueiredo, "Pathologies of Federalism, Russian Style: Political Institutions and Economic Transition"; Ekaterina Zhuravskaya and Sergei Guriev,

notion of distortion similarly presumes an idealized, functioning market economy free of such flaws. Capture approaches have also tended to focus on one side of the state-oligarch pacts – market-distorting concessions. Because of this focus on distortion and dysfunction, this literature systematically underestimated the extent to which market mechanisms were instituted. The most common assessment of Russia's economic reforms is that they have run aground and that they created an incomplete market order. Market institutions – and political institutions, for that matter – are generally seen as underdeveloped or delayed.[44] Hellman's framework, for example, sought mainly to explain the absence of reforms during the 1990s, hence his framework cannot account for the tremendously important structural changes that have taken place. More recently, another observer has even argued that "Russia has proven resistant to change."[45] This assessment belies and obscures the enormous reorganizations of Russia's economy during the two post-Soviet decades.

Andrei Shleifer and Daniel Treisman, in *Without a Map*, provided a more nuanced version of the capture account, arguing that there have been failures and successes in implementing market reforms. In their framework, change happened when reformers made "an accurate assessment" of opportunities and constraints, when they managed to "play off some groups against others" to pass a policy, by building a "pro-reform coalition" that was stronger than the "status quo coalition."[46] Shleifer and Treisman's account conceives of liberal reforms as policies rather than as institution building and market construction. Partly as a result of this, they overestimated the importance of shrewd strategy by reform-minded politicians and underestimated the complexity of structural change and the variability of outcomes.[47]

"Why Russia Is Not South Korea," *Journal of International Affairs* 63, no. 2 (2010), accessed March 15, 2014, http://hal.archives-ouvertes.fr/halshs-00754457/; Timothy Frye, *Building States and Markets after Communism: The Perils of Polarized Democracy* (Cambridge: Cambridge University Press, 2010); Hellman, Jones, and Kaufmann, "Seize the State, Seize the Day"; Åslund, *How Capitalism Was Built*; Hellman, "Winners Take All"; Frye and Shleifer, *The Invisible Hand and the Grabbing Hand*.

[44] Most explicitly, Zhuravskaya and Guriev, "Why Russia Is Not South Korea." but also work cited in previous footnote.

[45] Neil Robinson, "Introduction: The Political Problems of Russian Capitalism," in *The Political Economy of Russia*, ed. Neil Robinson (Lanham, MD: Rowman & Littlefield, 2013), 6.

[46] Shleifer and Treisman, *Without a Map*, 18.

[47] See Hanson for a comprehensive review of several assessments of reforms in the early 2000s; Hanson, "The Russian Economic Recovery."

A related problem is that many of the distinctions between private
and public actors, between "winners and losers," between "reformers"
and "capturers," that predatory and capture approaches rely on fail to
map onto post-Soviet realities. Gazprom was both an early winner – in
Hellman's framework, a potent "capturer" – and a state-owned company
compelled to subsidize Russian industry. Rusal is a private company, but
its interaction with other companies and the regional and federal governments were not arms-length transactions, nor simply determined by the
law of the land. The moment we seek to explain the terms of the bargains
between the government and Gazprom, Rusal and the electricity sector, we
need to understand what have been called "pre-contractual" elements –
who sits at the bargaining table and what defines their relationship to
each other?[48] And when we try to answer these questions, we cannot but
enter the realm of accounts of how Russia's energy system was built in
Soviet times and the varied roles actors play in its transformation.

My main point here is that a reliance on analytical categories such as
"self-interested actors" and "competitive markets" has limited our understanding of the origin and dynamics of new market institutions. As noted
in the introduction, this book in no way disputes that corruption and
predation were extremely prevalent, even endemic in post-Soviet Russia.
Nor do I want to whitewash the serious flaws of Vladimir Putin's rule
by emphasizing long-term developmental strategies. Rather than setting
out to disprove capture theories, I instead hope to shed light on aspects
of market reforms often obscured by capture theories. And while the
capture argument and this book's emphasis on long-term developmental
strategies are not necessarily incompatible, they entail important theoretical differences in how state-market relations are conceived. Finally, while
challenging capture theories, this book also confirms a mainstay of post-
Soviet political economy: Russia's emerging oligarchic conglomerates did
indeed play an important role in explaining Russia's post-Soviet trajectory. Whether old Soviet enterprise directors turned owners, nomenklatura youths turned oligarchs, or state-owned industrial complexes turned
global conglomerates, such actors exercised more influence than parties,
social movements, and unions.[49]

[48] John Lie, "Sociology of Markets," *Annual Review of Sociology* 23 (January 1, 1997):
341–360.
[49] For an account on the relative strength of unions in post-Socialist settings, see Rudra
Sil and Calvin Chen, "Communist Legacies, Postcommunist Transformations, and the
Fate of Organized Labor in Russia and China," *Studies in Comparative International*

Beyond Capture – Developmental Strategies as Legitimizing Narratives

Capture and predatory state approaches are rationalist accounts of post-Soviet politics that neglect ideational frameworks. "Politics" is conceptualized as the battle between vested interests. With some important exceptions, rationalist conceptualizations dominate analyses of post-Soviet political economy. Similarly, Russian capitalism is often described as a post-ideological space, a type of Wild West Capitalism where "ideas" do not matter while interests rein supreme.[50] The centrality of post-Soviet developmentalism in the marketization of electricity, by contrast, affirms the relevance of ideational and discursive dimensions and opens opportunities to theorize how ideas and interests are intertwined.

Developmental strategies legitimize interests by providing credible narratives and visions of future prosperity. Gunnar Trumbull's *Strength in Numbers* – a critique of theories wedded to interests and their influence on economic policies – illustrates how the notion of legitimizing narratives is useful. Trumbull refutes Mancur Olson's logic that concentrated interests are inherently more powerful than diffuse interests, proposing instead that interests' perceived legitimacy and their participation in "legitimacy coalitions" was more important in deciding who shaped policy. He argues that industries succeed in influencing policy only when they align their agenda with a broader set of diffuse interests via legitimating narratives.[51] Post-Soviet developmental strategies provide a kind of legitimating narrative: they link the influence of oligarchs on reform outcomes, and hence authorities' decisions in their favor, to broader social goals. In the case of the electricity sector, these narratives were

Development 41, no. 2 (2006): 62–87. For two accounts of the political dynamics of utility privatization in Latin America, see María Victoria Murillo, *Political Competition, Partisanship, and Policymaking in Latin American Public Utilities* (Cambridge: Cambridge University Press, 2009); and Alison E. Post, "Pathways for Redistribution: Privatisation, Regulation and Incentives for pro-Poor Investment in the Argentine Water Sector," *International Journal of Public Policy* 4, no. 1 (January 1, 2009): 51–75.

[50] This is a quote by Dmitry Trenin, who argues that in today's Russia "ideas hardly matter, whereas interests reign supreme. It is not surprising then that the worldview of Russian elites is focused on financial interests. (...)Values are secondary or tertiary issues (...)." Dmitri Trenin, "Russia Redefines Itself and Its Relations with the West," *The Washington Quarterly* 30, no. 2 (2007): 95. The most explicit and notable exceptions to the rationalist dominance in post-Soviet political economy are Yoshiko Herrera, Rawi Abdelal and Rudra Sil.

[51] Gunnar Trumbull, *Strength in Numbers the Political Power of Weak Interests* (Cambridge, MA: Harvard University Press, 2012), 26.

regional, and reform trajectories were tailored to distinct geographical contexts.[52]

Understanding development strategies in this way also helps us overcome the dichotomy of interests and ideas that pervades much of political economy and contributes to a central theoretical goal of constructivist political economy.[53] Competing with materialist and rationalist accounts, ideational accounts tend to argue that ideas matter more than a bundle of economic or material factors do.[54] Hillary Appel, for example, explained distinct privatization outcomes in Russia and the Czech Republic by emphasizing that ideology was the key variable that accounted for these differences, while rational interests could not.[55] While I emphasize that regional development strategies were ideational constructs, I am not making the argument that ideas trump interests, nor that actors acted against their interest, but in accordance with developmental ideas. Interests mattered crucially in shaping reform outcomes: Gazprom was certainly interested in choice assets of European Russia's power sector, for example. Yet neither interests nor ideas alone explain the particular patterns of how the electricity sector marketized, as Chapter 3 elaborates.

Constructivist studies often seek to stabilize cultural factors in order to demonstrate their causal force and treat ideational factors as a relatively fixed set of ideas, often a set of shared norms or ideology that preexist the explanandum. In *National Purpose in the World Economy*, Rawi Abdelal explains divergent paths in foreign economic policies with reference to relatively static national identities. While he notes that nationalist projects are always contested, he is most interested in the agreements societies

---

[52] The selective and strategic reliance on a repertoire of resonant ideas supports Nicolas Jabko's notion of "strategic constructivism." Jabko, *Playing the Market*.

[53] For other critiques of the ideas/interest dichotomy, see Regine Abrami and David Woodruff, "Toward a Manifesto: Interpretive Materialist Political Economy", 2004. For a study of the relevance of ideas in developmental strategies, see Kathryn Sikkink, *Ideas and Institutions: Developmentalism in Brazil and Argentina*, Cornell studies in political economy (Ithaca, NY: Cornell University Press, 1991).

[54] Hilary Appel, "The Ideological Determinants of Liberal Economic Reform: The Case of Privatization," *World Politics* 52, no. 4 (2000): 520–549. The distancing from material factors varies in the contributions to Rawi Abdelal, Mark Blyth, and Craig Parsons, eds., *Constructing the International Economy* (Ithaca, NY: Cornell University Press, 2010); and Yoshiko M. Herrera, *Imagined Economies: The Sources of Russian Regionalism*, Cambridge studies in comparative politics (Cambridge: Cambridge University Press, 2005). See also Rawi Abdelal, *National Purpose in the World Economy: Post-Soviet States in Comparative Perspective*, Cornell studies in political economy (Ithaca, NY: Cornell University Press, 2001).

[55] Appel, "The Ideological Determinants of Liberal Economic Reform."

reach, the "outcomes" of societal debates.[56] The ideological variable that Appel isolates is the pervasiveness of anticommunism. Like Abdelal and Appel, I found that ideational contexts matter. Like Yoshiko Herrera in *Imagined Economies*, I found that regionally patterned developmental agendas are deeply influenced by inherited notions about a region's role in domestic and international economies.[57] At the same time, the actual, concrete decisions about who was to become new owner of a power plant, about the pace of tariff increases, and myriad other decisions were the outcome of compromises, not of a stable consensus. Hence, it was not one ideology or one dogma that shaped outcomes, but the contingent agreements reached in bargains between various actors. Post-Soviet developmentalism is not one set of consistent norms; it is a contested, dynamic ideational framework. On one level, this complicates the task of demonstrating its relevance. While I reveal some constant features – a concern over keeping factory doors open, for example – strategies to achieve this goal were contested and varied across Russia. *Post-Soviet Power* then demonstrates the importance of evolving and unmoored ideational frameworks for explanations of complex market arrangements.[58]

In countering the dominant interest-based approaches in political economy, my research draws on the methods and ontology of economic sociology.[59] Sociological approaches to post-Soviet political economy document the emergence of market institutions in a particular historical, political, and social context. These studies have analyzed the complicated ways in which foundational market institutions have changed, each suggesting that the political logic of liberal reforms is deeply implicated in particular

---

[56] Abdelal, *National Purpose in the World Economy*. A minority of constructivist research projects treat norms as subject to ongoing construction. See Jabko, *Playing the Market*; and Catherine Weaver, "The Meaning of Development: Constructing the World Bank's Good Governance Agenda," in *Constructing the International Economy*, ed. Rawi Abdelal, Mark Blyth, and Craig Parsons (Ithaca, NY: Cornell University Press, 2010), 47.

[57] Herrera, *Imagined Economies*.

[58] In this understanding of how ideational constructs function, my work is closer to Stephen Collier's work that examines neoliberalism not as an ideology antithetical Soviet modernity, but as a reflexive critique of the Soviet social state. Collier, *Post-Soviet Social*.

[59] Smelser and Swedberg's Handbook provides overview of various approaches to economic sociology: Neil J. Smelser and Richard Swedberg, eds., *The Handbook of Economic Sociology*, 2nd ed. (Princeton, NJ: Princeton University Press, 2005). See also Koray Çalışkan and Michel Callon, "Economization, Part 1: Shifting Attention from the Economy towards Processes of Economization," *Economy and Society* 38, no. 3 (2009): 369–398; and "Economization, Part 2: A Research Programme for the Study of Markets," *Economy and Society* 39, no. 1 (2010): 1–32.

historical circumstances. They have also, to varying extents, identified developmental concerns by Russian authorities as part of the post-Soviet story.[60] Andrew Barnes's *Owning Russia* showed that actors' motivations in Russia's privatization struggles were highly political, hence broader than rent-seeking and capture explanations suggest. Niobe Thompson's account of economic development and modernization in the Northern Region Chukotka, *Settlers on the Edge*, and Jessica Allina-Pisano's study on land privatization, *Post-Soviet Potemkin Village*, both discuss the relevance of authorities' concerns with economic development.[61] David Woodruff's account of Russia's barter economy, *Money Unmade*, placed developmental motives of regional leaders at the center of his explanation of the rise of Russia's tenacious barter economy. Regional governors' efforts to keep factory doors open were a defining aspect of the state-business relationships Woodruff observed in the 1990s: "[F]or a local government, the failure of a single factory employing several thousand people seemed an unacceptable disaster."[62] Regional leaders endorsed the use of barter and nonmonetary means of exchange to prevent enterprises from going out of business.

This book is grounded in the intellectual tradition that informs David Woodruff and Stephen Collier's work – one that sees markets as fundamentally constructed social entities, and I utilize the methodologies that unite the research by Barnes, Thompson, Allina-Pisano, Woodruff and Collier – detailed empirical process tracing of how market arrangements and institutions were forged. *Post-Soviet Power* draws on and confirms many of their specific findings; subsequent chapters address convergences in more detail. Landmark studies in economic sociology outside of Russia have looked at the electricity sector as a compelling lens to demonstrate

---

[60] Woodruff, *Money Unmade*; Herrera, *Imagined Economies*; Barnes, *Owning Russia*; Juliet Johnson, *A Fistful of Rubles: The Rise and Fall of the Russian Banking System* (Ithaca, NY: Cornell University Press, 2000); and Jessica Allina-Pisano, *The Post-Soviet Potemkin Village: Politics and Property Rights in the Black Earth* (Cambridge: Cambridge University Press, 2008).

[61] Allina-Pisano's *Potemkin Village* shows how different versions of rural development pitted national policy makers against district officials loath to implement liberal reforms. Thompson's *Settlers on the Edge* traces how successive modernization projects reshaped the northern region of Chukhotka.

[62] David Woodruff, *Money Unmade: Barter and the Fate of Russian Capitalism* (Ithaca, NY: Cornell University Press, 1999), 115 and pp.130. Woodruff's focus is regional governor's acceptance of barter and various non-monetary means of settling tax debt, see p.135 in particular.

how interacting political, social, and technological forces shape econo-mies.[63] The story of the Russian electricity sector presented here follows this tradition too, relying on electricity to shed light on how markets, politics, and physical facts shaped Russia's post-Soviet transition. But the book also advances the sociological tradition in political economy: by relying more explicitly on economic sociology's notion of markets as social constructs, it offers a novel approach to study state-led develop-ment, to be discussed next.

State-Led Development as an Evolving, Contested, and Reflexive Project

Post-Soviet developmental strategies intended to enhance domestic com-petitiveness at a particular time and in a particular geographical space. Much like in the state-directed industrialization in East Asian and Latin American countries, statist views ultimately proved more influential than hands-off liberalism, which then defined ensuing state-market pacts. These characteristics align post-Soviet developmentalism with other state-led development projects. It is also different in many ways. What can we gain from leveraging similarities and differences? What can we learn from the post-Soviet case for state-directed development projects elsewhere?[64]

There were a series of important differences between the Russian con-text and the East Asian countries, where developmental state theories orig-inated. Post-Soviet development strategies were devised in the context of large-scale *de*industrialization rather than as a strategy to industrialize a rural economy. Post-Soviet strategies had little choice but to grapple with the inherited Soviet patterns of industrialization, shaped by the Soviet

---

[63] Thomas Parke Hughes, *Networks of Power: Electrification in Western Society, 1880–1930* (Baltimore, MD: Johns Hopkins University Press, 1983); and Mark Granovetter and Patrick McGuire, "The Making of an Industry: Electricity in the United States," in *The Law of Markets*, ed. Michel Callon (Oxford: Blackwell, 1998), 147–73.

[64] My research is influenced by central aspects of the developmental state literature, such as the notion of economic development as a historically embedded project. See Chalmers Johnson, *MITI and the Japanese Miracle: The Growth of Industrial Policy, 1925–1975* (Stanford, CA: Stanford University Press, 1982); Peter B. Evans, *Embedded Autonomy: States and Industrial Transformation* (Princeton, NJ: Princeton University Press, 1995); Robert Wade, *Governing the Market: Economic Theory and the Role of Government in East Asian Industrialization* (Princeton, N.J: Princeton University Press, 1990); Alice H. Amsden, *The Rise of "the Rest": Challenges to the West from Late-Industrialization Economies* (Oxford: Oxford University Press, 2001); and Atul Kohli, *State-Directed Development: Political Power and Industrialization in the Global Periphery* (Cambridge: Cambridge University Press, 2004).

state's vision of social modernity.[65] The Russian also state had virtually no experience as a regulator of private actors. And post-Soviet market institutions were built during an exceptionally turbulent period, as the collapse of the Soviet Union simultaneously undid an established economic order and triggered a crisis of state sovereignty. The roughly twenty years that are examined in the pages that follow are marked first by a severe economic crisis and the fragmentation of sovereignty, and later by attempts to strengthen state authority during an oil boom. Finally, partly because of this turmoil, the period under discussion was exceptionally fluid. In other words, the institutional foundations of politics and markets have been changing dramatically over the last fifteen years.[66]

This fluidity and institutional change stand in contrast with existing research on the developmental state. The focus of this research on continuity rather than change stems from an overriding concern with the evaluation of states' and planning bureaucracies' efforts to promote economic growth and development. These studies aim to distill the forms of state intervention that have propelled some countries ahead, distinguishing them from others that created large bureaucracies without boosting economic growth. The origins of institutional foundations are located in the past and are presumed to be relatively stable over time. Atul Kohli's study of the developmental state details cross-country institutional differences such authority structures, state capacity, and bureaucratic organization to explain variation in the efficacy of state-directed development programs.[67] *Post-Soviet Power*, by contrast, focuses on foundational aspects of market institutions not as ex-ante national peculiarities, but as prizes in ongoing political struggles over the architecture of market institutions. The story that unfolds here addresses the political preconditions for the electricity sectors' marketization *and* draws attention to the political consequences of market reforms. What this book has to offer to debates on state-led development beyond Russia is an analysis of the relationship between market reforms and authority as reflexive and mutually constitutive processes. Not only are particular market arrangements premised on certain political structures; the political and social status of

---

[65] A landmarks study of Soviet high modernism is Stephen Kotkin, *Magnetic Mountain: Stalinism as a Civilization* (Berkeley: University of California Press, 1995). See also Collier, *Post-Soviet Social*.

[66] Andrew Barnes and Stanislav Markus also draw attention to this. See Barnes, *Owning Russia*; and Stanislav Markus, "Capitalists of All Russia, Unite! Business Mobilization Under Debilitated Dirigisme," *Polity* 39, no. 3 (2007): 277–304.

[67] Kohli, *State-Directed Development*.

market-making actors is also produced (either consolidated or undermined) by the markets they create.

Regarding state-led development as an evolving and contested project is more than a methodological preference. It entails a shift in focus
toward the political and social processes in which development projects
are forged and progress, which has empirical and theoretical implications
for how we understand economic development.[68]

Empirically, it allows us to trace how developmental projects are
politically contested terrain, and conversely, to see transformations of the
political arena as part and parcel of economic reforms. Typically, political economy examines how power structures produce market outcomes,
paying far less attention to how particular market arrangements in turn
empower some market participants while sidelining others.[69] Tracing
the politics of ownership, subsidies, and expertise, I found that political struggles surrounding market reforms were battles not only – or not
primarily – over resources but also over the ability to shape markets and
over the political consequences of reforms. Opponents of liberal reforms
were motivated not only by short-term rent seeking or by the fear of losing access to resources. At stake was the ability to influence the terms of
regional integration into domestic and international markets, and ultimately the authority to shape market arrangements. Governors and other
groups opposing liberal reforms were loath to relinquish control of the
electricity sector not because it meant losing resources – in fact only very
few electricity companies in the 1990s were generating profits for regional

---

[68] Debates on the evolution of institutional underpinnings market economies draw mostly
on examples of advanced market economies. The fault lines of these debates concern the
weight of agency versus inherited structures in shaping/constraining institutional change.
Key texts are Kathleen Ann Thelen, *How Institutions Evolve: The Political Economy of
Skills in Germany, Britain, the United States, and Japan*, Cambridge studies in comparative politics (Cambridge: Cambridge University Press, 2004); and Paul Pierson, *Politics in
Time: History, Institutions, and Social Analysis* (Princeton, NJ: Princeton University Press,
2004). Most recently, the volume *Political Creativity* has contributed pragmatist perspectives to these debates, underscoring the value of research that understands structure and
agency as mutually constitutive. Berk, Galvan, and Hattam, *Political Creativity*.

[69] In these studies, political conditions are modeled to assess how reforms redistribute
resources. They then go on to examine whether constituencies that stand to gain have
sufficient collective action potential, or conversely, whether constituency that stand
to lose (monopoly rents or public sector wages, for example) are able block reforms.
See for example, Stephan Haggard, *The Political Economy of Democratic Transitions*
(Princeton, NJ: Princeton University Press, 1995); and Adam Przeworski, *Democracy
and the Market: Political and Economic Reforms in Eastern Europe and Latin America*,
Studies in rationality and social change (Cambridge: Cambridge University Press, 1991)
in addition to Russia specific literature cited above.

budgets. It meant losing a powerful tool to influence regional economies and it undermined their authority to govern. Similarly, Putin centralized political power not only to neutralize political opponents and gain access to resources, but more broadly to regain the ability and authority to govern and regulate economic activity from the center. And once reforms were implemented, they indeed shifted the political terrain. New zones of governance emerged during the marketization: regional (*oblast*) level regulation was effectively supplanted by regulation at the level of newly constituted supra-regions, where new political actors shaped the future of the sector. Much like other aspects of marketization, boundaries of regulatory zones were shaped in contingent political conflicts.

The literature on state-led development tends to rely on static national models. In other words, national economic transformations are determined by the manner in which they are embedded in political and social structures. Peter Evans' work on embedded autonomy established the importance of relationships between state planners and businesses.[70] Other studies subsequently emphasized the importance of reciprocity in state-business relationships in East Asia.[71] The bargains in Russia's electricity sector were embedded in regional social and political relations, and they very much rested on reciprocal concessions and thus confirm these points. Yet, the evidence in this book also highlights how concessions by both sides were politically contested terrain, and that the political terrain shifted as reforms were implemented and new actors emerged. Evans leaves open the possibility that bargains change over time, as he notes that new actors and social groups might be empowered by the results of a chosen developmental strategy.[72] Yet, this process and how it could in turn shape developmental strategies is essentially outside the purview of his study. The core chapters of *Post-Soviet Power* describe the evolution of three foundational market institutions and show how the implementation of market reforms shifted the political arena over time: ownership patterns, tariff and subsidy regimes, and expertise. Ownership transfers during privatization created de-territorialized holding companies, tariff liberalization created new regulatory institutions, and corporate

---

[70] Evans, *Embedded Autonomy*.
[71] Richard F. Doner, Bryan K. Ritchie, and Dan Slater, "Systemic Vulnerability and the Origins of Developmental States: Northeast and Southeast Asia in Comparative Perspective," *International Organization* 59, no. 02 (2005): 327–361; Amsden, *The Rise of "the Rest,"* 8; and Robert Wade, "After the Crisis: Industrial Policy and the Developmental State in Low-Income Countries," *Global Policy* 1, no. 2 (2010): 155.
[72] Evans, *Embedded Autonomy*, 227.

restructuring installed new cadres with no ties to incumbent elites – each with profound consequences for the political dynamics that would continue to shape the sector.

At its broadest, my research suggests that market institutions are continuously reshaped in contingent political contests. Liberalization and marketization not only transform economic institutions; they also reshape authority structures. A corollary of this observation is a dynamic notion of embedded institutions. Rules and regulations underpinning markets institutions are premised on politics and society – hence embedded – but they also fundamentally shape them. The chapters that follow demonstrate how political and social actions were both bound by structures and able to adapt them. I am particularly interested in material structures – that is, the physical manifestations of Soviet-era industry and how they were reconfigured during the course of market integration. I argue that inherited physical structures shaped outcomes but that they did not function as structural determinants. They could influence post-Soviet markets only if they were successfully mobilized and validated in political arguments about sector restructuring.[73] This nondeterministic notion of embeddedness recasts debates on the developmental states, opening opportunities to understand state-led development as continuously evolving construction projects rather than as national models. A number of more recent contributions in this literature have identified and theorized a new, "flexible" developmental state.[74] These studies show that states mediate the dynamic interaction of domestic actors with global markets, describing policies that foster "post-Fordist networks of production and innovation," increasingly seen as the drivers for growth in postindustrial knowledge economies.[75] One salient insight is that even in

---

[73] The focus of my research on sub-national outcomes provides a perspective on state responses to the differing vulnerabilities and industrial geographies of particular regions. Wade suggests "policies that are tailored to the different vulnerabilities" as a way to think beyond the current liberal consensus on development. Robert Wade, "What Strategies Are Viable for Developing Countries Today? The World Trade Organization and the Shrinking of 'development Space,'" *Review of International Political Economy* 10, no. 4 (2003): 621–644. For the landmark study on post-communist institutional recombination, see David Charles Stark, *Postsocialist Pathways: Transforming Politics and Property in East Central Europe*, Cambridge studies in comparative politics (Cambridge: Cambridge University Press, 1998) see, e.g., p. 12.

[74] Sean O Riain, "The Flexible Developmental State: Globalization, Information Technology and the 'Celtic Tiger,'" *Politics and Society* 28, no. 2 (June 2000): 157–193; and Fred Block, "Swimming Against the Current: The Rise of a Hidden Developmental State in the United States," *Politics & Society* 36, no. 2 (June 1, 2008): 169–206.

[75] O Riain, "The Flexible Developmental State."

the age of highly globalized markets, statist policies are the norm rather
the exception. At the same time, the focus of this literature is often on the
state's role in nurturing new sectors and industries, such as IT and biotechnology, and they tend to be less interested in the political contestation
over the role of "old" sectors and institutions in new developmental strategies.[76] The recognition of the reflexive, dynamic, and contingent relationship between authority and market development suggest that both
old sectors and new strategies are important. But rather than tracing how
actors are confined by inherited, "old" institutions and structures, studies
could draw attention to how they are reconfigured in political negotiations about new developmental models.

Finally, a shift toward a more dynamic approach to state-led development dovetails with new approaches in development economics that
emphasize the importance of institutional innovation, experimentation,
and learning for economic development.[77] Dani Rodrik has been at the
forefront of this approach on "economic development as self-discovery."
He argues that economic development outside the industrialized West
does not rely on the reproduction of market and regulatory institutions
that follow the trajectory of advanced industrial countries; instead, development hinges on country's ability to "learn at what they are good at
producing."[78] Evans and Block have also stressed the importance of institutional innovation for economic development.[79] Charles Sabel finds
these processes essential as well, although he qualifies the possibilities
of self-discovery, emphasizing the relevance of established relationships
and institutions that coordinate economies.[80] These arguments go far
beyond the "good governance" agenda and the consensus that markets

---

[76] This is due to a focus on knowledge-based economies of Europe and the US. See for
example John Zysman and Abraham Newman, eds., *How Revolutionary Was the Digital
Revolution? National Responses, Market Transitions, and Global Technology*, Innovation
and technology in the world economy (Stanford, CA: Stanford Business Books, 2006).

[77] See Ricardo Hausmann and Dani Rodrik, "Economic Development as Self-Discovery,"
Journal of Development Economics 72, no. 2 (December 2003): 603–633; and Charles
F. Sabel, "Self-Discovery as a Coordination Problem," in *Export Pioneers in Latin
America*, ed. Charles F. Sabel et al. (Washington, DC: Inter-American Development Bank,
2012), 1–46.

[78] Dani Rodrik, *One Economics, Many Recipes: Globalization, Institutions, and Economic
Growth* (Princeton, NJ: Princeton University Press, 2007).

[79] Fred Block and Peter Evans, "The State and the Economy," in *The Handbook of Economic
Sociology*, ed. Neil J. Smelser and Richard Swedberg, 2nd ed. (Princeton, NJ: Princeton
University Press, 2005), 505–526.

[80] Sabel, "Self-Discovery as a Coordination Problem."

cannot function without institutions – Douglas North's rules of the game. They open opportunities for studies how institutions evolve in learning processes. If institutional innovation is key for development, the messy processes of disagreement and contestation, and the uneven, heterogeneous market institutions that are thereby forged, are inherently part of economic development. But while this turn in development economics is promising, economists tend to lack the tools to examine social and political processes that underpin learning and self-discovery. Economic sociology, on the other hand, while attuned to the social construction of markets, is often relatively oblivious to politics.[81] *Post-Soviet Power*'s account of how market institutions were forged spans a bridge between economic sociology and the debates on the political economy of development.

Methodology and Logic of Comparison

The research conducted for this study of post-Soviet electricity sector was essentially inductive: I started looking at the transformation of the sector, followed the reorganization of the power grid and power plants, and sought out explanations that sector insiders provided. As noted in the Introduction, there is no doubt that electricity is an "easy case" to demonstrate that developmental considerations are relevant to the political dynamics that underpin market construction. Placing the electricity system at the heart of economic planning has a long tradition in Russia; since the early days of the Soviet Union's existence, planning went hand

---

[81] The notion of markets as fundamentally constructed and socially embedded is well established in economic sociology, in particular for performativity approaches. Some contributions in this field also provides interesting notions of power, as a quality that is conferred by market participants' position within market relations, rather than as something external to market relations. See Koray Çalışkan, *Market Threads: How Cotton Farmers and Traders Create a Global Commodity* (Princeton, NJ: Princeton University Press, 2010). But while attune to power, politics often remains an afterthought in economic sociology. (Marion Fourcade's work is exception. See Marion Fourcade, *Economists and Societies: Discipline and Profession in the United States, Britain, and France, 1890s to 1990s*, Princeton studies in cultural sociology (Princeton, NJ: Princeton University Press, 2009).) If at all, politics is conceptualized as lobbying, i.e. attempts to influence legislation by organized interest groups, see Donald A MacKenzie, *Material Markets How Economic Agents Are Constructed* (Oxford: Oxford University Press, 2009), 159. The concept of lobbying is limiting in the post-Soviet context for a number of reasons, mainly because channels of interest group influence are not formally institutionalized. Also, lobbying implies a distinction between private actors and government officials that is not realistic in Russia.

in hand with electrification.[82] Electricity is also an interesting lens to study the politics of market making for a few reasons that are not specific to Russia. Utilities are regulatory intensive in all countries. Power is a key input for most economic interests as well as a socially important service; reform outcomes matter for a broad spectrum of constituencies and are often highly political. It is also a sector where liberal reforms are both very common and very challenging. From the United Kingdom to Chile to California, creating markets for power has proven more difficult than liberal reformers anticipated. The 2000 California energy crisis, for example, led to price increases for years to come (by most accounts, the crisis was a direct result of new market participants manipulating the sector's regulation, creating bottlenecks that led to price increases benefiting these very actors).[83] Yet, even though developmental strategies were particularly influential for the restructuring of Russia's electricity provision, they were also relevant for other sectors, including railways and gas. And while power is a special sector, the complex patterns of liberal and illiberal elements that characterize market arrangements in electricity characterize other sectors and markets elsewhere, as the Introduction argued. The Conclusion of the book comes back to these points.

The evidence that supports the empirical narrative and theoretical claims of this book follows from the objective to explore how the qualitative patterns of electricity markets emerged in the post-Soviet period. I rely mainly on two structured but interwoven comparisons – an over-time comparison and a cross-regional comparison. Each chapter contains an over-time comparison, tracing the shifts in "Power Politics" between Yeltsin and Putin eras and comparing successes and failures of respective attempts to reform the Soviet-era monopoly. Chapters 3, 4, and 5 compare the sector's trajectory across Russia's regions. Spatial – that is, cross-regional – comparisons trace how subsidy and ownership regimes evolved differently across Russia's regions. For both comparisons I rely on two types of evidence. The first type consists of statements by regional and federal authorities and by private stakeholders that explicitly describe how the electricity sector was a key element of social

---

[82] Soviet industrialization, and even more broadly, the project of Soviet economic development was intricately linked to electrification. See for example, Jonathan Coopersmith, *The Electrification of Russia, 1880–1926* (Ithaca, NY: Cornell University Press, 1992).

[83] Paul L. Joskow, "Markets for Power in the United States: An Interim Assessment.," *Energy Journal* 27, no. 1 (2006).

and economic development. For the 1990s I rely extensively on statements about regional economic development by regional stakeholders. References that connected the reforms in the electricity sector with regional development were ubiquitous in the first post-Soviet decade, both in interviews and in regional and national media sources. As the political arena for electricity sector politics shifted from the regions to the center, my focus moves to federal level development strategies. For both periods I show that the cross-regional differences in reform trajectories align with regionally specific developmental bargains, as Table 1.1 summarized.

Research on power and influence in post-Soviet countries is often difficult, as political influence is not easily intelligible, at least compared with countries where established and well-organized interest groups exist. More often than not, influence is exerted informally rather than via partisan politics, business association, or labor unions. A few methodological decisions underlying this research therefore bear explanation. I utilize a variety of different sources: interviews, a variety of Russian-language newspaper accounts, and two original data sets on tariffs and ownership. Each of these sources has its own merit: I found ongoing and detailed coverage of the politics pertaining to the electricity sector's transformation in regional newspaper accounts (see Appendix 1 for a list of the major newspapers that I relied on). Expert interviews were invaluable for contextualizing media reports. I conducted more than sixty-five interviews during eleven months of fieldwork in 2006 and 2007; interviews with experts and observers included representatives of electricity companies, bureaucrats, regulators, academics, journalists, and sector analysts with Moscow-based financial institutions (see Appendix 2 for a list of interviews). Finally, I obtained unpublished data on regional electricity tariffs, which I used to compile a data set on subsidies and tariff liberalization. The subsidy regimes that I identify in Chapter 5 are based on thirty regions across Russia (twelve largest electricity producing regions in European Russia, ten such regions in Siberia, and eight in the Far East). The claims on ownership regimes in Chapter 4 are based on data that I compiled from media sources on ownership transfers.[84]

---

[84] For the calculations of subsidies I initially analyzed the all regions. In a second step of the analysis, I exclude the smallest regions in terms of electricity production in each supra-region from the analysis. I end up with 30 regions, each representing larger producing

Given the attention to different kinds of market institutions, the appropriate level of analysis of new institutional outcomes is subnational.[85] The unit of analysis of my research was initially the Russian region (*oblast'*)[86] and their respective Energos, the regional vertically integrated electricity monopolies. Regions and Energos are useful units of comparison because they share similar post-Soviet histories and were the target of the same set of reform attempts by UES and the central government. It was the regional Energos that were subject to ownership battles for most of the post-Soviet period, and regional political dynamics were decisive for the subsidy politics. The cross-regional comparison includes in-depth case studies of three regions – Moscow, Irkutsk, and Primorskii Krai – with their respective regional Energos: Mosenergo, Irkutskenergo, and Dal'energo. In each of these regions, the electricity sector has played an important role in regional politics over the last fifteen years. Ownership and tariff data support the claim that Moscow, Irkutsk, and Primorskii Krai – the regions where I conducted in-depth fieldwork – are typical cases for the larger, supra-regional patterns that the book traces.[87] Finally, while I am emphasizing these broad patterns that divide European Russia, Siberia, and the Far East, a number of regions do not fit neatly into this framework. Tatarstan and Bashkortostan will turn up as exceptional

regions within their supra-region. I use a data set on electricity tariffs obtained from the UES Strategy Committee for Reforms in December 2006; it contains the tariffs set by all Regional Energy Commissions between the years 1995 and 2005, broken down also by household, rural and industrial prices. See chapter 5 for details. As far as I know, this data is not publicly available. For the calculation of ownership regimes I proceeded differently: as the regional Energos were dissolved during the reforms, I use ownership data of power plants to calculate the share of ownership by dominant owners; see chapter 4 for details.

[85] On the merits of sub-national comparisons, see Wade, "After the Crisis"; and Richard Snyder, *Politics after Neoliberalism: Reregulation in Mexico*, (Cambridge: Cambridge University Press, 2001).

[86] For the remainder of the book, will call regional level governments *oblast'* governments, although not all of Russia's federal regions are *oblast's*, they also include *ethnic republic, oblast', krai, okrug* and municipalities. The Russian Federation is asymmetric: different types of regions vary in the degree of autonomy they enjoy, depending on their status. These formal differences mattered more during the 1990s, as overall regional autonomy has lessened drastically over the last years. When I did fieldwork, the Federation consisted of 89 regions. A 2008 administrative reforms merged some of the smallest regions with larger neighbors; when this book manuscript was finalized there were 83 regions.

[87] I also compare results from these typical regions with selected neighboring regions, examples from Krasnoyarsk complement the story from Irkutsk, and the same is true for evidence from Khabarovsk for Primorskii Krai Krai.

cases and so will European Russia's most Northern regions, Komi and Arkhangels. The war-torn regions of the North Caucasus faced their own challenges. The Far East is divided into two parts – the Southern Far East, with interconnected electricity grids, and the territories in the North where electricity is produced in isolated systems; these cases are discussed in more detail in the thematic chapters of Part II.

2

Power Politics

> *"Infrastructure development is a key tool for the*
> *socio-economic development of Russia's regions."*[1]
>
> Ministry of Regional Development

Power Politics

For most of the post-Soviet period, the future of Russia's electricity was political. Partly because of electricity's link to authorities' legitimacy, partly because of widespread blackouts and the economic crisis of the 1990s, politics in Russia centered on issues such as ownership battles and access to subsidized energy. What were the fault lines and dynamics of "power politics" – the politics that shaped the restructuring of the electricity sector? According to one veteran policy analyst, the politics surrounding electricity reforms was all about "short-term politics and long-term strategy."[2] While many political economy accounts privilege short-term interests, I focus on long-term strategies that shaped the process of institutional change. This chapter details how these strategies shaped alliances between political factions at the regional and federal level; the next chapter turns to the pacts between the state and Russia's oligarchs.

---

[1] *"Важнейшим инструментом влияния на социально–экономическое развитие субъектов Российской Федерации ... является размещение и развитие ... инфраструктуры."* In "Концепция совершенствования региональной политики в Российской Федерации 2008" (hereafter *Концепция 2008*), Ministry of Regional Development, 3.
[2] Interview #19 with academic and policy analyst, Moscow, 20061122.

Power politics refers to shifting coalitions among a set of actors, to their motivations, and to their views for the future of the electricity sector. Four actors take center stage: the liberal reformers, regional and federal governments, and Russia's oligarchic conglomerates. The chapter traces power politics over roughly twenty years, from the late Soviet period through the end of the second Putin administration in 2008. Throughout this period, the government was a divided entity: regional, or *oblast'* administrations and the federal government often had antithetical aims, and the federal government itself was constituted of different factions. It was a turbulent period in Russian history. Characterized by several rounds of elite replacements and ephemeral coalitions, political conditions for economic reforms constantly changed. Change came fast and recurring crises shook up alliances. Despite or perhaps because of this turmoil, we will see that various tiers of the Russian government pursued developmental strategies as an important aspect of political alliances. Regional and federal actors' economic planning crucially influenced liberalization trajectories in the electricity sector.

Before examining the sector's political underpinnings, the chapter introduces the intentions of liberal reforms to modernize the electricity sector between the early 1990s and 2008. A series of presidential decrees, legislative acts, regulations, and corporate restructuring plans deeply unsettled the inherited organization of the sector, and restructured relationships between the government, the electricity sector's firms, their customers and suppliers. Each of the documents that charted the sector's transformation sought to be authoritative, comprehensive, and final. In fact, every step of the reforms was modified in the process of being implemented and superseded by further plans and laws, either developing or compromising elements of previous plans. The reform process proceeded in incremental and contingent steps. This may sound obvious, but it is important to take these modifications and compromises seriously: no single ideology, lasting consensus, or particular combination of market and statist policies shaped post-Soviet electricity markets. Reforms were neither liberal nor statist. They were not the result of a liberal reform blueprint or the statist vision of Gazprom executives. Each faction was forced into a series of compromises over particular reform steps, continuous bargains that shaped the institutional underpinnings of the sector. These compromises are precisely the new and evolving market institutions in the power sector. They underpin the variation across regions and over time that characterize new electricity markets across Russia.

With *Post-Soviet Social*, Stephen Collier recast the debate over the role of neoliberalism in the post-Soviet transformation. He makes the case that neoliberalism functioned not as a totalizing ideology, but as a form of critique of existing governmental practices, of social welfare mechanisms in particular,[3] and argues that neoliberal reforms were programs that "*selectively* reconfigure inherited material structures, demographic patterns and social norms."[4] Post-Soviet reforms then resulted in "a *new patterning* of social welfare mechanism."[5] I share Collier's perspective that liberal reforms shaped economic institutions through interaction and compromise between the liberal vision and other intellectual traditions, even while our emphases differ. I focus on the contingent domestic political compromises that shaped new market patterns, while his account traces neoliberalism and its effects as a global intellectual movement that traveled from Chicago to Russia.

Electricity Sector Reforms – Chubais's Liberal Vision and "5+5"

The liberal vision paved the way for the historical changes in the electricity sector. From the start of Yeltsin's economic reform program, electricity was a particularly important sector for the "young reformers" (*молодые реформаторы* or *младореформаторы*), the team of liberal economists who shaped economic policy under President Boris Yeltsin. First, electricity is a key infrastructure sector – "the heart of the economy."[6] For most of the first two post-Soviet decades, UES (United Energy Systems, or *Единые Энергетические Системы*) and its subsidiaries produced about 70 percent of Russia's electricity.[7] UES was one of the "natural monopolies" (*естественные монополии*), a particular concern for the liberal reformers and Western advisors. This was the case because natural monopolies were important infrastructure sectors; in addition to electricity, gas, and

---

[3] More precisely, following Foucault, his study traces "liberalism and neo-liberalism not as ideologies, hegemonic projects or governmental rationalities" but as forms of "critical reflection on governmental practice." Collier, *Post-Soviet Social*, 18.

[4] Ibid., 3. Emphasis added.

[5] Ibid., 26. Emphasis added.

[6] Chubais in А. В. Колесников, *Неизвестный Чубайс: Страницы Из Биографии* (Захаров, 2003), 133. And interview #39 with electrical engineer/electricity sector expert, Vladivostok, 20071004.

[7] In 2005, UES produced 655 terawatt hours of electricity. UES is also the country's largest heat producer, with 465 million gigacalories delivered in 2005. Other electricity producers include the few independent Energos and Rosenergoatom, a fully state-owned company, which assumed the responsibility for all nuclear generators. Nuclear reactors remain state owned and were excluded from privatization.

railroads were in this category. While electricity had enjoyed privileged status in the allocation of investments during the Soviet era, in the post-Soviet period the Energos were plagued with a myriad of problems – nonpaying customers, mounting debt, fuel shortages, and aging facilities. Despite these problems though, they owned enormously valuable assets. A majority of the country's power plants, transmission, and distribution networks were part of UES. The company formally controlled majority stakes in most of the Energos, the regional, vertically integrated electricity monopolies.[8] It also had direct ownership of thirty-four of the country's biggest, most valuable power plants – the so-called *GRES* (*Государственная районная электростанция*, state district electric station, in direct translation.)[9] Like other Soviet enterprises, UES further owned a whole host of non-related assets (*непрофильных активов*). According to one source, these included more than sixty research institutes, more than twenty construction companies, scores of employee housing units in many Russian cities, as well as sanatoria, kindergartens, and various other assets administered by the Energos.[10] UES was also the countries' largest producer of central heat. This was an important function in a country where most urban housing units are heated centrally by heat produced in municipal steam plants rather than in individual dwellings. Last but not least, UES was also one of the biggest employers in Russia, with more than 700,000 employees in the mid-1990s.[11]

Any account of Russian electricity reforms should introduce its main protagonists, Anatoly Chubais, the chief architect of reform plans conceived in Moscow. Trained as an economist at Leningrad University in the 1970s, he became a lecturer in economics, also in Leningrad. His publications on the merits of markets and free price systems published in the 1980s were an early indication of the path he would later take. During Gorbachev's *Perestroika*, Chubais became the leader of a group of pro-market economists that also included Yegor Gaidar and Aleksei Kudrin. This group later formed the core of the young reformers. After

[8] As Chapter 4 details, UES's stake in a number of Energos was disputed and smaller than the law mandated.
[9] During the post-Soviet transformation, the abbreviation GRES was retained, although it lost its literal meaning. It is now used to refer to the large thermal power station.
[10] *Эксперт*, No.14, April 13, 1998, p. 27. According to one expert, Dal'energo even owned a pig farm, in addition to hospitals and childcare centers; interview #39 with electrical engineer/electricity sector expert, Vladivostok, 20071004.
[11] Since Chubais took the helm of UES, this number has been reduced to slightly more than half a million; see successive UES annual reports, http://www.rao-ees.ru/ru/investor/reporting/show.cgi?content.htm

serving in the St. Petersburg city council, Chubais first political appointment in Moscow was in Yeltsin's cabinet, heading the State Committee for Property Management (*ГКИ, Госкомимущество*). He later became deputy prime minister. In these capacities he was responsible for Russia's negotiations with foreign lenders. Far more important for Russia's transformation, he became the chief architect of Russia's voucher privatization – the critical but by all accounts deeply flawed transfer of ownership of the Soviet Union's factories and myriad other property. For most of the 1990s, Chubais was one of the most influential members of Yeltsin's cabinet as well as one of its most controversial figures (earning him many an epithet, including that of being a "neoliberal Rasputin at Yeltsin's court.")[12] In April 1998, he became chairman of UES. In 2000, he founded and became one of the leaders of the liberal political party, the Union of Rightist Forces (*Союз правых сил*).

Power sector reforms were on the agenda in Moscow even before Chubais took up the cause. The last Soviet government drew up the earliest blueprints for electricity sector reform in 1990. A team of British consultants, sent and funded by the British government under Margaret Thatcher, was invited to a workshop in Moscow to advise the Soviet Minenergo (*Минэнерго*) on how to restructure what was then called the All-Union Electricity System.[13] With the collapse of the Soviet Union just a few short months later, the context in which these plans were to be implemented changed dramatically: the world's largest, most centralized planning bureaucracy was fragmenting along multiple lines. Amid the turmoil, plans to restructure the electricity sector were initially shelved. Not for long, however. The spontaneous privatization of electricity companies started soon after the collapse of the Soviet Union, and the Yeltsin government wanted to assert control over the sector's transformation (see Chapter 4).[14] The young reformers came to see the reform of the

---

[12] Perry Anderson, "Russia's Managed Democracy," *London Review of Books*, January 25, 2007.

[13] Interview #16 with electricity sector expert/consultant, Moscow, 20061030.

[14] In the turmoil of the early 1990s, valuable power plants changed hands in the "spontaneous privatizations"; see Andrew Barnes and Stephen Solnick's accounts, both are landmark studies of privatization and property battles: Steven Lee Solnick, *Stealing the State: Control and Collapse in Soviet Institutions*, Russian Research Center Studies 89 (Cambridge, MA: Harvard University Press, 1998); Andrew Scott Barnes, *Owning Russia: The Struggle over Factories, Farms, and Power* (Ithaca, NY: Cornell University Press, 2006). See Alina-Pisano's work for rural Russia and Ukraine: Allina-Pisano, *The Post-Soviet Potemkin Village*. For a detailed discussion of privatization, see Chapter 4.

natural monopolies as something like a test case of the efficacy of market forces. By the mid-1990s, plans to restructure, privatize, and liberalize the electricity sector gained Yeltsin's approval.

The reform plans of the early and mid-1990s were drawn up in consultation with and at the request of international lenders keen on reforms of the natural monopolies. In the midst of Russia's 1997 financial crisis, IMF and World Bank structural adjustment loans were tied to a commitment by the Russian government to reform these powerful and important Soviet-era monopolies.[15] As part of these efforts, the federal government's reform team appointed a new director of UES in 1997, Boris Brevnov. He was a banker and personal friend of Boris Nemtsov, the deputy prime minister at the time. Along with Chubais, Nemtsov was an early proponent of electricity sector reforms. What happened next epitomized the fate of the liberal reforms devised in Moscow during the 1990s. A coalition of Energo directors opposed Brevnov's candidacy, seeing him as a threat to the decentralized governance of the electricity sector. They rallied behind the incumbent director, Anatoly D'iakov, boycotting Brevnov. Because he was an outsider, "nobody took him [Brevnov] seriously."[16] D'iakov, who had been part of the Soviet power elites, promised to leave the decentralized nature of the system intact and give regional authorities discretion in how to run the Energos.[17] Unable to force regional Energos and regional governors to comply with his steps to reform the system, Brevnov only lasted a few months as the director of UES.[18]

Clearly failing to transform UES from within the company, Boris Nemtsov turned to President Yeltsin, convincing him to put the liberalization of natural monopoly on the government's reform agenda. A 1998 presidential decree on the reform of electricity, rail, and gas meant to chart and coordinate the unbundling of networked infrastructure services (*Указ Президента РФ N. 426 "Об основных положениях структурной реформы в сферах естественных монополий,"* April 1998).[19] In reality, however, this presidential decree was essentially ignored for years, and

---

[15] See for example, *Известия*, April 9, 1997.
[16] "Его никто не воспринимал всерьез." М. Бергер и О. Проскурина, "Крест Чубайса," *М.: Колибри* (2008), 30.
[17] For a fascinating account of this conflict by Brevnov himself, see Boris Brevnov, "From Monopoly to Market Maker? Reforming Russia's Power Sector" (Belfer Center Programs or Projects: Strengthening Democratic Institutions Project, 2000). See also Бергер и Проскурина, "Крест Чубайса," 197; Woodruff, *Money Unmade*, 197.
[18] Brevnov, "From Monopoly to Market Maker? Reforming Russia's Power Sector."
[19] Бергер и Проскурина, "Крест Чубайса," 43.

the path that UES, the Russian railways, and Gazprom subsequently took
had little to do with its stipulations.

Reformers continued to push for liberalization of the electricity sector.
After Brevnov failed, Anatoly Chubais took on the power sector. He saw
in it the "most vital piece of unreformed socialism."[20] His stated aim was
to "liquidate the Soviet-style monopoly [UES]"[21] and to radically liberalize the provision of electric power. Even before becoming chairman of
UES in 1998, Chubais pursued a consistent liberal reform agenda for
the electricity sector.[22] Key priorities were the unbundling of vertically
integrated monopolies, the divestiture of state ownership in most generation and retail assets, the creation of wholesale markets, and the end of
widespread practice of subsidizing various groups of consumers. These
goals reflected his unflinching commitment to the creation of markets in
Russia. Chubais was in many ways a true believer in the power of markets: "The market is the ideal and a unique model to allocate resources....
It is simply the most effective way."[23] He was also a skilled and pragmatic
political actor, fully able and willing to accept compromises in pursuit of
his main goal.[24] For example, Chubais was weary of Gazprom's influence
in Russia's economy, but to make reforms happen he had to accept the
company's role in the newly "privatized" electricity sector.[25] Although
an effective politician, in the first few years after becoming UES chairman, Chubais failed to initiate liberal reforms. The opposition he faced is
outlined in more detail later in the chapter. It was not until 2003 that a
concrete liberal reform program passed the Duma and was enshrined in
a federal law (*N.35-ФЗ "Об электроэнергетике"*).

This federal law marked the beginning of reforms directed from
the center. And 2003 turned out to be a watershed moment for liberal

---

[20] Chubais, interview in Craig Mellow, "Is This a Way to Create Capitalism? Maybe so,"
Institutional Investor, June 1 (2003).

[21] Бергер и Проскурина, "Крест Чубайса," 36.

[22] For summaries of the reform process, see, for example, Peter Rutland, "Power Struggle:
Reforming the Electricity Industry," in *The Dynamics of Russian Politics: Putin's Reform
of Federal-Regional Relations*, ed. Peter Reddaway and Robert W. Orttung, vol. 2, 2 vols.
(Lanham, MD: Rowman & Littlefield, 2005), 267–294; and Leon Aron, "Privatizing
Russia's Electricity," *American Enterptise Institute Russian Outlook* (Summer 2003): 10.
The most comprehensive account is Бергер и Проскурина, "Крест Чубайса."

[23] Remark by Chubais at a conference "Electricity: Locomotive or Brake on Economic
Development?/Энергетика: тормоз или локомотив развития экономики?" Moscow,
February 13, 2007.

[24] According to the portrait of Chubais in David E. Hoffman, *The Oligarchs: Wealth and
Power in the New Russia* (Public Affairs, 2003).

[25] Interview #63 with electricity company executive, Moscow, 20071212.

reformers (we will see in a later discussion why this was the case and how the political balance had tipped to make this possible). Unlike the earlier presidential decrees, the 2003 legislation paved the way for the reorganization of the sector along market lines, charting a path to unbundle the regional vertical monopolies, privatize generation assets, and create new regulatory bodies and a wholesale market that allowed "free" transactions – that is, contracts outside the framework of regulated tariffs. The law endorsed a reform document drawn up by Chubais and his team, the "5+5 Strategy." The "5+5" was a two-staged five-year plan to unbundle monopolies and privatize important generation assets. The two 5s stand for the years it has been in gestation (1998–2003) and the years it was projected to require for implementation (2003–2008). Attentive to the symbolic resonance of the electricity sector modernization, the name borrows the number 5 from the authoritative Soviet "piatiletka" (*пятилетка*) – the centrally orchestrated five-year plans that determined the pulse of the Soviet economy from 1928 to 1991.

With the passage of the 2003 law and the adoption of "5+5," Anatoly Chubais claimed an early victory: "This plan fits in with the logic of everything I have been doing in the past fifteen years to break up state enterprises and create a free market. The fight for restructuring is over. The market and the business community accepted the logic and mechanism of the UES restructuring. Now there is no way back."[26] Time proved him both wrong and right. The fight for restructuring was far from over in 2003. It continued for years, as different actors continued to negotiate and renegotiate their share in bargains. He was right, however, that there was no way back to vertically integrated monopoly structure in the electricity sector. By 2008, the Energos were history.

All liberal reform plans, including the "5+5" plan, had a number of common denominators. They envisaged a multi-stage process that can be summarized under the following five headings. I am outlining the contours of each of these steps here, as a background for the processual accounts of how they were actually implemented in subsequent chapters.

(1) *Commercialization* refers to the conversion of state-owned power asset into joint stock companies, to be operated on a commercial basis. On paper, the conversion of power assets into joint stock companies happened in Russia in 1992, when two presidential decrees created the following commercial entities: one federal holding company, UES, one company

---

[26] Arkady Ostrovsky, "UES chief puts his faith in capitalism," *Financial Times*, June 2, 2003, p. 26.

for all the atomic energy assets, Rosenergoatom (*Росэнергоатом*), and seventy-one vertically integrated regional monopolies, the Energos.[27] With the same decrees, the Energos were mandated to transfer majority ownership to UES as well as full ownership of a number of the country's most valuable power plants. In reality, the mandated transfer of ownership was contested in multiple ways, as Chapter 4 demonstrates. Moreover, while these newly created organizations were commercially operated companies on paper, they retained many of the characteristics of Soviet-era ministerial structures for years. "Commercialization" was a project embraced only many years later, by a new group of managerially trained experts who were placed at the heads of power companies by Chubais, as Chapter 6 demonstrates.

(2) **Demonopolization** refers to the breaking up of vertically integrated monopolies and consists of two reform steps – "unbundling" and the creation of wholesale markets.

Unbundling refers to the separation of subsectors with varying competition potential: generation, transmission (high-voltage grids), distribution (low-voltage grids), and retail. For generation and retail, reformers wanted to introduce competition between independent, private companies. Unbundling was one of the most important and contested elements of electricity reforms. Anatoly Chubais and Boris Nemtsov devised a first concrete strategy to unbundle the Energos and UES in 1997, but it was not until after 2003 that unbundling commenced in earnest. Unbundling was the centerpiece of the "5+5 Strategy." It laid out, for example, how generation assets were to be reorganized into new companies, the "territorial generating companies" (TGKs/*ТГК*) and "wholesale generating companies" (OGKs/*ОГК*) that were to be privatized. Control of high-voltage grids, by contrast, was to be consolidated in the hands of the state, to secure free and fair access to grids by new private owners of power plants. Chapter 4 makes the case that the unbundling of regional monopolies fundamentally changed who could make the most fundamental decisions in the sector.

Wholesale markets: New companies and their customers increasingly traded electricity not bilaterally, but via newly created wholesale markets. An initial prototype of a wholesale market, called FOREM, was created in 1995. Managed by UES, FOREM oversaw only very few

---

[27] Presidential Decrees no. 922, 923, and 1334 as well as other legal documents are available on UES's site under the section *Нормативно-правовая база реформирования*, http://www.rao-ees.ru/ru/reforming/laws/show.cgi?laws.htm

transactions, which were bound by regulated tariffs. An independent electricity exchange was created in 2001, with the Administrator of Trading Systems (ATS/*ATC*) as the organization to oversee trading in different market segments (day-ahead contracts, long-term bilateral contracts, and balancing markets). The volume of electricity traded in this way gradually increased after 2002, although until 2007, most trades (90 percent took place at regulated prices. The rules of the wholesale market were updated in 2007, when the transition of the bulk of trading to the open market (from a regulated segment of the market) began.

(3) *Regulation* refers to the creation of an authoritative, predictable, and independent regulatory framework. It included bodies such as anti-monopoly regulators, network operators, and wholesale market regulators. Since 1995, various legislative acts and presidential decrees addressed regulatory issues. In 1995, a federal regulatory commission on natural monopolies was created, the Federal Energy Commission (FEK/*Федеральная энергетическая комиссия*), with subordinated regional branches, the Regional Energy Commissions (REKs/*Региональная энергетическая комиссия*).[28] In 1997, a federal law transferred authority away from regional governors and gave the REKs independent legal status. However, in practice, they remained subordinated to regional governments for years, and FEK had little sway over REKs. A 1999 legislative proposal intended to clarify price-setting authority placed the Ministry of Anti-Monopoly (today the Anti-Monopoly Service, FAS /*Федеральная антимонопольная служба*) in control of the FEK, but this legislation was never implemented.[29] The division of responsibility between FEK and FAS remained unclear for the period discussed in this book. Chapter 5 details the uneven progress of these reforms.

(4) *Privatization* refers to the sale of shares in state-owned energy suppliers and their assets to private shareholders. As a natural monopoly of strategic importance, the electricity sector was initially exempt from the privatization program of the mid-1990s.[30] Despite this exemption, regional Energos as well as UES sold minority shares during the 1990s. By 2000, Russia's large conglomerates owned significant stakes in most Energos. "5+5" envisaged state divestiture of most generation assets via share sales of UES, the independent Energos, and the newly created TGKs

---

[28] Федеральный закон от 17 августа 1995 г. № 147-ФЗ *"О естественных монополиях."*

[29] Rutland, "Power Struggle: Reforming the Electricity Industry," 279. Chapter 5 provides a detailed discussion of the FEK/REK dynamics.

[30] Федеральный закон N.147-ФЗ *"О естественных монополиях"* 1995 г.

and OGKS. Chapter 4 will detail which assets were actually sold, who the major purchasers were, and how these assets were valued – fiercely contested political issues for the entire period of study here.

(5) *Tariff reform* refers to the end of government regulation of electricity prices, a liberalization of prices that was negotiated freely between sellers and buyers. In theory, tariff liberalization promised lower prices, as capital infusions by private actors should have led to increased competition and lower prices. In reality, this was an elusive scenario for Russia. Prices had been kept very low during the 1990s. A belief that prices should increase to reflect long-term costs and to generate profits in some market segments led to an increase in regulated tariffs as the first step to price liberalization. Tariff liberalization also implied a phasing out of various subsidization schemes. One of the first steps in the long process of tariff reforms was a 1998 federal decree that allowed Energos to cut off nonpaying customers, which was meant to put an end to the de facto subsidization of much of their customers. Hitherto, utilities were not allowed to eliminate customers and had no choice but to extend in-kind credit to those that failed to pay.[31] Even though collection rates increased, regulated prices were kept low for the remainder of the decade (especially relative to the rising cost of other industrial inputs). From 2001 onward, federal-level regulators (FEK) followed liberal reform plans and approved yearly price increases of regulated prices. Particularly significant tariff increases in 2001 and 2003 led to waves of protests and opposition in the Duma.[32] Price reform continued to be one of the most contentious elements of the electricity sector restructuring. Chapter 4 will detail how price liberalization varied across regions and progressed unevenly over the years.

Reform Implementation: Opposition, Dissonance, and Shifting Agreements

While liberal reformers were successful in charting a path and undoing important aspects of the inherited Soviet-era organization of the sector – relegating UES and the Energos to history – the actual implementation

[31] After 1998, helped by the economic recovery following the devaluation of the ruble, the electricity sector was able to gradually improve collection rates. See also Rutland, "Power Struggle: Reforming the Electricity Industry."

[32] Irkutsk had among the lowest prices on electricity during the 1990s; see OECD (2003). By 2003 the FEK set a limit for price increases at 14%, but regional tariffs increased on average by 29%, reflecting larger increases in regions that had previously kept tariffs low. Ahead of 2004 presidential elections, United Russia launched a Duma initiative to keep prices low. See Chapter 5 for a discussion.

TABLE 2.1. *Evolving bargains that shape electricity sector outcomes*

	Yeltsin Presidency	Putin's First term 2000–2004	Putin's Second term 2004–2008
Proponents of reform	Liberal reformers and the federal government wanted reform	Governors' influence is eliminated. Oligarchs' influence shifts to federal level	*Bargains between fed. government and industrial and energy conglomerates shape the terms of reforms*
Opposition to liberalization	*Bargains between regional governors and industrial and energy companies prevented implement. of liberal reforms designed at the center.* *These regional bargains shaped ownership transfers and subsidies*	*Liberal reformers succeed in in initiating reforms, due to an alliance between liberals and siloviki*	No formal opposition to reforms; but liberal reformers have to make concessions to conglomerates

of electricity reforms depended on shifting political alliances. As alliances formed and fell apart, plans to modernize the sector evolved and changed. The changing role of foreign investors provides an example of this fluidity. Yeltsin's team of liberal reformers enthusiastically courted the big European power companies for their capital, technology, and expertise. During the 1990s, a number of foreign strategic investors acquired important minority stakes in Russian power companies. While some of these foreign companies remained involved as reforms progressed, others were edged out after 2003, when more statist factions in the Putin government influenced privatization decisions in favor of domestic energy companies.

The next three sections outline the shifting alliances of Russia's power politics. The first examines the Yeltsin years and the autonomy of regional governors, which essentially meant that attempts by the federal government to reform the system were boycotted. A second section explores the power shift from Yeltsin to Putin, the years around 2000, which marked the rise of an unlikely alliance between liberal reformers and statist *siloviki (силовики)*. Finally, I turn to the five years of the Putin presidency between 2003 and 2008, when reforms were implemented. For each of these periods, summarized in Table 2.1, I show how political opposition and provisional alliances, disagreement and consensus, shaped the restructuring of the electricity system. Note that the dichotomy of reform "opponents" and "proponents" broke down during Putin's first presidency. What remained constant over the years was that the sector was reshaped in pacts between Russia's emerging conglomerates and different tiers of the government.

Power Politics I: Regional Bargains During the Yeltsin Years

For much of the 1990s, the transformation of the electricity sector was shaped by bargains between regional governors, the Energos, and emerging private owners. In Moscow the young reformers planned to comprehensively restructure and reform the Russian economy.[33] But opposition to these plans by regional elites sharply limited the center's ability to implement market reforms. Alliances of regional governors with Energo directors, sometimes called the Electricity Generals, and enterprise directors (both the old nomenklatura and new entrepreneurs) defied directives and boycotted reforms emanating from Moscow. The tension between liberal reformers and regional authorities in the electricity sector – a struggle over jurisdiction, authority, resource allocation, and control – reflected one of the major fault lines in Russian politics during the Yeltsin period.[34] A handful of the most influential regional governors organized as a powerful political group in federal-level politics in the second half of the 1990s, vying for influence in Moscow and for the chance to nominate a successor to the ailing President Yeltsin.[35] A weak federal government

---

[33] For an interesting account by the insiders, see Sergei Vasiliev, A. B. Chubais, and Andrei Illarionov, *Ten Years of Russian Economic Reform: A Collection of Papers* (London: Centre for Research into Post-Communist Economics, 1999).

[34] See Gail W. Lapidus, "Asymmetrical Federalism and State Breakdown in Russia," *Post-Soviet Affairs* 15, no. 1 (1999): 74–82; and Philip Hanson, "The Center versus the Periphery in Russian Economic Policy," *RFE/RL Research Report* 3, no. 17 (1994): 23–28.

[35] Regional governors formed a political coalition led by Evgeni Primakov, the Fatherland – All Russia (*Отечество – Вся Россия*) Party, at their strongest in the late 1990s. For some time, they were seen as the most viable successors to Yeltsin and as such clearly the most threatening elite group for the *siloviki* and Vladimir Putin. The role of the Fatherland coalition was greatly diminished by 2003; see discussion later in the chapter.

challenged by powerful subnational power centers led many commentators to speculate about the return of a feudal power system under Yeltsin.[36] The feudal analogy was also applied to the fragmentation of regulation in the electricity system: the term "feudalism" was used to describe the de facto independence of regional monopolies from UES's headquarters in Moscow, and the federal government's inability to direct UES itself.[37] According to one insider, "during [the] period of 1994–97, the government has effectively lost control over UES' activities."[38]

Local and regional newspapers reported extensively on unpaid wages, double-digit inflation that wiped out savings, on strikes, everyday misery and the uncertainty of the local population. All of this registered as "social tension" (*социальное напряжение*).[39] Regional governors were often called to action in these reports, for the sake of resident's well-being and to assure "social stability."[40] Reports noted that regional authorities passed resolutions, decrees, and decisions aimed at helping regional enterprises, to quote one observer, "find their place in the market."[41] This would allow them to employ and pay regional residents, which in turn would reduce social tensions.[42] Regional responses varied widely during

---

[36] For a discussion of the feudal analogy, see Charles H. Fairbanks, "The Feudal Analogy," *Journal of Democracy* 11, no. 3 (2000): 34–36; and Vladimir Shlapentokh, *Contemporary Russia as a Feudal Society: A New Perspective on the Post-Soviet Era*, 1st ed. (New York: Palgrave Macmillan, 2007).

[37] See "Энергетика абсурда," *Эксперт*, No. 14, April 13, 1998, p. 29; the term "энергетический федерализм" was also used in this article. The term "energy principalities" is another reference to feudal structures and power of region; "Удельные княжества копят энергию," *Сегодня*, December 18, 1998.

[38] Alexander Burganskij and Irina Elinevskaya, *Hydro Power: Super-Profits or Super-Regulation?* Moscow: Renaissance Capital, 2005), 13.

[39] These difficulties were reported almost daily in the regional media. A report in 1995 states that "a significant part of enterprises have not yet found their place in the market economy, they do not have a healthy number of orders to complete, and they work irregularly." Full quote in Russian: "Значительная часть предпринимателей еще не нашла своего места в рыночной экономике, не имеет устойчивых заказов и работает неравномерно" in "Как живется – можется?" *Восточно-Сибирская правда*, September 7, 1995.

[40] Reference to social tensions in "Ради социальной стабильности," *Утро России*, February 8, 1994. David Woodruff stressed that regional governors were the first in line to respond to social consequences of the economic collapse; Woodruff, *Money Unmade*, 114.

[41] "Как живется – можется?" *Восточно-Сибирская правда*, September 7, 1995. The expression "finding their place in the market" was also used by a businessman, Irkutsk, Interview #54, 20071120.

[42] One among many examples, a decree by the governor of Krasnoiarsk oblast', "Decree on measures to reduce social tensions on enterprises," in Russian: "Постановление: 'О мерах по снижению социальной напряженности на предприятиях,' in "В Администрации края," *Красноярский рабочий*, June 10, 1994.

this period, as governors had different resources and perspectives on what was to be done in the face of these crises. Observers have explained this variation by emphasizing different aspects of regional independence. Yoshiko Herrera has drawn attention to the variation in the kind of economies that regional authorities envisioned for their regions, what they demanded from the center and what they managed to achieve.[43] Kathryn Stoner-Weiss saw some of them as "local heroes" who governed well in turbulent times.[44] Joel Hellman's account of regional autonomy privileged the governors' ability to block market reforms, wanting to protect monopoly rents.[45] While there are different interpretations of the governor's motivations, all accounts point to a fundamental tension between the central government, which wanted to push ahead market reforms, and the regional governors, who had to deal with the effects of dismantling the Soviet command economy.

Regional autonomy had initially been encouraged by Boris Yeltsin as an incentive to unite support in the fight to defy the forces intent on conserving the Soviet Union.[46] In 1991, he famously called on the regions to grab as much autonomy as they could digest.[47] Centrifugal forces, once unleashed, then led to the fragmentation of political and bureaucratic authority. This in turn meant that regions were essentially on their own: regions ended up with significant de facto autonomy in several realms of political and economic life.[48] In the words of one regional observer, this autonomy ushered in a difficult period in which "there was no direction, no cooperation and everything threatened to fall apart."[49] The challenges this created for regional authorities were enormous. As one Primorskii Krai observer noted, "Primorskii Krai was de facto burdened with a whole

---

[43] Herrera, *Imagined Economies*.

[44] The core of Stoner-Weiss's study is an examination why "local heroes," which are "higher-performance governments," existed in some regions but not in others. Kathryn Stoner, *Local Heroes: The Political Economy of Russian Regional Governance* (Princeton, NJ: Princeton University Press, 1997), 10.

[45] "Local officials ... have prevented market entry into their regions to protect their share of local monopoly rents" see Hellman, "Winners Take All," 204.

[46] For an account of these dynamics of the Yeltsin-Gorbachev struggle, see George W. Breslauer, *Gorbachev and Yeltsin as Leaders* (Cambridge: Cambridge University Press, 2002).

[47] Ibid., 125. See also Richard Sakwa, *Russian Politics and Society*, 4th ed., Fully rev. and updated. (London; New York: Routledge, 2008), 246. These centrifugal forces and the threat of secession were among the most hotly discussed issues of the 1990s.

[48] Lapidus, "Asymmetrical Federalism and State Breakdown in Russia."

[49] Interview #39 with electrical engineer/electricity sector expert, Vladivostok, 20071004.

series of government functions, without the necessary means, financial or otherwise, to fulfill these functions."[50]

While this was clearly a burden, many governors also embraced regional autonomy. This was true of the governors of the three regions I examine here. Moscow city's mayor, Yuri Mikhailovich Luzhkov, was charismatic and highly influential in shaping the capital's post-Soviet transformation in general and electricity sector reforms in particular. Primorskii Krai's governor, Evgeny Nazdratenko, was known for seizing the opportunity to devise his region's integration into domestic and international markets. Irkutsk oblast's governor, Yuri Nozhikov, was also exceptionally independent, explicitly pursuing an economic policy strategy that protected the region from the detrimental effect of Moscow's policies. Many governors felt like Nozhikov, who argued: "Each region has its particular circumstances, particular relationship, each region is inhabited by people with a different frame of mind, and each region has a different climate,"[51] adding that not everything could, or even should, be decided in Moscow. Yuri Nozhikov remembered being propelled to action by citizens surrounding him in the streets, telling him of their hardship and hunger: "When you, the head of the administration, the governor, are surrounded by people on the street, who tell you that they have nothing to feed their children, then that hardship cannot appear secondary. Then, to change this situation, no effort should be spared."[52] Nozhikov may have been among the most responsive governors. But governors everywhere devised their own solutions to the problems and challenges of the post-Soviet transformation. Whether governors willingly embraced regional autonomy, or whether it was foisted on them, the effect was that political decisions, battles, and alliances often became localized. Concretely, this meant that while Moscow's liberal reform attempts in the electricity sector formed the background for regional initiatives, most issues were resolved locally,

[50] "... целый ряд ... общегосударственных задач оказался фактически возложенным на Приморский край без предоставления ему достаточных для реализации этих функций финансовых и иных ресурсов," in "Ради социальной стабильности," *Утро России*, February 8, 1994.
[51] "На каждой территории – свои условия, свои отношения, свой менталитет населения, свой климат, наконец." Nozhikov recounts these events in his biography, Ю. А. Ножиков, *Я Это Видел, Или Жизнь Российского Губернатора, Рассказанная Им Самим* (Иркутск: Иркутская областная типография №1, 1998), 155.
[52] "Когда тебя, главу администрации, губернатора, на улице окружают люди и говорят, что нечем кормить детей ..., то это кажется ... второстепенным. И, чтобы изменить эту ситуацию, никаких сил не жалко." Ibid., 166.

in conflicts between regional governors and the mayors of major cities, for example.[53]

During the 1990s, the regional development strategies were more diverse and less formalized than the strategies formulated later, during the Putin era. Often strategies were devised in an ad hoc fashion, responding to the crises that engulfed regions, often in alliances between governors, Energos, and the region's largest employers. Former director of Irkutskenergo, later an oblast senator, described collaborating with regional industries and administration in the following terms: "We worked with regional industries and with the regional administration to provide (*обеспечить*) for the region's people."[54] Whether concluded with oligarchs or small-scale businessmen, such local arrangements protected regional businesses from closure and helped them adjust to new market conditions.[55] Electricity subsidies and privatization decisions were just one of many tools that governors used to direct the transformation of regional economies. Local media are replete with references to a variety of benefits – credits, tax breaks, in-kind benefits – granted to firms and workers by regional authorities.[56] In the aluminum sector, for example, an arrangement known as "tolling," exempted smelters from import and export duties, and proved crucial to the stellar rise of Russian aluminum smelters.[57]

[53] The constant battles between the mayor of Vladivostok and the governor of Primorskii Krai were well known and well documented; see, for example, "Паны дерутся ...," *Утро России*, January 21, 1997, among many articles in *Утро России* on this issues. See also Stoner-Weiss's work on regional governments; Stoner-Weiss, *Local Heroes*. She finds that in regions where industry is concentrated, governance is better, as alliances are more stable.

[54] Interview #59 with politician/former electricity executive, Irkutsk, 20071130. He used the word *обеспечить* – to provide for/care for, a term deeply rooted in Soviet-era planning terminology.

[55] Protection of regional industry was mentioned several times as the motivation for regional governor's interest in electricity, for example, in interview #60 with energy company executive, Irkutsk, 20071203. See also Woodruff, *Money Unmade*, 115.

[56] "Город накормить непросто," *Восточно-Сибирская правда*, January 26, 1994, an article about how local sausage factory got a credit from regional administration, which allowed its continued operation. Tax collection was a fundamental challenge for both federal and regional authorities; see, for example, *Восточно-Сибирская правда*, "Бюджетное послание Губернатора области," October 17, 1995. On the importance of in-kind benefits, see Susanne Wengle and Michael Rasell, "The Monetisation of L'goty: Changing Patterns of Welfare Politics and Provision in Russia," *Europe-Asia Studies* 60, no. 5 (2008): 739–756.

[57] Yuko Adachi, *Building Big Business in Russia: The Impact of Informal Corporate Governance Practices* (London: Routledge, 2010), 66.

The task of reliably providing electricity to residents and industry was both an urgent imperative for keeping local economies going and an opportunity to regulate regional economies. Matters relating to electricity became important issues in regional politics. "Without fail, all problems of regional administration in the realm of regional economic and social development were in one way or the other related to electricity," noted one Far Eastern observer.[58] Controlling the Energos served governors well.[59] Governors could influence regional development by distributing energy subsidies, by authorizing privatization decisions, or by influencing property disputes, as subsequent chapters show in more detail. One regional commentator put it succinctly: "Regional authorities were rather quickly convinced that the regional energy companies [the Energos] remained the only lever (*рычаг*) to influence the economic and social processes in a region."[60]

Governors used electricity subsidies in a variety of ways during the 1990s. Keeping household tariffs low was a successful strategy to cushion the effect of skyrocketing inflation. Rural households, and households with electric instead of gas appliances, had paid less than other household consumers for electricity in Soviet times and continued to be entitled to special rates.[61] Other categories of consumers, such as hospitals, education facilities, research institutes, and military facilities, which were affected by the collapse of government budgets in the 1990s, also usually paid very low rates or did not have to pay at all.[62] Controlling power plants was a way to subsidize industrial consumers. In return for lower rates, loyal enterprises employed local residents and often made in-kind contributions to regional well-being. For some governors, the electricity

[58] "Все проблемы регионального развития в экономической и социальной сфере местными властями в той или иной степени обязательно связываются с энергоснабжением." Анна Лобунец, "Перспективы развития энергетики Приморского края с учетом интеграционных процессов в Северо-Восточной Азии," Автореферат диссертации, Владивосток, May 17, 2004, 15.

[59] Just like other large regional companies, electricity companies were also asked to make in-kind contributions to regional well-being. Vladivostok's soccer stadium was sponsored by Dal'energo; Amurenergo was asked to do the same. Interview #30 with policy analyst, Vladivostok, 20070914.

[60] "Региональные власти достаточно быстро убедились, что для воздействия на экономические и социальные процессы у себя в регионе у них остался только один рычаг – местные энергокомпании." In "Энергетика абсурда," *Эксперт*, No. 14, April 13, 1998, p. 29. The word "leverage/рычаг" is often used in this context; interview #32 with electricity sector economist, Vladivostok, 20070918 and 20070925.

[61] See Chapter 4 for sources of price and subsidy data.

[62] Interview with Kudriavyi published in *Эксперт*, No. 14, April 13, 1998, p. 32.

sector also at times served as a treasure trove, allowing them to extort, bribes from regional industrialists in return for cheap rates.[63] Governors also strove to control electricity sector tax revenues at the regional level, limiting the amounts flowing to Moscow.[64] Whatever the mechanism, ensuring service – keeping power flowing and companies operating – was always a chief rationale. Not only were service interruptions problematic per se; they were also seized upon in political battles to discredit governing elites.[65]

Regions with a surplus of electricity had another option to put the sector in the service of regional development: exporting electricity abroad. In the heyday of regional independence, in the mid-1990s, Irkutskenergo was ambitiously planning to build an energy bridge to China: a high-voltage transmission line to export electricity from the region's huge hydroelectric power plants.[66] "It will create jobs and benefit the financial situation of the region," explained the director of Irkutskenergo.[67] UES and liberal reformers were hardly pleased with this strategy, as the center wanted to convince low-cost/high-volume regions to feed electricity into the grid. The governor of Irkutsk oblast then had to make a choice: he could follow UES's directives and subsidize neighboring Buriatiia, where utilities were inefficient and power was expensive, or he could insist on energy policies that secured lower rates for local industry and local residents. We will see that he tried to do the latter as long as he could.

In theory, the Energos were subordinate to UES and directed via a hierarchical, centralized bureaucracy. In reality, governors maintained firm control of the Energos. As one commentator put it, "the structure of ... UES is such that the resolution of many key questions is impossible

[63] Though references to this kind of corruption in the electricity sector were made in conversations, I am uncertain that these cases were documented with concrete evidence. Documenting corrupt practices by Russian elites has been the reserve of Russia's most courageous investigative reporters. Masha Geesen provides an account of some of these investiations; Geesen, Masha. *The Man Without a Face: The Unlikely Rise of Vladimir Putin.* New York: Riverhead Books, 2012.

[64] "Президент тоже ошибается," *Красноярский рабочий,* September 25, 1992.

[65] This was especially evident in the conflict between the mayor of Vladivostok and the governor of Primorskii Krai; see, for example, "Паны дерутся…," *Утро России,* January 21, 1997.

[66] А. С. Щербаков и И. Тертышник, "Мировая экономика и внешнеэкономическая деятельность Иркутского Предбайкалья," Иркутский государственный университет, Иркутск, 2000, p. 235. See also "Китай отверг российскую электроэнергию," *Коммерсантъ,* September 15, 2000.

[67] Viktor Borovskii, *Moscow Times,* October 28, 1997.

without the agreement of governors."[68] Close ties between regional elites and the electricity sector are a legacy of the Soviet era. As a vital infrastructure, Energos had been subordinated to the control of the Communist Party elites before the collapse of the Soviet planned economy. Energo managers were often part of the old regional nomenklatura. They remained in charge for most of the 1990s, which facilitated the tight connection between regional administrations and the Energos in the first post-Soviet decade.[69] UES accepted these kinds agreements: "[I]n its commitment to supplying energy, UES ... followed a Soviet-style priority for providing regional industries with electricity regardless of their ability to pay," noted one observer in the mid-1990s.[70] Such practices drained the finances of Energos and the UES and drove a number of Energos into bankruptcy.[71]

The broader context of regional autonomy and defiance of central government's directives was the dissolution of many Soviet-era bureaucratic structures during the 1990s. Commenting on a dispute about Tyumenenergo, an observer noted that "the authority of the federal government and of federal laws has fallen to such low levels that many do not consider it necessary to take them into consideration."[72] Against this background, regional governments used bilateral treaties with central authorities to clarify jurisdiction and solidify autonomy over electricity sector regulation.[73] The combination of a weak central government and the apparent carte blanche that Yeltsin offered the regions resulted in what has been called Russia's asymmetric federalism. Regions with natural resources and strong leaders negotiated special status and privileges

---

[68] "Как известно, холдинг РАО ЕЭС России представляет собой структуру, в которой решение многих ключевых вопросов невозможно без согласия губернатора"; *Известия*, August 12, 2000.

[69] These connections between regional authorities and Energo directors are discussed in Chapter 6. They were mentioned in several interviews, for example, interviews #45 with employee of electricity company and #46 with academic, both in Khabarovsk, 20071011.

[70] *Moscow Times*, March 11, 1997.

[71] Although formal bankruptcy proceedings were rare for most of the 1990s, one source mentions that about twenty Energos were in bankruptcy proceedings by the 1990s: Михаил Бергер и Ольга Проскурина, *Крест Чубайса*, p. 58.

[72] "Авторитет федеральной власти и законов упал так низко, что считаться с ними многие уже не считают необходимым." This was a comment on the Tyumen government's attempt to gain ownership of Tymenenergo in blatant defiance of federal directives; see "Удельные княжества копят энергию," *Сегодня*, December 18, 1998.

[73] Irkutsk Oblast's treaty and the provisions on electricity is mentioned in "Опять двадцать пять – энергетический спор продолжается," *Восточно-Сибирская правда*, January 17, 1997.

that went beyond those granted in the constitution. Yeltsin also granted these treaties to regions with the most credible threat of secession – ethnic republics and regions with natural resources and with strong governors.[74]

The same logic held for the electricity sector: "All the [electricity] surplus regions ran to Yeltsin ... asking for special rules," recalled one observer.[75] Treaties granted de jure autonomy in the electricity sector to the strongest regions, whose governors enjoyed the support of the Yeltsin administration: Tatarstan, Bashkortostan, Sverdlovsk, Irkutsk, Khabarovsk and Yakutiia had treaties with special clauses on the electricity sector.[76] Some regions without a treaty agreement negotiated price levels directly with the federal government. This was the case for regions with a strong bargaining position owing to the fact that they were electricity surplus regions. Khakassiia, one of Siberia's big electricity producers, negotiated a ten-year moratorium on price increases with the federal government.[77] Other regions sought special prerogatives to regulate the sector in times of crisis, when outages threatened to disrupt local economies.[78] These treaties and agreements were a double-edged sword for the federal government. On the one hand, they regularized the relationship between the region and the federal center on important issues in the sector, such as fiscal authority and tariff regulation. On the other hand, they created a patchwork of regulation that privileged the stronger regions and did not allow the federal government to redistribute across regions.

More important was the de facto autonomy that regional governors enjoyed during the 1990s. De facto regional sovereignty manifested itself in multiple ways. They could, for example, stop fiscal transfers to the federal government.[79] Or they could appoint loyalists as representatives to federal agencies in the oblasts, which augmented their control over issues

[74] Treisman, *After the Deluge*; Daniel Treisman, "Deciphering Russia's Federal Finance: Fiscal Appeasement in 1995 and 1996," *Europe-Asia Studies* 50, no. 5 (1998): 893–906.

[75] Interview #39 with electrical engineer/electricity sector expert, Vladivostok, 20071004.

[76] Губогло, М. "Федерализм Власти и Власть Федерализма." Москва: ИнтелТех 1997. The Irkutsk treaty was discussed in interview #50, Irkutsk, 20071115.

[77] Burganskij and Elinevskaya, *Hydro Power*.

[78] "Красноярск отобрал собственность у РАО ЕЭС," *Сегодня*, December 4, 1998.

[79] For example, "Иркутская область отказывается платить в федеральную казну," *Восточно-Сибирская правда*, February 2, 1994. See also Vadim Volkov, "Standard Oil and Yukos in the Context of Early Capitalism in the United States and Russia," *Demokratizatsyia* 16, no. 3 (2008): 250.

that were formally beyond regional jurisdiction.[80] The sale of electricity to consumers abroad was another manifestation of regional governors' exercise of de facto autonomy in the electricity sector. UES and federal-level politicians objected to this practice, because, as mentioned earlier, *they* wanted to decide about how to allocate the low-cost electricity and profit directly from foreign sales (rather than leaving this up to the regions). Regional initiatives were particularly unwelcome in the case of Irkutsk, the region that was trying to fetch a much higher price for electricity abroad, ignoring the government's plea to subsidize neighboring Buriatiia.[81] Although the ambitious high-voltage line ultimately remained an unfulfilled dream, Irkutsk was selling electricity to nearby Chinese and Mongolian regions via existing lines. Overall, Siberian governors were particularly autonomous in the electricity sector, including Viktor Kress from Tomsk, Leonid Polezhaev from Omsk, Aman Tuleev from Kemerovo, Viktor Tolokonskii from Novosibirsk, Aleksander Surikov from Altai, Aleksander Lebed from Krasnoiarsk, and, of course, Yuri Nozhikov from Irkutsk. These governors spearheaded the opposition to the liberal reform plans formulated at the center.[82]

In sum, the politically relevant actors during the Yeltsin government were thus the following: (1) the liberal reformers at the center, who had the ear of the Yeltsin government but lacked the strength to implement controversial reform steps without the support of governors or other powerful groups; (2) the regional governors; and (3) the emerging oligarchic conglomerates, some regional, others with national reach. Alliances of regional governments and emerging private owners successfully resisted implementation of market reforms planned at the center. Yeltsin's liberal reform team, some of whom continued to hold important positions in the Putin administration, realized that liberalization would require a "de-politicization" of electricity; measures were needed to prevent regional political authorities from using electricity as a tool to regulate regional economies.

For much of the 1990s, politics in the electricity sector mirrored broader center-region tensions. This was the situation when Anatoly Chubais became head of UES in 1998. The young reformers and Chubais

---

[80] See Sakwa, *Russian Politics and Society*, 227. Subsequent chapters show that this mattered crucially for the appointments to the regional energy commissions (REKs) and as the directors of Energos.

[81] This was mentioned in interview #54 with businessman, Irkutsk, 20071120.

[82] Максим Шандаров, "Анатолия Чубайса холодно встретили в Сибири," *Коммерсантъ*, November 11, 2000.

were well aware of the importance of the sector for regional governors, and were displeased with regional control of the Energos. Much like regional authorities, Moscow's liberal reformers understood the intricate connection between Energos and regional economies. But they remained powerless to make real changes during the 1990s. When he became director of UES, Chubais brought with him reform plans he had devised while in Yeltsin's cabinet. One of his first and most important goals was to dissolve the vertically integrated Energos. This step, he thought, was a prerequisite for undercutting the hold of regional governors on the sector. Not surprisingly, these plans were highly unpopular in the regions – "nobody liked Chubais' plan."[83] His opponents claimed that he had little understanding of the "social aspects" of economic governance. One regional administrator noted that Chubais "considers the social sphere secondary." The same official lamented that Chubais did not hesitate to drastically cut UES expenditures on "social programs,"[84] contrasting federal-level indifference with regional compassion for the "social sphere."

Regional governors were not alone in their opposition to liberalization. Chubais recalled the waves of opposition he encountered: "Who was against us when we started? … governors, most parties in parliament, big business, minority shareholders, scientists from the academies, and that's not the whole list."[85] Governors and "big business" were the key opponents of reforms: governors wanted to secure their ability to influence the future of the electricity sector and large firms turned to regional governors to secure advantageous terms for their electricity provisions.[86]

In the Duma, liberal reformers faced a broad, but heterogeneous, opposition coalition led by regional governors and industrialists and joined by a group of reform opponents that included the Communist Party, the social-democratic or left-liberal Yabloko Party (*Яблоко*), and a group of electricity sector professionals, the *energetiki* (*энергетики*).[87] Opponents feared that national resources would be squandered, that well-connected insiders would grab valuable assets, often referring to the outcome of the voucher privatizations under the auspices of Chubais as

[83] Interview #39 with electrical engineer/electricity sector expert, Vladivostok, 20071004.
[84] Opinion of Pavel Shtein, head of the Bureiskaya district of Amur oblast'; he notes, "социальную сферу он считает делом второстепнным"; interview with Shtein in "Конфликт интересов разрешаем дипломатично," *Дальневосточный капитал*, No. 5/57 (May 2005): 44.
[85] Interview with Chubais, in Mellow, "Is This a Way to Create Capitalism?"
[86] See "Выборы," *Восточно-Сибирская правда*, February 15, 1994.
[87] *Yabloko* was Russia's first liberal democratic party, founded in the early 1990s.

theft (*прихватизация*, a word play, combining the words *приватизация* and *хватать* – the noun "privatization" and the verb "to grab").[88] They also worried about the impact of rising electricity tariffs on the social and economic development of their regions. This fear split the liberal political position, as Grigory Yavlinsky, the head of Yabloko, Russia's oldest liberal party, opposed the "young reformers" of the Yeltsin team on this point.[89] Electricity sector experts (the "scientists in the academy" referred to by Chubais in the earlier quote) opposed to reform included prominent bureaucrats in the energy ministry, such as deputy energy minister, Viktor Kudriavyi.[90] They were highly skeptical of introducing markets as an organizational principle for providing electricity.[91] Together, these groups managed to stall electricity reforms in the Duma for years – from the mid-1990s up until 2003.[92]

While the Duma was an important arena of power politics, regional governors and their firm hold over the Energos were the main impediments to sector reform. Yeltsin took some steps to centralize power, but it was only during the Putin presidency that the strengthening of the federal government attained paramount importance. With the rise of Vladimir Putin, liberal reformers found an important ally in their crusade against regional independence, increasingly regarded a dangerous threat to the Kremlin's ability to govern, let alone "modernize," the country.

Power Politics II: An Unlikely Alliance

When Putin became president, the political dynamics in Russia changed dramatically. Putin's efforts to eliminate two perceived challenges to the central government's sovereignty – the governors and the oligarchs – dominated Russian politics. A third aim of the federal government was the reassertion of the center's ability to regulate the economy, to centralize economic policy making, and to create a unified economic zone.[93]

---

[88] "Энергетика России: реформа или прихватизация?" *Восточно-Сибирская правда*, November 14, 2000.

[89] Aron, "Privatizing Russia's Electricity."

[90] Kudriavyi, deputy minister of energy, was an outspoken critic of electricity reforms; see interview in *Эксперт*, No. 14, April 13, 1998, p. 32. See Chapter 6 for more on Kudriavyi's role.

[91] Chapter 6 deals with this in more detail.

[92] *Yabloko* and Communist factions voted against reforms even in 2002/2003, but were a minority by then; see Aron, "Privatizing Russia's Electricity."

[93] For an assessment of the trend of the centralization of economic policy making, see "Региональная Экономика," *Вопросы экономики*, No. 7, 2006, p. 73.

These aims were wrapped in a promise to increase economic prosperity across all of Russia. Speaking in Kazan, the capital of Tatarstan, a very independent region, President Putin criticized what he saw as excessive regional discretion in policy making: "We must aim to make life equally good in all Russian regions. We will not achieve that without a unified legal and economic space in Russia."[94] While the fight against oligarchs and regional governors is much better known than the third goal is, the steps taken toward all three mutually reinforced each other.

President Putin largely succeeded in centralizing power during the first four years of his presidency.[95] Centralization also helped set in motion far-reaching changes in the electricity sector, as Putin united two different political factions unhappy about the autonomy of the regions. The liberal reforms in the electricity sector overcame the stalemate of the 1990s because of an unlikely alliance between the *siloviki* and the liberal wing of the Putin administration led by Alexei Kudrin, German Gref, Mikhail Kasyanov, and Aleksander Voloshin.[96] The *siloviki* were a group of FSB insiders at the core of Putin's power base. Both factions in this unlikely, and often overlooked, alliance shared the goal of wanting to end the influence of regional authorities.[97] For the *siloviki*, the defiant regions were an unacceptable challenge to the central government's authority. They were also an acute threat to their interests as a political group, as governors were well placed to succeed the ailing Yeltsin and his political allies as the dominant faction in the Kremlin in the late 1990s. For the liberal reformers, regional autonomy complicated implementation of reforms: Chubais wanted to separate electricity sector reforms from regional politics, to "de-politicize" electricity.[98] Undercutting the governors' autonomy would weaken their hold on Energos. The aims of the liberal reformers and the *siloviki* thus coincided. Putin supported Chubais in his reform

---

[94] Speech reported in *Putin calls for new, improved Federalism*, RFE/RL Newsline, March 23, 2000.

[95] For an account of Putin's political reforms, see Peter Reddaway and Robert W. Orttung, eds., *The Dynamics of Russian Politics: Putin's Reform of Federal-Regional Relations*, volume 1 and 2 (Lanham, MD: Rowman & Littlefield, 2004 and 2005).

[96] Many of the liberal faction of the Putin government were appointed by Putin; Voloshin had served in the Yeltsin administration.

[97] For an account of the rise of the *siloviki*, see Olga Kryshtanovskaya and Stephen White, "Putin's Militocracy," *Post-Soviet Affairs* 19, no. 4 (2003): 289–306; and Ian Bremmer and Samuel Charap, "The Siloviki in Putin's Russia: Who They Are and What They Want," *The Washington Quarterly* 30, no. 1 (2007): 83–92.

[98] Interview #63 with electricity company executive, Moscow, 20071212.

efforts.[99] And when Putin vowed to strengthen the authority of the state by establishing a "vertical of power" (*вертикаль власти*), he could count on the support of the liberals and the *siloviki*.

Putin's support of Chubais and liberalization of the sector puzzled many observers, because the *siloviki*'s position on the role of the state, in general and in the electricity sector in particular, was really quite different from the liberal vision. A core belief in statism as an economic program was the central shared notion of this group.[100] Liberals referred to the *siloviki*'s statism as *goskapitalism (госкапитализм)*, literally "state-capitalism." The reassertion of state control over the oil and gas sectors was a critical element of the *siloviki*'s vision of a strong state to direct Russia's economic future.[101] The *siloviki* and their allies in the Kremlin favored the creation of an energy behemoth that unified the control of all energy assets – oil, gas, and electricity – in the hands of Gazprom. A report by a Russian think-tank summarizes their position as follows: "Consolidating Russia's energy sector into a state-controlled goliath and channeling financial flows through the hands of the siloviki is their main goal." The report adds a list of specific energy companies and includes UES as the target of this strategy.[102] A prominent proponent of *goskapitalism*, Igor Shuvalov, frequently argued against the privatization of electricity on the grounds that the state needed to retain control of the energy sector, with Gazprom – as "an arm of the government" – at its center.[103] In the electricity sector, there were more specific differences: the statist position tended to view subsidies and differentiated price regimes as an

---

[99] Rutland notes Putin's "firm support" of Chubais and his reforms; see Rutland, "The Business Sector in Post-Soviet Russia," 294.

[100] Bremmer and Charap, "The Siloviki in Putin's Russia," 89. Also note, however, that *siloviki*'s position was more amorphous than the liberals'; this was the case partly because it was a faction that was not defined by their economic policy agenda (unlike the liberal), and partly because it was probably a less coherent group than it appeared to be.

[101] Putin had apparently formulated these ideas in a doctoral dissertation, according to Harley Balzer, "The Putin Thesis and Russian Energy Policy," *Post-Soviet Affairs* 21, no. 3 (2005): 210–225.

[102] The report is said to reflect the views of Vladislav Surkov, a powerful *silovik*, although the think-tank insists on its independence and on the report's "objective view of the situation within the Kremlin." See comment by Greg Walters, "Study: Siloviki's Struggle for Assets Not Over," *Moscow Times*, June 27, 2005.

[103] Igor Shuvalov said in an interview: "We don't need Gazprom purely as a business – we want Gazprom to be an arm of the government." Interview in *Russian Investment Review*, Vol. 3/3, p. 9, available online at http://www.russiainvestors.com/pdf/v3n3/theRIRinterview.pdf

important governance tool, while liberals saw them as market distortions and wanted to phase them out.[104]

Despite these differences, cooperation was inspired by the mutual goal of creating a state that can create and enforce rules. That liberals were willing to ally with forces intent on strengthening the authority of the central government is an interesting irony, given that they also ultimately wanted to *limit* the role of the state in the electricity sector. Chubais was very explicit in his rejection of *goskapitalism* – "In my eyes, state-capitalism is a dead end."[105] In response to a question about why the state could not provide the needed investment for power plants, he answered: "The state can put up maps with lamps (*плакаты с лампочкой*)" – a reference to Lenin's map with light bulbs to model the Soviet electrification project – "but that does not resolve the problems [in the sector]."[106]

But political goals were just as important as the economic agenda was: "disempowering regional governors and REKs [the regional regulatory bodies] was a key consideration in the reforms," confirmed an insider.[107] More precisely, the overlapping of goals of liberals and statists demonstrates just how much the projects of market making and state-building were related. Although the liberal reforms explicitly rested on creating as much distance as possible between politics and the structures of the new electricity sector – electricity should be "all business" and "no politics"[108] – to achieve this goal, liberals allied with the *siloviki* to sideline the opponents of reforms. Just as much as he needed to de-politicize electricity, Chubais wanted to create "one market for electricity, with one set of rules."[109] For a period, the transformation of the electricity

[104] For an argument for price increases, see interview with UES executive, "Низкие цены – враг экономики," *Коммерсантъ*, December 6, 2001.
[105] "Я считаю госкапитализм тупиком." Remark in response to a question asked by Catherine Belton, journalist for the *Financial Times*, about an announced merger between SUEK and Gazprom, at a conference "Electricity: Locomotive or Brake on Economic Development?/Энергетика: тормоз или локомотив развития экономики?" Moscow, February 13, 2007.
[106] Chubais's remark at the same conference.
[107] Interview #11 with electricity sector expert, Moscow, 20061018.
[108] "All business" and "no politics" are the words of electricity company executive, interview #63 in Moscow, 20071212. Another observer noted that the reorganization of the electricity sector was motivated by the ideal that there should be "less political involvement in business" and that the practice of "politically appointed heads of enterprises" should end; interview with an electricity sector economist, interview #43, Khabarovsk, 20071010. For the same ideas, see also "Низкие цены – враг экономики," *Коммерсантъ*, December 6, 2001.
[109] Interview #63 with electricity company executive, Moscow, 20071212.

sector was then shaped by a limited agreement that united these two groups. The alliance was important, but it ultimately proved unstable. As the reforms progressed, the liberal and statist camps diverged again. We will see that liberal reformers continued to chart the broad direction of the sector's transformation, but they were also forced to compromise and bend to the demands of other factions and to particular oligarchs.

For now, during the early years of the Putin presidency, various opponents of electricity sector reforms (many of whom were also a threat to the ascendancy and consolidation of power by the *siloviki*) lost ground. These included the governors, the *energetiki*, the Communist Party, and the left-liberal wing led by *Yabloko*. The last two groups had played a role in blocking reforms from passing in the Duma. A number of parties had had a certain influence on reforms, including the Communist Party, the party backed by regional governors, Fatherland – All Russia (*Отечество – Вся Россия*), and *Yabloko*. They were all either marginalized or disappeared altogether after United Russia (*Единая Россия*), the president's "party of power," started dominating the Duma in 2003. *Yabloko* did not clear the 5 percent hurdle to make it into the Duma in the 2003 elections. The liberal party Union of Rightist Forces (*Союз правых сил*) supported reforms, as Chubais was the leader of *SPS* at the time.[110] The remaining parties in the Duma rubber-stamped legislation introduced by United Russia.[111] This is how the watershed law of 2003 came to pass, and the "5+5" plan was approved.

Putin's political strategy was of course not confined to promoting United Russia and dominating the Duma. Governors were a key target of Putin's attempts to shore up the authority of the central government. Under Putin, some particularly defiant governors were "forced" to resign, notably Primorskii Krai's Nazdratenko.[112] In a well-documented series of events, governors became subject to increasing oversight from the central government starting in 2000. In a zero-sum struggle for authority,

---

[110] Some say SPS was funded through money from the electricity sector. This was mentioned in interview #39 with electrical engineer/electricity sector expert, Vladivostok, 20071004.

[111] In addition to the weakened communist successor party, two parties continue to exist as a "shadow" opposition – Just Russia (*Справедливая Россия/SR*) and Zhirinovsky's Liberal Democratic Party of Russia (*Либерально-демократическая партия России/ LDPR*). SR and LDPR have been unwilling and/or unable to oppose Kremlin policies.

[112] Nazdratenko was offered a leadership position in the fisheries ministry in Moscow to remove him from the governorship, clearly an offer he could not refuse (2001). Interview #31 with journalist covering electricity sector, Vladivostok, 20070915.

regions began losing and the center began winning.[113] The first step was the creation of seven new supra-regional administrative structures – the federal *okrugs* (*федеральные округа*). Each of these seven *okrugs* was placed under the supervision of a *polpred* (*полпред* or *полномочный представитель*), also called the "super-governor"[114] or presidential envoy, charged with ensuring that central government policies were enacted. A number of measures then subordinated regional administrative structures to these envoys, whose powers expanded rapidly.[115] Probably the most important and radical shift in center-region relations was the 2004 law that abolished the regional level election of governors, who were instead to be appointed by the president. The governors' constituents were no longer citizens, but rather Kremlin's power brokers.[116] As a regional journalist noted about the governor of a Far Eastern region: his status among Moscow's power elites became far more important than his reputation in the region.[117]

These centralizing strategies were mirrored in the transformation of the electricity sector. Subsequent chapters will describe this process in more detail; I want to preview three important aspects of these developments in a nutshell here. The Putin government eliminated the privileges of regional governors negotiated under Yeltsin. In property and tariff disputes federal agencies gained authority, and federal courts consistently ruled in favor of UES and the central government, something that was not the case in the 1990s (see Chapter 4).[118] A set of administrative reforms reorganized the regulatory agencies in a way that increased oversight of

113 Petrov, "How Have the Presidential Envoys Changed the Administrative-Political Balance of Putin's Regime?"; and Steven Solnick, "The New Federal Structure: More Centralized, or More of the Same?" *New Approaches to Russian Security (PONARS) Policy Memo* 161 (2000): 1–6.
114 Interview #8 with electricity sector expert at financial institution, Moscow, 20061006.
115 Petrov, "How Have the Presidential Envoys Changed the Administrative-Political Balance of Putin's Regime?" By 2007, *Новая газета* concluded that regional governors were left with so little autonomy that the presidential envoys were no longer needed; Андрей Рябов, "Орден – За взятие регионов," *Новая газета*, October 8, 2007.
116 Apparently this is a relatively small circle of Putin's advisors in charge of appointments. Interview #19 with academic and policy analyst, Moscow 20061122. See also Николай Петров, *Карнеги Брифинг*, 8/3, 2006.
117 This is referred to as "capital city status/столичный статус," a concept to which I was introduce in interview #33, journalist covering electricity sector, Vladivostok, 20070921.
118 Chapter 4 outlines details of the court battle surrounding Irkutskenergo. Another example is a ruling by the federal arbitrage court in favor of Dal'energo, against the decision of the Primorskii Krai Regional Energy Commission; "Дальэнерго нашла защитников," *Коммерсантъ*, February 18, 2000.

regional regulators by the *polpredy*. "Without the agreement of the office of the presidential envoy [*полпредство*], nothing happens," said an electricity sector executive in Primorskii Krai.[119] The result of these shifts in power to the center was summarized by one observers as follows: "The political power of local monopolies, [the Energos], was broken down progressively." This led to the "evaporation of regional control."[120] Since then "regional authorities have not been influential in shaping reforms [in the power sector]."[121] Finally, an observer from Primorskii Krai noted that the new governor, who relies on the approval of the Kremlin for his appointment, had little influence over the electricity sector's direction: "[Governor] Dar'kin had no choice but to implement [Chubais'] reforms."[122]

The role of the oligarchs and Russia's new private owners changed during this period as well. As with the governors, they were key targets in the Kremlin's attempt to regain sovereignty. The power of the Russian oligarchy in the 1990s can hardly be overestimated.[123] Their strength vis-à-vis the government declined radically during the first four years of the Putin administration.[124] Oligarchs were weakened in various ways. First, after the crisis in 1998, many small, regionally based enterprises were swallowed by larger conglomerates – often the FIGs (financial-industrial groups) – and assets were consolidated in the hands of a few powerful conglomerates.[125] The remaining oligarchs were rendered compliant or

[119] Interview #37 with electricity sector executive, Vladivostok, 20071002.
[120] Interview #16 with electricity sector consultant, Moscow/phone, 20061030. Statement to the same effect, "now governors hardly play a role," was made in interview #57 with electricity sector economist, Irkutsk, 20071122.
[121] Interview #1 with electricity sector expert at international financial institution, Moscow, 20060721. Another observer noted that the governor of Primorskii Krai, Dar'kin, "is pro-market, but that has nothing to do with electricity." This was reportedly based on an agreement between Chubais and Dar'kin, where Chubais promised to solve the region's energy problem and "create order," but asked the governor to stay clear of electricity. Interview #39 with electrical engineer and electricity sector expert, Vladivostok, 20071004.
[122] Interview #34 with academic and employee of electricity company, Vladivostok, 20070923. Interview #39 with electrical engineer and electricity sector expert, Vladivostok, 20071004
[123] Their role in President Yeltsin's reelection to his second term unambiguously signaled their dominance, which manifested itself in many other ways; see, for example, Hoffman, *The Oligarchs*.
[124] Petrov, "How Have the Presidential Envoys Changed the Administrative-Political Balance of Putin's Regime?"
[125] For the changing nature and role of FIGs, see Barnes, *Owning Russia*. For an account specifically about Siberian enterprises, see Maksim Shandarov, "Siberian Federal Okrug," in *The Dynamics of Russian Politics: Putin's Reform of Federal-Regional Relations*, ed.

"loyal" because the newly strengthened presidency could wield a whole "cornucopia of carrots and sticks."[126] The stick for a few of the high-profile oligarchs was arrest, labor camp, or exile.[127] The most notorious move to eliminate oligarchic power was the re-nationalization of Yukos and the imprisonment of Mikhail Khodorkovsky. The government offered two sweet carrots to loyal oligarchs: immunity for those assets already won and the ability to acquire more assets to complete their vertically integrated business empires.[128] Not wanting to jeopardize assets acquired during the tumultuous last decade of the twentieth century, most remaining oligarchs "behaved well" and followed the wishes of the center. The taming of the oligarchs had a direct influence on the electricity reforms. The role of many oligarchs in the regional pacts that characterized the first post-Soviet decade was eliminated. The regional or "local oligarchs have been significantly less influential,"[129] in the words of one observer. A number of the big national oligarchic empires were broken up, most infamously Yukos. (Yukos had owned Tomskenergo and on several occasions had challenged UES's plans for unbundling, corporate restructuring, and the creation of the new supra-regional generation company.[130]) At the same time, some of the largest and "well-behaved" conglomerates were able to retain their influence. We will see in subsequent chapters that with the taming of the oligarchs, the site of their influence shifted from the regional to the federal level.

Peter Reddaway and Robert W. Orttung, vol. 1 (Lanham, MD: Rowman & Littlefield, 2004), 214. The most important ones include Potanin's Interros and Deripaska's Rusal.

[126] Peter Rutland, "The Oligarchs and Economic Development," in *After Putin's Russia: Past Imperfect, Future Uncertain*, ed. Stephen K. Wegren and Dale Herspring (Lanham, MD: Rowman & Littlefield, 2010), 167.

[127] Including the media tycoons Berezovsky and Gusinsky and the oil magnate Mikhail Khodorkovsky. As is well known, these moves were the basis for virtually complete state control over broadcast media, the de facto "re-nationalization" of Yukos, the largest private oil company, and more generally, the neutralization of oligarchs as political actors. For accounts of the Yukos affair, see for example, Sakwa, *The Quality of Freedom*; and Keith Gessen's review, Keith Gessen, "Cell Block Four," *London Review of Books*, February 25, 2010. See also Stephen Fortescue, *Russia's Oil Barons and Metal Magnates: Oligarchs and the State in Transition* (Basingstoke, Hampshire; New York: Palgrave Macmillan, 2006); and Sim, *The Rise and Fall of Privatization in the Russian Oil Industry*.

[128] Masha Lipman called this "property rights earned by good behavior." Talk given at ISEEES/BPS, UC Berkeley in March 2007.

[129] Interview #7 with electricity sector analyst at financial institution, Moscow, 20061005.

[130] Nadia Popova, "Court Postpones Ruling on TGK-11 Asset Split," *St. Petersburg Times*, April 1, 2008.

Once political opposition by the governors, Duma representatives, and oligarchs was neutralized, significant legislation was passed between the fall of 2002 and early 2003 establishing the basic contours of electricity sector reforms.[131] These laws marked the beginning of more orderly reform in the sector. They ended a period of "legal disorder" in which "everybody could do what they wanted."[132] They also charted the broad liberalization course that was to define the next stage: the unbundling of regional monopolies, divestiture of the government stake in generation and retail, but reassertion of state control over transmission networks.[133] With the passage of the 2003 legislation, Chubais claimed an early victory. Yet, the fight for restructuring was far from over in 2003. Electricity was *not* de-politicized and the "big battle" continued[134] for years, as different actors negotiated and reevaluated their share in bargains. One observer thought, "the 2003 version of the law was very radical, [and] corrections were called for."[135] Liberal reformers officially won some of the key battles in the sector by 2003, but these "corrections" were political concessions they had to make in order to see their vision realized. Corrections and concessions ended up creating the three different zones

---

[131] These laws passed in three readings in the Duma; see, for example, Alla Startseva, "Deputies Vote to Break Up Power Grid," *Moscow Times*, October 10, 2002. The electricity package consists of six legislative measures: two federal laws 'On electricity' and 'On the implementation of the law "On electricity"' (Federal Law No. 35-FZ dated March 26, 2003 "On the Electric Power Industry" and Federal Law No. 36-FZ dated March 26, 2003 "On the Specifics of Electric Power Industry Functioning during the Transition Period") as well as four bills amending other pieces of legislation: the Civil Code (part 2), the law 'On natural monopolies', the law 'On the state regulation of electricity and heating tariffs', and the law 'On energy saving.' William Tompson, "Electricity Legislation Passes Second Reading," in *Prospects for the Russian Federation Project* (London: Royal Institute of International Affairs: Russia and Eurasia Programme, 2003).

[132] According to one observer, the lack of a legal basis for the changes in the 1990s was partly responsible for the electricity crises of that decade; interview #39 with electrical engineer/electricity sector expert, Vladivostok, 20071004.

[133] The state wanted to secure control of transmission networks, partly because it is a natural monopoly, partly because it can be a very profitable subsector, a "cash cow," in the words of one analyst. Interview #15 with electricity sector analyst at financial institution, Moscow, 20061027.

[134] In Russian, "большая борьба," interview #39 with electrical engineer and electricity sector expert, Vladivostok, 20071004.

[135] Interview #52 with electricity sector economist, Irkutsk, 20071117. How "radical" these laws were was also mentioned in Interview #57 with electricity sector economist, Irkutsk, 20071122. Note that both these informants were *energetiki*, the old guard of electricity sector professionals.

in European Russia, Siberia, and the Far East. This outcome was not at all clear in 2003.[136]

Power Politics III: Post-Soviet Economic Planning Under Putin

A different set of political forces influenced reforms after the passage of the 2003 laws. Policies were no longer contested in the Duma, and governors had lost much of their clout, but this did not mean that the electricity reforms were no longer subject to political battles. Conflicts continued between different factions of the government as well as between conglomerates with different interest vis-à-vis the electricity sector.

Liberal reformers initially wanted to create thousands of new power companies and one market, with one set of rules.[137] The reforms wound up creating only twenty-two new companies while regional differences in ownership and regulatory regimes persisted. These differences reflected compromises that liberal reformers made with Russia's large energy and industrial conglomerates and the *siloviki*. The political dynamic that necessitated these compromises was rooted in relationships between Putin, oligarchs, and two factions he relied on – the statist *siloviki* and the liberal reformers. As earlier, the logic of electricity sector bargains combined short-term political calculations with long-term developmental goals.

Electricity sector bargains reflected a balancing strategy: with a newly strengthened central government, Putin accommodated both liberal and statist factions, but also forced both sides to compromise. Liberals won important victories: they were granted free reign to dismantle vertically integrated monopolies, UES, and the Energos; institutions were created to regulate private entities and a liberalized wholesale market; managers committed to the liberal vision of markets were appointed to run most electricity companies; and most of the country's power plants were privatized in reasonably (though not fully) transparent auctions. Note that none of these steps would have made sense for a predatory state, which was increasingly how the Russian state under Putin came to be characterized after the attack on Yukos in 2004.

At the same time, liberals had to adapt plans and revise goals, because liberalization was never Putin's primary goal. Just as preventing

---

[136] The federal law, for example, designated the Far East a "special case" but made no explicit provisions whether or how reforms were to proceed there.

[137] Interview with Chubais in Mellow, "Is This a Way to Create Capitalism?"

deindustrialization had been a primary concern of regional governors in the 1990s, it was now the federal government that pursued this agenda. The federal government under Putin sought to avert deindustrialization and its destabilizing consequences by devising comprehensive strategies to diversify economic activity beyond the oil sector. Echoing regional authorities in the 1990s, it was now the federal government that often referred to electricity as a "mechanism for development."[138] Initially, two competing models of how to achieve diversification continued to coexist and compete. In 2001, shortly after becoming president, Vladimir Putin asked two important actors at the federal level, who broadly represented market liberal and *goskapitalist* factions, to devise a long-term development strategy for Russia – German Gref and the more statist governor of Khabarovsk, Viktor Ishaev, respectively.[139] They shared a belief in markets and a commitment to modernize the Russian economy, but they had divergent views concerning the origins of competitiveness. The liberal faction of the Putin government insisted that eliminating subsidies, liberalizing energy sectors, and ridding industry of special protections best achieved economic modernization and diversification. They insisted that only "genuine winners" would be competitive in the long run.[140]

Putin eventually supported a middle path: embracing liberal markets while confirming that the "state has a powerful role to play in promoting growth, revitalizing core industries, and reforming and regulating natural monopolies."[141] While supporting liberal ideas about introducing competition into natural monopolies, he ultimately sided with an activist strategy that privileged select "national champions" or "strategically important enterprises."[142]

[138] Interview #52 with electricity sector economist, Irkutsk, 20071117; he also called it an "economic mechanism to develop regions."
[139] Commentary of these strategies by Yevgeny Yasin, a well-known Russian economist and economy minister in the mid-1990s; available at http://www.project-syndicate.org/commentary/putin-s-undercover-liberalism
[140] "Genuine winners" is an expression used in the World Bank's *Russian Economic Report*, March 2005, p. 14, available at http://web.worldbank.org/
[141] According to Yasin, noted earlier in the chapter.
[142] Putin's doctoral dissertation (entitled "Strategic Planning of the Reproduction of the Resource Base") elaborated on the merits of national champions; see Harley Balzer, "Vladimir Putin's Academic Writings and Russian Natural Resource Policy," *Problems of Post-Communism* 53, no. 1 (2006): 48–49. See also Laura Solanko, *The Policy of National Champions and Russian Competitiveness*, Expert Position (Institute for Economies in Transition at the Bank of Finland, June 2007), available at http://www.bof.fi/; and Marshall I. Goldman, *Petrostate: Putin, Power, and the New Russia* (Oxford: Oxford University Press, 2008), 97. State funding of high-tech and science initiatives is a core part of this agenda as well; see Loren R Graham, *Lonely Ideas: Can Russia*

The concessions that liberals made to the large energy and industrial conglomerates in the 2003–2008 period reflected the political dominance of the activist/statist conception of economic development. Demographic implications, in particular concerns over labor mobility, help explain the ascendency of statism during this time. The liberal model is premised on the axiom that Soviet planners bequeathed Russia a profound "spatial misallocation of people": cities and towns located in regions too cold (thermal misallocation), too remote, or too dominated by a single industry, typically the shrinking military-industrial complex.[143] Unconcerned with returns on investment, Soviet planners had made investment decisions based on political grounds. Post-Soviet liberal reformers, found that such "misallocations" of capital were too costly and must be corrected by letting northern and mono-industrial towns shrink to a size viable in a market economy. The liberal advice was to "somehow undo the past."[144] This could only happen once special privileges for remote fringe regions were eliminated.[145]

Regional governors, and later the more statist faction at the center, were deeply troubled by the implications of this position. Rather than abandoning cities, regional leaders wanted to transform and modernize existing population centers. Not surprisingly, regionalist movements rejected the arguments that depopulation of remote cities was inevitable.[146] By the second term of the Putin administration, with the influence of regionalist movements having waned and with the centralization of

Compete? Graham details the state's efforts to build a high-tech industrial cluster at Skolkovo. See also "Dubna's Tale," *The Economist*, July 31, 2008, accessed March 18, 2014, http://www.economist.com/node/11849278. A list of strategically important enterprises was approved by with a presidential decree (decree No. 1009, August 4, 2004). The list is available on the Kremlin's website, http://archive.kremlin.ru/text/docs/2004/08/75174.shtml

[143] Clifford G. Gaddy, *The Price of the Past: Russia's Struggle with the Legacy of a Militarized Economy* (Washington, DC: Brookings Institution Press, 1996). The Russian debates on this were sparked by the work of Andrey Parshev, quoted in Hill and Gaddy, *The Siberian Curse*; and Andrew Kuchins, ed., *Russia after the Fall* (Washington, DC: Brookings Institution Press, 2002).

[144] Hill and Gaddy, *The Siberian Curse*, 117.

[145] See Michael Rasell, "Neoliberalism in the North: The Transformation of Social Policy in Russia's Northern Periphery," *Polar Geography* 32, no. 3–4 (2009): 99. The policy document that Rasell highlights is the Gref Program 2000.

[146] The Siberian regionalist movement, for example, demanded that local resources be retained, with the aim to transform Soviet-era cities into their modern equivalents. See, for example, James Hughes, "Regionalism in Russia: The Rise and Fall of the Siberian Agreement," *Europe Asia Studies* 46, no. 7 (1994): 1133–1161. Though Siberian regionalism outlasted the Siberian Agreement, it weakened by the late 1990s.

political power and economic resources, the federal government assumed responsibility for regional planning. Statist factions at the federal level were anxious about population loss, migration, and the specter of more ghost towns in remote areas, and argued for state support to modernize Russian industry. With the liberal and statist factions pulling in opposing directions, the federal government often pursued a dual strategy. Direct state entitlements for citizens in remote regions were either eliminated or greatly reduced.[147] The federal government remained committed, however, to supporting Soviet-era industrial enterprises, to both foster economic diversification and avoid turning provincial cities into ghost towns.[148]

There is clear evidence that the government was also concerned with long-term developmental goals closely tied to its legitimacy beyond the walls of the Kremlin. While reasserting the center's authority over the regions, Putin still had to provide solutions to the problems that regional governors had been grappling with since the 1990s. In particular, he needed to demonstrate a credible intention to restore prosperity and stability. That "[g]overnment abstention from [industrial] regulation [is] the most important factor in the destruction of regional industries throughout Russia" was a widespread sentiment.[149] While regional governors had been first in line to respond, now the central government was called upon to coordinate industrial policy, to "systematically help" regional industry integrate into global and domestic markets.[150]

Under Putin, the central government then turned increasingly to regional development strategies to shape the country's post-Soviet transformation. Moscow, or more precisely the Ministry for Regional Development, once again planned *for* the regions, although in a very different way than during the Soviet period. State-directed planning (also referred to as *стратегическое планирование*) included strategies for socio-economic development at the regional level and the level of the federal okrug (*стратегии социально-экономического развития*). These strategies

---

[147] Wengle and Rasell, "The Monetisation of L'goty"; and Rasell, "Neoliberalism in the North."

[148] See also Collier, *Post-Soviet Social*; and Niobe Thompson, *Settlers on the Edge: Identity and Modernization on Russia's Arctic Frontier* (Vancouver: University of British Columbia Press, 2009).

[149] "Выражу мнение, и не только мое, что самую большую роль в развале промышленности регионов и всей России сыграло то, что государство полностью отказалось от ее регулирования." Opinion by Shepshelev, an industrialist from Barnaul; in *Эко*, No. 2, 2006, p. 96.

[150] Ibid.

were also referred to as territorial planning documents (*территориальное планирование*) and targeted strategies (*целевые стратегии*).[151] Although the relationship and hierarchy between various documents was often unclear, the federal government explicitly wanted to improve upon the ad hoc responses of regional governors during the 1990s. The Ministry of Regional Development produced a series of framework documents that laid out targets and methodologies to guide the formulation of regional development programs. New legislation meant to provide the basis for meta-level regional strategies.[152] In part regional development plans relied on strategies that had been formulated by the regions in the 1990s and earlier, in collaboration with academics in the field of regional studies, a well-established discipline at Russian universities. In part they were drawn up anew by a cottage industry of consultants that advised regional and federal administrators in their formulation.

Electricity is mentioned in one of these documents as a "mechanism for the social and economic development" of Russia's regions.[153] Improving electricity infrastructure was included as an important development strategy for the eight federal okrugs. Noting that aging electrical infrastructure plagued many regions, these framework strategies suggested capital investments and modernization of electricity infrastructure.[154] One okrug-level document stated, for example, that "realizing the promise of energy production is a priority in the formulation of the North-Caucasus Federal District's strategy for social and economic development."[155] Along the same lines, the "Program for the Economic

---

[151] These terms are partly used interchangeably. For a discussion of these strategies and their proliferation under Putin, see Елена Овчинникова, "Расширение горизонта," *Эксперт*, No. 22 June 8, 2008. Regional development strategies exist for almost all regions; for example, the development program for Primorskii Krai: Администрация Приморского края, "Стратегия социально-экономического развития Приморского края на 2004–2010 гг.," под общей редакцией С. М.Дарькина, Владивосток, Издательство ТЦСП, 2004.

[152] Including the 2005 "Federal Conceptual Framework for Projecting the Problems, Targets, Tasks and Mechanisms of the Social and Economic Development of the Regions of the Russian Federation," and a series of "Conceptual Strategies for the Social and Economic Development of the Regions of the Russian Federation," for example, the *Концепция Стратегии социально-экономического развития регионов Российской Федерации 2005* (hereafter Концепция 2005; available at the Minregion site: http://archive.minregion.ru/WorkItems/DocItem.aspx?PageID=148&DocID=136

[153] See section 4: Механизмы социально-экономического развития регионов Российской Федерации, and 4.1, on p. 64 of the Концепция 2005, as well as p. 3 of the Концепция 2008.

[154] Концепция 2005, p. 4, as part of section 1.1. "Экономические структурные проблемы."

[155] "Реализация энергетического потенциала Северо-Кавказского федерального округа – приоритетное направление разрабатываемой в настоящее время стратегии социально-экономического развития СКФО."

and Social Development of the Far East and the Pre-Baikal Region for
the Period until 2013" contained three large projects in the electricity sector.[156] The National Priority Projects (*Федеральные целевые программы
России*) were another set of developmental planning documents.[157] These
were state-funded investment projects in a variety of sectors, often including infrastructural updates and electricity sector reforms.[158]

An important aspect of these developmental plans was their emphasis on regional and geographic specificity. They were often referred to as
"territorial planning" documents (*территориальное планирование*) and
relied on the term "spatial development" (*пространственное развитие*).
Explicit attention to geographical differences across regions was a key
rationale of these plans. The need for "complex analysis of internal and
external factors that influence regional development" is highlighted
by the Ministry of Regional Development, and includes an analysis of
existing "infrastructural provisions, including the provision of electricity services."[159] Overall, such federal and regional development strategies
and state-funded projects proliferated during the eight years of the Putin
administration under discussion here.

These plans were highly ambitious, and many commentators emphasized problems with strategies and targets. Russian observers were critical
of their tendency to prioritize oversized prestige projects, or "mega-proj-
ects," as well as their top-down character, noting that the mechanisms
to achieve specified targets were underdeveloped. The lack of appropriate financing for regional development strategies was another concern.[160]
One commentator noted the lack of coordination between strategies
and between different levels of government, questioning whether these

---

[156] See the "Program for the Economic and Social Development of the Far East and the Pre-
Baikal Region until 213/Программа экономического и социального развития Дальнего
Востока и Забайкалья на период до 2013 года." Also available on the Minregio site:
http://www.minregion.ru/state_programs/56.html

[157] These national projects are detailed on a dedicated site by the Russian government; see
http://fcp.economy.gov.ru

[158] Putin introduced these national priority projects in 2005 in pursuit of his stated goal of
social and economic development; see http://www.rost.ru/ for details

[159] "Комплексную оценку ключевых внешних и внутренних факторов, оказывающих
влияние на социально-экономическое развитие региона," and "Инфраструктурная
обеспеченность территории региона (в т.ч. обеспеченность электроэнергетической
инфраструктурой)." This meta-document details how regional strategies are to be formulated and specifies how infrastructure should be assessed as part of this process.
"Требования/технический стандарт к стратегии социально-экономического развития
субъекта РФ" (p. 4), available on the MinRegio site: http://archive.minregion.ru/
WorkItems/ListNews.aspx?PageID=278

[160] Granberg, Pelyasov, and Vavilova, "Programs of Regional Development Revisited."

strategies facilitated investment and capital inflows into a region – one
of their main rationales.[161] Another observer held out hope for the future
but noted that "temporary disorganization" prevailed.[162] Nevertheless,
we will see in the following chapters that, similar to the ad hoc responses
of regional governors in the 1990s, these strategies proved influential.

A last aspect of the rise of regional development strategies under
Putin that I want to introduce here is their reliance on the cooperation
of Russia's conglomerates. Just as with regional governors in the 1990s,
the central government enlisted Russia's conglomerates. As Peter Rutland
points out, oligarchs were "expected to play an active role in helping
the Kremlin to realize its political, economic and social agenda."[163] Aside
from providing tax revenues and employment, the big regional employers
were enlisted in many different ways, small and large. A small example
may be gleaned from the youth soccer tournament, sponsored by the Far
Eastern regional electricity company, that I stumbled upon in Vladivostok
during fieldwork in 2007. A larger example may be found in the case
of Chukotka, a region in the most northern Far East. Niobe Thompson
documents how the oligarch Roman Abramovich became the guarantor
of well-being and modernization in Chukotka, where his team designed
ambitious structural and institutional reforms for the region, while also
serving as the "provider of humanitarian aid in the form of flour, sugar, oil,
fish hooks and nets."[164] A theatrical example of a powerful conglomerate
being encouraged to work in support of regional development transpired
in the town of Pikalevo in 2007. When the town's largest plant stopped
operating, Putin very publicly criticized Oleg Deripaska, another prominent oligarch, the owner of Rusal and of the said plant, on state-owned
TV networks, making the point that oligarchs could not get away with
closing factories and abandoning heat and electricity plants that keep
the city's apartments warm.[165] The event was widely interpreted as an

[161] Елена Овчинникова, "Расширение горизонта," *Эксперт*, No. 22, June 8, 2008.
[162] The Ministry of Regional Development admits that there is a problem with coordinat-
ing these various levels of economic planning; see Концепция 2008. See also Sozhinov,
who discusses how this "temporary disorganization" (*временная дезорганизация*) is the
result of a number of contradictions in the way regional regulation is attempted; В.
А. Сожинов, "Регулирование экономического развития на уровне субъекта федерации,"
Эко, No. 3, 2006.
[163] Rutland, "Business-State Relations in Russia."
[164] Thompson, *Settlers on the Edge*. Quoted by Mumin Shakirov "Chukotka's Smitten with
Roman Abramovich," *St. Petersburg Times*, August 7, 2001.
[165] Reported widely in the Russian news, for example, in "Путин заставил Дерипаску вновь
запустить завод в Пикалево," *Известия*, June 4, 2009, as well as abroad: Ellen Barry,
"Putin Plays Sheriff for Cowboy Capitalists," *New York Times*, June 4, 2009.

attempt by Putin to ward off social unrest. Such a public rebuke, reminding loyal oligarchs of their social function and enlisting them for broader social and developmental goals, was an important aspect of developmental bargains. In what follows we will see that in return for fulfilling these functions, conglomerates were endowed with state resources and special provisions to increase their international competitiveness.

Generally, Russia's conglomerates pursued vertical integration as a strategy to insulate their core activities against the uncertainties of doing business in the postcommunist environment.[166] In the electricity sector, vertical integration lowered the risks of unpredictable contracts with suppliers and consumers. Importantly, we will see that energy and industrial conglomerates had very different interests vis-à-vis the electricity sector, targeting different assets and pushing for different kinds of subsidy regimes. Russian state policy selectively accommodated different private interests. A Russian textbook on electricity sector regulation described the state's role by noting that one of the government's most important function in the sector was to "balance the interests of electricity providers and [electricity] consumers."[167]

A Contested and Shifting Consensus Shapes Market Arrangements

UES, the vertically integrated monopoly dating back to Lenin's electrification, ceased to exist on July 1, 2008, with all its operations taken over by new successor companies. As he had done in 2003, when key legislation passed in the Duma, Anatoly Chubais once again claimed success in creating a market for electricity. At the same time, after eight years as Russia's president, Vladimir Putin claimed success in unifying the country and defeating challengers to the central government's sovereignty. These projects were intertwined, each premised on temporary alliances and evolving bargains.

---

[166] This tendency has been widely observed, for example, by Rutland, ibid. According to Volkov, "target selection for hostile takeovers was governed by the logic of vertical integration" in Vadim Volkov, "Standard Oil and Yukos in the Context of Early Capitalism in the United States and Russia," p. 252. This applies to the electricity sector in particular, according to interview #9 with electricity sector analyst at financial institution, Moscow, 20061008. For a reference to this strategy, see "Кто правее, Есапов или Чубайс?" *Комсомольская правда*, November 13, 2002.

[167] "Достижение баланса экономических интересов поставщиков и потребителей электрической энергии." This is listed as one of the key functions of government regulation of electricity markets, in В. В. Хлебников, *Рынок Электроэнергии в России.* Гуманитарный издательский центр ВЛАДОС, 2005, p. 181.

This chapter introduced power politics. Initially, Chubais's liberal reform strategies, which emphasized marketization of the electricity sector, conflicted with the regional development strategies of the governors, who sought to protect their regions from the impact of liberal reforms. Governors tried to enlist regional industrialists, at times writing their own laws while circumventing those of the federal government. The oblast level became the de facto site of political bargains and economic regulation. President Putin's successful centralization of political power undercut the governors. Regional pacts were replaced by bargaining at the federal level. Putin selectively accommodated the oligarch's demands in the electricity sector, in return for their contribution to regional development.

My account of power politics emphasized the importance of contested ideas and compromises in shaping outcomes of the electricity sector's transformation. While liberal reformers were remarkably successful in undoing monopoly structures inherited from the Soviet period, they also had to make important compromises. For constructivist political economy, such compromises suggest the need for research on how ideas evolve in contested arenas. Constructivist focus on shared norms and the constructed nature of economic interest has provided a critical corrective to the dominance of interest-based models. Yoshiko Herrera, for example, directed our attention to local understandings of the economy – imagined economies – to explain variation in the way economic interests were formulated in political demands for more sovereignty. Her framework captured how regional economic projects resulted from a shared understanding of local economic conditions, the "imagined economic interests," rather than "objective" economic conditions, such as how hard a region was affected by the economic collapse of the nineties.[168] Regional developmental strategies reflected negotiated compromises, and post-Soviet developmentalism was an ideational framework that was fundamentally contested, rather than a set of shared, relatively stable ideas. The post-Soviet case then suggests that "unmoored" ideational frameworks are critical for our understanding of complex, real-life market institutions.

[168] Herrera, *Imagined Economies*. Herrera singled out a pessimistic understanding of the local economic situation in one case, Sverdlovsk, and contrasted it with a more positive assessment, in the case of Samara, to explain variation in the emergence of local sovereignty movements.

3

Regionally Patterned Pacts and the Political
Life of Things

"There is no single recipe; restructuring ... took into account regional differences, economic and natural particularities."[1]

Three Regions, Three Bargains, and the Political Life of Things

Different actors kept lights on across Russia. Market arrangements in the electricity sector varied across regions because of negotiated and evolving political pacts. The preceding chapter introduced power politics – political negotiations between central and regional authorities, and between different factions at the center. This chapter turns to the evolving pacts between the government and Russia's new economic actors. As in the previous chapter, I emphasize the adaptability of the liberal reform program. When Moscow struggled to reassert centralized control over the economy, regional governments worked to find their own ways to integrate regional economies into new market relations. Both central and regional governments devised various mechanisms of state support to promote the regional and national competitiveness of Russian companies. The first aim of this chapter is to give an account of these bargains and to show how they aligned with regional development strategies. I introduce the government's pact with Gazprom in European Russia, with Rusal in Siberia, and with electricity companies in the Far East. Policies and reforms in the electricity sector were adapted to the specific needs and interests of each of these privileged economic actors.

---

[1] "Кто правее, Есапов или Чубайс?" *Комсомольская правда*, November 13, 2002.

Inherited material facts – transmission lines, pipelines, and fuel types underlying power production – played an important role in the trajectory and outcome of market reforms.[2] A second task of this chapter is to clarify the role such material facts played in post-Soviet power politics. The Soviet Unified Electricity System relied predominately on gas-fired power plants in European Russia, on enormous hydroelectric dams in Siberia, and on regionally mined coal in the Russian Far East.[3] Physical realities, or to be more specific the material ties between the electricity sector and its upstream suppliers in the gas and coal sectors and its downstream customers in the electricity-intensive industries, hence differed across regions. But did Stalin-era decisions that transformed coal-fired plants in European Russia into gas-fired plants determine the way post-Soviet power markets emerged? Physical facts helped define the three supra-regions in the post-Soviet period, but they were not structural determinants. Tracing the political role of physical ties and materialities, I found that material ties were indeed important, but also that only some of them persisted, while others were idled. If we think of the former Soviet, now Russian, industrial geography as a multidimensional material construct, the post-Soviet collapse was a sharp blow that destroyed many of its constitutive elements. Yet as relations between these elements came undone and were reshaped during the period of market reforms, some of the physical ties proved resilient and portions of the Soviet-era industrial order were left intact.[4]

This chapter makes the case that it was the political resonance of a particular set of ideas, which validated certain inherited structures, rather than the mechanistic workings of geographic or structural determinism, that best explains this selective retention of Soviet-era structure. The liberal reform team around Chubais wanted to create "one market," governed by one set of rules. Russian conglomerates, by contrast, frequently strove to preserve inherited, particularistic ties to the electricity sector and privileged relationship with power providers. Conglomerates argued that the interconnectedness between their industries and the electricity sector

---

[2] Anthropologists have been much more concerned with materiality than other social sciences are. Fernando Coronil notes, for example, that "material properties of these resources are made to matter by the network of social relations woven around them." Fernando Coronil, *The Magical State: Nature, Money, and Modernity in Venezuela* (Chicago: University of Chicago Press, 1997), 41. See also Collier, *Post-Soviet Social*; and Rogers, "The Materiality of the Corporation."

[3] These are the dominant patterns: there are hydroelectric plants in European Russia as well, and many of the outlying regions in Siberia rely on coal-fired power plants.

[4] For the concept of industrial order, see Gary Herrigel, *Industrial Constructions: The Sources of German Industrial Power* (Cambridge: Cambridge University Press, 2000).

was natural, essential, and efficient. These arguments helped legitimize and therefore secure concessions for Russia's oligarchs. Electricity sector reforms, while quite liberal by design, wound up creating a regionally fragmented organization of power provision, with many elements that reflected the inherited industrial order. Market reforms came to reflect regional context, as one observer concluded – "There [was] no single recipe; restructuring ... took into account regional differences, economic and natural particularities." [5]

Industrial geography, then, conditioned the outcomes of political bargains. Inherited material ties delimited the set of possibilities for bargains between conglomerates and the government in two distinct ways: they shaped conglomerates' interests and they mattered as politically resonant narratives that construed physical facts as natural givens. Material ties did indeed at times act as structural conditions shaping oligarchic interests. At the same time, material ties did not necessarily survive the post-Soviet turmoil, and it would be misleading to argue that they determined reform trajectories. We will see that material ties shaped reforms in the form of powerful rhetoric that physical ties *should* remain intact by Russian conglomerates, conferring legitimacy on their demands. Chapter 1 introduced the idea that oligarchic conglomerates relied on "legitimizing narratives" to justify their demands for concessions by the government and pointed out that this strategic use of ideas defies the ideas/interest dichotomy that pervades much of political economy. A striking common feature of such narratives was their emphasis that certain elements of Soviet-era industrial geography need to remain intact. [6]

---

[5] "Кто правее, Есапов или Чубайс?" *Комсомольская правда*, November 13, 2002.

[6] I should add a methodological note particular to this chapter. While I don't have access to the words used in bargains between oligarchs and the government, the inference that conglomerates shaped public and academic discourses is not particularly controversial. Arguments about the naturalness, the necessity, and the efficiency of maintaining the connection between the electricity sector and adjacent sectors surface in various documents. I draw mostly on regional newspaper sources, regional development reports, and business strategies to illustrate how Russia's conglomerates mobilized physical ties to justify the ownership and subsidy regimes that characterize the three zones. Most Russians are convinced, for example, that regional newspaper coverage is often swayed by what is called "white PR" – reporting that reflects the views of the company and makes the company itself appear in a good light, while demonizing competitors or opponents. The director of Krasnoiarskenergo, Kolmogorov hints at this in "Раскалять амбиции не продуктивно," *Красноярский рабочий*, March 5, 1998. The same is sometimes said of academic institutions, although academics generally enjoy a better reputation than journalists do. The proximity of the Siberian branch of the Russian Academy of Sciences to regional industrialists was mentioned in interview #58 with academic, Irkutsk, 20071124.

A third, even broader inquiry woven through this chapter then examines how interests and ideas are intertwined in power politics. We will see that conglomerates' arguments naturalized physical ties as necessary and efficient: they *should* own particular power plants, they argued, because they are physically connected via pipelines and transmission lines. Referring to physical facts allowed conglomerates to shift concessions out of the realm of politically negotiated privilege. Put more generally, physical realities mattered as ideas that legitimized interests.

In its effort to disentangle arguments about the role of economic geography and physical "things" in political bargains, this chapter first explores connections between the economic geography of the reform period and that of the late Soviet era. It then details developmental bargains struck between the regional and later federal governments and Russia's conglomerates in each of the three zones. I describe the ties that bound the electricity sector to the gas sector in European Russia, to industrial consumers in Siberia, and to coal companies in the Far East, and how these ties shaped interests and political bargains. The chapter's conclusion considers how these observations depart from debates about Soviet-era legacies and how they contribute to constructivist political economy.

Soviet-Era Planning and Post-Soviet Industrial Geography

Human geographers have long stressed that social activity is embedded in spatial contexts: landscapes and geographies are reshaped by human activity, but they also in turn condition social life down the road.[7] Soviet planning fundamentally altered the geography of the Russian empire, collectivizing farms, building factories, power plants and dams, company towns, and military installations. Elements of the intricate but very tangible web of Soviet factories, power plants, and pipelines that matured over decades, in turn, shaped post-Soviet trajectories of social change. I follow Oleg Kharkordin and Stephen Collier, who noted that the material structures built by Soviet-era planners proved remarkably resilient, taking seriously the "vital importance of these material structures."[8] I focus

---

[7] See, for example, Mike Crang and N. J. Thrift, eds., *Thinking Space*, Critical Geographies 9 (London; New York: Routledge, 2000).

[8] Collier notes that "the substantive economy created by Soviet city builders proved stubbornly intransigent." Collier, *Post-Soviet Social*, p. 7. See also Oleg Kharkordin, *Main Concepts of Russian Politics* (Lanham, MD: University Press of America, 2005), chapter 8; and Stephen J. Collier, "Pipes," in *Patterned Ground: Entanglements of Nature and Culture*, ed. Stephan Harrison, Steve Pile, and N. J. Thrift (London: Reaktion, 2004), 50–51.

here on the physical connections between electricity and neighboring sectors, bequeathed by Soviet-era economic planners to post-Soviet actors, although other aspects of Russia's geography also mattered (references to climatic conditions in particular regions, or to Siberia and the Far East as frontier regions, for example).

During the early Soviet period, electrification and, later, the production of ever-increasing amounts of electrical power were among the highest priorities of economic planning. Lenin's determination to bring light to all corners of the Soviet state rendered the projection of state power over the economy synonymous with the modernization of social life brought about by the expansion of the electricity grid. Even as electricity was increasingly taken for granted over the decades of the twentieth century, it continued to carry a symbolic association with modernity as a basic prerequisite for modern life. This priority status meant that during seventy years of planning, every aspect of the physical structure of the electricity system was shaped by the imperatives of Soviet industrialization, however imperfectly plans were implemented and negotiated along bureaucratic hierarchies.

The geographical distribution of industries, the monopolistic structure of the economy, and the geographical map of power plants and transmission grids profoundly reflected the logic of Soviet industrialization.[9] The production of electric power was designed to be an integrated system, the backbone of the planned economy. Electrification and industrialization were parallel projects, which meant that the electricity system evolved closely with industrial capacity and gas production.[10] When a factory, gas pipeline, or coalmine was planned and built, electric power plants were simultaneously constructed, often in close proximity to enhance efficiency. The co-construction of hydroelectric dams and industrial towns in Siberia was a particularly striking example of this coordination. These dams remain physically connected to the region's most important industrial centers, a fact that is plainly obvious to regional observers: "[A]s a result of the development of hydroelectric plants during Soviet times, [we have] tight links between industry and electricity."[11] Similar ties also

---

[9] For the ideal-typical formulation of the planned economy, see János Kornai, *The Socialist System: The Political Economy of Communism* (Princeton, NJ: Princeton University Press, 1992). For an anthropologist's perspective, see Katherine Verdery, *What Was Socialism, and What Comes Next?* (Princeton, NJ: Princeton University Press, 1996). See also Gaddy on the militarized economy, in Gaddy, *The Price of the Past*.

[10] Coopersmith, *The Electrification of Russia, 1880–1926.*

[11] Interview #57 with electricity sector economist, Irkutsk, 20071122

existed in the industrial towns of European Russia, which were built together with gas pipelines, and in the towns of the Far East that clustered around coalmines. These ties were not accidental: Soviet planners saw them as the basis for efficient production and stressed their importance. The strength and integrity of these ties continued to play a political role in post-Soviet political economy.[12]

The construction of power plants and industrial capacity during the Soviet period was also closely associated with urban development, with where and how people lived. Soviet planners famously preferred company towns and so-called city-forming enterprises (*градообразующие предприятия*), which meant that huge, integrated companies were the primary employers in many Russian cities.[13] Soviet city planning was based on the premise that production and living space were integrated systems. This meant that electricity grids and heating pipes literally became the physical ties that kept people's workplaces and living quarters connected, viscerally important for Soviet as well as post-Soviet life. While the disorganization that followed the introduction of market reforms undid many of the Soviet-era industrial structures, many have remained intact. The remainder of the chapter demonstrates how inherited industrial structures and material ties shaped post-Soviet market reforms differently across Russia.

As I am drawing attention to how physical ties mattered as ideas, it is perhaps useful to sketch two opposing positions how these ties mattered, to set the stage for the rest of the chapter. Liberal views of sector reform pushed for market arrangements that would overcome existing

---

[12] Another way in which Soviet-era planning influenced post-Soviet political economy is that in the Soviet economy there typically were far fewer firms in each industry than in Western capitalist economies; see Olivier Blanchard and Michael Kremer, "Disorganization," *The Quarterly Journal of Economics* 112, no. 4 (November 1, 1997): 1093. As a result of this and of the post-Soviet property redistribution, ownership in the Russian economy was fairly concentrated. The gas and aluminum sectors have among the most highly concentrated ownership in the Russian economy, which probably contributed to Gazprom's and Rusal's role in development bargains. Sergei Guriev and Andrei Rachinsky, "The Role of Oligarchs in Russian Capitalism," *The Journal of Economic Perspectives* 19, no. 1 (2005): 131–150. Also in Sergei Guriev and Andrei Rachinsky, "Ownership Concentration in Russian Industry," *Background Paper for Country Economic Memorandum for Russia, World Bank* (2004), accessed March 16, 2014, http://www.cefir.ru/papers/WP45_OwnershipConcentration.pdf

[13] Gregory D. Andrusz, Michael Harloe, and Iván Szelényi, eds., *Cities after Socialism: Urban and Regional Change and Conflict in Post-Socialist Societies* (Cambridge, MA: Blackwell, 1996); Collier, *Post-Soviet Social*; and Collier, "Pipes."

geographies. For the liberal reformers at UES, technology and geography were constraints that could and should be overcome in the course of market reforms. Existing relationships and physical ties were considered malleable, subject to transformation in the process of market reform. Upstream and downstream ties between electricity companies, fuel providers, and industrial consumers should be recast to reflect market forces. Each kilowatt, each cubic meter of gas, and every ton of coal should go to the highest bidder. Existing energy assets should likewise be sold to the investor who values ownership most, and thus offers the high bid.[14]

An opposing political argument in post-Soviet Russia places a great deal of importance on the integrity and importance of industrial structures in shaping reform outcomes. This view draws in many ways on Marxist economic determinism that underpinned socialist economic policy for decades. In the post-Soviet political arena it is largely congruent with political positions that wanted to preserve industrial capacity in remote locations that I introduced in the last chapter. When asked about the logic of ownership changes, prices, and subsidies, a typical response in my interviews was "it's not politics, it's technology," with technology referring to the sector's different types of physical assets, whether they were gas- or coal-fired, nuclear- or hydro-powered.[15] What this implied was that *Soviet*-era decisions about the type of power generation – Stalin's gasification campaign (*Газификация*), for example – determined who would gain influence over the *post*-Soviet electricity sector. One observer argued, for example, that Siberian industrial consumers enjoyed lower prices, because "here, 50 percent of electricity is generated via hydroelectric plants" and "because the regions' industry is very energy intensive."[16] In this account, industrial geography features prominently to explain downstream industries' influence on sector reform and the privileges they secured. This suggests a strong form of geographic determinism: Soviet industrial geography hardwired post-Soviet privatization and reform outcomes. According to this logic, the division of the Russian electricity sector into three zones is natural, rather than political, because it mirrors underlying production technologies. What I argue here, however, is that

---

[14] This view was expressed in interviews with financial analysts who specialized in the sector, for example interview #7, Moscow, 20061005 and interview #9, Moscow, 20061008, both with electricity sector analysts at financial institutions.

[15] Interview #37 with electricity sector executive, Vladivostok, 20071002.

[16] Interview #52 with electricity sector economist, Irkutsk, 20071117.

just like the liberal requirement for fluid material ties, "naturalness" is a discursive position rather than a necessary, mechanistic dynamic.

Development Bargains and How "Things" Matter across Russia

Regionally patterned developmental pacts were conditioned by the inherited industrial order. The three sections that follow focus on pacts in European Russia, Siberia, and the Russian Far East, detailing in each case the ways in which bargains followed from industrial geographies. While material ties were important, they shaped outcomes in ways that neither liberals nor conglomerates fully anticipated: they mattered both as inherited structures and as rhetorical devices. Industrial geographies clearly configured conglomerates' interests and relationships within the electricity sector, hence their position on reform proposals. As a gas company, Gazprom was particularly interested in acquiring European Russia's gas-fired utilities. Rusal, a conglomerate based on the energy-intensive smelting of aluminum, targeted the acquisition of Siberian hydroelectric power plants to ensure abundant, affordable energy. Far Eastern electricity companies sought controlling interest in regional coalmines, since electrical power plants in this region were fired mainly by coal.

These relationships were important, but they did not determine reform outcomes; they shaped reforms only when and where they were validated in the post-Soviet political and economic context. This proved to be the case for Gazprom, Rusal, and the Far Eastern electricity and coal sectors. As we shall see, Gazprom's arguments about the "integrity of energy production chains," Rusal's insistence on the "unity of territorial production complexes (TPKs)," and the Far East's emphasis on the affinities between coal and electricity convincingly articulated the "naturalness" of physical facts. The argument that these relationships were ultimately contingent and not predetermined gains credibility by two types of counterfactuals – physical ties that were undone because of the success of the liberal faction, or others that were idled as nobody stood to gain from mobilizing their importance. A critical case of the first is the unbundling of the monopoly structure that underpinned UES and the Energos. Liberal reformers succeeded in "undoing" the physical ties that linked generation, transmission, and retail in the electricity sector – each subsector now has different owners. An example of an idled physical link is a high-voltage transmission line that connected Siberia to European Russia via Kazakhstan, which fell into disrepair after the collapse of the Soviet Union. Built in the 1980s, by the early 2000s the line was still defunct because nobody was interested in connecting Siberia with European Russia at the time.[17] There were many other connections between the power sector and its downstream and upstream neighbors that did *not* serve as catalysts for ownership and control. One electricity sector insider noted that municipal ownership would make sense from a perspective that recognizes the physical interconnectedness of housing units, factories, and power and heat plants, but that this was never a politically viable option.[18] There were other physical ties that did not translate into ownership rights. Gazprom was connected to many other downstream industries that did not fit its corporate strategy; the company was uninterested in assuming control of the communal housing sector (*Жилищно-коммунальное хозяйств, ЖКХ*), for example.[19]

These cases demonstrate that even though transmission lines connecting power plants to consumers implied physical and economic realities (sunk cost, for example) that could shape outcomes, they did not necessarily compel a particular outcome. In the end, material ties clearly mattered, but whether or not they did was contingent on post-Soviet power politics. The sections that follow detail how Gazprom, Rusal, and Far Eastern electricity were able to successfully stave off some aspects of liberal reforms, selectively protecting certain inherited industrial structures that fit their vision of the power sector's future.

Developmental Bargains in European Russia

European Russia refers to the western and central areas of Russia, bordered in the East by the Ural Mountains. Roughly three-quarters of Russia's population live in European Russia, even though it comprises only one-quarter of the country's territory. European Russia is a diverse region, and development strategies reflect this diversity. Moscow and Petersburg, Russia's most prosperous metropolitan areas, are located within European Russia, but so are the war-torn regions of the North Caucasus. Energy and electricity subsidies were a central feature of

---

[17] This line connects Itat in Kemerovo oblast' via Ekibastuz in Kazakhstan to Shagol in Chelyabinsk. In 2012, updating this line was mentioned as a possible investment, although no concrete steps were in sight at that point. See "Олег Дерипаска заглянул в светлое прошлое: Проект энергомоста через Казахстан могут возродить," *Коммерсантъ*, April 12, 2012.

[18] Interview #39 with electrical engineer/electricity sector expert, Vladivostok, 20071004.

[19] A further example of the indeterminacy of physical ties is the role of foreign investors; Gazprom did not end up owning all of European Russia's power plants; foreign energy conglomerates successfully acquired ownership stakes of thermal plants that were connected to Gazprom.

European Russia's development strategy. The counterparties to a key developmental bargain in European Russia were the government, Gazprom, and gas-fired power plants. A core aspect of this developmental pact revolved around Gazprom's role in providing subsidized gas to European Russian power plants and industrial consumers. Gazprom's importance to the Russian economy can hardly be overstated: the company produced a large majority of Russian gas, and gas production accounted for an important share of GDP and of Russia's export revenue.[20] During successive rounds of electricity privatization, Gazprom cherry-picked and increased its control of valuable assets in European Russia, including the generation assets of Mosenergo and Lenenergo. Tariff reforms and increasing prices for electricity ensured Gazprom steady income streams from domestic electricity generation based on subsidized fuel costs.[21] Subsequent chapters detail how ownership and subsidy regimes evolved in the electricity sector of European Russia. A monopoly on Russian gas exports – by far the most lucrative agreement between the state and Gazprom – made Gazprom the sole beneficiary of international sales of one of the world's largest natural gas reserves.[22] While this monopoly on exports was long a de facto reality, as Gazprom owned the high-pressure gas transmission lines necessary to export gas, in 2006 it was legally secured. These arrangements in the electricity and gas sectors clearly reflected Gazprom's preferences. How, then, has Gazprom served the government's development strategies?

The Gazprom-government pact was complex and subject to shifting priorities, but a key feature of Gazprom's contribution to the Russian developmental agenda has remained constant.[23] Since the very beginning

---

[20] According to Jonathan Stern, the share of non-Gazprom production has increased over the years, from 6% in 1995 to 13% in 2003. Stern, *The Future of Russian Gas and Gazprom*, 27. Gazprom's share of GDP varied over the years; a range between 5% and 10% is cited (5% for 2003) by ibid., 56; 8% for 1999 by Åslund, *How Capitalism Was Built*, 141; and 10% by the Economist, "Careful What You Wish for," *The Economist*, July 14, 2012, accessed March 16, 2014, http://www.economist.com/node/21558433

[21] To clarify this point: if Gazprom invests in fuel-saving technologies in the domestic electricity sector, this frees up gas for profitable exports.

[22] Marina Tsygankova, "An Evaluation of Alternative Scenarios for the Gazprom Monopoly of Russian Gas Exports," *Energy Economics* 34, no. 1 (January 2012): 153–161. This monopoly position seems very secure. Igor Sechin, one of the Kremlin's most powerful insiders, confirmed in 2010 that "we will not cancel Gazprom's monopoly on exports," in "Sechin says Gazprom must raise game," Katya Golubkova and Polina Devitt, *Reuters Newswire*, June 21, 2010.

[23] Gazprom is also Russia's largest taxpayer. For an analysis of the shifting relations between Gazprom and the government, see Stern, *The Future of Russian Gas and Gazprom*.

of the post-Soviet period, Gazprom supplied gas to domestic industry and consumers at heavily discounted prices, gas that it could sell for far more to Western Europe.[24] Gas exported to Western Europe typically sold for around five times the price of domestic gas.[25] It has been long understood that "the main reason for dual gas pricing has been to provide a gas subsidy to the Russian economy," and that this has been "a measure to promote growth in predominantly the manufacturing branches of industry."[26] In policy circles, this is referred to as the "dual pricing" system; it exists because "[f]ederal authorities have substantial legal power over the natural gas sector in order to improve the social and economic environment."[27] The government's energy strategy assures affordable energy for residential and industrial consumers: "Guaranteeing the provision of affordable energy resources to the population, to socially and strategically important entities is one of the most important tasks of the state's energy policy."[28] This commitment relies on Gazprom's ongoing cooperation. Gazprom annually negotiates what is called the "gas balance" with the government – the amount of gas it has to supply to domestic industry and residential consumers and at what price.[29] Importantly, Gazprom has for the whole post-Soviet period supplied electricity companies with gas far below the

[24] According to Gazprom's website, the average regulated gas price for industrial consumers in 2010 was 2,495 ruble/thousand m^3 and 1,860 rubles/thousand m^3 for gas that was to be resold to household; see http://gazpromquestions.ru/?id=35#c251

[25] According to Stern, *The Future of Russian Gas and Gazprom*. See also Roland Götz "Nach dem Gaskonflikt: Wirtschaftliche Konsequenzen für Russland, die Ukraine und die EU." *Stiftung Wissenschaft und Politik: SWP-Aktuell* no. 3 (2006): 1–4.

[26] Aldo Spanjer (2007), "Russian Gas Price Reform and the EU-Russia Gas Relationship: Incentives, Consequences and European Security of Supply." *Energy Policy Journal* 35, no. 5: 2889–2898, p. 2891.

[27] According to Spanjer, "Russian Gas Price Reform and the EU-Russia Gas Relationship." On the dual pricing systems, see also Rudiger Ahrend and William Tompson, "Unnatural Monopoly: The Endless Wait for Gas Sector Reform in Russia," *Europe-Asia Studies* 57, no. 6 (2005): 801–821; David G. Tarr and Peter D. Thomson, "The Merits of Dual Pricing of Russian Natural Gas," *World Economy* 27, no. 8 (2004): 1173–1194; and International Energy Agency, *Russia Energy Survey 2002* (Paris: OECD/IEA, 2002), http://www.iea.org/publications/freepublications/publication/russia_energy_survey.pdf

[28] "Одной из важнейших задач государственной энергетической политики является гарантированное обеспечение энергетическими ресурсами населения, социально значимых и стратетичесих объектов по доступным ценам," Energy Strategy of the Russian Federation to the year 2020/Энергетическая стратегия России на период до 2020 года, p. 45.

[29] According to Spanjer, "The domestic gas market is rationed by the government, with Gazprom in charge of the rationing. It negotiates an annual gas balance with the governmental authorities. The balance is distributed to the regions and the industrial consumers." Spanjer, "Russian Gas Price Reform and the EU-Russia Gas Relationship," p. 2892.

prices it could fetch if exported internationally, although the actual volumes and prices are renegotiated in ongoing political struggles.[30]

The concessions Gazprom secured during electricity sector liberalization can only be understood as part of this larger pact. Here too, the price and volume of gas delivered to electricity companies rested at the nexus of a bargain involving Gazprom, the government, UES, and newly privatized electricity companies.[31] Electricity companies have long been Gazprom's largest domestic customers, and the price of gas supplied to power plants has been subject to enduring battles between the company, its downstream customers, and the government. For most of the 1990s, conflicts over how much gas to supply at what price lingered. The struggle came to a head in 2000, during the period of elite turnover between the Yeltsin and Putin administrations. In an example of how energy prices were precisely what drove Russian real-life politics, the chairman of Gazprom, Rem Viakhirev, threatened to cut gas deliveries to electricity companies in April 2000 unless the companies' debt was paid in full and paid at prices that had previously been agreed to. After a few days of uncertainty, Putin resolved the UES-Gazprom standoff by supporting the electricity sector, ordering Gazprom to supply UES and the Energos with the required gas. Similarly, Gazprom's demands for higher gas prices were denied.[32] Putin sided with domestic industry and the electricity sector, continuing the policy that they should be entitled to subsidized energy. Soon after Viakhirev's rebellion, he lost his position as board chairman, and Putin made sure the company's board and managers were replaced with loyalists.[33]

Most analysts agree that under the new leadership Gazprom adhered to its side of the bargain and continued to subsidize domestic industry by supplying cheap gas, occasionally below cost.[34] Russia has been

---

[30] "Цены на газ в России всегда будут ниже, чем в Европе" [Gas prices in Russia will always be lower than in Europe], *RBK News Daily*, June 30, 2011.

[31] Although other aspects of the relationship between gas and electricity companies were also at stake; see, for example, Stern, *The Future of Russian Gas and Gazprom*; and Laura Solanko, *The Policy of National Champions and Russian Competitiveness*.

[32] Instead of the 26 billion cubic meters, Gazprom threatened to provide only 22 billion for the second quarter of 2000. *Известия*, April 12, 2001. For a similar dispute, see also *Коммерсантъ*, April 11, 2000.

[33] To ensure that Gazprom would play the role the Kremlin devised for it, one of the first moves of Putin as president was to make sure that Gazprom's board and managers were replaced with loyalists. Miller replaced Viakhirev and the board was staffed with Putin's loyalist from St. Petersburg in 2001.

[34] See for example J. Litwack and W. Thompson, *OECD Economic Survey of the Russian Federation* (Paris: OECD, 2002); Stern, *The Future of Russian Gas and Gazprom*;

pressured for years to end domestic gas subsidies, and introduced a "unified pricing system" during WTO negotiations. Despite this pressure, the price differential has persisted. A somewhat separate issue is the relationship between Gazprom and the electricity companies it now owns. Crucial for our purposes, Gazprom has supplied gas at very low rates for the power plants the company acquired. Given the low, regulated prices for domestic gas, the company wanted to profit from electricity that was generated with cheap gas.[35] This issue was made explicit during negotiations concerning the merger of KES, European Russia's second-largest owner of power plants, and Gazprom in 2011. According to Viktor Veksel'berg, one of Russia's most powerful oligarchs and majority owner of KES, lower gas prices were the main rationale for merging his energy assets with Gazprom: "The deal would save hundreds of millions of dollars a year because [we/KES] would be able to buy gas more cheaply from Gazprom."[36] Additionally, Gazprom's control of power plants allowed it to free up gas for the more lucrative export market by increasing the efficiency of these plants. These are only the very broadest parameters of Gazprom's complicated pact with the government; the gas company was involved in a vast array of corporate social responsibility programs that blur the boundary between public service and philanthropy.[37]

Spanjer, "Russian Gas Price Reform and the EU-Russia Gas Relationship"; Marina Tsygankova, "When Is a Break-up of Gazprom Good for Russia?," *Energy Economics* 32, no. 4 (July 2010): 908–917; and Tsygankova, "An Evaluation of Alternative Scenarios for the Gazprom Monopoly of Russian Gas Exports." The Gazprom website documents that these price subsidies continue to exist: "regulated prices for gas are subsidized" (*директивно регулируемые цены на газ являются заниженными*). The extent of the subsidy is not specified, although the company notes that "low regulated prices did not allow the company to cover cost ... for many years, until 2009." (*Много лет, вплоть до 2009 года, этот фактор не позволял покрыть затраты на производство, транспортировку и реализацию газа.*) http://gazpromquestions.ru/?id=35#c251. It is not specified what costs this refers to. For a Russian observer's prediction that gas subsidies for residential consumer and other budget organizations are likely to continue, because of their "social importance" – "в связи с большой социальной нагрузкой" – see Е. Л. Логинов и др., "Либерализация национального рынка газа: проблемы реформирования российской экономики," *Экономика региона*, 8/23, 2005, p. 35.

[35] What price Gazprom charges the power companies it owns for gas supplies is unclear; the comment by Veksel'berg, quoted later in the chapter, suggests that prices are even lower than the low regulated prices.

[36] Popova and Groholt-Pederson, "Gazprom Powers Up," *The Wall Street Journal*, July 8, 2011.

[37] These arrangements are only beginning to be documented in scholarship on Russia; Douglas Rogers and Laura Henry, cited in the Introduction, provide compelling accounts of these types of pacts for oil companies. The artist Guillaume Herbaut has documented

Physical Link between Gazprom and the Electricity Sector in European Russia

Gazprom's influence on economic policy is undoubtedly national rather than regional. The company's influence – pithily encapsulated by their slogan "What is good for Gazprom is good for Russia"[38] – far exceeded the electricity sector.[39] With the acquisition of important electricity assets in European Russia, Gazprom moved a step closer to becoming a global vertically integrated energy company. But why has Gazprom been particularly influential in European Russia's electricity reforms? Gazprom crucially shaped European Russia's electricity sector transformation by virtue of the physical links forged between the gas giant and European Russian power plants. Gazprom's privileges were justified by arguments that the company *should* own these power plants, that an integrated energy production chain was the most efficient way of organizing production and most conducive to economic development.

Domestic pipelines date back to the gasification campaigns initiated under Stalin in the mid-1940s.[40] Like electrification, gasification was an ambitious project, aiming to connect Russian regions via an expanding gas pipeline system. While gasification brought gas to many corners of Russia, the pipeline system remained concentrated in European Russia – only European Russian factories were connected via an extensive network of gas pipelines (see Figure 3.1). By 2008, the vast majority of Russian domestic gas sales supplied European Russian industry; roughly 90 percent of Gazprom's domestic gas was sold west of the Urals.[41] Gazprom's largest customers were power plants: 30–40 percent of Gazprom's domestic supplies went to power companies. For European Russia's electricity companies, in turn, Gazprom was the single largest supplier: more than 80 percent of European Russia's electricity is produced in gas-fired plants, and Gazprom produces almost 90 percent of Russian gas.[42] While major

the role of Gazprom in the Siberian city of Novy Urengoy; see http://www.instituteart-ist.com/feature-Gazprom-s-Capital-City-Novy-Ourengoy-Guillaume-Herbaut

[38] See, for example, Götz, "Nach Dem Gaskonflikt."
[39] See Goldman, *Petrostate*.
[40] The first natural gas pipeline between Moscow and Saratov was constructed in 1946. See Stern, *The Future of Russian Gas and Gazprom*.
[41] Gazprom website, http://www.gazprom.com/marketing/russia/. The information on the domestic gas sales by sector and region in the remainder of this paragraph and the map that follows were also obtained on the Gazprom website.
[42] *Тепловые генерирующе компании РАО ЕЭС РОССИИ*, РАО ЕЭС, Москва, 2006. On Gazprom's overall role in Russia, see Simmons and Murray, "Russian Gas: Will There Be Enough Investment?"

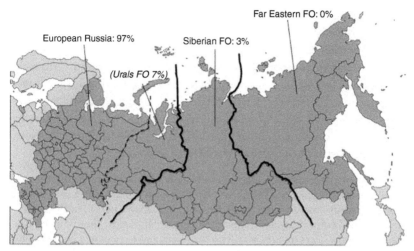

Far Eastern FO: 0%

European Russia: 97%   Siberian FO: 3%

(Urals FO 7%)

FIGURE 3.1. Regional distribution of Gazprom's Russian domestic gas sales, 2008.

Source: Gazprom. Note that FO stands for the newly formed federal districts, *federal'nye okruga*. The 97% of gas sales for European Russia are divided into Southern FO (14%), Central (34%), Volga (32%), Northwest (11%), and Urals (7%).

Siberian and Far Eastern cities were gasified, large industrial consumers outside of the European Russia/Urals region largely relied on other forms of energy. Unlike electrification, which reached almost all corners of the Soviet Union by the 1970s, many Russian regions still await gasification.[43] Siberian and Far Eastern power plants lacked ties to Gazprom, because power plants there are largely hydro-powered or coal fired. Even though the vast majority of gas originates in Western Siberia, and plans existed to expand domestic gas pipelines, most of Siberia was not reliant on gas in 2008. Siberia accounted for only 3 percent of Gazprom's domestic sales; no gas was supplied to the Far East.

How and why were these physical links between the two sectors translated into special privileges for Gazprom during electricity sector reforms? The physical ties between the gas and electricity sectors made European

---

[43] The Sakhalin peninsula in the Russian Far East, for example, is the site of one of Gazprom's largest gas fields, but much of the island was still awaiting gasification at the time I was conducting research for this project. The fields are located in the north of the peninsula and off shore in the Sea of Japan, but Sakhalin's main urban center, Yuzhno-Sakhalinsk, was never connected to the gas grid. The pipeline was supposed to be built in 2003, but nothing happened – a fact that became the subject of a political scandal. Interview #38 with academic, Vladivostok, 20071003.

Russian electricity assets particularly attractive targets for takeover and integration into the Gazprom empire; they shaped Gazprom's interest vis-à-vis the electricity sector. The company inherited supply-chain relationships between the gas industry and gas-fired power plants in European Russia that had existed for decades. These ties and relationships persisted during post-Soviet reforms, partly because Gazprom successfully mobilized arguments why it *should* own electricity assets. An observer, clearly partial to the company, framed this idea under the heading, "A New National Project – The Creation of a Mega-Company":

> If Russia is to participate and compete in the global free market, she has to construct major global players. Under Putin the formation of a pool of such major players has begun – these are the future Russian participants in the big global race [to compete]. Gazprom has been a pioneer. Against the odds, the company has managed over the years to remain in Russian hands and to remain a unified company. Time has shown that we were right to preserve the unity and the greatness of the company, to not let it fall prey to charges of ineffectiveness, which the likes of Chubais used to intimidate and to threaten to split up Gazprom.[44]

This is a telling acclamation of Gazprom's steadfastness in maintaining its own unity because it explicitly states that the company's success was a political feat, one that was not to be taken for granted, given the power and arguments of Chubais and his liberal allies.

The company also relied on the argument that its control of the entire production chain – from the production of extraction equipment, oil and gas extraction, and transport and distribution pipelines to electricity production and energy retail – was a necessary attribute of a successful global energy company.[45] The rationale of "unity" that underpins Gazprom's

---

[44] "Если Россия собирается участвовать в свободной глобальной конкуренции, она должна создать крупных глобальных игроков. При Путине началось формирование такого пула крупнейших игроков – будущих российских участников большого глобального экономического забега. Пионером выступил 'Газпром'. В свое время с огромным трудом удалось отстоять российскую принадлежность 'Газпрома' и сохранить его как единую компанию. Время показало, насколько мы были правы тогда: сохранившая единство и величину компания не пала под напором неэффективности, как стращали тогда такие, как Чубайс, который умолял раздробить 'Газпром' (а набрала огромный вес, став третьей в мире компанией по капитализации)." Sergey Markov, "Новый национальный проект – создание мегакомпаний." *Независимая газета*, September 14, 2006.

[45] "Зачем Газпром участвует в энергетическом бизнесе? Для завоевания глобального лидерства на энергетических рынках Газпрому необходимо развиваться как компании, ведущей свою деятельность по всей производственной цепочке – от добычи до сбыта – как первичных энергоносителей, так и конечных продуктов, одним из которых является электроэнергия." http://gazpromquestions.ru/?id=27#c202

strategy to become an energy empire is evident in its business plan.[46] Gazprom's business plan stated that the company wants to "achieve synergies by combining natural gas and electric power businesses. The major focus is ... improving the efficiency of natural gas fired power generation, which will provide for the effective use of natural gas in the context of growing energy demand of the Russian economy."[47] An integrated production chain is portrayed here as key for economic development.

The importance of economic geography in explaining Gazprom's influence on the electricity sector is confirmed by a closer look at those European Russian regions without a close link to Gazprom. Tatarstan, Bashkortostan, and Sverdlovsk are three regions where regional leaders in the 1990s were exceptionally independent. In Tatarstan and Bashkortostan, ownership of energy assets – primarily in the oil, but also in the electricity sector – went to the families of regional leaders. As Gazprom did not own gas pipelines, it did not supply fuel and lacked a physical connection to these regions' electricity sector. In Sverdlovsk, gas is supplied by Itera (*Итера*), Russia's largest independent gas company.[48] As we will see in Chapters 4 and 5, Gazprom has not had a similar influence on the electricity sector in these regions; most notably Tatenergo (*Татэнерго*) and Bashkirenergo (*Башкирэнерго*) remained independent electricity companies and were not part of the UES umbrella. Note again, however, that my argument about the importance of the physical link between the two sectors is not one of geographic determinism; Gazprom's control of European Russia's vast power assets (as well as regional ownership of Tatenergo and Bashenergo) was neither natural nor necessary, despite company rhetoric. It was a politically negotiated outcome, in which Gazprom was allowed to cherry-pick assets in return for its contribution to a broader developmental agenda.

---

[46] This strategy goes beyond the electricity sector and includes a proposed merger with SUEK, a major coal company, and the construction of LNG facilities, for example. Interviews #26 and #27 with energy sector experts, Berkeley, 20070613; interview #17 with electricity sector expert at financial institution, Moscow, 20061101. Note that both the state's energy strategy and Gazprom's corporate strategy relied on consolidating ownership of the energy production chain.

[47] Gazprom business strategy and electricity sector strategy, available on Gazprom website, http://old.gazprom.ru/eng/articles/article8523.shtml. Alexey Miller, Chief Executive of Gazprom, has also frequently stated that Gazprom wants to be a "global vertically integrated energy company"; see, for example, his statement at the XXIII World Gas Conference, Amsterdam, June 6, 2006.

[48] See Stern (2005), *The Future of Russian Gas and Gazprom*, p. 181. See also Логинов и др., "Либерализация национального рынка газа," p. 35.

Developmental Bargains in Siberia

Since the late tsarist period, successive Russian governments pushed the development of heavy industry in Siberia. Siberia's economy was transformed in the postwar period with the construction of gigantic hydroelectric dams built to harness the formidable flow of the Angara and Yenisei rivers to power the region's largest industrial plants.[49] Siberian power plants were hailed as construction sites of Soviet socialism and symbols of man's victory over nature.[50] Post-Soviet developmental strategies were shaped by these inherited material facts. A historical quirk made Siberian hydroelectric power plants particularly valuable; having been built under the Soviet planned economy, where capital was allocated rather than borrowed, post-Soviet enterprises did not inherit any debt service obligations with the hydropower plants.[51] This is particularly important for hydropower plants, where initial construction costs are enormous. Absent the debt-servicing costs typical of large-scale hydroelectric projects, the power produced by Irkutskenergo and Krasnoiarskenergo is among the world's cheapest.[52]

Rusal, a powerful metals conglomerate, was successful in negotiating privileged access to Siberia's cheap hydroelectric resources, gaining both ownership and access to subsidies, as we will see in Part II. What did the aluminum conglomerate provide in return for these concessions? Concessions to Rusal were part of a regional development strategy that supported large employers and providers of social services in Siberian industrial towns. During the economic collapse of the 1990s, the threat of deindustrialization loomed large throughout Russia, but it was particularly acute in company towns in remote territories of Siberia and the Russian Far East. Liberal reformers argued that remoteness and the "cost of the cold" – the disproportionate costs associated with maintaining

[49] These were often technologically highly ambitious projects (note that Cold War–era competition for size of turbines was also an element of this construction boom); technological feats were stressed, for example, in interview #55 with employee of electricity company, Irkutsk, 20071120.

[50] In the 1950s and 1960s, joining the work crews that built Siberian dams was the thing to do for enthusiastic young patriots; see В. В. Алексеев, *Электрификация Сибири*, Наука, Siberian Branch of the Russian Academy of Sciences/ Сибирское отделение Российской академии наук, Новосибирск, 1973.

[51] Interview #16 with electricity sector expert/consultant, Moscow/phone, 20061030, and interview #21 with electricity sector economist, Moscow, 20061214. The sheer value of Irkutskenergo's assets in a market economy was also stressed in other interviews, for example, interview #54 with businessman, Irkutsk, 20071120, and interview #60 with energy company executive, Irkutsk, 20071203.

[52] See Chapter 4 for details on electricity tariffs.

population centers in extreme northern climes – made them ultimately unviable in the context of market economies. Liberals urged evacuation rather than continued subsidization.[53] Not surprisingly, Siberian regional leaders and industrialists vehemently opposed this liberal logic that threatened to depopulate the northern regions.

Successive bargains between industrialists and the regional and federal authorities centered on employment in the northern regions. But being an employer in a Russian company town (*градообразующее предприятие*) meant more than just providing a job and paying taxes. Yuko Adachi, for example, traced the role of Oleg Deripaska's first aluminum smelter, SaAZ (later integrated into the Rusal empire), in the town of Saianogorsk during the late 1990s. In addition to providing jobs, most of the region's revenues (60 percent of Khakassiia's income), and virtually all of the city's revenues (95 percent), SaAZ built roads, schools, and new housing. The company eventually even took control of the former state farm, to assure Saianogorsk's food supply. In an interview, one employee summarized this role as follows: "The company has to be part of ... society and a part of the region, to be accepted [and] in order to work successfully. The company has to make [a] contribution to ... society."[54]

In the 1990s, when regional authorities were de facto charged with charting regional economies' post-Soviet path, regional governors were looking to emerging oligarchs for tax revenues, employment opportunities for local residents, and help with infrastructural updates of all kinds. Under Putin, the federal government turned to Siberian oligarchs to update existing hydroelectric power plants and for the construction of new hydroelectric dams. The latter was a key part of the Siberian development bargain. During the last decades of the Soviet Union, a whole series of hydroelectric dam projects were planned or initiated. These capital-intensive projects were abandoned in the turmoil of the late 1980s and early 1990s. No financing was available for these unfinished dams (*недострои*) during the 1990s. "The government is in no state to finish these projects, there is no money," lamented an electricity sector insider at the

---

[53] Gaddy and Hill elaborate this concept based on a discussion by Russian geographers. See Hill and Gaddy, *The Siberian Curse*. For a discussion of politics of the north, see Anna Stammler-Grossmann, "Reshaping the North of Russia: Towards a Conception of Space," in *Northern Research Forum*, 2007, 24–27, accessed March 16, 2014, http://nrf. is/Open%20Meetings/Anchorage/Position%20Papers/StammlerGrossman_5thNRF_position_paper_session4.pdf

[54] Adachi, *Building Big Business in Russia*, 73. Note the translation by Adachi adds the definitive article to "society" ("part of *the* society" ... "contribute to *the* society"), though the paragraph referes to society writ large, not to a particular society.

time.[55] After 2000, a number of these projects were revived, including the enormous Boguchansk hydroelectric dam (*ГЭС, гидроэлектростанция*), located in Krasnoiarsk oblast on the Angara River. A representative of the government's hydroelectricity company enthusiastically referred to this resumption of large-scale dam projects as the "second wave of investment in hydro-capacity," comparing it to the glorious heyday of dam building in the late 1960s and 1970s.[56] Since the completion of these dams was under discussion again, co-financing by the enterprises in the thriving metals sector was part of the government's plan.

The Boguchansk dam was the largest of these projects. It had been initiated in 1980 but was then abandoned during the 1990s. While the Soviet Union had invested large sums in the construction of this dam, the Russian state needed a projected $1.7 billion of private financing to complete construction.[57] While Rusal agreed to provide part of this sum, the conditions of financing were highly contested for years. Rusal agreed to participate if UES and the federal government guaranteed a significant ownership stake and long-term agreements to sell electricity at reduced prices. Rusal and the Russian government eventually agreed to share ownership, each with a 50 percent stake.[58] They also agreed that the price of electricity for Rusal was to be tied to the London Metal Exchange price for aluminum, although negotiations about how much capital Rusal had to provide in return for these concessions continued for years.[59] The aluminum company contributed significantly to the construction

---

[55] "Государство не в состоянии ее достроить, денег нет." The remark was made by Victor Borovskii about the Boguchansk project, in an interview in *Эксперт*, no. 14, April 13, 1998, p. 35.

[56] A remark by a Hydro-OGK representative at a conference "Second annual conference on the functioning of electricity companies in a market context/Вторая ежегодная конференция – Работа электроэнергетических компаний в рыночных условиях," Moscow, December 13, 2006. These projects came up often in the interviews in Siberia, for example, in interview #55 with employee of electricity company, Irkutsk, 20071120, who described these projects as "lining Siberia's rivers like pearls on a necklace."

[57] See "РАО ЕЭС ищет партнера, который мог бы достроить Богучанскую ГЭС," *Ведомости*, March 24, 2003. See also "Станционные правители: РАО ЕЭС и 'Русал' поделили Богучанскую ГЭС," *Коммерсантъ*, July 11, 2005. See also Adachi, *Building Big Business in Russia*, 85.

[58] Only the contours of the negotiations between UES and Rusal, and the political battles that accompanied them, were public knowledge. As each side was trying to align support in the Kremlin on their side, some of the terms of their negotiations surfaced in the media over the years; see "Станционные правители: РАО ЕЭС и 'Русал' поделили Богучанскую ГЭС," *Коммерсантъ*, July 11, 2005.

[59] "Конец большой дружбы," *Ведомости*, June 1, 2000. The *aluminshchiki*'s attempts to link the price of electricity with the world market prices for aluminum are also mentioned in interview #60 with energy company executive, Irkutsk, 20071203. For an account of the

cost of Boguchansk and technological updates of other major dams. Siberian development relied on large infrastructure projects, on increasing hydro-capacity, and on maintaining and creating industrial plants. They industrial facilities controlled by Rusal were an important part of this strategy: not only did it own many of the existing industrial facilities adjacent to existing damns; it constructed a new aluminum smelter linked to the new Boguchansk dam (BEMO). President Putin interpreted the Rusal-government bargain as the outcome of a successful public-private pact: "The construction of the [Boguchansk hydro-electric] station can be seen as an example of successful realization of a mechanism of a state-private partnership."[60] The project's completion was widely interpreted as a beneficial to Rusal and for the economic development of the region. "It is obvious that Rusal is a winner. ... Siberia as a whole, and Krasnoiarsk Krai in particular are also winners. The realization of the project [of completing the dam with the adjacent BEMO] creates 10,000 new jobs and tangibly promotes the development of the lower Priangara region."[61]

One could interpret the evidence of Rusal's role in Siberia as state capture; the company did indeed receive support in many forms and now controls lucrative smelters and power plants all over Siberia. Yet, capture arguments obscure the developmental aspect of the bargain and fail to explain why it centered on this particular hydroelectric project. Similar to the case of Gazprom in European Russia, the government's arrangement with Rusal was based on shared interests and mutual interdependence characteristic of post-Soviet developmentalism.

Siberian Aluminum and Electricity Tied Together in the "Territorial Industrial Complexes"

Rusal's prominent role as an employer in the region helps explain the outcome of electricity sector reform in Siberia.[62] Yet, nothing guaranteed

ongoing negotiations between Rusal and the government, see Yuriy Humber, "RusHydro Sees Rusal Power Financing Accord by Summer." *Bloomberg*, April 21, 2009. Not only financing of the dam itself was at stake, Rusal also initiated the construction of a new aluminum plant adjacent to Boguchansk. Over a disagreement, Rusal threatened to delay construction, after which Vneshekonbank, controlled by the government, agreed to extend credit. For this support Rusal received permission to construct the new aluminum smelter at Boguchansk; see "Последний долгострой" *Эксперт Сибирь*, No. 42/350.

[60] "Последний долгострой," *Эксперт Сибирь*, No. 42/350, October 22, 2012.

[61] Ibid.

[62] See for, example, А. С. Щербаков и И. Тертышник, *Мировая экономика и внешнеэкономическая деятельность Иркутского Предбайкалья*. Иркутск: Иркутский государственный университет, 2000.

that Rusal would receive special privileges; few industries were able to negotiate special electricity rates, and industrial facilities crumbled in many towns unable to forestall deindustrialization and outmigration. The aluminum industry was able to secure ownership and special subsidy regimes because it made the case that these concessions were vital to the region's well-being. Rusal was linked to Siberia's most valuable electricity assets through a close physical connection that originated in Soviet industrial planning. This connection was routinely mentioned and mobilized in arguments about the future of the electricity sector: "We are closely connected with our industrial consumers, we depend on them. Therefore we need to care for them and together adjust our price policies,"[63] argued one prominent electricity sector executive. References to the necessity of the link between aluminum and hydro-power served to legitimize its privileged position.

More specifically, particular Siberian industrial interests were able to capitalize on their material connectedness with the electricity sector because they were part – and, they argued, complementary elements – of so-called Territorial Industrial Complexes (*TPK, территориально-производственный комплекс*). *TPK*s were the Soviet version of industrial clusters or company towns, consisting of closely connected industries that utilized local resources. Importantly, the Soviet-era rationale of a *TPK* was that its unity – the synergies that are created through the proximity of upstream and downstream industries – was its strength. *TPK*s were Soviet planners' solution to the problem of underdeveloped remote areas. The city of Bratsk, in Irkutsk oblast', is a typical Siberian *TPK*. Created on a river bend of the Angara River in Eastern Siberia, Bratsk was a tiny rural settlement until a prison camp was located there in 1947 and tens of thousands of prisoners arrived to serve as the first labor force of Siberia's industrialization.[64] The crowning height of Bratsk's Soviet-era history is the construction of the hydroelectric dam that powered the industrial enterprises located in the town.[65] Bratsk became one of the

---

[63] This is a quote by S. Kuimov. "Мы жестко интегрированы с нашими промышленными потребителями, зависимы от них. И поэтому мы вынуждены вслед за ними корректировать свою тарифную политику." *Эксперт*, No. 14, April 1998, p. 35.

[64] Prison labor was used for the construction of the railway link from Bratsk to Ust-Kut (http://www.gulag.memorial.de). Many of the labor camp inmates were political prisoners and victims of Stalin's purges. Prison camps existed at least until 1960. Construction on the Bratsk hydroelectric dam started in 1954 and ended in 1967.

[65] Dams served as monuments of the Soviet path to modernity; Yevtushenko's poem "Bratsk Station" illustrates this well; Yevgenii Yevtushenko, *The Bratsk Station and Other Poems* (London: Hart-Davis, 1967).

Soviet Union's most famous company towns and a prime example of the close ties between electricity generation, industrial production, and urban development.

Soviet planning invested great symbolic value in the unity of the *TPKs*. It thereby fixed the connectedness of power plants and adjacent factories as a natural fact in the minds of regional residents; they were memories, in other words. In the post-Soviet period then, regional elites and regional politicians continued to argue that the unity and integrity of the *TPKs* should not be destroyed. They mobilized the Soviet-era rationale.[66] In political battles over the ownership of Siberian hydroelectric plants, post-Soviet actors relied on the inherited physical and discursive reality to justify regional control. Proponents of granting ownership and subsidies to regional industrial powers frequently made reference to the *TPK*, to the fact that industry and power production were part of one and the same economic cluster, and that elements of the *TPK* relied on each other.[67] It was argued that tearing out power plants from the "industry+hydro-power plant+dam" agglomeration would be harmful for the region's economy, because industry depended on their connectedness.[68] One academic summarized these claims: "The unification [of electricity and adjacent industrial plants] is necessary for the stabilization and healthy growth of the region's economy. The unification of the TPK should take place not only on the level of production, but on the level of financial and organizational structures."[69] Such arguments justified Rusal's control of electricity assets. Rusal secured ownership partly because the discourse in favor of maintaining the integrity of the *TPK*

<hr />

[66] See, for example, reference to "единый территориально-технологический комплекс" in an article about the fight between Chubais and Lebed about Krasnoiarsk's hydroelectric power plant and the adjacent aluminum factories in "Политическая энергетика," *Известия*, September 2, 1999. Interview #60 with energy company executive, Irkutsk, 20071203.

[67] *Основные проблемы и направления обеспечения энергетической безопасности*. Иркутск: Сибирское отделение Российской академии наук, 2001, p. 19. *TPKs* also feature prominently in Krasnoiarsk's development strategies, for example.

[68] A comment on the presidential directive that tried to transfer ownership of power plants away from regional owners to federally owned UES is telling. "Передача трех гидростанций в состав РАО ... разрушает сложившийся единый производственно технологический и хозяйственный комплекс." ["The transfer of three hydro-electric power plants to UES would destroy the existing unity of the productive-technological and the economic complex."] In "Указ против Нас," *Восточно-Сибирская правда*, October 20, 1992. See also *Основные проблемы и направления обеспечения энергетической безопасности*. Иркутск: Сибирское отделение Российской академии наук, 2001, p. 19.

[69] *Материалы к энергетической стратегии Сибири*. Новосибирск: Сибирское отделение Российской академии наук, 1997, p. 89.

had broad resonance among those concerned with preserving Siberia's industrial capacity. (With the construction of the Boguchansk power plant and a new aluminum smelter, a post-Soviet version of a *TPK* was even constructed.) Maintaining and strengthening *TPKs* became a cornerstone of the Siberian development strategy – they were the "champions" of Siberian industry.

Rusal also benefited from a discourse that aimed to keep Siberia's resources under regional control. In the case of electricity, the argument was that the power generated by Siberian rivers should be used locally. In regional academic and public discourse, a series of arguments were put forth to justify the aluminum company's claims to ownership and control. The most basic claim was that regional well-being required regional control of electricity assets: "[T]o preserve regional interests, we need regional control [of the Energo]."[70] Regional control of hydroelectric dams became part of a larger movement to keep Siberian resources for local use and to uphold the rights of residents to proceeds from local energy resources.[71] These rights were backed by the argument that Siberians have a right to self-determination, because "Siberia is not a colony."[72] Moreover, Siberia was not responsible for regions lacking local energy resources with high electricity costs. The exclusive right of local residents was often justified with reference to past suffering that resulted from dam building, such as population resettlement and environmental pollution. Regional media coverage of Moscow's claims to Irkutsk's electricity emphasized that the negative consequences of industrialization and dam building conferred

[70] This is a quote by Sergey Kuimov, a senior Irkutskenergo executive, in "Высокие энерготарифы – крах для Приангарья," *Восточно-Сибирская правда*, February 23, 1999.
[71] "Энергия территории и сила ведомства," *Восточно-Сибирская правда*, October 28, 1992 makes the argument that local resources belong to Siberians. In "Политическая энергетика," *Восточно-Сибирская правда*, February 25, 1992, the journalist argues that Siberians have a right to the proceeds of Siberian resources. This is an ongoing theme, in "Чьи богатства прирастают Сибирью?" *Восточно-Сибирская правда*, January 6, 1996. This was also the broad agenda of the "Siberian Agreement" (see Hughes, "Regionalism in Russia: The Rise and Fall of the Siberian Agreement"). This claim was mobilized not only with regard to hydroelectric resources. UES tried to gain control of Irkutsk's coal reserves, for example, and the oblast' opposed it; see "Проглотит ли РАО ЕЭС сибирские экспортные угли?" *Восточно-Сибирская правда*, February 25, 1999. Note that this implies that the sense of shared community does not extend to regions beyond Siberia.
[72] See, for example, "Сибирь – не колония," *Восточно-Сибирская правда*, September 22, 1992.

rights to Siberians: to the proceeds of the hydroelectric power plants, to own assets, and to keep prices low.[73]

As in the case of Gazprom, there was nothing natural or necessary about the special privileges afforded to Rusal. The ownership and subsidy privileges were the result of a negotiated pact between a powerful industrial interest and the government. The liberal reformers in the Putin government wanted to create a uniform regulatory zone and to abolish all special privileges for companies and the population in the north.[74] Siberian industrialists won important victories, partly because they were able to mobilize politically resonant memories about the need to maintain the integrity of the *TPKs*.

Russian Far East: Developmental Bargains in a Weakly Industrialized Frontier Region

Much of the Russian Far East's industry had been devoted to the Soviet Union's defense sector, which contracted dramatically after the collapse of the Soviet Union, leaving the region weakly industrialized and isolated from both Europe and Asia. As the homeport of the Soviet Union's Pacific fleet, Vladivostok had been a closed city, sealed off from neighboring countries as well as other Russian regions.[75] In 1991, Vladivostok, only a few hundred miles away from South Korea and Japan, could not have been more distant from these booming sites of postwar capitalism.

---

[73] Several articles in Irkustk's regional newspaper, *Восточно-Сибирская правда*, make these arguments. One article asks the rhetorical question: "Is it fair that electricity in Irkutsk Oblast' costs 60 rubles, and in Primorskii Krai, for example, it costs 400?" The answer the article gives is, yes, it is fair, because *Irkutiantsi* (oblast' residents) have been suffering the ecological cost of the dams: the resettlements and the catastrophic ecological consequences, the inundation of agricultural and forestry land, the loss of villages, and the decline of fishery reserves. The article notes that local residents were never compensated for these losses and these cost, and that the state has a debt vis-à-vis local residents because of this past suffering, "Чьи богатства прирастают Сибирью?" *Восточно-Сибирская правда*, January 6, 1996. Interview #60 with energy company executive, Irkutsk, 20071203. See also "Не дележ, а грабеж," *Восточно-Сибирская правда*, February 2, 1993, another article in which the region's strong opposition to the presidential decree is based on the region's suffering.

[74] The Gref program 2000 aimed to abolish all special privileges for the north; see Chapter 2 and Rasell, "Neoliberalism in the North: The Transformation of Social Policy in Russia's Northern Periphery."

[75] In Primorskii Krai, for example, this meant that regional economic activity was reduced to fisheries and cross-border smuggling of used Japanese cars. A few exceptions were retooled defense companies; interview #41 with journalist covering electricity sector, Vladivostok, 20071005. For a rich account of the post-Soviet collapse in one Far Easter region, Chukotka, see Thompson, *Settlers on the Edge*.

For years following the end of the Soviet Union, the prognosis for Far Eastern electricity companies, such as Primorskii Krai's Dal'energo (*Дальэнерго*), remained bleak. For much of the 1990s, these companies were caught between nonpaying customers and their reliance on local coal miners. The military-industrial sector and the so-called budget-organizations (schools, hospitals and other public organizations financed from government budgets) were either exempt from electricity bills or simply did not pay.[76] A large portion of household consumers, such as veterans and pensioners, were entitled to reduced rates.[77] Even more than other Energos, Dal'energo was saddled with unpaid bills, constant short-age of cash, and mounting debt. This meant that Dal'energo could not pay repair workers and coal miners, whose situation led them to strike on many occasions during the 1990s.[78] This breakdown led to blackouts in many regions – referred to as the Far Eastern energy crisis – the most severe of which were in Primorskii Krai, where for years electricity was often only available for a few hours a day.[79]

Reform outcomes in the Far East followed a very different path from those in European Russia or Siberia. Energy and development strategies for the region were a reaction to the Far Eastern energy crisis and to the contraction of military-related industries. While most responses to the energy crisis in the 1990s were ad hoc palliative measures – sending funds to allow Far Eastern governors to cover budget shortfalls – both regional and federal governments wanted to formulate a more sustain-able solution to help and reform inefficient, cash-starved, coal-fired power plants. Unlike in Siberia and European Russia, the government retained control of generation assets: only minority stakes in the newly formed electricity companies were sold to private investors, and prices remained fully regulated. Far Eastern electricity companies were com-pensated for low prices through direct budget transfers. These measures

---

[76] Interview #41 with journalist covering electricity sector, Vladivostok, 20071005. See also Michael Bradshaw and Peter Kirkow, "The Energy Crisis in the Russian Far East: Origins and Possible Solutions," *Europe Asia Studies* 50, no. 6 (1998): 1043–1063.

[77] As many as 70% of households in the Far East were entitled beneficiaries of various types of in-kind benefits (*льготы*); see sources in note 76. See also Wengle and Rasell, "The Monetisation of L'goty."

[78] Wengle and Rasell, "The Monetisation of L'goty"; Bradshaw and Kirkow, "The Energy Crisis in the Russian Far East"; and Woodruff, *Money Unmade*.

[79] There are repeated references to blackouts in regional newspapers of Primorskii Krai, for example, "Посмотрел бы на нас Цюрупа," *Утро России*, February 12, 1994; "Что же происходит?" *Утро России*, April 8, 1997; "Кто отключает свет?" *Утро России*, April 16, 1997; and "Почему сидим во тьме?" *Утро России*, April 19, 1997.

protected Far Eastern electricity companies from low-cost Siberian electricity.

Under Putin, the reform trajectory of the Far Eastern electricity sector became part of the federal government's strategy for integrating the region into the markets of East Asia.[80] Integration with Northeast Asia, China, Japan, and Korea, in particular, became the cornerstone of the government's regional development strategy.[81] The most important aspect of the Far East's integration was cross-border cooperation on energy-related issues.[82] The Russian Far East combined low demand for energy with abundant untapped hydrocarbon resources. Adjacent countries had high demand for energy but fewer of their own energy resources.[83] At the same time, Russian integration strategies aimed at moving away from exporting raw materials and toward value-adding production. Rather than exporting gas and coal, therefore, the government's regional development strategy also wanted to process energy resources domestically. This had important implications for the government's strategy in the electricity sector. One regional electricity sector professional stressed, "exporting electricity is worth it. It is much more profitable than selling coal or gas. Electricity is a processed good, and thus more expensive than the underlying raw materials."[84] The development strategy of one of the larger Far

---

[80] The federal government's development strategy was mentioned by several interviewees in the Far East, including interview #32 with electricity sector economist, Vladivostok, 20070918.

[81] This is the premise of the texts on energy integration, including P. A. Minakir, *Economic Cooperation between The Russian Far East and Asia-Pacific Countries* (Khabarovsk: RIOTIP, 2007); see also work by Kalashnikov and Gulidov cited in the next note. This was also often mentioned in interviews, for example, interview #38 with academic, Vladivostok, 20071003.

[82] В. Д. Калашников и Р. В. Гулидов, "Основные предпосылки в анализе развития ТЭК Дальнего Востока," *Стратегия развития Дальнего Востока: возможности и перспективы, Том I.* Хабаровск, 2003, p. 99; В. Д. Калашников, "Инфраструктура международного экономического сотрудничества в СВА," *Перспективы развития российских регионов: Дальний Восток и Забайкалье.* Хабаровск, 2001, p. 49. Also interviews #43 and #44 with electricity sector economists, Khabarovsk, 20071010. See also Анна Лобунец "Перспективы развития энергетики Приморского края с учетом интеграционных процессов в Северо-Восточной Азии," Автореферат диссертации, Владивосток, May 17, 2004, p. 19.

[83] Minakir, *Economic Cooperation between the Russian Far East and Asia-Pacific Countries*, 7.

[84] "Электроэнергию стоит экспортировать. Это гораздо выгоднее, чем продавать за границу уголь или нефть. Энергия, это конечный продукт, который дороже, чем исходное сырье." Remark by Victor Minakov, director of Vostokenergo, as Dal'energo was called for some time, in an interview in *Дальневосточный капитал*, October 2003, No. 10/38, p. 49. The dissertation of Anna Lobunetz concludes practically with the same recommendation: "Мы считаем развитие экспорта электроэнергии и создание межгосударственных

Eastern oblast's, Primorskii Krai, thus called for investment in a series of infrastructural upgrades in the region's power plants.[85] Rather than creating one nationwide market, the government continued to protect the Far Eastern electricity sector. Because of the deleterious effects of competition with Siberian plants, price liberalization was not in the interest of Far Eastern energy companies.[86]

Electricity sector bargains in the Far East were less contested than elsewhere, as the overarching goal of preserving and expanding Far Eastern electricity production was shared between the main actors. At the same time, the terms of the bargain were continuously debated: the incremental increase in regulated prices, the size of direct subsidies, who should have control over operations and investment projects, and so on. These issues were negotiated as part of the region's international energy cooperation projects and, more broadly, its integration into Northeast Asia.

Tying Together the Future of Far Eastern Electricity and Coal

As was the case elsewhere in Russia, electricity sector reform in the Far East was negotiated and outcomes were not preordained. Liberal reformers initially wanted to include the power plants of this region in a national market: "subsidies were supposed to be phased out and markets phased in."[87] However, by 2008, the electricity companies of the Far East remained under state control and continued to receive substantial subsidies. As in Siberia and European Russia, Far Eastern electricity companies benefited from a discourse that linked their fate to that of a neighboring sector – coal, in this case.

Far Eastern power plants largely relied on regionally mined coal to fuel them. During the economic crisis of the early 1990s, energy demand fell and Far Eastern coal production shrank drastically.[88] Far Eastern coal

---

электроэнергетических связей ... более перспективным и выгодным вариантом как для Дальнего Востока в целом, так и для Приморского края в частности." Анна Лобунец, "Перспективы развития энергетики Приморского края," p. 20.

[85] Development program for Primorskii Krai, "Стратегия социально-экономического развития Приморского края на 2004–2010 гг."

[86] The connection with Siberia was a real possibility and would have been technically feasible for the largest regions in the Far East, which are connected to the national grid, including Primorskii Krai, Khabarovsk, and Amurskii Krai. A number of Far Eastern regions are not connected to the grid, including Chukotka, Kamchatka, and Sakhalin; price liberalization was not likely to be an option in these isolated systems.

[87] Interview #39 with electrical engineer/electricity sector expert, Vladivostok, 20071004.

[88] The 1995 level of coal production in all of the Russian Far East was 68% of the 1990 level (although coal production had already been declining between 1985 and 1990). Minakir, *Economic Cooperation between The Russian Far East and Asia-Pacific Countries.*

mining, in particular that of Primorskii Krai, was relatively inefficient. Low-caloric coal, located deep underground and accompanied by methane gas, meant that the region's coal mining was expensive and unprofitable relative to that of other regions. Liberals called for the closure of these mines, and between 1990 and 1995 many were indeed closed, while others were privatized and restructured, with drastic effects on the regional workforce.[89] However, miners were a politically active group in Primorskii Krai and fought hard to prevent mine closures. "Coal miners were prepared to fight."[90] Miners' strikes in the Far East started in 1993,[91] escalating into the "coal war" that would dominate regional politics throughout the 1990s.[92] Key points of contention included the price of coal supplied to regional electricity providers and what fraction of federal subsidies designed to alleviate the Far Eastern energy crisis should target the coal sector. Ultimately, federal subsidies kept both electricity and coal companies afloat during the 1990s.

Outcomes of ownership battles further consolidated links between electricity and coal. Coal and power plants were combined into energy companies so that they might more easily agree on prices, more effectively deal with nonpayment, and minimize transport costs.[93] This rationale dominated regional and federal political discourse in this period.[94] While unification of coal and electricity companies was planned for other regions where electricity production was reliant on coal-fired plants,

---

[89] International Energy Agency, *Coal Mine Methane in Russia: Capturing the Safety and Environmental Benefits* (Paris: OECD/IEA, 2010), 16, http://www.iea.org/publications/freepublications/publication/Coal_Mine_Methane_Russian.pdf

[90] "Дальэнерго меняет партнеров?" *Утро России*, January 14, 1997. Regional coal miners appealed to the federal government, for example, in an open letter to Chernomyrdin titled "Ситуация вышла из-под контроля," *Утро России*, April 30, 1997.

[91] An account of the difficult years 1993 and 1994 by a local miner; see "Просим нас поддержать," *Утро России*, January 21, 1994.

[92] The coal war (*угольная война*) was a recurring theme in the regional media; see, for example, "Дальэнерго меняет партнеров?" *Утро России*, January 14, 1997; "Долой популиста Наздратенко," *Утро России*, May 17, 1997; "Стабилизация?" *Утро России*, May 20, 1997.

[93] "Согласно решению главы РАО ЕЭС России Анатолия Чубайса в настоящее время разрабатывается программа формирования энергоугольных компаний на базе электростанций и угольных предприятий." ["In accordance with a decision of the head of RAO UES, Anatoly Chubais, the company is currently working on a program to form joint electricity and coal companies on the basis of the assets of electricity companies and coal mines."] "Чубайс дает стране угля," *Известия*, December 3, 1998.

[94] "Одной из мер по спасению Приморского ТЕКа станет объединение Лучеторского угольного разреза с Приморской ГРЭС, а в перспективе, возможно, и всех предприятий угольной индустрии и энергетики края"; in "Повышения цен не избежать," *Утро России*, May 27, 1997.

not surprisingly, it started in the Far East. In Primorskii Krai, the largest power plant and an adjacent coal mine were merged to form the company LuTEK (*ЛуТЭК*), which then became one of the largest recipients of federal aid in the region.[95] After 2001, other Far Eastern coal companies were incorporated into larger coal companies, such as SUEK (*СУЭК*). SUEK, in turn, purchased shares of the power plants that were the main customers of regional coal.[96] While the government retained majority ownership of Far Eastern power plants, SUEK became the largest minority owner.[97] Much like Gazprom, SUEK argued that economic efficiency required it to own both coal companies and power plants. According to one of the company's executives, "the idea of achieving a synergetic effect from the integration of the coal mining and power supply business has been fundamental for SUEK from the very beginning of its activity. While building the vertically-integrated fuel and power supply company, we … have concentrated on the power grid systems that use coal as main fuel."[98]

In addition to favoring coal interests in decisions about who should own power plants after the reforms, and about who should or should not continue to receive subsidies, the federal government also made coal a national priority sector in 2004. During Putin's second term, the federal government pushed to expand domestic coal production and coal exports, encouraging investment in new mining technologies. Several federal and regional planning documents called for a switch from gas to coal.[99] Particularly in Far East towns where coalmines were an important source of employment, this strategy had enormous developmental implications. In the town of Partizansk, for example, coal mining dominated economic life – the coalmine paid salaries or pensions for most residents, while few other employers survived the post-Soviet collapse.

[95] For the announcement of a merger between a coal and an electricity company to form the Lutek, see "Пока просто товарищи," *Утро России*, June 3, 1997.
[96] СУЭК, Сибирская угольная энергетическая компания (SUEK, Siberian Coal Company), http://www.suek.ru/
[97] See the discussion of ownership changes in Chapter 4.
[98] According to Sergei Mironosetsky, Deputy Director General, Energy Supply, Mergers and Acquisitions of SUEK; interview available online, http://www.suek.ru/en/page.php?id=207
[99] This switch from coal to gas is reported in various government documents; see, for example, "General Scheme of Placing Electric Power Engineering Facilities for the Period Up to 2020." Strategy approved by Decree of the Government of the Russian Federation No. 215-r of February 22, 2008. Also mentioned by Chubais at a conference "Electricity: Locomotive or Brake on Economic Development?/Энергетика: тормоз или локомотив развития экономики?" Moscow, February 13, 2007.

The protection of inefficient coalmines and of coal-fired power plants was never a predetermined or a necessary result of the physical link between the electricity and coal sectors. Sakhalin's oil and gas fields, among the country's most abundant, could have provided an alternative energy resource. Russia's foreign economic advisors and liberals consistently argued that the Far Eastern electricity sector should be weaned from the region's low-caloric coal and instead linked to gas deposits, or that cheaper electricity could be imported from Siberia. The switch to gas was tempting. Regional governors in the 1990s sometimes pursued both strategies – gasification and the protection of local coal production.[100] The two strategies have conflicting regional constituencies – "there has been a conflict [over the issue of] coal versus gas"[101] – and most regional governors ended up supporting local coal miners. Even the federal government under Putin in reality pursued a dual strategy: protecting Far Eastern coal industries while also planning to build a gas pipeline between Sakhalin, Khabarovsk, and Vladivostok that would gasify the big regions in the Southern Far East, Khabarovsk, and Primorskii Krai. However, in 2008, when I was in the region to conduct field research for this project, many observers were skeptical that the gas pipeline would be ever be built. One observer explained the opposition to gasification: "Nobody here really wants coal-fired plants to switch to gas.… The coal miners are opposed. The [regional] administration is opposed.… Really, there won't be a switch to gas."[102] Ultimately, as many other aspects of the post-Soviet transformation, these decisions are being made in ongoing negotiations between gas and coal interests.

The Far Eastern electricity and coal sectors emerged as the provisional winners in the political negotiation about the region's reforms: they remained protected from cheap Siberian power and continued to be subsidized. Despite the liberal push to reduce the region's reliance on coal, the government opted to protect coal-fired power plants and coal mines rather than allow Far Eastern power plants to go under and switch from coal to gas. It was a decision to protect coal miners and coal-fired power

[100] Khabarovsk Governor Ishaev is personally credited with effecting the "gasification" of a power plant in Nikolaevsk-na-Amure, or more precisely for convincing domestic and foreign companies to invest in the technology to switch the power plant from coal to gas. The deal was brokered by a UN agency. Interview #45 with employee of electricity company and interview #46 with academic and journalist, both in Khabarovsk, 20071011

[101] Interview #39 with electrical engineer/electricity sector expert, Vladivostok, 20071004.

[102] "Переходить на газ не будем." Interview #41 with journalist covering electricity sector, Vladivostok, 20071005.

plants in a weakly industrialized frontier region. Important for the theoretical concern of this chapter, power plants and coalmines mobilized the physical link that tied their fates together in these negotiations.

Interests and Ideas

Reform outcomes in the electricity sector were negotiated in political pacts between governmental and private actors. Physical facts shaped interests in these political bargains; hence, they mattered as structures shaping interests. But the materialities also featured as ideas in political negotiations about whose interests were realized. This account of the role of industrial geography in shaping Russia's electricity sector transformation may be critiqued from two angles: either as too obvious (of course the physical infrastructure, the sunk cost, and the technology of fuel generation mattered), or as implausible (Gazprom's prominent political position is what matters, rather than an inherited industrial geography linking gas and electricity sectors).

The point here is that *both* the physical reality and the political positions mattered, and hence that the political life of things merits our attention. Inherited linkages between the electricity sector and adjacent upstream suppliers and downstream customers mattered because they shaped the interests of conglomerates and their relationships with the electricity sector. These interests alone did not guarantee that the demands of Gazprom, Rusal, and Far Eastern power plants were met. Just as important were discursive strategies that "naturalized" certain sector configurations as economically efficient or even technologically necessary. Physical links could not shape reform outcomes unless/until political battles were won. The liberal faction of the Yeltsin and Putin governments disagreed with privileges afforded to Gazprom and other champions, unviable behemoths best left at the mercy of market forces. Had the liberals been a stronger force, more of these particularistic ties would have been superseded, or at least loosened and eventually replaced by new relationships. The resilience of inherited ties, then, was the result of victories in political struggles, and not a predetermined outcome.

A broader theoretical claim concerning political economy's conceptualization of interests and ideas emerges from this understanding that economic geography is constituted both by material interests and discursively constructed realities. As Chapter 1 introduced, observers of Russian capitalism often describe it as a post-ideological space where

reality holds dominion over ideology: "ideas hardly matter, while interests rein supreme," argues Trenin.[103] Analytically distinguishing and
opposing ideas and interests in this way remains the default strategy of
most of political economy. While constructivist approaches draw attention to ideational factors, the theorization of how ideas and interests are
intertwined in political economy continues to be a challenge.[104] Social
theory has recently re-emphasized the role of "things" in politics, calling
attention to political discourses that construct physical facts as givens.[105]
The story told here, about how industrial geography enters politics both
as "real things" and as discursively mobilized reality, suggests a way
to theorize how interests and ideas are intertwined, rather than relying on one or the other to explain a particular outcome. Perhaps the
most interesting aspect of the cases discussed here is the effectiveness
of political strategies that manipulated the boundary between "things"
and "politics" – between what is politically negotiable and what is technologically necessary, economically efficient and naturally given.[106] The
role physical facts play in the way the economies restructure, or develop,
is not necessarily fixed, or given; instead, they are naturalized in specific
political discourses. Similarly, interests are validated through particular
ideas that naturalize and legitimize them. What this means is that we

[103] As Chapter 1 introduced, arguments that ideas hardly matter in Russia's Wild West
Capitalism are common; see Trenin, "Russia Redefines Itself and Its Relations with the
West."
[104] See discussion in Chapter 1.
[105] These studies point out, for example, how scientific evidence are constructed as indisput-
able facts and then marshaled as justifications for political agendas. Bruno Latour has
referred to "things" as the "res" in the "res publica" and has called on political science
to refocus attention on nonhuman matters; Bruno Latour, Peter Weibel, and Exhibition,
Making Things Public: Atmospheres of Democracy (Cambridge, MA: MIT Press, 2005).
See also the work by Oleg Kharkordin that draws on Latour; Dominique Colas and
Oleg Kharkhordin, *The Materiality of Res Publica: How to Do Things with Public?*
(Newcastle: Cambridge Scholars, 2009); Kharkhordin, *Main Concepts of Russian
Politics*. Like Latour's, Michel Callon's work is central in these debates; see, for example,
Michel Callon, ed., *The Laws of the Markets*, Sociological Review Monograph Series
(Oxford: Blackwell Publishers, 1998). See also Mitchell, *Rule of Experts*. Jane Bennet
has examined the politics of things in *Vibrant Matter: A Political Ecology of Things*
(Durham, NC: Duke University Press, 2010); also see Mitchell, *Rule of Experts*. With
the exceptions of Mitchell and Bennett, political science has, on the whole, neglected
material facts and tends to think of politics as the interaction of human interests and
ideas. This may be an important omission, as an ever-larger part of politics concerns
technical and technological features of social life. In debates about environmental politics, biotechnology, security, and complex infrastructure, arguments about physical reality and facts are key.
[106] Mitchell (2004) draws attention to this dynamic. Mitchell, *Rule of Experts*, p. 29.

must seek explanations for why many elements of the inherited infrastructure were idled and why many interests were neglected while others
were not.

Legacies and Memories

Finally, this discussion of the relevance of inherited, Soviet-era industrial structures also begs for an engagement with the debate on the relevance of Soviet legacies, on how institutional and cultural features of
the Soviet social, political, and economic order persisted, and how these
legacies shaped post-Soviet outcomes.[107] Legacies tend to be viewed as
static factors that shaped post-Soviet politics, causal factors situated
in the past and therefore unalterable.[108] This chapter has investigated
the role of industrial and economic geography as important legacies,
although the point is not to add another type of legacy to the long list
already examined.[109] Instead, I show that economic geography and
inherited industrial structures do not mechanistically determine outcomes. Instead, legacies were strategically and selectively used by various
motivated political actors. This suggests something about the workings
of legacies more generally during the transition period: legacies functioned, not because of any inherent resonance, but rather because political actors succeeded in naturalizing them to secure concessions. For
this reason, regarding legacies as memories might be a useful conceptual
move, one that sheds deterministic connotations that so often inhere in
"legacies."[110] Post-Soviet geography contained memories of Soviet reasoning, remembrances of what was necessary and efficient in things past.

---

[107] For a survey of this literature, see Jody LaPorte and Danielle N. Lussier, "What Is
the Leninist Legacy? Assessing Twenty Years of Scholarship," *Slavic Review* 70, no. 3
(October 1, 2011): 637–654.

[108] For this reason Markus is critical of approaches that overemphasize legacies, he sees leg-
acies based explanations as "historically deterministic." Stanislav Markus, "Corporate
Governance as Political Insurance: Firm-Level Institutional Creation in Emerging
Markets and beyond," *Socio-Economic Review* 6, no. 1 (January 1, 2008): 74.

[109] Some studies have included geography as a communist legacy; see Grigore Pop-Eleches,
"Historical Legacies and Post-Communist Regime Change," *Journal of Politics* 69, no. 4
(2007): 908–926. Others find geography to be "largely autonomous from the structures
and institutions of communist rule." See J. M. LaPorte and D. N. Lussier, "Revisiting
the Leninist Legacy: Conceptualization and Measurement for Meaningful Comparison."
Paper presented at the Annual Meeting of the American Political Science Association,
August 28–31, Boston, MA, 2008.

[110] Memory is theorized in political theory that draws on Freud; see Svetlana Boym, *The
Future of Nostalgia* (New York: Basic Books, 2001).

Memories were then mobilized in political struggles, arguments whose resonance helped create conditions for certain reform trajectories while prohibiting others.

In a discussion over tea, a friend likened the relevance of inherited industrial geography to a railway line. Railways are physical facts, based on built objects and relatively fixed technologies. Once completed, a railway line organizes how goods and people move; it is responsible for the thriving of some sites and the stagnation of others. Who travels, when and with what destination is up to the traveler. Some railway lines fall into disrepair and are abandoned. Railways create the conditions for the movement of people and goods; they enable certain human actions and prohibit others.[111] Industrial geography is a set of physical facts that enable human action. In the Russian electricity sector, they created the possibility for certain relationships in the post-Soviet economy. As the Trans-Siberian railway conditions the way cargo is transported across the Eurasian landmass, so hydro-power plants and gas pipelines conditioned the way post-Soviet industrial conglomerates shaped new electricity markets. The most interesting part of this story is why some physical ties such as transmission lines were abandoned while others were incorporated into vertically integrated conglomerates, updated, and heavily used. For the people and factories tied into these grids, this is ultimately the most important question, and the answer, it seems, conjoins interests and ideas and confounds observers wedded to keeping them separate.

[111] Contrast this with Marx's emphasis on the railways for the development of India that implies a strong version of material/economic determinism: "Modern industry, resulting from the railway system, will dissolve the hereditary divisions of labor, upon which rest the Indian castes, those decisive impediments to Indian progress and Indian power." See "The Future Results of British Rule in India," in *The Marx-Engels Reader*, ed. Robert C. Tucker, 2nd ed. (New York: Norton, 1978), p. 659.

Part II

4

Privatization – Competing Claims and New Owners

"Electricity – the heart of the economy"[1]

Anatoly Chubais

Privatizing Soviet Assets: Political Motives and Political Outcomes

By 1980, privatization was a favorite policy tool of conservative governments from Chile to the United Kingdom. The transfer of ownership from public to private entities was an apparently simple solution to a set of complex problems – an easy way to relieve public budgets of expensive state-owned enterprises, to undercut the political clout of public-sector unions, and to raise private capital for new investments in vital infrastructure sectors. In sync with this international trend, privatizing the states' vast holdings topped the list of priorities of many newly independent post-Socialist governments in the early 1990s. Privatization was the single most important political project of Yeltsin's liberal reform team. Yet, the process of privatizing Soviet and Eastern European assets proved vastly more complex than anticipated. Difficulties stemmed from weakly established property rights and the absence of institutions able to value assets.[2] As the Polish privatization minister acidly summarized, "Privatization is when someone who doesn't know who the real owner is and doesn't know what it is really

---

[1] Колесников, *Неизвестный Чубайс: Страницы из биографии*, 133.

[2] Empirically rich landmark studies of post-socialist privatization are Solnick, *Stealing the State*; Katherine Verdery, *The Vanishing Hectare: Property and Value in Postsocialist Transylvania* (Ithaca, NY: Cornell University Press, 2003); Barnes, *Owning Russia*; and Allina-Pisano, *The Post-Soviet Potemkin Village*.

worth sells it to someone who doesn't have any money."[3] Despite these difficulties, most post-Socialist countries had privatized large swaths of state holdings by the end of the 1990s.[4] This chapter details the processes and outcomes of ownership transfers in the electricity sector. The largest of the Energos, and the most valuable power plants within the Energos, were contested most ferociously. But why did some ownership claims fail while others succeeded, and what were the consequences of these outcomes?

Privatization of Russian state-owned assets was motivated by far more than simply a concern for improved economic efficiency. "Every enterprise ripped out of the state and transferred to the hands of a private owner was a way of destroying Communism in Russia," Anatoly Chubais, the architect of Russia's privatization program, once claimed.[5] Privatization made the collapse of the Soviet Union irreversible, preventing any possibility of return to a planned economy. The political effects of privatization were very much on the minds of liberal reformers in Russia throughout the early post-Soviet period. In the early 1990s, Yeltsin's hold on power was tenuous, as incumbent Communist Party elites, factory directors, and other stalwarts of the old order were trying to regain power.[6] Even more fragile was the position of the young reformers. Yeltsin's young reformers, including Chubais, had a clear political agenda: large-scale privatization would create a new class of property owners with a vested interest in a capitalist system.[7] In defense of newly acquired property, new owners would ensure against re-nationalization or the reconstitution of central planning.

Ownership transfers did indeed transform the political arena, but in ways that the young reformers could not have imagined. Russian privatization in the 1990s conspicuously failed to distribute Soviet-era property widely among its citizens, as promised at the beginning of the decade.[8]

[3] Quoted in Verdery, *The Vanishing Hectare*, 1.

[4] An example from a Russian oblast' illustrates the scale of privatization: in Irkutsk oblast', 1,608 enterprises had been privatized by January 1, 1994; "Иркутская область: шаги приватизации." *Восточно-Сибирская правда*, January 25, 1994.

[5] Anatoly Chubais, quoted by Hoffman in *The Oligarchs*. The political rationale of privatization is captured by Lynn D. Nelson, *Radical Reform in Yeltsin's Russia: Political, Economic, and Social Dimensions* (Armonk, NY: M. E. Sharpe, 1995).

[6] See, for example, Lilia Fedorovna Shevtsova, *Yeltsin's Russia: Myths and Reality* (Washington, DC: Carnegie Endowment for International Peace, 1999).

[7] Lynn D. Nelson, *Property to the People: The Struggle for Radical Economic Reforme in Russia* (Armonk, NY: M.E. Sharpe, 1994).

[8] Studies with a focus on the role of oligarchs include Nelson, *Property to the People*; McFaul and Perlmutter, *Privatization, Conversion, and Enterprise Reform in Russia*;

Instead of creating a well-endowed property-owning citizenry who would fight for capitalism and liberal democracy, privatization resulted in a handful of oligarchs with control over most Russian factories. What can an examination of electricity sector reform add to the established consensus that "winners took all" during Russia's "sale of the century," ostensibly little more than the corrupt transfer of valuable assets to political insiders?[9]

The privatization of Russia's electricity sector throws new light on the political consequences of the ownership changes in the sector. The privatization of electricity assets empowered new actors and sidelined others. Regional actors – governors, regional companies, and residents – lost out in ownership battles. The unbundling, restructuring, and sale of electricity assets orchestrated by liberal reformers undercut regional utilities. The regional monopolies – the Energos – were dissolved and the most valuable power plants were bundled into "de-territorialized" holding companies, the so-called OGKs (*Оптовая генерирующая компания/ОГК*).[10] "De-territorialized" meant that the power plants these companies owned were dispersed across Russia's regions, rather than being located in situ, as the Energo's assets had been. Dispersing the physical assets of new companies across different locations intended to divorce and insulate electricity assets from the sphere of influence and jurisdiction of regional governors.

Russia's oligarchic conglomerates acquired substantial stakes in the newly privatized electricity companies as they sought assets that assembled into vertically integrated production chains. While regional electricity monopolies were undone, conglomerates targeted and acquired electricity assets – the "missing links" to consolidate their own production chains. Three types production chains emerged across three supra-regions: Gazprom reintegrated electricity assets into energy production chains in European Russia; Rusal relied on electricity to vertically integrate production of non-ferrous

Joseph E. Stiglitz, "Who Lost Russia?" in *Globalization and Its Discontents* (New York: W. W. Norton & Co., 2002), 133–165; Åslund, *Building Capitalism*; and Hoffman, *The Oligarchs*.

[9] These terms are coined by Hellman, "Winners Take All"; and Chrystia Freeland, *Sale of the Century: Russia's Wild Ride from Communism to Capitalism*, 1st ed. (New York: Crown Business, 2000).

[10] Six OGKs were created on the basis of UES's holdings of the GRES (*Государственная районная электростанция*), the largest and most valuable thermal generation assets; these are OGK-1 through OGK-6. A seventh OGK was based on UES's hydroelectric holdings, Hydro-OGK. The benefits of de-territorialized electricity companies were widely discussed; see, for example, "Низкие цены – враг экономии," *Коммерсантъ*, December 6, 2001.

metals in Siberia; while in the Far East, the government retained control of power plants in an attempt to craft export-directed energy production chains. In each case, the integration of electricity assets into larger production chains played a significant role in national and regional developmental bargains. By drawing attention to production chains, this chapter contributes to a central claim of the book, that a meaningful understanding of new owner's interest situates them in the shifting context of electricity politics and in the economies they operate.

Paradoxically, the privatization of power assets meant that production and distribution of electric power came to be directed through *fewer* and more *centralized* structures. While in the 1990s there were seventy-one Energos, each tied to a regional government, by 2008 a handful conglomerates owned most electricity generation assets. OGKs' assets were both more physically dispersed as well as centrally managed than the Energos had ever been. Many OGKs were officially registered in one of Russia's regions while in reality headquartered in Moscow.[11] Along with this re-centralization of assets, relationships with authorities were redefined: following the unbundling of the Energos, new, Moscow-based owners negotiated the terms of liberal reforms and the future of power provision with federal authorities. The shift from regional to oligarchic control then fundamentally changed the conditions for political influence in the sector.

Andrew Barnes drew attention to the deeply political nature of the profound conflicts over assets that characterized the early post-Soviet Russia, where "incentives for acquiring property went beyond the pursuit of profit" and assets were "the key to establishing, defending, or expanding one's position in the new system."[12] Controlling assets was far more than a way to accumulate wealth – assets were "a source of political power," as "ownership could mean significant influence over politicians," or it could be an "effective tool to capturing [other] assets further down the production chain."[13] Evidence from the electricity sector suggests that we can take Barnes's argument about the relationship between privatization and politics one step further. Not only were ownership transfers motivated by political aims; they fundamentally transformed the political conditions for successive rounds of property struggles. Barnes pays

---

[11] OGK-3, for example, is registered in Ulan Ude, in the Buryatia region, but headquartered in Moscow; see http://www.ogk3.ru/
[12] Andrew Barnes, *Owning Russia*, 13.
[13] Ibid.

close attention to shifts in the political logic of property disputes, but he regards these shifts to be the result of exogenous shocks – "events [that] periodically shook up the system" and "upheavals such as a financial crash, the transformation of political structures, or the emergence of new politicians and policies" that transformed "the arena of competition over assets."[14] I stress that it was the property struggles themselves that not only remade fundamental market institutions, as they were intended to, but the political arena as well.

The privatization histories of the Energos also confirmed what is well known about Russia's privatization: the political connections of winning bidders were frequently decisive for the award of ownership rights.[15] Privatization auctions, and other processes of ownership transfer, often occurred in a murky legal zone with little oversight or transparency. De facto control was often more important the de jure ownership, and de facto owners frequently bent rules to gain de jure property rights.[16] The privatization of electricity sector assets was "non-transparent, much like other privatizations,"[17] and "marred by numerous examples of unfair, illegal or opaque deals."[18] This was particularly evident with respect to asset valuations, which were often "arbitrary, murky and inconsistent."[19] It would be shortsighted, however, to extrapolate from these character-istics of ownership change and conclude that corruption, predation, and capture sufficiently describe or explain the processes and outcomes of privatization. Reducing these complex dynamics to little more than strat-egies for self-enrichment among political elites obscures other important political rationales.

---

[14] Ibid., 8.

[15] This was not just a Russian phenomenon; see Regine Spector, "Securing Property in Contemporary Kyrgyzstan."

[16] Many observers noted this; for example one of the privatization's architects, Alfred Kokh (lecture at the Institute for East European and Eurasian Studies, Berkeley, in April 2009). Kokh was deputy prime minister under Yeltsin, and headed the State Property Committee for about a year between the fall of 1996 and 1997. The literature on the emergence of Russia's property rights is vast; for a view on how different Russia's property rights regime is from what Western investors are looking for, see, for example, Karla Hoff and Joseph E. Stiglitz, "After the Big Bang? Obstacles to the Emergence of the Rule of Law in Post-Communist Societies," *American Economic Review* 94, no. 3 (2004): 753–763; and Karla Hoff and Joseph E. Stiglitz, "Exiting a Lawless State," *The Economic Journal* 118, no. 531 (2008): 1474–1497.

[17] Interview #1 with electricity sector expert, international financial institution, Moscow, 20060721.

[18] Burganskij and Elinevskaya, *Hydro Power*, 12.

[19] Interview #7 with electricity sector analyst at financial institution, Moscow, 20061005.

Privatizing the Energos, from Spontaneous Privatization to
Competitive Tenders

Post-Soviet privatization involved multiple and complex shifts in ownership and control. Factories, oil rigs, coal mines, apartment buildings, electricity grids, hydroelectric dams, and myriad other assets
were subject to frequent and conflicting ownership claims during the
two post-Soviet decades. "Privatization" fails to adequately describe
these shifts and transformations. As Barnes detailed, different "winners" emerged from successive rounds of ownership transfers. I follow
Barnes' account in characterizing the privatization of electricity assets
as a long process of shifting, overlapping, and conflicting ownership
claims rather than a simple shift of property rights from the state to
private companies. Electricity sector assets changed hands by means
of privatization vouchers, debt-for-equity swaps, hostile takeovers,
auctions, and public share offerings, to name but the most important
mechanisms. Each involved different actors, with different political
connections and different interests vis-à-vis the electricity sector. At
times, several public and private owners simultaneously claimed ownership of the most valuable assets.

   To document the processes and outcomes of privatization battles
that played out over the roughly twenty years under discussion here,
I rely on the privatization histories of three Energos: Mosenergo,
Irkutskenergo, and Dal'energo, located in Moscow, Irkutsk oblast', and
Primorskii Krai, respectively (see Table 4.1). I trace the success and failure of ownership claims made by the federal government, by regional
governments, by new conglomerates, and by foreign investors. The narrative of Energos privatization that emerges, brings together a historical
analysis of each region's sector reform with a cross-regional comparison of outcomes.

   Mosenergo, Irkutskenergo, and Dal'energo illustrate the privatization
histories of Energos in the three new zones that emerged – European
Russia, Siberia, and the Far East, respectively. The three Energos were
the largest electricity producers in their respective geographical territories and were typical of the regions they represent. Mosenergo owned
mostly gas-fired generation assets, Irkutskenergo relied on a large hydroelectric power plant, and Dalenergo on coal-fired generators. Mosenergo
was the world's largest thermal power company and Russia's largest and
oldest Energo. Power consumption in Moscow city remained remarkably
stable even as the rest of the country's economy collapsed, and it grew

TABLE 4.1. *Case studies of three energos*

Region	*Energo*	Control and/or Ownership in 1990s	Majority Ownership after reforms (2008)
		Governor/Mayor	*Conglomerate*
Moscow (European Russia)	**Mosenergo**	Luzhkov	Gazprom = energy conglomerate
Irkutsk (Siberia)	**Irkutskenergo**	Nozhikov	Rusal = industrial conglomerate
Primorskii Krai (Far East)	**Dal'energo**	Nazdratenko	State remains majority stakeholder

rapidly with the post-1998 economic boom. Mosenergo was also one of the most profitable companies in Russia, and not plagued with as many nonpaying customers as was a typical Russian Energo.[20] Unlike most Energos, Irkutskenergo possessed some of the largest and most valuable hydroelectric power plants in the world and consequently was at the center of a particularly troubled ownership transformation. Both Russian and foreign investors coveted Irkutskenergo and Mosenergo (the two Energos were among the country's earliest "blue-chip" assets). By contrast, Primorskii Krai's Dal'energo was unprofitable.[21] Dal'energo, much like electricity companies throughout the Russian Far East, was caught between nonpaying customers and striking coal miners. Dal'energo's customers were unable to pay for the electricity they consumed: the military industrial sector and the so-called budget organizations (schools, hospitals, and other public organizations financed from government budgets) were either exempt from having to pay for electricity or simply did not pay.[22]

The ownership changes relevant for the electricity sector can be roughly grouped into four chronological types: spontaneous privatization (1989–1991), voucher and auction privatizations (1993–1994), hostile takeover (1998–2002), and the reform program led by Anatoly

---

[20] Mosenergo share prices were a mirror image of Russia's political history as perceived by the West. Whenever something happened – a sacked prime minister, for example – Mosenergo shares plummeted; this relationship was pointed out to me in interview #8 with economist at financial institution, 20061006.

[21] Interview #41 with journalist covering electricity sector, Vladivostok, 20071005.

[22] See Bradshaw and Kirkow, "The Energy Crisis in the Russian Far East."

Chubais (2005–2008).[23] Two types of evidence support the thesis that electricity assets were linked to economic development agendas devised by Moscow for Russia's regions: regional strategies for ownership changes of the Energos in the 1990s and federal policies for the sector's post-reform ownership that were formulated under Putin. The three Energos were each located in regions that were particularly independent during Russia's first post-Soviet decade. These regions pursued their own path in the electricity sector, providing excellent case studies to illustrate the center-region conflict that shaped privatization. Finally, a note on ownership claims. Particularly during the 1990s, it was difficult to discern the large shareholders of Russian firms. Even for publicly traded firms, reporting requirements were often disregarded and no meaningful ownership information was publicly available, or, alternatively, real owners hid behind shell companies. The narrative in this chapter is based on newspaper reports, company statements, brokerage reports, and information obtained in interviews with actors involved in these ownership struggles.

Ownership Battles in the 1990s

Claims by the Federal Government: Constitutionally Binding, Factually Contested

Because electricity was an important infrastructure sector, the federal government initially tried to keep control of the bulk of power plants and grids, though with varying levels of success across regions and over time. While the ownership claims by the federal government were constitutionally binding, in reality they were contested and controversial. To untangle overlapping and competing ownership claims, I start with an overview of the federal government's ownership of assets and then turn to the ownership claims of other actors and subsequent transfers.

While the Russian federal government de jure inherited the assets of the Soviet-era ministries, in reality many of these assets did not remain intact. The first wave of ownership transfers happened in what Steve Solnick and others referred to as spontaneous privatizations – ownership transfers in which well-placed nomenklatura insiders spun off profitable parts of state-owned enterprises for their own

---

[23] The ownership changes in the electricity sector mirrored some of the key events in other sectors, well documented in the literature on Russia's privatization. The privatization timeline of the electricity sector is unique in other ways, as this chapter documents.

businesses.[24] In the absence of a legal framework for privatization, this happened through various types of ad hoc deals. For example, a well-placed insider authorized the privatization of a valuable section of a company to a new owner in return for a stake in the company. In this way new stakeholders acquired property rights to electricity sector assets prior to the actual privatization of the Energos. Such spontaneous and ad hoc deals threatened federal control of valuable assets. In August 1992, the federal government passed two presidential decrees, Nos. 922 and 923, that required presidential decrees for any further privatization in the energy sectors.[25] The two decrees were passed at a moment of great jeopardy for the central government, as disintegrated Soviet-era chains of command were but tentatively reconstituted within the nascent bureaucracy of the Russian Federation.

Ironically, but perhaps unsurprisingly given the legal uncertainty at the time, the first step to privatize the Soviet-era Unified Electricity System was a presidential decree that *reserved* a large share of the sector assets for the federal government. A third decree (No. 1334) in November 1992 "corporatized" electricity assets of the Soviet ministry, creating UES and its daughter companies, the regional Energos. These decrees intended to keep most electricity assets under control of the federal government, granting the state a majority stake, if not full ownership. UES was to own the country's biggest power plants and receive majority stakes in all the regional Energos. Most controversial was the proposition that the country's largest power plants – insiders referred to them as the crown jewels of the electricity system – were to be directly controlled by UES and owned by the federal government rather than by the respective regional Energos. This included all hydroelectric power plants and the largest and newest thermal electric plants, the most valuable assets in the system.[26] While the decrees of the fall of 1992 did indeed reserve large parts of the sector for the federal government, like many other unpopular presidential directives, their legitimacy was disputed immediately by

---

[24] See Solnick, *Stealing the State*. For a reference to the ongoing spontaneous privatization in the electricity sector (*стихийное растаскивание имущества*), see "Какие монстры нам нужны," *Восточно-Сибирская правда*, July 8, 1992.

[25] Decrees No. 922 and No. 923 were passed on August 14 and August 15, 1992, respectively. See Barnes, *Owning Russia*, 84–85. For details on the decrees, see Хлебников, *Рынок электроэнергии в России*.

[26] Nuclear power plants had been excluded from reforms from the start. They had remained under the control of the federal government as a state-owned enterprise, *Росэнергоатом*.

many actors – governors, mayors, and the newly emerging private-sector interests – who opposed the federal government's claim to the "most delicious pieces" of the pie.[27]

Throughout Russia, valuable power plants and Energos were withheld from the federal government. "RAO-[UES] became the world's largest electricity company. [Yet] many pieces [of this pie] were gobbled up," noted one observer.[28] Governors and Energo managers transferred assets to new owners in ways that directly defied the 1992 decrees.[29] Many valuable power plants, and four whole Energos – Irkutskenergo, Novosibirskenergo, Tatenergo, and Bashenergo – passed into the ownership of actors *other* than the federal government.[30] Circumvention of the decrees left UES with a *minority* stake in nineteen Energos by the late 1990s. Breakdowns in federal enforcement led to overlapping and competing ownership claims that would plague the electricity sector for years to come, as the remainder of the chapter documents. With the exception of some high-profile clashes, such as in the case of Irkutskenergo, conflicts over competing claims simmered during much of the 1990s, and were only brought to light following the 1997 reforms of the electricity system, when it became clear that while the federal government was formally the legal owner of UES and the Energos, it was unable to force compliance with directives meant to transform the sector.

Although contested on many fronts, the 1992 presidential decrees did manage to reserve a large share of Russia's electricity sector for the federal government. Minority shares in many Energos were included in the 1993 privatization program (we will see in the later discussion that they often ended up consolidated in special investment funds, *ЧИФ – Чековый инвестиционный фонд*). A majority of the sector's assets, most of the catastrophically inefficient and money-losing enterprises but also many valuable power plants, remained in state hands throughout the 1990s. It

---

[27] An observer from Krasnoiarskii Krai asks whether the Krai will be able to resist the "cutting off of the tasty parts" of the electricity pie: "Сумеет ли край противостоять отрезанию лакомых кусков? На тебе, боже, что нам негоже," *Красноярский рабочий*, February 11, 1993. This analogy was also used in various interviews, for example, interview #49 with academic, Irkutsk, 20071114. See also Burganskij and Elinevskaya, *Hydro Power*.

[28] "РАО стало самой крупной в мире корпорацией по производству ... электроэнергии. Было от чего отхватывать куски." *Крест Чубайса*, 70.

[29] See, for example, Burgansky, who emphasizes the hydro-power plants. Burganskij and Elinevskaya, *Hydro Power*.

[30] The four "independent" Energos were Irkutskenergo, Tatenergo, Bashkirenergo, and Novosibirskenergo; see discussion later in the chapter on the privatization histories of these Energos.

also meant that many electricity assets were not included in the "loans-for-shares" deals, the egregious asset grab that led to the acquisition of some of the countries most valuable industrial assets by a few politically connected, emerging oligarchs.

Ownership Claims by Regional Governors: From Strength to Weakness

Ownership changes were strongly influenced by a center-region dynamic that characterized Russian politics during the first post-Soviet decade. Regional governors across Russia sought control of regional electricity generators to stave off factory closures and to secure the provision of cheap electricity, so important during a time of economic, political, and social crisis.[31] While side payments and other corrupt dealings influenced some decisions to privatize assets, the patterns of ownership transfers and the way these transfers were rationalized in public discourse provide strong evidence that governors considered regional electricity assets to be crucial for economic and social development.

Control of electricity sector assets took a variety of forms across Russia. In some regions, governors did not own a de jure majority stake, but instead wielded great influence via informal channels and personal connections to Energo directors – this was the case in Moscow and Primorskii Krai. In other regions, governors saw that spontaneous privatizations were already ongoing and wanted to rescue important assets from passing into private hands. In Irkutsk, for example, Governor Nozhikov considered a wave of early privatizations highly destructive.[32] In Tatarstan and Bashkortostan, regional authorities also sought control of the electricity sector. In these powerful and potentially separatist ethnic republics, Yeltsin allowed regional leaders control of Tatenergo and Bashkirenergo as part of a political horse trade meant to secure loyalty and votes.[33] In other regions, such as Novosibirsk, governors simply defied federal legislation and authorized transfers of ownership to regional administrations or loyal regional enterprises. Over the years, regional governments also often acquired ownership stakes gradually in lieu of tax arrears by

---

[31] The narrative that follows focuses on Mosenergo, Irkutskenergo, and Dal'energo. But regional governors elsewhere similarly sought control. In Tyumen, for example, the regional government contested UES's property rights through a Duma motion; see "Удельные княжества копят энергию," *Сегодня*, December 18, 1998.

[32] See Nozhikov's commentaries in his biography on this very early "wave" of privatization; Ножиков, *Я Это Видел, или Жизнь Российского Губернатора*, 139, 159.

[33] Бергер and Проскурина, "Крест Чубайса," 71.

regional Energos.[34] A number of ownership disputes between the federal and regional governments were brought to regional courts. Under the influence of regional authorities, regional courts decided in favor of regional actors during the 1990s. In almost all regions, governors had personal ties to the Energo directors, which served as a conduit for control even when governors did not formally gain ownership. Importantly, this meant that in all three cases discussed later in this chapter, the de facto control of Energos by regional administrations in the 1990s far outweighed their de jure ownership stake.

Mosenergo and De Facto Regional Control

Mosenergo was a token in a political contest between the mayor of Moscow, the charismatic and influential Yuri Luzhkov, and the federal reform team.[35] From the early days of privatization, the city's mayor took an interest in Mosenergo as one of Moscow's most valuable enterprises. The mayor was keenly aware of the value of the city's municipal infrastructure. He wanted to be the "master" (*хозяин*) of the city's electricity and proclaimed often and loudly that Mosenergo is "ours," even if UES technically controlled a majority stake of Mosenergo assets.[36] Luzhkov was often called "Chubais's worst enemy."[37] He clashed with Chubais over the size of the city's stake in Mosenergo and more generally about whether the electricity sector should be privatized at all. Because of his political prominence and charismatic personality, Luzhkov became one of the main opponents of Chubais, the young reformers, and electricity privatization.

Luzhkov argued that privatizing a socially important sector was too costly, too dangerous, and would lead the country down "the wrong

[34] During the nonpayment and barter crisis, Energos ran up debt vis-à-vis regional tax authorities; see Brevnov, "From Monopoly to Market Maker? Reforming Russia's Power Sector"; and Woodruff, *Money Unmade*. For how this translated into ownership, see, for example, Barnes, *Owning Russia*, 164.

[35] The conflict between Chubais and Luzhkov was extensively reported in various media outlets. See, for example, "Хроника энергетического конфликта," *Коммерсантъ*, September 25, 2002. Дмитрий Докучаев и Наталия Давыдова, "Закон сохранения энергии," *Московские новости*, October 8, 2002. Виталий Цепляев, "Чубайс–Лужков – боевая ничья," *Аргументы и факты*, October 16, 2002. Рыбалченко, "Электроэнергия 1991–2000," *Коммерсантъ*, November 13, 2001.

[36] "Чубайса рвет на родину ГОЭЛРО." *Московская правда*, October 9, 2002; "История 2000–2004: Укрощение региональных энергокомпаний," *Коммерсантъ Власть*, June 14, 2004.

[37] Interview #8 with economist at financial institution, Moscow, 20061006.

path."[38] He reasoned that "[the proposed privatization of UES] isn't just a privatization of a regular company. UES, aside from its economic functions, fulfills enormous social functions as well. Because of this ... the provision of electricity and heat is the responsibility of the state."[39] Private ownership of the sector was undesirable, he reasoned, as private investors would seek to reap returns on assets, which in turn would lead only to sharp rate increases for electricity and heat. He accused Chubais of wanting to make a short-term profit from electricity. He argued instead that there was no need for private investment, that the sector was the government's responsibility, and that the government should find the means to develop and modernize the sector – as it had done since GOELRO.[40]

Luzhkov wanted at least 50 percent of Mosenergo to be owned by the city.[41] Under municipal ownership, he claimed, the sector would thrive and electricity infrastructure would be able to keep up with post-Soviet change. This fit with Luzhkov's broader vision for Moscow's assets, which he considered invaluable tools for governing the city's economy. The mayor tried to strengthen his control of Mosenergo many times over the years, mainly through attempts to increase formal ownership and via personal ties to Mosenergo's leadership. Both the mayor and liberal reformers around Chubais used all available resources at their disposal to influence Mosenergo. As a way to exert control, Luzhkov maintained personal relationships first with D'iakov, UES's director until 1997, and then with Aleksander Remezov, Mosenergo's director. D'iakov was backed by Luzhkov and other regional governors because he did not threaten their control of the Energos.[42] Chubais tried to oust Remezov, the mayor's loyalist.[43] In response, Luzhkov used the city's administrative powers

---

[38] "Хроника энергетического конфликта," *Коммерсантъ*, September 25, 2002; "Реформа по Чубайсу – это опасно, считает Лужков," *Daily News Bulletin/Interfax*, May 19, 2001.

[39] "РАО ЕЭС – это не просто приватизация какого-то предприятия. ЕЭС, помимо хозяйственных, выполняет колоссальные социальные функции. При этом мэр сказал, что обеспечение электроэнергией и теплом является важнейшей задачей государства." In "Реформа по Чубайсу – это опасно, считает Лужков," *Daily News Bulletin/Interfax*, May 19, 2001. See also "Мэр Москвы выступает против приватизации энергетических объектов," *Daily News Bulletin/Interfax*, March 17, 2001.

[40] "Мэр Москвы выступает против приватизации энергетических объектов," *Daily News Bulletin/Interfax*, March 17, 2001, and "Чубайса рвет на родину ГОЭЛРО," *Московская правда*, October 9, 2002.

[41] Виталий Цепляев, "Чубайс–Лужков – боевая ничья," *Аргументы и факты*, October 16, 2002.

[42] Stephanie Baker-Said, "Chubais' Shocking New Job," *Moscow Times*, June 30, 1998.

[43] Remezov was replaced in July 2001; Рыбалченко, "Электроэнергия 1991–2000," *Коммерсантъ*, November 13, 2001.

to blackmail Chubais. He ordered a "raid" on Mosenergo, a tax audit ordered by the city administration, supposedly to investigate unpaid taxes and prove UES's mismanagement of Mosenergo.[44] Luzhkov repeatedly tried to increase the city's stake in the Energo through an additional share issue, something that could only work with the support of Remezov.[45] Even as he failed to increase the city's stake, Luzhkov insisted on a say in the new ownership of Mosenergo. He was well known for his role in "picking winners" during the privatizations of high-profile assets in his city, as a way to reward loyalty to his vision of post-Soviet change.[46]

Luzhkov and Chubais continued to be political foes for most of the 1990s, partly because their views on liberalization differed, but also because each headed a political party and both were potential successors of Yeltsin. Luzhkov led the Fatherland–All-Russia Party, which controlled sixty-seven Duma seats when electricity reforms were discussed in the late 1990s. These Duma seats, together with support from a number of other allies, allowed him to block key legislation necessary to restructure of the sector.[47] Luzhkov used power blackouts as occasions for vitriolic attacks on Chubais, blaming him for accidents, bad leadership, UES's reaping of "excess profits" in the sector, and, once again, selling off the country's most valuable assets. ("Again" because Chubais had been architect of the voucher privatization, and was much reviled by ordinary Russians for selling Soviet-era factories on the cheap).[48] Luzhkov mobilized support in the Duma and in street protests to prevent passage of Chubais's legislation. Although the city administration never ended up with more than a small share of the Energo (3 percent), while UES owned a majority (51 percent by 2007), the mayor's ability to control Mosenergo was always greater than Moscow's formal ownership suggested.

---

[44] "Хроника энергетического конфликта," *Коммерсантъ*, September 25, 2002. "Raids" in the Russian context refer to audits of various kinds, sometimes achieved by force; they were a tool often used in Russia's hostile takeover battles; see Volkov, "Standard Oil and Yukos in the Context of Early Capitalism in the United States and Russia."

[45] The city was trying to increase its stake to 5% through an additional shares issue. This was a plan that the city's municipal property department came up with, it was never approved by UES.

[46] Hoffman, *The Oligarchs*. See also Michael Brie, "The Moscow Political Regime: The Emergence of a New Urban Political Machine," in *The Politics of Local Government in Russia*, ed. Alfred B. Evans and Vladimir Gel'man (Lanham, MD: Rowman & Littlefield, 2004), 203–234.

[47] Виталий Цепляев, "Чубайс–Лужков – боевая ничья," *Аргументы и факты*, October 16, 2002; Alla Startseva, "Deputies Vote to Break Up Power Grid," *Moscow Times*, October 10, 2002; and Mellow, "Is This a Way to Create Capitalism?"

[48] "Mosenergo government audit ends," *RFE/RL Business Watch*, August 16, 2001. Note that the term "excess profits" echoes Soviet-era language.

By 2001, however, Luzhkov's ability to influence reforms was increasingly limited. When the Duma became dominated by Putin's United Russia in 2003, Luzhkov ultimately gave up his opposition to electricity privatization. Although he held out until the last minute, resenting and agitating against the legislation that paved the way for liberalization, he finally relented. Officially, he was promised "greater control over the distribution of ... companies that will be created from Mosenergo's current assets," and other sources noted that this promise included a larger stake in the network companies that were to be spun off from Mosenergo. Chubais is said to have had to use his whole arsenal of carrots and sticks (gingerbread and horsewhips, in Russian), although it is ultimately unclear what brought the two old foes together.[49]

Irkutskenergo under Regional Control

Irkutskenergo was one of the country's four important Energos that were "privatized" to the regional administration and were therefore independent of UES and the federal government. The first post-Soviet governor of Irkutsk oblast', Yuri Nozhikov, explained that he pursued this strategy to protect the region from the detrimental effect of Moscow's policies. The legality of the ownership transfer to the regional government was contested for most of the 1990s. The struggle over Irkutskenergo's assets made national headlines, mostly because Irkutskenergo owns a few of the country's most valuable power plants – the Bratsk, Ust'-Ilimsk, and Irkutsk hydroelectric power plants.

The value of Irkutskenergo was particularly obvious to two groups: electricity sector insiders, the *energetiki*, and regional enterprises reliant on cheap electricity – most of all the *aliuminshchiki*, the aluminum industries. Yuri Nozhikov belonged to the former group: he was a high-profile member of the *energetiki*. Before becoming governor of Irkutsk, Nozhikov was a high-ranking official at the Bratsk hydroelectric station, one of the world's largest power plants.[50] He had close personal connections to the *energetiki* and was thoroughly familiar with the electricity sector's importance to the regional economy. Nozhikov proved to be

[49] Татьяна Егорова и Дмитрий Симаков, "Пакт Лужкова–Чубайса," *Ведомости*, March 27, 2003; Alla Startseva, "Deputies Vote to Break Up Power Grid," *Moscow Times*, October 10, 2002.

[50] See Nozhikov's biography for his experience at Bratskgesstroi (the construction of the Bratsk hydroelectric plant) and in the electricity sector spanning over thirty-two years; Ножиков, *Я Это Видел, или Жизнь Российского Губернатора*, 110, 117. His connection with the *energetiki* was also mentioned in interview #49 with an academic, Irkutsk, 20071114, and in interview #60 with energy company executive, Irkutsk, 20071203.

one of the most independent governors of the early Yeltsin years, and a
leader of governors opposed to federal reforms of the electricity sector.[51]
A strong regional support base and economy helped Nozhikov defy presidential decrees. Irkutsk was an electricity surplus region, as well as being
a relatively rich oblast' and a net contributor to the national budget.
Residents of Irkutsk tended to stress that Nozhikov was a free spirit and
a critical thinker, willing and able to resist federal directives detrimental
to the region's wellbeing.

When Yeltsin sought the allegiance of regional elites in the fight against
communist hard-liners, he promised them "as much sovereignty as they
can digest."[52] Taking Yeltsin by his word, Nozhikov claimed ownership
of Irkutskenergo for the regional administration.[53] To avoid spontaneous
privatizations, the regional administration acted swiftly, "taking on the
responsibility," in the words of one regional observer, to determine who
will become the new owners.[54] The key stake was a 40 percent share of
Irkutskenergo – which was claimed by both the regional administration's
and the federal government's property committees.[55] Nozhikov wanted
to "defend our electricity"[56] by asserting regional control over hydroelectric resources.[57] His rationale was simple: "The economy of our region
relies on it," and "if our electricity belongs to us, it will be cheap – goods
and services will be cheap, utility bills [*kvartplata*] will be cheap, etc. If
our electricity will not be ours – everything will become more expensive,
and profits will be diminished."[58] Finally, as Irkutskenergo was one of the

[51] In "Губернаторы показали силу," *Восточно-Сибирская правда*, January 20, 1994. See
also Nozhikov's biography, *Я это видел*, 179. Nozhikov refused to support Yeltsin in
this regard, and almost lost Yeltsin's support, because he vehemently disagreed with the
unequal treatment of the different subjects of the federation. Nozhikov's ability to defy
federal-level directives was mentioned in several interviews, for example, interview #48
with academic, Irkutsk, 20071113.

[52] Nozhikov explicitly remembers this carte blanche; Ножиков, *Я Это Видел*, 138.

[53] See Nozhikov, *Я это видел*, 173. Also in interview #13 with academic, St. Petersburg,
20061023; interview #49 with an academic, Irkutsk, 20071114; interview #53 with
employee of electricity company, Irkutsk, 20071119.

[54] "Какие монстры нам нужны," *Восточно-Сибирская правда*, July 8, 1992.

[55] М. А. Уколова, "Передел собственности: борьба за Иркутскэнерго," in *Актуальные
вопросы государственного регулирования регионального развития*, Baikal State
University of Economics and Law, Irkutsk, 2002. Also discussed in Burganskij and
Elinevskaya, *Hydro Power*.

[56] Ножиков, *Я Это Видел*, 173.

[57] Interview #49 with an academic, Irkutsk, 20071114.

[58] "Мы отстояли нашу энергетику. На ней держится все хозяйство области, она – основа всей
экономики. Будет своя, дешевая энергия – будут дешевые товары и услуги, квартплата и

biggest taxpayers in the region, the regional government reasoned that it would have an easier time collecting taxes and securing them for the regional administration's coffers if it controlled a significant stake in the company.[59]

When the Kremlin's reformers tried to reassert the central government's control over the power sector with Decree No. 922, the Irkutsk governor resisted.[60] Nozhikov not only refused to give back the region's share in Irkutskenergo; he also mobilized a coalition of Siberian governors to produce an alternative sector reform plan, putting regional administrations in charge of their Energos.[61] The Siberian governors rejected Decree No. 922 as harmful to regional economic well-being, and as unconstitutional.[62]

Irkutskenergo became the center of a decade-long ownership battle, as the region refused to cede ownership to UES. Several rounds of federal and regional court cases did not bring clarity.[63] The case was brought to Russia's constitutional court by the Irkutsk regional parliament.[64] After extended deliberation and political maneuvering, the court ruled very ambiguously that both the regional and the central government should

---

так далее. Не будет своей – все будет дороже, и доходы тоже уйдут на сторону." Ножиков, *Я Это Видел*, 173.

[59] "Энергетическая схватка продолжается," *Восточно-Сибирская правда*, January 13, 1993. The article mentions that the ownership struggle around Irkutskenergo continues, precisely because it is one of the biggest taxpayers of the region.

[60] Irkutsk oblast's opposition to the federal government's regulation of the electricity sector is well documented in the regional newspapers. One of the earliest references is the following article – "Республиканцы поддержали Ножикова," *Восточно-Сибирская правда*, September 9, 1992.

[61] "Выкручивание рук энергетикам Приангарья продолжается," *Восточно-Сибирская правда*, November 19, 1992. Also discussed in interview #49 with an academic, Irkutsk, 20071114. The other Siberian governors were Kress of Tomsk, Tuleev of Kemerovo, and the governor of Krasnoiarskii Krai, see also Chapters 2 and 6.

[62] See "Республиканцы поддержали Ножикова," *Восточно-Сибирская правда*, September 9, 1992; "Решение: Об обращении в конституционный суд Российской Федерации," *Восточно-Сибирская правда*, November 26, 1992; "Иркутская делегация встретилась с Гайдаром," *Восточно-Сибирская правда*, September 30, 1992, for an account of a high-level delegation from Irkutsk that traveled to Moscow to try to prevent the passing of the decree or to negotiate an exception for the oblast' during the fall of 1992.

[63] For an account of the conflict by one of the insiders, general director of Irkutskenergo in the late 1990s, Victor Borovskii, see *Эксперт*, No. 14, April 13, 1998, 34. Also, interview #50 with businessman, Irkutsk, 20071115. Legal uncertainty was also mentioned in interview #56 with journalist, Irkutsk, 20071120, and interview #60 with energy company executive, Irkutsk, 20071203.

[64] "Решение: Об обращении в Конституционный суд Российской Федерации," *Восточно-Сибирская правда*, November 26, 1992.

"have a say" in the future of Irkutskenergo. For several years, governor
Nozhikov, UES, and Yeltsin continued their debate.[65] UES and the federal government tried to resolve the issue several times, but the tariffs
that regional consumers were to pay remained a sticking point.[66] While
the legal status of Irkutskenergo was disputed, the regional government
effectively controlled the Energo; close personal relationships persisted
between the regional administration and Irkutskenergo.[67] Regional *energetiki*, such as Victor Borovskii, sat on the board of Irkutskenergo while
serving as elected chairman of the Irkutsk oblast' legislature.[68] It was not
until 2001 that a federal court decision restituted control to the federal
government.[69] Even after this, however, Irkutskenergo remained legally
independent of UES, and was therefore not bound by the corporate
restructuring that the Energo's owned by UES followed.

In Khakassiia, another Siberian region with significant electricity production, the regional governor also tried to prevent Saiano-Shushenskaia
Hydroelectric Power Plant (*SShGES*, Russia's largest power plant)
from passing into federal ownership in the mid-1990s. The governor of
Khakassiia was less successful than his counterpart in Irkutsk: the hydro-
damn continued to be controlled by UES, although Khakassiia managed
to negotiate a moratorium on price increases.[70] In 2003, Khakassiia's
regional administration launched a lawsuit to contest UES ownership of
SShGES, claiming that the region should own a larger stake. UES threatened to register *SShGES* in neighboring Krasnoiarsk, which would have
had catastrophic effects on Khakassiia's budget. By 2003, the center-
region power balance had shifted in favor of the center: the case went
nowhere, *SShGES* was incorporated into the UES reform plan and is now
the federal government's largest hydroelectric power plant.

[65] The region's electricity assets were included in the bilateral agreements between the oblast'
authorities and the Yeltsin government; see chapter 2 in М. Н. Губогло, *Федерализм
Власти и Власть Федерализма*, Москва: ИнтелТех, 1997.
[66] "Пять вариантов кабалы," *Восточно-Сибирская правда,* January 19, 1993.
[67] For the ties between regional governments and the *energetiki*, see also Chapter 6.
[68] His title was *председатель законодательного собрания* (chair of the legislative committee). See М. А. Уколова, "Передел собственности: борьба за Иркутскэнерго," in
Актуальные вопросы государственного регулирования регионального развития, Baikal
State University of Economics and Law, Irkutsk, 2002.
[69] Уколова, "Передел собственности." The final court decision was taken on February 5,
2001. See also "Борьба за Иркутскэнерго вступила в завершающую стадию," *Новая
газета*, September 30, 2001.
[70] In fact, Saiano-Shushenskaia Hydroelectric Power Plant is Siberia's only large power
plant in which UES (and now Hydro-OGK) and the federal government own a large
majority.

In Krasnoiarsk, the region's largest power plant, and the country's second largest hydroelectric power plant, Krasnoiarsk Hydroelectric Plant (KHP), was privatized to the regionally controlled aluminum plant in the 1990s and later transferred to Rusal. UES hence lost control of KHP but kept control of Krasnoiarskenergo.[71] In the early 1990s, the Krasnoiarsk regional government also tried to transfer a second major hydroelectric plant, Boguchansk.[72] This never happened. Instead, the federal government took control of Boguchansk with the help of Rusal, as we will see in the later discussion.

Dal'energo and Regional Control
In the 1990s, Dal'energo was not likely to be a very profitable company. At the epicenter of the Far Eastern energy crisis, its production costs were astronomical because of antiquated capital stock and because it relied on either burning local low-caloric coal or transporting better coal from Siberia.[73] Yet, like all the Energos, it was a regional monopoly that provided a basic infrastructure service. Regional control, though not ownership, became a source of contention in the conflict between the regions' notoriously defiant governor, Evgeny Nazdratenko, and federal reformers, in particular Boris Nemtsov, Sergey Kirienko, and Anatoly Chubais.[74] While the regional government did not formally own a stake in Dal'energo, Nazdratenko managed to control the company through the regional energy commission and by installing his loyalists as directors of Dal'energo and important regional power plants, much as Luzhkov had with Mosenergo.[75] In another echo of the battles between Chubais and Luzhkov, the Far Eastern

---

[71] "РАО ЕЭС восстановила контроль над Красноярской ГЭС," *Коммерсантъ*, April 4, 1998.

[72] "Берем чужое – отдаем свое," *Красноярский рабочий*, May 22, 1992.

[73] "Дальэнерго меняет партнеров?" *Утро России*, January 14, 1997. Also interview #31 with journalist covering electricity sector, Vladivostok, 20070915.

[74] The conflict between Nazdratenko and Chubais was mentioned in several interviews, for example, in interview #39 with electrical engineer/electricity sector expert, Vladivostok, 20071004, and interview #31 with journalist covering electricity sector, Vladivostok, 20070915. An aspect of the conflict that was often mentioned is that Nazdratenko's regional opponents sided with the young reformers in Moscow and Chubais. See, for example, "Губернатор намерен стоять до конца," and "Оставьте губернатора в покое," both articles in *Утро России*, June 17, 1997. Also "Приморский кризис: возможные варианты," *Утро России*, June 18, 1997.

[75] Nazdratenko's appointments were particularly controversial after 1999, when Chubais actively tried to install a new management team. Nazdratenko managed to install his loyalists – Yuri Likhoida to lead Dal'energo, and Yuri Basharov at Lutek. Lutek is comprised of Primorskii GRES and Luchegorsk coal mine. The Primorskii GRES is Primorskii

electricity sector was a key site of conflict between regional heavyweights and Moscow reformers. The enmity between Nazdratenko and the young reformers started in the early 1990s, when the governor consolidated his power by building a regional alliance of factory owners who defied federal regulations in all kinds of ways – from fishing quotas to restrictions on the import of used cars from Japan.[76]

Chubais and Nazdratenko differed fundamentally on the future of the sector – Nazdratenko was "against markets and for 100% state ownership."[77] The region's energy crisis turned out to be a focal point of the conflict between Nazdratenko and the liberal reformers, who sought a reason to remove him from office. Unwilling to lose influence over the sector, Nazdratenko blamed the energy crisis on liberal reformers, making them responsible for the skyrocketing cost of living in the Far East, for the nonpayment crisis, and for the "darkness" brought about by electricity outages.[78] Most regional observers however, linked the resistance to reform (and the crisis) to the threat this presented for regional influence: "If the current way of managing the sector is abolished, the government will lose its ability to influence it."[79]

Nazdratenko's grip was so tight that Nemtsov and Chubais decided that removing the governor from office was necessary to solve the energy crisis.[80] Despite concerted efforts, it took years to remove the governor. He finally resigned in early 2001, forced out by his opponents in Moscow.[81] Soon thereafter, the management of Dal'energo was completely changed: Chubais put in place an "anti-crisis team," a group of outside managers

---

Krai's most valuable power plant, and was one of the large power plants transferred to federal ownership according to Decree No. 922. The appointment of Likhoida against the will of Chubais was an explicit provocation, since Chubais was legally entitled to appoint Energo directors; see "Чубайс сдал Приморье," *Коммерсантъ*, August 8, 2000, and "Чубайс сменил начальников Приморья," *Известия*, August 9, 2000.

[76] Bradshaw and Kirkow, "The Energy Crisis in the Russian Far East"; and Peter Kirkow, "Regional Warlordism in Russia: The Case of Primorskii Krai," *Europe-Asia Studies* 47, no. 6 (1995): 923–947.

[77] Interview #39 with electrical engineer/electricity sector expert, Vladivostok, 20071004.

[78] A detailed statement of the regional government's position was published by the press service of the regional administration in "О ситуации в топливно-энергетическом комплексе Приморья," *Утро России*, August 19, 1997; an interesting perspective is an open letter by the governor himself on the cover or *Утро России*, October 11, 1997. Chubais blamed Nazdratenko in no uncertain terms for the electricity crisis; "Чубайс проиграл Приморье," *Коммерсантъ*, February 11, 2000.

[79] "...нарушится управляемость отраслью, уменьшится возможность государственного влияния на нее." Op-ed by Вероника Белоусова, *Утро России*, January 14, 1997.

[80] "Приморский кризис: возможные варианты," *Утро России*, June 18, 1997.

[81] Interview #31 with journalist covering electricity sector, Vladivostok, 20070915.

determined to reform the Far Eastern Energo (see also Chapter 6).[82] While Primorskii Krai and the open defiance of Nazdratenko were certainly particularly provocative, other Far Eastern governors acted similarly.[83]

Privatization, Centralization, and the Consolidation of Control

The histories of Mosenergo, Irkutskenergo, and Dal'energo are remarkably similar in the rise and decline of regional influence over the course of the first post-Soviet decade. While regional governors had considerable leverage over the electricity sector in the 1990s, Putin's recentralization of the political system deprived them of autonomy in the setting of economic policy, including their ability to control assets in the electricity sector. This recentralization paved the way for the liberal reforms: regional Energos were unbundled and power plants were privatized. Privatization, paradoxically, meant that electricity assets accumulated in the hands of a small number of new private owners, far fewer than when regional governors held sway in the 1990s. This mirrors a larger trend in Russia's political economy: political centralization was paralleled by a consolidation of economic assets into the hands of ever smaller numbers of oligarchs.

Privatization Under the 5+5 Plan
The last important ownership transfer during the period under discussion here took place in the years between 2004 and 2008. It was initiated after the "5+5" plan was approved in 2003. The ownership changes laid out in "5+5" were based on Chubais's vision of a competitive electricity generation market. A key step was the reduction of the role of the state in the competitive segment of the sector, most importantly in power generation. Chubais set the bar high, letting everybody know that "the aim is to have zero state ownership in the generation sector."[84] This required unbundling vertically integrated Energos, no small feat as subsequent chapters will show. Power plants we separated from grid and network assets beginning in 2004, followed by the creation of a host of new companies in the

---

[82] "Чубайс остается," *Известия*, February 2, 2001. The new team was rather dramatically called *антикризисный штаб* (anti-crisis headquarters); interview #33 with journalist covering electricity sector, Vladivostok, 20070921.

[83] Khabarovsk governor Ishaev was also a long-standing proponent of regional control; interview #39 with electrical engineer/electricity sector expert, Vladivostok, 20071004, and interview #43 with electricity sector economist, Khabarovsk, 20071010.

[84] Remark by Chubais at a conference "Энергетика: тормоз или локомотив развития экономики?" Moscow, February 13, 2007.

generation, transmission, distribution, and retail segments of the sector. In the power generation subsector, the following companies were created: seven OGKs (*Оптовая генерирующая компания*, OGKs/*ОГК*, including Hydro-OGK) and fourteen TGKs (*Территориальные генерирующие компании*, TGKs/*ТГК*).[85] After 2004, these power companies traded shares on the RTS (Russian Trading System) and MICEX (Moscow Interbank Currency Exchange). Between 2005 and 2007, larger stakes were sold in a series of tenders to reduce the state's ownership, with the first tenders of OGKs stakes taking place in 2007.

This final round of asset redistribution was not without opposition. During the years leading up to the state's divestiture of generation assets, minority and foreign shareholders feared that oligarchs would receive the most valuable assets without having to pay market prices. Yeltsin-era oligarchs had eyed electricity assets for years. According to one source, Chubais was approached in the late 1990s, when he was privatization minister, with a plan to carve up UES among a group of high-profile oligarchs. Chubais insisted that electricity assets be sold to the highest bidder. Perhaps he explicitly intended to repudiate the reputation he had acquired for giving away assets in rigged auctions during the "loans for shares" deals in the mid-1990s.[86] Tenders for controlling stakes of the most valuable assets – the OGKs – did indeed fetch what were considered competitive prices; in other words, electricity companies were auctioned off at or above their share prices. Important for the sector's future, these tenders contained commitments by new owners to make substantial investments in their newly acquired power companies.[87]

The "5+5" plan also laid out that the government was to regain control over other elements of the electricity sector, some of which it had lost during ownership battles in the 1990s. These included first and foremost the noncompetitive segments of the sector, the high-voltage networks. The government considered ownership of networks a priority, because networks are natural monopolies and guaranteeing equal access

---

[85] Note that Russian electricity insiders call this process "privatization" even when new owners were not only private companies; see, for example, UES Press Release, June 30, 2008, or in the summary of reform up to the summer of 2008 by Nadia Popova, *Moscow Times*, July 1, 2008.

[86] Hoffman tells the story how two rival oligarchs, Potanin and Smolensky, wanted to divide up the telecoms and electricity sector between themselves. Hoffman, *The Oligarchs*.

[87] After the 2008 economic crisis, these companies were accused of not living up to the investment plans they committed to; see Conclusion for a discussion.

is generally thought of as a prerequisite for competition in the generation and retail segment.[88] The Federal Grid Company (FGC) was created in 2002. By law, the government was to control at least 75 percent of FGC, although initially it fell well short of this mark. Between 2003 and 2008, the government regained control of networks through assets swaps with owners that had acquired them during the 1990s. These negotiations were fraught and complicated by the fact that the valuation of assets not publicly traded was often highly arbitrary.[89] But by 2007, the government owned 78 percent of the FGC. The federal government also wanted to regain and consolidate its control of hydroelectric dams; it created the company Hydro-OGK in 2004 for this purpose. Finally, the federal government wanted to secure its monopoly over foreign sales of electricity; the company Inter-RAO was to be tasked with foreign sales and holdings (its role will be discussed later in this chapter).[90]

Electricity's Integration into Oligarchic Conglomerates

Russia's oligarchs were very interested in choice assets of the electricity sector. While the presidential decrees 922 and 923 reserved majority stakes in most Energos for the federal government in the early 1990s, minority shares were sold and resold from the earliest days of the post-Soviet period. Oligarchs and their conglomerates gradually consolidated their control over power provision. But oligarchs were more than just rent-seeking individuals; oligarchic conglomerates had very different interests vis-à-vis the electricity sector because they controlled different types of production chains. Gazprom was interested primarily in acquiring electricity assets to reassemble an energy production chain, whereas Rusal targeted hydroelectric plants to power its electricity intensive factories. As the major counterparties to the developmental pacts introduced in previous chapters, these conglomerates emerged as the dominant owners of power plants.

---

[88] Interview #15 with electricity sector analyst at financial institution, Moscow, 20061027. This insider also pointed out that transmission is said to be a source of easy revenues as a reason why the government wanted to control transmission.

[89] These deals were negotiated behind closed doors and there was not much publicly available information about their terms, according to interviewee #15, electricity sector analyst at financial institution, Moscow, 20061027.

[90] Concretely, this means that the federal government is in charge of negotiating with foreign governments about the operation and construction of cross-border transmission grids, for example, the high-voltage line planned in the Far East, from Blagoveshensk to China; interview #33 with journalist covering electricity sector, Vladivostok, 20070921.

In the 1990s oligarchs cooperated with regional governors to gain ownership rights, while under Putin they negotiated with the federal government and UES. Changes in the electricity sector and the political arena were mutually reinforcing: as regional governors lost their hold on electricity companies and their loyalists were expelled from the Energos' boards of directors, vertically integrated conglomerates were able to further consolidate their holdings. The means by which oligarchs gained control and the assets that were available also changed over the years. Conglomerates sometimes acquired Energo shares via rigged auctions in which regionally influential oligarchs were able to "convince" regional authorities to sell stakes to loyalists.[91] But the oligarchs also had the requisite cash to simply buy assets. The most common way in which oligarchs initially consolidated their holdings of electricity assets was by buying shares that were publicly traded. Holders of privatization vouchers could bid for shares of Energos and then sell them on to various intermediaries. The voucher privatization of 1993–1994 is a story of shattered hopes: citizens were promised valuable stakes in the country's factories and farms, which on the whole rarely materialized.[92] As this is a story that is extensively documented elsewhere, I will keep the discussion of these events short and focused on electricity assets.[93]

An important outcome of voucher privatization is that it actually facilitated the concentration of ownership rather than its dispersal. Investment funds emerged as a new type of business in Russia's young post-Soviet economy. These funds, the *ЧИФ (Чековый инвестиционный фонд)*, were weakly regulated financial intermediaries, specifically created for the management of privatization vouchers, which mushroomed in the mid-1990s as people started selling and reselling privatization vouchers.[94] These funds used information unavailable to most Russian citizens to target and buy vouchers from citizens for companies of value. Funds sent emissaries all over Russia to buy vouchers from local residents

[91] Interview #54 with businessman, Irkutsk, 20071120.

[92] See, for example, "Энергия – народу," *Восточно-Сибирская правда*, January 5, 1994. This article describes how people opted to buy vouchers of Irktuskenergo, after being encouraged by the regional administration to do so. The stated rationale of the regional administration was to try to give access to Energo vouchers to poor regional residents (бюджетники и малоимущие), and not let them pass into the hands of "powerful investors from Moscow" (крупные московские инвесторы). Over the years, the former lost ownership to the latter.

[93] See, for example, Hoffman, *The Oligarchs*; Allina-Pisano, *The Post-Soviet Potemkin Village*; and Barnes, *Owning Russia*.

[94] Hoffman, *The Oligarchs*.

in exchange for cash, or "live money" as it was called in Russia in the 1990s, and sell them on to larger investment funds based in Moscow.[95] A young entrepreneur, turned fund manager, explained to me why Energo shares were a particularly good business. Cash was scarce everywhere in Russia and particularly outside of Moscow, especially during the years of the nonpayment and barter crisis. "Live-money" was worth much more to people than the vouchers that promised an elusive future profit. As one commentator noted, "[Energo] vouchers fell into the hands of speculators (*спекулянты*)" – a word that for a long time implied illegitimate economic activity in Russia and implies a contrast with legitimate owners.[96] The small funds that acquired electricity sector vouchers from regional residents could always find a willing buyer for them in regional oligarchs or in Moscow.[97] Certain Energo shares in particular were highly sought after by both Russian and foreign investors. In this way, "regional oligarchs acquired blocking stakes [in Energos]."[98]

Oligarchs further increased their shares in Energos during the heyday of the period of hostile takeovers, from about 1998 to 2002. Hostile takeovers in Russia entailed the use of administrative or coercive means by the buyer to force a change of management, which often ultimately resulted in a change of ownership.[99] Sometimes, these literally involved "guys with guns," either private security firms or the special armed forces sent by tax authorities, who helped one group of managers displace another. When formal ownership of Energos was contested, what mattered most was placing loyalists on the company's board (*совет директоров*).[100] Chubais

---

[95] Interview #50 with businessman, Irkutsk, 20071115.

[96] Interview #39 with electrical engineer/electricity sector expert, Vladivostok, 20071004.

[97] Initially, only Mosenergo and Irkutskenergo shares were publicly traded. By the early 2000s, however, as investors started to believe that Chubais would pull through his reforms, other Energo shares were sought after by Moscow's brokerages. Between 2003 and 2007, the key was knowledge and information about the new generation companies that were created on the basis of the old Energos, some bound to be more valuable than others. I interviewed two of these investment fund entrepreneurs in Irkutsk and Vladivostok: interview #50 with businessman, Irkutsk, 20071115 and #47 with businessman, Vladivostok, 20071017.

[98] Interview #7 with electricity sector analyst at financial institution, Moscow, 20061005.

[99] See Vadim Volkov, "Hostile Enterprise Takeovers: Russia's Economy in 1998–2002," *Review of Central and East European Law* 29, no. 4 (2004): 527–548. In the electricity sector, a change in the board of directors often resulted in a change of ownership in the following way: the new management could issue new shares that were then sold to the owner that controlled management, thereby increasing its stake.

[100] Even at UES itself there were often changes in the composition of the board; interview #11 with electricity sector expert, Moscow 20061018.

and competing oligarchs all tried to place loyalists on the Energo boards. Where UES had uncontested control of an Energo, Chubais could staff the board of directors to his liking.[101] In regions where UES did not have controlling stakes or where minority shareholders boycotted the restructuring of the Energos, replacing boards of directors was accomplished in a number of "creative" or extralegal ways. Novosibirskenergo, for example, was one of the four independent Energos, as UES owned only a 14 percent stake. This was partly due to an earlier share issue orchestrated by a rebellious board of directors, which reduced the UES's stake. UES's efforts to change Novosibirskenergo's management were met with fierce resistance and took years to accomplish.[102]

During the 2005–2008 round of privatizations, the conglomerates targeted select electricity assets that filled missing links in their production chains.[103] Gazprom's chairman Alexey Miller, for example, noted in 2006, "Gazprom [is making] good progress, developing into a global, vertically integrated energy company."[104] The ability of conglomerates to make such purchases depended on capital and on their connections with the federal government. Export-oriented conglomerates – which included Gazprom and Rusal – had the requisite means to acquire companies to consolidate their vertical production chains. After about 2003, influence in Moscow mattered most to determine who became the new owners in the privatization of generation companies. Powerful and well-connected Russian conglomerates used political influence to gain ownership, and foreign competitors gained only limited access.

The outcome of this battle was a compromise. Chubais was able to restructure the electricity sector and abolish vertically integrated regional monopolies. New owners of power plants agreed to extensive

---

[101] See Chapter 6 for details on the changing management of Energos.

[102] "Запрет не подействовал," *Ведомости*, April 26, 2001; "РАО ЕЭС готовит силовые акции в Новосибирске," *Коммерсантъ*, May 11, 2001; "Новосибирскэнерго без боя не сдается," *Коммерсантъ*, May 16, 2001. Finally, "РАО ЕЭС России решило конфликт в Новосибирскэнерго," *Известия*, July 13, 2001. It is rumored that UES and Novosibirskenergo came to be under the same patronage roof – the Yeltsin "family." As a result, several key managers of Novosibirskenergo moved to the highest position at UES, including the board of directors.

[103] Interview #9 with electricity sector analyst at financial institution, Moscow, 20061008. Vadim Volkov shows that "oligarchs undertook vertical integration to ensure that their core enterprises remained stable and to prevent takeovers by competitors"; see Volkov, "Hostile Enterprise Takeovers," 254.

[104] "Energy for the Planet," statement by Alexey Miller, chief executive of Gazprom, at the XXIII World Gas Conference, Amsterdam, June 6, 2006; available at http://www.gazprom.ru/eng/articles/article19731.shtml

infrastructural modernization plans and capital upgrades. The sale of the government's stake in the OGKs and TGKs was a clear victory for the liberal reformers. One insider noted that from a corporate finance perspective, these asset sales in OKGs were not necessarily called for: "Russian electricity companies are still under-leveraged," compared with utilities elsewhere. She pointed out that "[the new electricity companies] could have increased the amount of debt, they do not necessarily need to sell equity ... everybody knows that equity sales are not necessarily called for." These large equity stakes were sold for political reasons, to "dilute the government's stake and decrease the role of the government."[105] But the reform process also allocated electricity assets to the "loyal oligarchs" and could not ward off their influence on the liberals' vision. Chubais had initially planned to create "thousands" of new private electricity companies, modeled on the U.S. electricity market.[106] The creation of a mere twenty-one new private generation companies (or twenty-two including Inter-RAO) was a compromise that appeased factions of the government reluctant to yield control of a strategic sector. And, as introduced at the outset, the new de-territorialized holding companies, the OGKs, represented a relative centralization of decision making.

New Owners Differ across Regions

The assets of Mosenergo, Irkutskenergo, and Dal'energo changed hands in a similar pattern: over the years each gradually became incorporated into a vertically integrated production chain, and they consolidated the holdings of Russia's most powerful conglomerates. Many observers have pointed out that Russia's conglomerates consolidated control over vertically integrated production chains as a way to reduce uncertainty and vulnerability to hostile takeovers.[107] These strategies included the assets in the electricity sector. As noted in 2002, "in many regional electricity companies, we observe an increase of the share of industrial enterprises as shareholders."[108] In the next section I outline how the assets of

---

[105] Interview #23 with electricity sector expert, international financial institution, Moscow, 20070210. The sale was achieved through what were called initial public offerings. This was a misleading term, however, since OGKs and TGKs comprised the assets of the old Energos, which had long issued shares on the market, but it served to emphasize that OGKS and TGKS were *new* companies.

[106] Mellow, "Is This a Way to Create Capitalism?"

[107] See, for example, Volkov, "Hostile Enterprise Takeovers."

[108] "Кто правее, Есапос или Чубайс?" *Комсомольская правда*, November 13, 2002.

Mosenergo, Irkutskenergo and Dal'energo were integrated into different production chains.

Mosenergo's Integration into New a Vertically Integrated Energy Empire

Gazprom, the country's largest and most powerful semi-statal energy conglomerate, increased its control of Mosenergo steadily over the two post-Soviet decades. During the 1990s, Mosenergo, like most other European Energos, ran up a mounting burden of debt vis-à-vis Gazprom, its main fuel provider.[109] Rem Viakhirev, Gazprom's first director, was keen to settle Energos debts by increasing Gazprom's stake in UES. Debt-for-equity swaps were common practice in Russia's early transition years. By the late 1990s, Gazprom had secured a 25 percent stake Mosenergo and a 5 percent stake in UES, mainly through these kinds of transactions. By 2003, Gazprom's stake in Mosenergo had increased to 30 percent.[110] This set the stage for ownership transfers that followed the restructuring of the Energo under the "5+5" Plan. Mosenergo's power plants were unbundled and "re-bundled" into the company TGK-3 (which stands for Territorial Generation Company No. 3). During the 2007–2008 round of privatization, Gazprom was able to increase its stake in TGK-3 to 75 percent.[111] Gazprom apparently had privileged access, or "first dibs," on the most valuable electricity assets in European Russia. Although Chubais openly complained that Gazprom was not the new private actor he had been hoping for,[112] he had little choice but to compromise, or in his words, to be a "pragmatist." He reasoned as follows:

I relate to this issue as a pragmatist. Here we have Mosenergo that relies on gas for 97% of its fuel supplies, and that needs private investment. It is entirely obvious that from a technical, as well as from a political standpoint, Gazprom, of course, is one of the most natural solutions [to Mosenergo's problems]. Despite all my liberalism, I would consider the idea of giving a majority stake in Mosenergo to

---

[109] This is a recurring theme of the relationship between the Energos and Gazprom; see, for example, "Автономное плавание," *Известия*, April 7, 2000.

[110] Stern, *The Future of Russian Gas and Gazprom*, 186.

[111] "Gazprom continues electricity sector expansion," *RFERL Newsline*, September 12, 2007.

[112] Chubais has made several remarks to this effect, for example, at a press conference outlining the investment program in electricity attended by the author; Simon Shuster, "Chubais Says UES Requires $118bln," *The Moscow Times*, February 14, 2007.

a foreign strategic investor with great care. And at this point, the state does not want to even consider this. Hence Gazprom.[113]

How representative is Mosenergo's history of the Energos in European Russia? It is representative in that Gazprom gained ownership of European Russia's most profitable electricity assets. In 2008, Gazprom owned at least 30 percent of European Russia's electricity assets (see Table 4.2), and the gas giant's role in the sector has only been strengthened further since then. After years of controversy, Gazprom formed a joint venture with KES, the second-largest owner of gas-fired power plants in European Russia, to increase its control of electricity in 2011. The KES-Gazprom venture was subject to an unresolved political battle for at least four years before that date. The deal was opposed by a coalition that included Anatoly Chubais, the liberal faction of the Putin administration, and the State Antimonopoly Agency. But once the merger was approved, it paved the way for an even more prominent role for Gazprom's merger with European Russia's power sector.[114]

Overall, European Russia ended up with a somewhat more diverse set of new owners than Siberia and the Far East did, largely because it is more a diverse and larger territory. Table 4.2 shows the major new owners of generation assets in European Russia in 2008, including the prominent position of Gazprom. There is more to ownership than these overall figures can show: Gazprom was able to gain ownership of the most profitable new companies – including Moscow and St. Petersburg's TGKs (TGK-3 and TGK-1) and some of European Russia's most valuable power plants bundled into the new OGKs. Gazprom owns large stakes in OGK-2 and OGK-6, with assets mostly located in European Russia.[115] This created a

---

[113] "Знаете, я отношусь к этому прагматически. Вот есть "Мосэнерго", у которого 97% в топливе – газ и которому нужны частные инвестиции. Совершенно очевидно, что и с технологической точки зрения, да и с политической, конечно, "Газпром" является наиболее естественным вариантом. При всем моем либерализме я бы с осторожностью отнесся к идее отдать контрольный пакет "Мосэнерго" иностранному стратегу. В то же время государству он тоже ни к чему. Вот отсюда и "Газпром"." Interview with Anatoly Chubais, "Анатолий Чубайс: Из полного нерынка в полный рынок," *Коммерсантъ*, December 5, 2006.

[114] For KES holding by Viktor Vekselberg, see Nadia Popova and Jacob Groholt-Pederson, "Gazprom Powers Up," *The Wall Street Journal*, July 8, 2011. This deal has been discussed since at least 2007, but was opposed by the more liberal faction of the Putin government as well as by the Russian Federal Anti-Monopoly Agency (FAS).

[115] This includes OGK-2 and OGK-6; "Gazprom continues electricity sector expansion," *RFERL Newsline*, September 12, 2007. The FAS also followed the expansion

TABLE 4.2. *New owners in European Russia's power sector (2008)*

European Russia	Installed Capacity* %	Type of New Owner
Gazprom	30	Energy conglomerate (Russian/government)
Hydro-OGK	13	Russian government's hydro-electric holdings
KES	12	Industrial conglomerate (Russian/private)
Enel	9	Energy conglomerate (foreign)
Inter-RAO	8	Electricity company (Russian/government)
E.On	6	Energy conglomerate (foreign)
Tatenergo	6	Energy company (regional government/private)
Noril'skii Nickel	5	Industrial conglomerate (Russian/private) Russian/private
Lukoil Others	3	Energy conglomerate (Russian/private)

* Installed capacity: 100% = all major power plants of European Russia, excluding nuclear power plants.
Sources: combined press reports on ownership changes in 2007 and 2008; UES publications for installed capacity; see Appendix 3 for details.

conflict between Gazprom and at least one foreign strategic investor that was interested in the same assets. In the case of St. Petersburg's generation company (formerly Lenenergo, now TGK-1), Gazprom found itself competing against a Finnish company, Fortum.[116] Fortum had acquired a sizable share of Lenenergo (25 percent by 2004) and had also played a role in the company's operations via a management contract. Fortum was interested in acquiring a majority stake in TGK-1 with the retreat of UES from Lenenergo in 2007. Given the Finnish company's involvement in St. Petersburg's power sector, it was widely expected that it would receive the sizable block of shares up for auction at the time. Yet, after a statement by the government that Moscow and St. Petersburg's generation companies were "strategically important" and that foreign companies were unsuitable owners for such assets (see also Chubais' statement

of Gazprom in the electricity sector; see "Gazprom controls 50% of Mosenergo," FAS Press Release, available at http://www.fas.gov.ru/english/news/n_12937.shtml
[116] The Finnish company Fortum had gained about a 40% stake in Lenenergo/TGK-1 during the decade leading up to reforms. This was accompanied by a broader agreement between Finland and Russia to cooperate on matters related to energy trade. The Fortum/Lenenergo partnership was often mentioned as a successful example of foreign ownership; interview #9, Moscow, 20061008, and interview #15, Moscow, 20061027, both with electricity sector analysts at financial institutions.

quoted earlier), Gazprom won the auction of the TGK-1 stake that was for sale.[117] Gazprom ended up with majority control of the most profitable electricity asset in European Russia.

Two important exceptions in European Russia's ownership pattern were Tatenergo and Bashkirenergo; they had been independent of UES during the 1990s, and by 2008 they remained outside of Gazprom's reach. They are located, respectively, in Tatarstan and Bashkortostan, two "ethnic Republics," subnational regions that managed to claim the most extensive formal autonomy in Russia's asymmetric federalism during the 1990s. UES tried to gain 51 percent of Bashkirenergo's assets following the presidential decree of the early 1990s, but received only 15 percent.[118] Along with other energy-related assets in these regions – oil resources and refineries – the regional governor of Tatarstan, Mintimer Shaimiev, and of Bashkortostan, Murtaza Rakhimov, gained control of their respective Energos.[119] They remained under the ownership of the respective regional governor's family, and neither UES, the federal government, nor Gazprom was able to regain ownership by 2008. However, because they were owned by the same owners as Tatneft' and Bashneft', the region's respective energy conglomerates, Tatenergo and Bashkirenergo also became part of vertically integrated energy-led conglomerates.

Irkutskenergo's Integration into Vertical Production Chains

As discussed earlier, Irkutskenergo was a highly coveted asset initially under regional control. The aluminum interests – the *aliuminshchiki* – entered the battle for Siberia's electricity assets in the second half of the 1990s. During the early and mid-1990s, the aluminum sector was undergoing its own consolidation struggles that came to be known as the aluminum wars. Pitting an illustrious cast of ruthless entrepreneurs against one another, this episode was highlighted by illegal corporate takeovers, contract killings, and a marriage of convenience to a member of Yeltsin's family.[120] Striking deals with regional leaders was an important tool in

---

[117] An 18% stake in TGK-1 was for sale in 2007. Through a number of assets purchases, Gazprom controlled TGK-1 via a 46% stake by 2011; see TGK-1s website, http://tgc1.ru/

[118] Burganskij and Elinevskaya, *Hydro Power*, 12.

[119] Interview #9 with electricity sector analyst at financial institution, Moscow, 20061008. See also Robert W. Orttung, "Business and Politics in the Russian Regions," *Problems of Post-Communism* 51, no. 2 (2004): 48–60.

[120] The history of KrAZ was at the epicenter of the aluminum wars. See Barnes, *Owning Russia*, 137. See also Kramer, "Deripaska's Climb from Farm to Empire," *Moscow Times*, August 22, 2006.

the repertoire of the *aliuminshchiki*, including deals in the electricity sector. Oleg Deripaska, the owner of Rusal, eventually emerged victorious, not only in becoming Siberia's undisputed aluminum czar but in building a global empire that includes bauxite mines in Guyana as well as practically all of the former Soviet Union's largest aluminum smelters from the Volga to Tajikistan.[121] Importantly, during these battles, "the *aliuminshchiki* realized that they cannot exist without cheap electricity," in the words of one observer.[122] In Siberia, Rusal owned aluminum smelters in Bratsk (BrAZ), Novokuznetsk (NkAZ), Saianogorsk (SaAZ), and Irkutsk (IrkAZ) – each of which was located close to a hydroelectric dam that Rusal sought to control.

Over the course of the 1990s, Rusal acquired around 40 percent of Irkutskenergo's capital. Rusal bought shares offered by regional and national investment funds, which had been gathered from holders of privatization vouchers.[123] Shifting and ambiguous boundaries between federal and regional authorities meant that control over the board of directors was what mattered most. In a classic case of a hostile takeover, the *aliuminshchiki* usurped control of board of directors and installed a loyal director by mobilizing regional courts and the assistance of the regional governor at the time, Boris Govorin, who needed the support of Rusal for an upcoming election.[124] This happened in 2001, when a minority shareholder of Irkutskenergo, representing aluminum interests, called for a shareholder meeting that conflicted with the meeting set up by the existing board of directors. Their intention to replace the board of directors, rewrite company statutes, and install a new director was an open secret. The simultaneous meetings were each supported by different district court

[121] Chubais is said to have helped Deripaska consolidate aluminum holdings at key moments. For example, Chubais helped Deripaska change the management of the Novokuznetsk Aluminium Plant (NkAZ): Kuzbassenergo brought bankruptcy proceedings against NkAZ, which resulted in a successful hostile takeover of NkAZ by Deripaska. These events were widely reported; see "Энергетический тупик," *Независимая газета*, June 27, 2000, and "На том же месте в тот же час: энергетики и алюминщики снова поругались," *Известия*, May 15, 2001. See also Volkov, "Standard Oil and Yukos in the Context of Early Capitalism in the United States and Russia," 235.
[122] Interview #60 with energy company executive, Irkutsk, 20071203.
[123] Interview #50 with businessman, Irkutsk, 20071115 and interview #60 with energy company executive, Irkutsk, 20071203.
[124] According to a regional observer, Govorin decided to support the *aluminshchiki* because he depended on their support for his relection – "на предстоящих летних выборах алюминщики могут оказать неоценимую поддержку, если он поддержит их...." Уколова, "Передел собственности: борьба за Иркутскэнерго," 148.

decisions. In the end, a standoff with armed guards of the regional court ensured that the first shareholder meeting – the one called by the existing Irkutskenergo leadership – did not take place.[125] By the end of the incident, the *aliuminshchiki* won the battle by installing both their own director – Kolmogorov, who had previously worked for a Rusal-owned hydroelectric power plant in Krasnoiarsk – and by placing their representatives in the majority of board positions.[126] When I did fieldwork in Irkutsk in 2007, local Irkutsk residents call Irkutskenergo Deripaska's *карманная компания*,[127] literally a "pocket company" as Rusal controlled probably about half, if not more, of Irkutskenergo's capital and its board of directors.[128]

The outcome of the ownership battle of Irkutskenergo is representative of the trajectory followed by other Siberian Energos. By 2008, Rusal controlled around 42 percent of Siberia's electricity production and either a large or a controlling stake in all of the regions hydroelectric plants (see Table 4.3). The federal government's Hydro-OGK controlled the remaining stakes in hydroelectric plants, and it was rumored that Deripaska could easily sway Hydro-OGK, having placed his loyalists on its board of directors.[129]

---

[125] With the ambiguity over the state's share in Irkutskenergo persisting, the minority shareholders Rusal and Sual (the *aluminshchiki*) were able to challenge the existing board of directors (*совет директоров*). Two competing shareholder meetings were called for April 28, 2001 – one at 10 AM, called by the existing Irkutskenergo management, and a second one at 3 PM, called by the *aluminshchiki*, the minority shareholders; Уколова, "Передел собственности: борьба за Иркутскэнерго," p. 149.

[126] A telling sign that Rusal had won control was that the July 2001 board meeting took place in Moscow, rather than in Irkutsk – far removed from regional events; Уколова, "Передел собственности: борьба за Иркутскэнерго," p. 150.

[127] Interview #53 with employee of electricity company, Irkutsk, 20071119.

[128] It is not entirely clear how much of Irkutskenergo's capital is controlled by Rusal, since intermediary companies might be holding shares in custody for Rusal. In 1999, Rusal's share was already close to 40%, according to Уколова, "Передел собственности: борьба за Иркутскэнерго." According to one interview source, Rusal's ownership stake today is closer to 60%; interview #48, with academic, Irkutsk, 20071113.

[129] Following a major accident at the Saiano-Shushenskaia Hydro-Power station in August 2009, *Коммерсантъ* reported in October 2009 that the company's Siberian holdings are now managed by somebody loyal to Deripaska: "все ее сибирские станции, в том числе проект восстановления Саяно-Шушенской ГЭС, будет теперь контролировать выходец из структур Олега Дерипаски." In "'РусГидро' сливает команду," *Коммерсантъ*, October 27, 2009. A further sign of these power struggles is the replacement of the director of Hydro-OGK in November 2009. The new director, Evegnii Dodd, is rumored to be close to Igor Sechin, one of the key Kremlin power brokers, who is also on the board of Inter-Rao; see "Vor Strom-Fusion in Russland; Neuer Chef für Russhydro" *Neue Zürcher Zeitung*, November 24, 2009, 29.

TABLE 4.3. *New owners of Siberia's power sector (2008)*

Siberia	Installed capacity %	Type of new owner
Rusal	41.5	**Industrial conglomerate** (Russian/private)
Hydro-OGK	20.1	Russian government's hydro-electric holdings (Russian/government)
SUEK	19.5	Energy conglomerate (Russian/private)
Novosibirskenergo	5.5	Electricity company (Russian/private)
Norilsk Nickel	4.8	**Industrial conglomerate** (Russian/private)
E.On	3.3	Electricity company (foreign)
Gazprom	2.7	Energy conglomerate (Russian/government)
Others: Mechel, Evras	2.5	**Industrial conglomerates** (Russian/private)

Source: Combined press reports on ownership changes in 2007 and 2008; see Appendix 3 for details.

Siberia's hydroelectric plants are the region's most valuable assets. So, although the combined percentage of energy conglomerates that have become new owners (SUEK, E-On, and Gazprom) is not negligible, it is Rusal that has captured the most valuable power plants, including Irkutskenergo and Krasnoiarsk Hydroelectric Power Plant with almost 13,000- and 6000-megawatt hours of installed capacity, respectively.[130] Krasnoiarsk power plants were similarly coveted by aluminum magnates. While Krasnoiarskenergo was owned by UES, Krasnoiarsk Hydroelectric Power Plant (Krasnoiarskaia GES – *Красноярская гидроэлектростанция*), the regional Energo's most valuable asset, was owned by Rusal since the mid-1990s. Krasnoiarsk's second large hydroelectric dam, Boguchanskaia GES, is also under "shared custody" of Rusal and the government.[131] In sum, industry-led conglomerates gained control over large parts of Siberia's power plants, in particular the valuable hydroelectric plants. In Siberian regions with hydroelectric dams, we then see a very similar pattern: regional administrations tried to keep control of the most valuable

---

[130] See Rusal website, http://rusal.ru/history.aspx
[131] Construction had started under Brezhnev, but was halted during the economic turmoil of the late 1980s and 1990s. UES needed Rusal to contribute to the huge cost of finishing the construction of the dam; see Chapter 2.

electricity assets for some years, but lost their share to the *aliuminsh-chiki* or to the federal government. Regions without hydroelectric power plants – Chita, for example – followed a different pattern of ownership change in Siberia. Regions reliant on coal-fired plants were less interesting to Rusal. Instead, coal companies (SUEK and MDM) acquired power plants in these regions.

Dal'energo's New Owners

In the Far East, no private interests were vying to gain control, and Dal'energo did not become the target of an oligarchic's expansion strategy. The Russian government ended up with a controlling stake in the Far Eastern electricity sector. This was not a foregone conclusion, however; Sergei Kirienko, one of Yeltsin's young reformers (and appointed as energy minister just a few months later), visited the Far East in the summer of 1997 and concluded that the solution to the region's energy crisis should be built on "market forces" and that unprofitable power plants should be closed.[132] Chubais also initially wanted to sell the state's majority stake there and privatize Dal'energo like any other Energo.[133] Ultimately, however, "the federal government did not want to give away control of Far Eastern generation plants to private owners,"[134] and they "decided against competition,"[135] and electricity companies remained majority owned federal government.

While Chubais conceded to opponents of power sector privatization in the Far East, he did not want these Energos to remain regional monopolies controlled by regional administrations. The Energos of Primorskii Krai and of neighboring Khabarovsk Krai were de-politicized through a series of corporate reforms. First they were unbundled, separating respective subsectors from each other. These elements were then combined into new supra-regional generation, transmission, and retail companies, and then, finally merged into a holding company, DVEUK (Far East Energy Management Company – *ДВЭУК, Дальневосточная энергетическая управляющая компания*), in 2001.[136] DVEUK later merged with other Far

[132] Interview by Veronica Belousova with Kirienko, *Утро России*, June 10, 1997.
[133] Interview #43 with electricity sector economist, Khabarovsk, 20071010.
[134] Interview #41 with journalist covering electricity sector, Vladivostok, 20071005.
[135] Interview #43 with electricity sector economist, Khabarovsk, 20071010.
[136] DVEUK (Дальневосточная энергетическая управляющая компания, ДВЭУК) was initially created on the basis of the assets of Dal'energo and Lutek; in 2003, the assets of Kamchatenergo and Sakhalinenergo were also integrated. DVEUK was a holding company, with full control of the newly formed Far Eastern generation, transmission, and retail companies, respectively called DGK (generation), DRSK (transmission), and DEK (retail).

Eastern Energos to form RAO ES Vostoka (Energy systems of the East – *РАО Энергетические система Востока*). Both DVEUK and RAO ES Vostoka are majority owned and controlled by the federal government. The aspirations of governors to play a larger role in the sector was discussed as late as 2005, when governors were trying to place representatives on the boards of directors of newly formed electricity companies.[137] This idea was ultimately rejected, and by the time I visited the region in 2007, regional governors were widely considered to be uninvolved in the electricity sector.[138]

While the Far Eastern electricity sector was not as coveted as were power plants Siberia or some of European Russia's prized assets, it was not the case that government ownership was simply a default option because no private investors could be mobilized. Russia's largest coal company, SUEK, gradually increased its share in DVEUK. Like Gazprom, the coal company sought to acquire downstream assets. However SUEK's share in DVEUK is hardly a key to great wealth: Primorskii Krai's coal reserves are important for the local economy, but are small compared to SUEK's Siberian reserves. It is likely that SUEK was put in charge of the region's coalmines in the type of developmental pact described for Rusal and Gazprom in Chapter 2. Finally, I should add that Primorskii Krai was representative of the other Energos in the Far East; ownership outcomes for other Energos in the region was very similar. All Far Eastern Energos were unbundled and their constituent generation and retail companies controlled by the holding company RAO ES Vostoka, which came to be referred to as the Far Eastern UES or "mini-UES" – as it was controlled by the federal government.[139] The Far East's only hydroelectric power

---

[137] The persistence of regional governors' influence was noted by one observer as yet another way in which the region's sector differs from the rest of Russia. "Еще одно отличие дальневосточного варианта энергореформы – участие в них местных властей. Предполагается, что в совет директоров Дальневосточной энергетической компании войдут некоторые губернаторы краев и областей Дальнего Востока." Opinion by Олег Клименко, in *Дальневосточный капитал*, p. 10.

[138] Interview #34 with academic and employee of electricity company, Vladivostok 20070923.

[139] The expression "mini-UES" or "mini-RAO" was mentioned in interviews #43 and #44 with electricity sector economists, Khabarovsk, 20071010. There are more fine-grain distinctions between Far Eastern regions; Khabarovsk and Primorskii Krai, the two largest regions, have fought over the location of the headquarters and tax revenues of the new RAO-ES Vostoka. Khabarovsk is said to have secured a better deal than did Primorskii Krai, as the headquarters and therefore tax revenues of the new generation company are located there. Interview #34 with academic and employee of electricity company, Vladivostok 20070923.

plant, Bureiskaia Hydroelectric Company, was owned by Hydro-OGK, which was itself majority owned by the federal government.[140]

Other Claims and New Owners: Foreign Owners and Inter-RAO

Foreign Investors

Until about 2006, foreign investors were drawn to Russian electricity assets for one simple reason: they were undervalued as measured by asset price per kilowatt-hour of capacity.[141] While UES and a few of the most profitable Energos had been selling shares to foreign investors since 1996, such investments promised a favorable return only if Chubais succeeded in de-politicizing the electricity sector and liberalizing prices. Liberal reformers long considered foreign strategic investment a major rationale for liberalization. Chubais stressed the importance of attracting foreigners – first and foremost as a guarantor for investment and technology transfers, but also to support his reform agenda.[142] "It is a sign of the quality [of the Russian electricity sector] that world leaders want to invest," he argued.[143] While Chubais succeeded at some key junctures, and foreign investors have played an important role at times, foreign stakeholders were not significant protagonists in ownership battles over electricity assets.

Two types of foreign investors tend to be distinguished: portfolio investors and strategic investors. While the actual line between them became blurred over time, the former were concerned with short-term capital gains, while the latter were interested in gaining market shares and long-term involvement in Russia's electricity sector.[144] Portfolio investors

---

[140] The 2003 legislation stipulates that Hydro-OGK should be 75% owned by the federal government. See, for example, Хлебников, *Рынок электроэнергии в России.*

[141] Asset price/kilowatt-hour is the rough comparison that is used by traders. Even if discounted for political risk and the need for capital investments, Russian electricity assets seemed undervalued for the years while reforms were debated. Most analysts admit, however, that models based on this valuation are best guesses (see also Chapter 6). I learned about different models for valuing the electricity sector and about analyst's perceived need for new models at a conference, "Second annual conference on the functioning of electricity companies in a market context/Вторая ежегодная конференция – Работа электроэнергетических компаний в рыночных условиях," Moscow, December 13, 2006.

[142] Interview #8 with economist at financial institution, Moscow, 20061006.

[143] Remark by Chubais at a conference "Энергетика: тормоз или локомотив развития экономики?" Moscow, February 13, 2007.

[144] Interview #5 with electricity sector expert, international financial institution, London, 20060920. At that point, in mid-2006, he doubted that there was going to be much interest by strategic investors.

played an important role during first years of Chubais's chairmanship. When Chubais became director of UES in 1998, he skillfully used the fact that foreigners controlled a minority package in the company to remain at its helm. One of his first moves as head of UES was to push through a modification of the company shareholder agreement, increasing to 75 percent the quorum of votes needed to replace the chairman of the board. At that point, UES already had almost 30 percent foreign shareholders.[145] This move thus positioned control over his fate as chairman beyond Russian borders and outside of Russia's political arena.[146] It proved to be a crucial strategic move: during his first six years at UES, the Duma passed numerous motions to remove him from chairmanship.[147]

Foreign strategic investors played an important role at different times. The European Bank for Reconstruction and Development (EBRD), a regional development bank, first invested in UES in 2001, and created the UES Restructuring Committee as a condition for the loan.[148] This committee became a key institution for debate over reform issues.[149] Foreign strategic investors became new owners of a few select power plants. The German firm E.ON gained a large stake in the power company OGK-4 and the Italian company Enel in OGK-5.[150] Foreign companies, which targeted the most profitable of Russian electricity sector assets, frequently clashed with Gazprom, as in the Fortum case, described earlier in the chapter. Although it is difficult to ascertain a coherent logic in these deals, foreign owners might have been allowed ownership positions based on informal quid-pro-quo agreements in politically negotiated asset swaps.

---

[145] A 1998 law had formally restricted foreign ownership to 25%, although foreign investors circumvented the law by using local companies as intermediaries. Petrosyan, "What Is the Current Status of Russian Electricity Sector in the Light of Restructuring Laws and RAO UES Breakup Strategy?" 9.

[146] At the same time, Chubais was popular in the United States; according to one source, he spent many a lobbying dollar in Washington, DC to further his popularity among U.S. policy-making circles; "Чубайс платит американским лоббистам по 700 тыс. долларов в год," *Газета*, April 1, 2005.

[147] According to one source, more than sixty motions were passed in the Duma between 1998 and 2004 to remove Chubais. Petrosyan, *What Is the Current Status of Russian Electricity Sector in the Light of Restructuring Laws and RAO UES Breakup Strategy*, 11.

[148] EBRD is the European Bank for Reconstruction and Development. See EBRD press release, "Powering change in Russia's electricity sector," September 8, 2006. See http://www.ebrd.net/new/stories/2006/20060908.htm.

[149] Interview #11 electricity sector expert at financial institution, Moscow, 20061018.

[150] Both stakes were around 40% in 2008, but both companies have stated the intent to raise their stakes to more than 50%, according to *The Economist*, November 22, 2007.

Foreign companies were allowed ownership stakes of important (albeit "non-strategic") assets in return for a Russian company's access to foreign assets and joint ventures. The European Union has been reluctant to allow Russian companies to participate in European energy retail as long as European companies are prevented access to Russian energy assets.[151] For years, Gazprom tried to acquire stakes in German and Italian gas distribution assets to directly profit from retail sales in Western Europe. While no formal reciprocity agreement was reached, it is likely that the electricity sector arrangements between Gazprom and German and Italian energy companies were negotiated as part of other, larger energy partnerships. Gazprom and E.ON have collaborated on large joint ventures, such as the Nord-Stream pipeline that will bring Russian gas under the Baltic Sea to Western Europe.[152] As with the domestic bargains, the cooperation between foreign energy companies, Gazprom, and the Russian government was shaped by developmental bargains with long time horizons, rather than by the narrow rent-seeking motives of the actors involved.

Inter-RAO

Other than foreign owners, the company Inter-RAO deserves mention in a discussion of Russia's link to foreign electricity companies. Inter-RAO is a government-owned holding company initially created as a subsidiary of UES that acquired electricity assets abroad, mostly in CIS countries (CIS stands for Commonwealth of Independent States, a group of former Soviet Republics excluding the three Baltic countries.) Inter-RAO then incorporated Russian power plants that did not find private investors during the 2004–2008 reforms. I briefly sketch the history of Inter-RAO here because it illustrates how electricity sector reforms created new political actors outside of Russia.

At the same time that UES's role in Russia's electricity market and electricity politics declined after the unbundling of the Energos, Inter-RAO entered power politics in a number of CIS countries – Moldova, Georgia, Armenia, Kazakhstan, Kyrgyzstan, and Tajikistan – acquiring prime power plants and transmission companies.[153] By 2008, Inter-RAO was

---

[151] See, for example, Goldman, *Petrostate*.

[152] Nord-Stream and Siberia's Yuzhno-Russkoye oil and gas field are only the largest and the most high profile of a number of ongoing asset swaps and joint ventures between E.On and Gazprom.

[153] These are Moldavskaya thermal power plant in Moldova, Telasi transmission company and Mtkvari and Khrami power plants in Georgia, Metsamor nuclear power plant and Armenian Power Network in Armenia, Ekibazstuz thermal power plant in Kazakhstan,

the largest owner of privatized electricity assets in CIS countries, owning some of the most valuable electricity assets in Soviet successor states.
In Georgia and Armenia the company became a particularly prominent
actor, acquiring large parts of the electricity generation and transmission
subsectors. Assets were initially acquired through debt-for-equity swaps
between the Russian and CIS governments. Later investments were made
through the use of Russia's stabilization fund, awash with cash during
the period of high oil prices.[154] The Russian government controlled Inter-
RAO together with a number of Russian government-owned companies,
including Gazprom.

Armenia is a particularly interesting case. During the Soviet period, the
power systems of Georgia, Armenia, and Azerbaijan had been designed
as an interconnected whole rather than having to serve the needs of each
Soviet Republic. As violent conflicts erupted between these countries
after the collapse of the Soviet Union, cooperation in the electricity sector
broke down and each electricity system needed to function independently.
Armenia ended up with surplus generation capacity but little indigenous
energy resources, while Georgia had to deal with chronic shortages.[155]
In all three countries, serious technical problems and prolonged system
outages characterized much of the 1990s. As was the case for most post-
Soviet countries, Armenia's electricity companies were unable to collect
receivables and were plagued by debt.[156] Inter-RAO acquired significant
assets in Armenia's power sector, initially through debt-for-equity swaps.
Over the years, it increased its share in most larger electricity assets,
acquiring, for example, shares from a U.S. company that abandoned its
investment in Armenia because of the difficulties in collecting electricity
bills and in restructuring the sector. By 2008, Inter-RAO owned around
50 percent of Armenia's installed capacity and operated the country's largest power plant – the Medzamor nuclear power plant. [157] It also fully

Sangtuda hydroelectric power plant in Tajikistan, and Kambarata hydroelectric power
plant in Kyrgyzstan.

[154] Theresa Sabonis-Helf, "The Unified Energy Systems of Russia (RAO-UES) in Central
Asia and the Caucasus: Nets of Interdependence," *Demokratizatsiya* 15, no. 4 (2007):
429–444.

[155] Ibid., 435.

[156] Gevorg Sargsyan, Ali Balabanyan, and Denzel Hankinson, *From Crisis to Stability in the
Armenian Power Sector: Lessons Learned from Armenia's Energy Reform Experience*,
World Bank working paper no. 74 (Washington, DC: World Bank, 2006).

[157] According to one source, Inter-RAO controls more than 85% of generation capacity in Armenia, although this seems to include the contract to operate Medzamor.
Дальневосточный капитал, July 2004, No. 6/58, p. 11.

owned Armenia's distribution network, the Electric Networks of Armenia. The Armenian government welcomed Inter-RAO's acquisitions for a number of reasons. The government had acquired large debts for fuel, as nuclear energy and nuclear fuel supplied by Russia made up a large part of the country's generation capacity. After assuming ownership, Inter-RAO wrote off debts, provided technical assistance for Medzamor's nuclear reactor, and supported the Armenian government in resisting international pressure to shut down Medzamor, deemed unsafe by many international observers. It also helped Armenia deal with overcapacity, selling electricity to Iran and Turkey (transiting via Georgia, since Armenia does not have official relationships with Turkey).[158] Inter-RAO owned more of Armenia's power assets than of any other country, but it played a similarly important role in the power politics of many other CIS countries.[159]

A Focus on New Owners and Shifting Authority

In sum, different actors emerged as new owners in the electricity sector, acquiring electricity companies as key links in vertically integrated production chains that played a large role in regional economic development. Ownership struggles and their outcomes were closely tied to larger political dynamics in Russia, in particular to center-regional dynamics and the government's relationship to emerging oligarchic conglomerates. Competing ownership claims were resolved in many different ways over the years: sales were the most common way assets changed hands, but debt-for-equity swaps, corporate restructuring, hostile takeovers, and court decisions were also important at times.

[158] Sabonis-Helf, "The Unified Energy Systems of Russia (RAO-UES) in Central Asia and the Caucasus," 436.
[159] For example, the 2010 riots in Kyrgyzstan that led to a change in government were sparked by an increase in living costs, in particular electricity tariffs that followed sector liberalization; see Madeleine Reeves, "The Latest Revolution," *London Review of Books*, May 13, 2010. While this point requires further research, it seems that Kyrgyzstan's relatively democratic parliament was opposed to tariff increases for household consumers that liberal reforms called for, but had little leverage to actually impose its will on the reform program negotiated by the Kyrgyz president and Inter-RAO. In contrast with Kyrgyzstan, Kazakhstan is a resource-rich country and seems to have been able to be more selective in shaping Inter-RAO's involvement. For example, the Kazakh government was able to reserve government ownership of an important transmission line that Inter-RAO coveted. The involvement of Russia and Inter-RAO in the domestic politics of CIS countries is interesting; I am not aware of a systematic analysis of RAO's role in CIS countries, other than Sabonis-Helf's account that treats the CIS country's domestic dynamics only cursorily.

We saw that successive waves of privatization struggles changed the political arena for the state-oligarch bargains that underpinned new electricity markets. New market institutions – here the new ownership structures – shifted authority, empowering one set of actors at the expense of others. Regional governors lost their influence and regional property owners lost their stakes everywhere, while large conglomerates became important actors. The second crucial point is that ownership trajectories and outcomes clustered into three large supra-regional patterns, and in each of these regions, electricity sector assets were incorporated into a new vertically integrated production chain: a semi-statal energy conglomerate gained dominant ownership in European Russia, an industrial conglomerate did so in Siberia, while the government retained majority ownership of electricity assets in the Far East.

A closer look at how reforms created new owners and who these new owners were contributes to the literature on the political economy of privatization. This is a large and diverse research field, often dealing with privatization as an element of a broader liberalization agenda. The case of the Russian electricity sector suggests that rather than thinking of new owners either as law-abiding private companies or, alternatively, as rent-seeking oligarchs, we should think of them as economic and political actors whose interests are defined by the regional and international economies in which they operate. As we will see in the next chapter, positions in the debate on price liberalization and tariff regulation differed depending on the type of production chain new owners controlled.[160] Production chains are networks that link producers and consumers from raw material to finished product and final consumer.[161] In the Russian electricity sector, the relevant production chains were energy and energy-intensive metallurgical industries. Russian electricity companies produced power for domestic

---

[160] Much of the literature on the post-Soviet transition lumps individual oligarchs and the economic empires they control into one category. I am not aware of studies that have investigated how their political influence depends on their interest as different types of businesses, tied in to different types of production chains.

[161] The production chain literature originates in economic sociology and tends to stress the importance of the regulation for the evolution and organization of production chains. Charles Sabel and others have analyzed regulation and production chains in the context of industrial districts and regional economic clusters; see, for example, Sabel, "Flexible Sepcialisation and the Re-Emergence of Regional Economies." Overall the focus of this research, however, has been to explain divergent economic outcomes rather than to question the origin and evolution of different regulatory regimes. I am borrowing the concept of a "lead firm" from the production chain literature; Gary Gereffi, "Shifting Governance Structures in Global Commodity Chains, with Special Reference to the Internet," *American Behavioral Scientist* 44, no. 10 (June 1, 2001): 1616–1637.

consumption, but the products at the ends of the two chains – gas and aluminum – were sold to consumers across the world. While Russia's new class of oligarchs were indeed early "winners" and influenced reforms, classifying them as corrupt rent seekers does not help us understand how interests and influence differed across time and space or help us make sense of winners versus losers. Placing new owners in the contexts of production chains and regional economies reveals the network of relations that embedded the sector in regional and global markets, and helps us understand the role of upstream and downstream firms linked to the sector. It enables analysis of how these firms uniquely influenced the electricity sector in question, for example why a particular conglomerate's claims mattered, and how they sought to influence reform and sector regulation.

The privatization literature, on the whole, has considered "new owners" to be a relatively uncomplicated category, characterized by a motivation to decrease labor costs and make former state-owned enterprises profitable.[162] New post-Soviet owners, however, retained complicated relationships with the state. The very distinction between public and private companies is problematic in this context. During Russian electricity sector privatization for example, "privatized" assets frequently ended up in the hands of state-owned companies. Observers of Russia's electricity privatization cast doubt on the success of reform by pointing to Gazprom's increasingly prominent ownership role in the sector. While it is certainly true that many new owners were not "private," this does not mean that the transfer of ownership was less consequential. Trying to fit new owners into a public/private spectrum is particularly futile in the post-Soviet context, because neither publicly nor privately owned companies necessarily stood in any particular relationship with the state. As discussed in Chapter 1, the obligations of both private and public companies vis-à-vis the state were subject to evolving bargains with the government.[163]

---

[162] See, for example, Maxim Boycko, Andrei Shleifer, and Robert W. Vishny, "A Theory of Privatisation," *The Economic Journal* 106, no. 435 (March 1996): 309–319. There are notable exceptions to this trend. For example the literature on privatization of welfare services and the policy literature on public-private partnerships (PPPs) have recognized that privatization of public services can lead to a whole host of arrangement that mix and divide responsibilities between the state and private entities in vastly different ways. Jane Gingrich examines this for Western European welfare states; Jane R. Gingrich, *Making Markets in the Welfare State: The Politics of Varying Market Reforms* (Cambridge: Cambridge University Press, 2011).

[163] The general point that the public-private dichotomy is precarious has long been made across the social sciences. Paul Starr, "Meaning of Privatization, The," *Yale Law & Policy Review* 6 (1988): 6–41.

180 *Post-Soviet Power*

While the privatization literature dealing with the post-Soviet experience has been more attentive to the complex roles played by new owners, this work has focused on predicting the new owners' propensity to restructure enterprises, whether or not they could cut costs and increase efficiency after privatization.[164] Initial studies sought to distinguish two classes of emergent owners: insiders – factory directors and labor collectives; and outsiders – investors not related to the management of a firm. In the political discourse of the early transition period, insiders were thought to have both moral and practical claims to these assets, a right earned during decades of work in the factories. Indeed, insiders were a political force that Yeltsin's reform team had to appease.[165] At the same time, liberal reformers and their foreign advisors were far less enthusiastic about the role insiders should play after privatization. They thought outsiders would do a better job transforming new private enterprises into competitive companies by streamlining the labor force and ending reliance on government subsidies. Over the years, the insider/outsider distinction has lost much of its relevance, partly because new actors have entered the stage and partly because the privatization literature has moved to new questions. At the same time, new private actors' failure to establish arm's-length interactions with the government (and with other private actors for that matter) within the framework of well-defined laws remained an important question, even if it no longer concerned insiders. Given the rise of the oligarchs and their ability to shape reforms, "winners took all" became an almost axiomatic summary of post-Soviet privatization.[166]

While it is true that oligarchs reaped the benefits of privatization, this chapter argued for situating new owners and their interests in particular interconnected contexts – of the production chains they control and the political battles over the future of electricity, rather than thinking of them as decontextualized actors with given preferences. Such a qualitative analysis of private interest and corporate influence is useful because it links privatization with the subsequent need to regulate new private actors – a link that ongoing debates in the privatization literature have

[164] J. David Brown, John S. Earle, and Scott Gehlbach, "Privitization," in *The Oxford Handbook of the Russian Economy*, ed. Michael V. Alexeev and Shlomo Weber (Oxford: Oxford University Press, 2013), 161–188. See also Susan J. Linz and Gary Krueger, "Enterprise Restructuring in Russia's Transition Economy: Formal and Informal Mechanisms," *Comparative Economic Studies* 40, no. 2 (1998): 5–52.
[165] For an account of the debates about insiders/outsider privatization, see Hoffman, *The Oligarchs*; and Nelson, *Property to the People*.
[166] Hellman, "Winners Take All."

recognized. Privatization of public service entailed a promise that competition among private actors will turn inefficient and corrupt bureaucracies
into efficient enterprises, reduce cost, and improve service.[167] The political justification for the state's divestiture from state-owned enterprises
was always the long-term benefits for consumers, and a unifying theme
of the privatization literature has been the question of what it takes to
realize the privatization's promise. A first wave of answers took efficiency
gains for granted and was interested in the political conditions conducive
to the realization of reforms.[168] A second wave of studies has not assumed
that new private actors necessarily provide improved public service. A
key criticism by later approaches concerns a general lack of attention to
the institutional environment in which privatization is enacted and the
institutions needed to regulate newly privatized industries.[169] These studies are thus interested in new owners as private actors that need to be regulated, then go on to examine why this may not be an easy task, and why

---

[167] The liberal reform agenda in the electricity sector entails a further promise: more efficient use of scarce energy resources and therefore also of a "greener" way of producing
power for growing economies. This argument is salient in the post-Soviet economies,
where factories are particularly energy inefficient. More energy is used per GDP; see
Jan Cornillie and Samuel Fankhauser, "The Energy Intensity of Transition Countries,"
Energy Economics 26, no. 3 (May 2004): 283–295. Jan Cornillie and Samuel Fankhauser,
The Energy Intensity of Transition Countries, Working Paper Series (London: European
Bank for Reconstruction and Development, June 2002), http://www.ebrd.com/down-
loads/research/economics/workingpapers/wp0072.pdf

[168] Identifying potential winners and losers of reforms, they modeled the behavior of these
groups before, during, and after privatization; see, for example, Przeworski, *Democracy
and the Market*; Stiglitz, "Who Lost Russia?"; and Shleifer and Vishny, *The Grabbing
Hand*. A common presumption is that concentrated cost but diffuse benefits prevent
reforms: a large but weakly organized group stands to gain – all consumers of electricity, for example – while a smaller group, the producers and state-sector employees, lose
privileges they enjoyed under a state-owned system. For privatization to happen, the
large group of beneficiaries needs to overcome collective action problem, or the reformist government must be insulated from pressures that oppose privatization, is a key concern for this literature. This literature is particularly influenced by the Latin American
experience, where the post-ISI liberalizations were either conditioned by a simultaneous
democratization or happened under an authoritarian regime.

[169] This literature emphasized that for privatization to be successful and for efficiency gains
to materialize, states have to regulate new private actors in a way that benefits consumers. Van de Walle notes that "privatization is unlikely to generate major gains in efficiency, unless it is accompanied by other reforms, which alter the relative prices in the
economy." Nicolas van de Walle, "Privatization in Developing Countries: A Review of
the Issues," *World Development* 17, no. 5 (May 1989): 601–615. For a study of regulatory effectiveness in the electricity sector, see Jon Stern and John Cubbin, *Regulatory
Effectiveness: The Impact of Regulation and Regulatory Governance Arrangements on
Electricity Industry Outcomes* (Washington, DC: World Bank Publications, 2005).

reforms, once implemented, do not necessarily deliver on the promises they had entailed.[170] What the story of Russia's electricity privatization told here, together with the account of price regulation that follows in the next chapter, suggests is that regulatory challenges appear in a different light if we contextualize actors' preferences vis-à-vis the newly privatized sector, rather than relying on stylized models of interest motivations.

At the most general level, then, the consolidation of ownership in the power sector during liberalization suggests that a focus on the political actors created during privatization is useful to examine these questions about sector regulation. This kind of analysis is only possible if we think of political authority and market arrangements as reflexive and mutually constitutive. The next two chapters – on tariff liberalization and expert regimes – develop this argument further.

[170] Whether efficiency gains seem attainable or elusive, analysts agree that privatization entails redistribution of the costs, benefits, risks, and profits of service provision. The political weight of the actors able to shape the process of privatization are thought to be central to understanding both how the redistribution works and how the new private owners behave once they control the former SOEs. Different approaches rely on different political actor for their predictions – the first wave on interest groups and voter blocks, the second wave on corporate and industrial lobbies – and implicit assumptions of how these actors relate to the state. Privatization programs have fared differently in different parts of the world. See, for example, David M. Woodruff, "Property Rights in Context: Privatization's Legacy for Corporate Legality in Poland and Russia," *Studies in Comparative International Development* 38, no. 4 (December 1, 2004): 82–108; and van de Walle, "Privatization in Developing Countries." For Russia, see Massimo Florio, "Economists, Privatization in Russia and the Waning of the 'Washington Consensus'," *Review of International Political Economy* 9, no. 2 (2002): 374–415. This literature emphasized that effective regulation of privatized firms demands administrative capacities of the state and the ability to evade capture by powerful lobbies; van de Walle, "Privatization in Developing Countries," 602; and K. A Chaudhry, "The Myths of the Market and the Common History of Late Developers," *Politics & Society* 21, no. 3 (1993): 245–274. For an account of re-regulation after liberalization in advanced industrialized countries, see Steven Vogel. *"Freer Markets, More Rules: Regulatory Reform in Advanced Industrial Countries."* Ithaca, NY: Cornell University Press, 1996. Regulating infrastructure after liberalization may be particularly challenging; see Conclusion, note 10.

5

Liberalization – the Price of Power

"Tariffs are the most controversial part of reforms."[1]

"Kemerovo Oblast' Aman Tuleev ... confirmed his unwillingness to fulfill the [federal] government's resolution on electricity tariffs."

Kemerovo Oblast' Press Service, 2000

"We must aim to make life equally good in all Russian regions. We will not achieve that without a unified legal and economic space in Russia"[2]

Vladimir Putin, 2000

Introduction: Rules That Regulate Prices

In the electricity sector, no regulations were more contested than those that governed prices and subsidies – the price of power. "Tariffs are the most controversial part of reforms,"[3] determined one observer in Moscow. The price at which electricity was bought and sold and the mechanisms to determine prices and tariffs were subject to intense political battles because they profoundly affected costs of living and production.[4] In the

---

[1] Interview #1 with electricity sector expert, international financial institution, Moscow, 20060721.

[2] In a speech given in Kazan in March 2000, acting President Putin also said that relations between the center, the regions, and localities must be improved; reported by *Interfax*, March 22, 2000, also reported by *RFE/RL Newsline*, "Putin calls for new, improved federalism," March 23, 2000.

[3] Interview #1 with electricity sector expert, international financial institution, Moscow, 20060721.

[4] A number of observers also stressed the role of electricity subsidies in the "demonetization" of the Russian economy in the 1990s, as money surrogates were particularly

words of a journalist from Krasnoiarsk, "electricity tariffs play a very important role in the economic life of our region."[5] What is more, the state was widely expected to play a role in shaping the price of energy. Indeed, the "protection of citizens from unreasonable price increases of electricity and heat" was widely regarded as a core responsibility of the government.[6] Electricity tariffs and subsidies were hence tied up with larger question about the redistribution of energy wealth. The subsidization of industrial and household consumers via low-priced energy – referred to in Russian policy discourse as the "cheapening of energy resources"[7] – was indeed a central prize in post-Soviet energy politics.[8] Russia relied on its ability to determine the price of gas in its attempts to shape political developments in Ukraine, for example, increasing prices after the Orange Revolution in 2004 and then again in 2014, following the ouster of Viktor Yanukovych. There were many equivalents of such conflicts over the price of energy in Russian domestic politics, although they were rarely reported abroad. In very general terms, it is difficult to overstate the importance of the state's role as an arbiter of energy subsidies.

As with ownership, the process of price liberalization entailed fundamental decisions about how the sector was to be reorganized. The "price of power" – how much power companies could charge, whether tariffs were regulated or liberalized, and who obtained subsidies – was a basic building block of the sector's economic architecture. Whether or not the Energos could operate, make investments, and earn profits hinged on these decisions. Yet, the political stakes were equally important. Control over prices allowed authorities to use energy resources to subsidize select groups of consumers; this was a useful tool in pursuit of particular

prevalent in electricity; Litwack and Thompson, *OECD Economic Survey of the Russian Federation*; Woodruff, *Money Unmade*. See discussion below.

[5] "Тарифы на электроэнергию играют очень большую роль в экономической жизни нашего края." Interview with director of Krasnoiarskenergo, V. A. Bulankin, in "Тариф – экономика опора," *Красноярский рабочий*, January 15, 1999.

[6] Владимир Викторович Хлебников, *Рынок Электроэнергии в России* (Москва: ВЛАДОС, 2005), 180. Also interview #24 with bureaucrat at the Ministry for Economic Development, Moscow, 20070214, who mentioned that FEK decisions are always made with an eye to the inflationary effects of tariff increases.

[7] In Russian, "удешевление энергетических ресурсов"; see, for example, Е. Гурвич, "Оценка Эффекта Удешевления Энергетических Ресурсов," *Энергетическая политика*, 1997, no. 3.

[8] Litwack and Thompson, *OECD Economic Survey of the Russian Federation*, 127. This OECD report gives the following estimates of the magnitude of energy subsides: conservative estimates around 5% of GDP, up to 30% of GDP if energy prices are compared with international market prices. See also discussion in Chapter 3.

development strategies and social goals. Less control over prices meant an end to subsidies and entitlements, as local electricity prices would be to global energy markets. Liberals considered wholesale markets and price liberalization essential to their reforms. Reformers were adamant that "letting prices speak" was absolutely crucial; they considered the silencing of price signals under state socialism to be responsible for its demise.[9] Liberal reformers wanted to introduce the discipline of the market to the electricity sector, by teaching customers the "right" behavior as participants in market economies – by "teach[ing them] how to pay" and "how to economize."[10] In the 1990s, Russia's international creditors, the IMF in particular, insisted that Russia end subsidies in the electricity sector.[11] This was also a core demand in Russia's negotiations concerning accession to the WTO. In contrast, opponents of UES reforms, advocates of regional autonomy, statists, and industrialists preferred to preserve control over tariffs and to use electricity subsidies as a policy tool. Opponents of liberal reforms in regions with low electricity costs, such as Siberia, also resisted the equalization of prices across Russia.

Subsidy regimes are arrangements among different tiers of the government, regulators, utilities, fuel providers, and industrialists to provide electricity at below long-run average cost in exchange for political, economic, and social goals.[12] We will see that over the course of electricity sector reform in Russia, both proponents and opponents of price liberalization shaped emergent subsidy regimes in ways that evade stylized models of actor preferences. The statist faction that supported Gazprom's ownership claims, for example, preferred a *liberal* price policy and wanted to *reduce* electricity subsidies. New private owners of power plants in Siberia, by contrast, succeeded in *preserving* subsidies and special price zones. These conglomerate's preferences for tariff reforms differed depending on the type of production chain they controlled, which then meant that the subsidies negotiated with regional and federal authorities

---

[9] Ibid.
[10] The first remark that people should be taught how to pay for electricity was made by the minister of energy at the time, Yuri Shafranik, in "Надо научиться платить," *Утро России*, Februray 10, 1994. For the second, see "Экономить тепло и свет," *Утро России*, January 19, 1994. This emphasis might be interesting for debates on neoliberal subjectivity sparked by Michel Foucault's Collège de France lectures.
[11] *Open Media Research Institute/Daily Digest* (OMRI/DD in what follows), August 30, 1996.
[12] Arguably the term "subsidy" is misleading, as it implies a deviation from a neutral market price. This is a problematic assumption. I am relying on it for lack of an easily understood alternative.

TABLE 5.1. *Household and industrial tariffs: Regional differences over time*

RR/kWh	Mosenergo/ER		Irkutskenergo/SIB		Dal'energo/RFE	
	Household	Industrial	Household	Industrial	Household	Industrial
1995 /1998*	.13	.32*	.02	.09*	.10	.53*
2000	.35	.55	.10	.09	.60	.70
2005	1.08	1.13	.32	.28	.84	1.50

Note: Industrial tariffs were generally available for consumers with a connection rate of more than 750 kWh. The data listed by UES as industrial tariffs were average tariffs for industrial users; as outlined later, the actual tariffs for each enterprise could differ quite substantially. For household tariffs, I quote urban tariffs. Rural tariffs were different in the following cases: Mosenergo 1995: rural – 9. Irkutskenergo 2000: rural – 7, 2005: rural – 22.
Source: UES data set on regulated tariffs for Russia's regional Energos, 1995–2005. Industrial tariffs are only available starting 1998; Numbers marked with * are for 1998.

varied widely across regions. The empirical core of this chapter is devoted to tracing the emergence of different electricity subsidy regimes and then comparing them across three supra-regions – European Russia, Siberia, and the Far East. Energy subsidies were administered and distributed in myriad ways.

The persistence of different price levels for different consumers across regions was a concrete manifestation of varied subsidy regimes. Price differentials reflect cost variations in power generation across regions. The central argument of this chapter is that they were also a reflection of the complicated political dynamics that underpinned markets and that regional economic development played an important part in regional power politics. Table 5.1 provides an overview of tariffs across regions, before reforms were initiated (1995) and after an important period of price liberalization (2005). While tariffs increased in all three regions, they did so to varying extents; they remained lowest in Irkutsk both before and after liberalization. Household subsidies – the difference between industrial and household tariffs – persisted everywhere, but were most significant in the Russian Far East.

A second argument this chapter makes is that the implementation of price reforms had important effects on the politics of regulation. In the preceding chapter we saw that the ability of UES and its liberal-minded reform team to reclaim de facto control of regional electricity assets was crucial for the implementation of Chubais's reforms. In this chapter I examine price regulation, subsidies, and the cash flow of the Energos. We will see here, too, that market reforms changed the political arena in which prices and subsidies were negotiated. New zones of governance emerged during the sector's marketization: regional (oblast') level regulation was effectively supplanted by newly created federal regulatory institutions organized at the level of newly constituted supra-regions (the federal okrugs). The chapter details how a number of reforms that were intended to de-politicize regulation and curtail subsidies ended up centralizing regulation. Rather than de-politicizing electricity, the arena of politics moved from region to center, shifting along with it the site of negotiation over tariffs and subsidies. Liberalization of subsidy regimes and the centralization of political power (Putin's state-building project, in other words) were mutually reinforcing processes, because liberal reforms weakened regional governors by transferring authority to regulatory structures newly built and closely supervised by federal authorities.

Prices and Subsidies in the 1990s

In the 1990s, being able to determine the "price of power" – and to use electricity subsidies as a policy tool – was the main motivation for various political forces seeking control of the electricity sector. The ability to influence electricity prices was crucial for regional governors. As previous chapters argued, the federal government lacked the authority to regulate regional economies during much of the 1990s. The central government's inability to regulate tariffs for the regional electricity monopolies was a case in point. Regional governors devised their own complicated subsidy regimes, favoring select industrial consumers and either all households or certain subcategories. Whatever the subsidy regime, most governors concurred with Khabarovsk Governor Ishaev, who insisted that tariff regulation remain the domain of regional leaders, hence that "the electricity system's boundaries should coincide with political boundaries."[13]

During Soviet times, the State Committee on Prices – Goskomtsen (*Госкомцен*) – fixed prices across the Soviet Union for different classes of electricity consumers.[14] A shift toward increased regional autonomy in electricity regulation started during the late Soviet period. As

---

[13] Interview #43 with electricity sector economist, Khabarovsk, 20071010. That Ishaev wanted to regulate electricity on the regional level was also mentioned in interview #39 with electrical engineer/electricity sector expert, Vladivostok, 20071004.

[14] Федеральная служба по тарифам (ФСТ), *Информационно-аналитический бюллетень: тарифы в электроэнергетике*, ФСТ / Академия народного хозяйства, Moscow, September 2004, 11. The remainder of the discussion of the REKs in this section is based on information in this publication.

part of Gorbachev's decentralization efforts, a 1990 law gave regional authorities the right to increase or decrease electricity tariffs. The law set a strict ceiling on how much regions could diverge from the centrally determined tariff: governors could change tariffs by a limited coefficient, either increasing or decreasing the centrally mandated prices for electricity and heat in their region. After the collapse of the Soviet Union, a 1991 presidential decree "On the Liberalization of Prices" continued to give regional authorities a say in price regulations, though they were supposed to follow directives emanating from the center. The law created the Federal Energy Commission (FEK) and the Regional Energy Commissions (REKs); the responsibility for price setting was transferred from Goskomtsen to these newly established institutions.

Regional Energy Commissions, the regional price-setting bodies, were composed of representatives of regional administrations, electricity companies, and major industrial consumers. REKs were formally charged with implementing the energy policy and price directives recommended by the FEK, which was required to coordinate and supervise REKs. In reality, the FEK was often ineffective. Its price directives were ignored and governors routinely used REKs to influence electricity tariffs. In Kemerovo, for example, governor Tuleev had his own idea of what the appropriate price for electricity should be. He did not favor price hikes, because "tariff increases lead to factory closures and propel our region backwards."[15] He is one of a number of governors, throughout much of the 1990s, who consistently used their influence within REKs to challenge federal directives. An explanation of Tuleev's opposition to Chubais's reforms published as a press release in the regional newspaper is revealing:

The governor of Kemerovo Oblast' Aman Tuleev signed instruction entitled "On Electricity Tariffs for the Population," in which he confirmed his unwillingness to fulfill the [federal] government's resolution on electricity tariffs. The governor of Kemerovo officially supported the recent decision by the Kemerovo Regional Energy Commission (REK), confirming that ... tariffs for the population of Kemerovo oblast' should be kept at 15 kopek per kilowatt-hour. At the same time, a resolution by the federal government of the Russian Federation determined that household tariffs for Kemerovo should be 23 kopek per kilowatt-hour.... Aman Tuleev, with a strict position on this issue, allied with the Kemerovo REK in their defiance of the federal government. He hereby expresses his intention to remain

---

[15] "Рост тарифов приведет к закрытию предприятий, откинет регион назад," according to a press release of the Kemerovo Administration, "Пресс-релиз, Пресс-служба Администрации Кемеровской области," *Известия*, June 5, 2001.

steadfastly behind the REK. He will not allow this theft of [regional] residents, which the federal government's tariffs would amount to ....[16]

The FEK was unable to force the regional governors and REKs to comply with its directives. One insider described the federal body as either hopelessly overburdened or as a gentlemen's club, where important energy-related matters were discussed, but which lacked tools to monitor implementation.[17] REKs were often little more than offices within regional administration facilities that took cues from governors for price setting; in a number of regions REKs did not formally exist until the late 1990s.[18] In Krasnoiarsk, for example, the REK was a commission under the direction of the regional administration until 1998, rather than an independent regulator.[19] The proximity of regulators and regional officials was emblematic of REK decision making. In 1993, the Krasnoiarsk REK advocated for free electricity for a community hit hard by the economic crisis, for this would provide "enormous support for people during the difficult period of the economic collapse."[20] The Irkutsk REK went so far as to argue in favor of free electricity for all regional residents.[21]

Although tariff levels were the most vital point of contention between governors and Moscow, FEK authority was disputed on a number of levels. REKs challenged the length of time for which prices could be fixed; regional governors wanted favored increased flexibility and frequent tariff changes, while FEK wanted the predictability afforded by annual adjustments.[22] FEK also regulated the "subscription fee," a payment regional

[16] "Лампочка Амана Гумировича," *Известия*, August 3, 2000; see previous note. REK decisions were often publicized in regional newspapers, for example, "Тарифы – те же!" *Утро России*, February 4, 1997, or "Региональная энергетическая комиссия Приморского края: Постановление N. 46," *Утро России*, June 18, 1997.

[17] Interview #16 with electricity sector expert/consultant, Moscow, 20061030.

[18] Федеральная служба по тарифам, *Информационно-аналитический бюллетень: тарифы в электроэнергетике*, 13.

[19] The commission was one of the so-called "общественные органы при Администрации края [societal agencies within the Krai administration]," according to director of Krasnoiarskenergo, В. А. Буланкин, in "Тариф – экономике опора," *Красноярский рабочий*, January 15, 1999.

[20] "Жители Краснотуранского района будут бесплатно пользоваться электроэнергей до 1 января 1994 года. В сложный период экономического спада это огромное подспорье для людей." In "Электроэнергия – бесплатно," *Красноярский рабочий*, June 22, 1993.

[21] "Уже два с половиной месяца региональная энергосистема обслуживает потребителей бесплатно." ["The regional electricity system has served customers for free, for two months already."] Reported in "Энергия – даром?" *Восточно-Сибирская правда*, February 17, 1994.

[22] Interview #39 with electrical engineer/electricity sector expert, Vladivostok, 20071004.

Energos owed the UES. Ostensibly a fee for using high-voltage grids, in essence these payments continued the Soviet schemes to channel money collected in the regions to the center.[23] Regions often complained that this fee was too high, and that it lacked transparency and was therefore illegitimate. Kemerovo oblast' governor Tuleev argued that it was an illegitimate levy on regional residents.[24] Energos that owned their own high-voltage grids, including Irkutskenergo, were most successful in disputing the legitimacy of this payment, since the fee was to cover the cost of grid maintenance. But many other Energos skirted this payment for years.[25] As late as 2005, the most rebellious Energos – Bashkortostan, Tatarstan, Novosibirsk, Irkutsk, and Dal'energo – still failed to pay this fee.[26]

REKs played an important role in determining electricity tariffs because they calculated the cost of production. Officially, the mode of price regulation in post-Soviet Russia was the "cost-plus" method, where prices were set to recover cost plus an additional fixed "investment component," a sum intended for capital improvements. However, most observers believed that cost determinations were open to the governors' interpretation. "Electricity costs are politicized," observed one insider poignantly.[27] Determining the cost of electricity production and the investment component involves some degree of arbitrariness for any regulator. "Costs can be easily inflated," by tweaking the rate of asset depreciation, for example.[28] In the post-Soviet context, where the cost of capital was a relatively new concept, asset depreciation rested even more in the eye of the beholder. Governors were also sometimes blamed for inflating the investment component of cost accounting to finance pet projects or line their own pockets.[29]

---

[23] Interview #7 with electricity sector analyst at financial institution, Moscow, 20061005.

[24] "Пресс-релиз, Пресс-служба Администрации Кемеровской области," *Известия*, June 5, 2001.

[25] The dispute over the subscription fees (*абонентская плата*) was quite heated and in many ways carried more symbolic than actual monetary significance; it was a way for the Energos to resist Chubais. See "В сетях РАО ЕЭС растет напряжение," *Коммерсантъ*, July 21, 2001. Conflict over "subscription fees" discussed in interview #7 with electricity sector analyst at financial institution, Moscow, 20061005, and interview #53 with employee of electricity company, Irkutsk, 20071119. See also interview with Kuimov, Irkutskenergo executive, who disputes the legitimacy of the *абонентская плата*, in *Эксперт*, No. 14, April 1998, 36–37.

[26] See *Вестник региональной энергокомиссии Красноярского края*, January 2005, 9.

[27] Interview #32 with electricity sector economist, Vladivostok, 20070925.

[28] Interview #7 with electricity sector expert at financial institution, Moscow, 20061005.

[29] According to Bradshaw and Kirkow, the "investment component" was often the source for private money flows; Bradshaw and Kirkow, "The Energy Crisis in the Russian Far East," 1051.

Regional governments used means other than manipulating the REKs to regulate electricity tariffs. They also relied on their control over regional distribution networks. Controlling networks enabled governors in high-cost regions to prevent large-scale industrial consumers from buying low-cost electricity from other regions. Later, this same strategy prevented industrial consumers in some regions from gaining access to the newly established wholesale electricity market.[30]

Governors used electricity tariffs as a tool to subsidize household and industrial electricity consumers throughout the 1990s.[31] Three types of subsidies played a particularly important role in the electricity sector: *cross-subsidies* – the subsidization of household consumers through increased prices for industrial consumers; *industrial subsidies* – which either set prices for industrial consumers at a low level or established low-cost production zones in certain industrial regions; and *budget transfers* – direct payments to electricity companies. [32]

Household consumers benefited from cross-subsidies (*перекрестное субсидирование*). For most of the post-Soviet period, in most regions, households were charged less than industrial consumers, even though the cost of providing electricity to residential customers was generally far higher.[33] Low-cost residential electricity was initially a response to inflation in the early 1990s. But it has been a politically sensitive issue for most of the post-Soviet period. Household subsidies in the electricity sector are part of the politics of the *kvartplata (квартплата)*, a consolidated bill for a number of "communal housing services" – gas, heat, water, and repair services. During periods of high inflation in the 1990s, as wages lost their real value while the cost of living increased, households were particularly sensitive to increases in the monthly *kvartplata* payments. "What a silly idea to increase the *kvartplata*; nobody can pay

---

[30] Litwack and Thompson, *OECD Economic Survey of the Russian Federation*.

[31] In 2000, the FEK assessed only forty-eight of the existing sixty-eight REKS as functioning according to federal legislation; see Litwack and Thompson, *OECD Economic Survey of the Russian Federation*.

[32] Various types of electricity subsidies are common all over the world. Industrial subsidies in particular have kept tariffs low for electricity-intensive industries such as aluminum and chemical plants. More recently these kind of subsidies have been sought by companies like Google and Microsoft for their server farms; see "Down on the Server Farm: The Real-World Impliations of the Rise of Internet Computing," *The Economist*, May 24, 2008.

[33] One observer calls cross-subsidies a "terrible disease"; interview #39 with electrical engineer and electricity sector expert, Vladivostok, 20071004.

it," complained my landlady in Vladivostok.[34] As was the case for many low-income households, she spent a large part of her monthly pension income on the *kvartplata*. It was not uncommon for the *kvartplata* to account for one-half of household income.[35] Finally, in some cities and for some neighborhoods, the provision of these services, including electricity and the maintenance of the physical infrastructure, were so inferior – "inhuman," as residents of one building in Irkutsk put it – that they wondered, "what are we paying for?"[36]

Not surprisingly, promises to keep utility prices stable, or to lower payments, ahead of an election were popular strategies for politicians. "Cheap electricity was an effective slogan," noted one observer from the Far East.[37] The promise of low utility bills resonated in particular with pensioners, avid voters living on small, fixed incomes. A study found that governors tended to decrease tariffs before gubernatorial elections, only to increase them again after being reelected.[38] In addition to keeping household tariffs generally low via cross-subsidies from commercial users, it was also common to give subsidies to select categories of household consumers. For example, households in rural areas and residents of apartment buildings outfitted with electric stoves received special tariffs,

---

[34] Interview #40 with pensioner in Vladivostok, as well as in an ongoing conversation during September and October 2007, Vladivostok.

[35] This is based on an opinion survey by FOM (*Фонд Общественного Мнения*) conducted in 2005; see details in note 95 to this chapter.

[36] "What are we paying such a high *kvartplata* for, if we live in inhuman conditions? / За что мы платим такую большую квартплату, если живем в нечеловеческих условиях?" in the section "*Письма*" ["Letters"], *Восточно-Сибирская правда*, October 17, 1992. Apparently the problem has continued over the years. Prices have risen but services remained inferior, and people did not want to pay. They asked "What for? For radiators that don't heat up, and water that is turned off? / За что? То батареи не греют, то воду отключают," in "Почем литр воды? О квартплате и тарифах на коммунальные услуги," *Восточно-Сибирская правда*, September 14, 1995. The discussion of the problems of communal service provision (ЖКХ) in Russia is vast, both in national and regional media. For a description of the situation in the Far East, see "Жилищно-коммунальное бесхозяйство," *Дальневосточный капитал*, April 2004, No. 4/44, 12.

[37] Interview #32 with electricity sector economist, Vladivostok, 20070918.

[38] Yudashkina and Popochy analyzed regional tariffs during years of governor elections and found that between 1998 and 2003, regional governors decreased prices in the quarter ahead of elections. Galina Yudashkina and Sergey Pobochy, "Regulation of the Electricity Sector in Russia: Regional Aspects (in Russian)," *Quantile*, no. 2 (2007): 107–130. As reforms at the center tightened control over regional regulators, this practice became less common. Apparently the governor of Primorskii Krai made a noisy announcement in 2003 that he was lowering electricity prices, but this turned out to be only a temporary measure. Interview #33 with journalist covering electricity sector, Vladivostok, 20070921.

as did various categories of war and labor veterans, pensioners, and other populations considered vulnerable. These discounted rates were known as in-kind benefits (*льготы*), and they were also a highly political issue in post-Soviet Russia.[39]

The ability to set electricity prices for a region's industrial enterprises was just as important as controlling a household electricity bills. Industrial enterprises consumed just over half of Russia's electricity.[40] Keeping tariffs low for select industrial consumers was a way for regional administrations to prevent deindustrialization. The governor "was trying to prevent the negative influence on regional development," said one observer from Irkutsk.[41] An executive at Irkutskenergo remembers one instance in particular:

> Khimprom, one of eight major enterprises in our oblast', supports the whole region. It is a promising enterprise with export potential. But it ceased to operate for nine months. After we agreed on the basis for our cooperation, it is now it is back on its feet.... The factory survived thanks to the reduction of tariffs ....[42]

Governors kept lists of industrial customers eligible for reduced electricity tariffs. References to these lists were ubiquitous in interviews, although it was never entirely clear if these lists were real or metaphorical.[43] In each region, two or three companies were repeatedly mentioned as examples of beneficiaries: BOR (chemicals) and SPASK (cement) in Primorskii Krai and Amur Metall in Khabarovsk, for example. A place on the list was usually reserved for companies with many employees, who played an

---

[39] In Primorskii Krai, for example, veterans received special tariffs; see "За свет будем платить так," *Утро России*, May 26, 1998. That rural residents also often receive special tarrifs was mentioned in interview #43 with electricity sector economist, Khabarovsk, 20071010. The whole system of subsidies for pensioners, veterans, disabled people, and other *льготники* (beneficiaries of in-kind benefits) underwent a wholesale revision in 2005, with very mixed results. See Wengle and Rasell, "The Monetisation of L'goty."

[40] In 2006, for example, the main consumer groups were the following: industrial 53%, residential 23%, transport 11%, service sector 11%, and agriculture 4%; information provided by UES, available at http://www.rao-ees.ru/en/info/about/main_facts/show.cgi?str_potreb.htm

[41] Interview #52 with electricity sector economist, Irkutsk, 20071117.

[42] Interview with Kuimov, *Эксперт*, No. 14, April 1998, 35. In this case the "cooperation" refers explicitly to the cooperation between Irkutskenergo and Khimprom, but it implicitly includes the regional government that brokered and supported these kinds of deals.

[43] Interview #32 with electricity sector economist, Vladivostok, 20070918; interview #33 with journalist covering electricity sector, Vladivostok, 20070921; interview #34 with academic and employee of an electricity company; and interview #41 with journalist covering electricity sector, Vladivostok, 20071005.

important part in regional economies.[44] While governors had employment in mind, preferential tariffs were probably also part of the arsenal of favors that a governor could dispense to loyal elites and his "political friends."[45] Sometimes entrepreneurs without connections to regional elites were charged far more than were companies with regional owners.[46] This tended to be a problem for smaller and newer enterprises that lacked the connections that large, established factories enjoyed.[47] Alliances with regional oligarchs and industrialists were important for governors during the 1990s; their ability to act in defiance of the federal government – in the electricity sector and in other realms – often depended on the backing of regional industrialists or regional oligarchs.

In addition to selective subsidies, both regional and federal government agencies also compiled lists of consumers who could not be cut off for failing to pay their bills. The deputy energy minister, Viktor Kudriavy, noted in 1998 that "[electricity companies] were advised to not allow the cut-off of certain customers."[48] This usually included schools, hospitals, public transport, and other infrastructure. In a number of Siberian regions, railways had access to privileged price regimes for electricity and could not be penalized for payment arrears. The director of Krasnoiarskenergo reported that "[our] relationship with the railways function[ed] according to special contracts."[49] A host of other socially or strategically important organizations, military installations, and defense related industries, for example, were also on such lists, usually in the name of energy security.[50] In the Far East, where much of the local economy depended on the military industrial complex, stories circulated about Soviet-era defense

---

[44] Interview #32 with electricity sector economist, Vladivostok, 20070918 and interview #46 with academic, Khabarovsk, 20071011.

[45] Interview #34 with academic and employee of an electricity company, Vladivostok, 20070923.

[46] Bradshaw and Kirkow, "The Energy Crisis in the Russian Far East," 1051. See also reference to this in Krasnoiarsk, where companies outside the aluminum industry paid more; "Красноярск пошел по приморскому пути," *Сегодня*, September 12, 1997.

[47] Interview #34 with academic and employee of an electricity company and interview #50 with businessman, Irkutsk, 20071115.

[48] "Некоторых потребителей вам совесть не позволит отключить." Interview in *Эксперт*, No. 14, April 13, 1998, 33.

[49] "Мы работаем с железнодорожниками по специальным договорам," according to Kolmogorov, director of Krasnoiarskenergo in "Раскалять амбиции не продуктивно," *Красноярский рабочий*, March 5, 1998.

[50] The rationale of energy security is mentioned in the case of Krasnoiarsk. See reference to the Altai region's military installations not paying their electricity bills; "Энергетики Сибири борются с неплатежами военных," *Известия*, February 29, 2000.

industries that converted to producing other goods – refrigerators, for example – but continued to benefit from their special exempt status, and did not pay for their electricity.[51] Governors could use their authority to pressure consumers to pay for electricity, or, as happened frequently, to condone nonpayment.

Governors played a crucial role in the nonpayment and barter crisis, one of the most serious problems to afflict the Russian economy during the mid-1990s.[52] While Energo debt was partly due to the low *regulated* prices, it also arose from the fact that many industrial customers simply did not pay their bills. The cause of nonpayment of bills was, on one level, quite simple: "Why don't [industrial] consumers pay for electricity? Because *they* don't get paid for whatever they produce," explained one observer.[53] Local authorities tolerated nonpayment and barter transactions.[54] The governor of Krasnoiarsk, for example, allowed debtors of the electricity sector to settle accounts via barter, and in turn decreed that electricity companies could do the same to decrease their debt vis-à-vis the regional administration.[55] Woodruff shows that governors in many regions condoned nonpayment, in part by not authorizing the cutoff of nonpaying customers, in part by encouraging the rise of surrogate monies and barter. Governors rationalized that barter transactions allowed factories to remain open.[56] Even enterprises that collected revenues were reluctant to pay for electricity once they realized that nonpayment carried no real consequence, which was not the case for salaries and other day-to-day expenses. It has also been argued that Energo directors benefited from barter payments that helped conceal side payments and enabled creative bookkeeping practices.[57] One journalist speculated that, "the larger

---

[51] Interview #41 with journalist covering electricity sector, Vladivostok, 20071005.

[52] Woodruff, *Money Unmade*.

[53] "Почему потребители не платят за электроэнергию? ... Все очень просто: им тоже не платят за выпущенную продукцию," in "Стреноженный монстр," *Восточно-Сибирская правда*, August 12, 1992.

[54] In a note on the state of the regional budget, the Irkutsk oblast' administration declared that "the administration will continue to try to deal with the indebtedness and non-payment [of enterprises] with offsets and *veksels* [*векселя*]"; see "Бюджетное послание Губернатора области," *Восточно-Сибирская правда*, October 17, 1995.

[55] "В Администрации края," *Красноярский рабочий*, June 10, 1994.

[56] Woodruff shows how the de facto price concessions were condoned or even coerced by regional authorities; Woodruff, *Money Unmade*, 114.

[57] References to double bookkeeping tended to refer to attempts to end it and restore order; see, for example, "Раскалять амбиции не продуктивно," *Красноярский рабочий*, March 5, 1998.

the share of barter payments, the larger are the rooms in the country home of the Energo director."[58]

The result of the nonpayment crisis was that by the late 1990s UES and the Energos were owed very large sums: "RAO-[UES] is the creditor of *all of Russia.*"[59] Electricity companies negotiated various settlements of this debt, via barter, offset agreements, and by issuing promissory notes (the so-called *векселя*).[60] This response "infected" fuel suppliers with problems of the barter economy, widening the cycle of nonpayment. One insider outlined the situation as follows: "As the 1990s progressed, customers accumulated a huge debt of more than $4.3 billion – a figure comparable to the annual income of UES's holdings. In other words, the [electricity] industry has been subsidizing the Russian economy by continuing the supply of electricity and heat to nonpaying customers. Barter and mutual debt write-offs covered a large portion of these payments."[61] Boris Brevnov, who was briefly the chairman of UES, noted that in the late 1990s "over 90 percent of receipts were in non-cash forms of payment, principally barter, mutual settlements, and *векселя* (promissory notes)."[62] It is difficult to know just how much of UES and the Energo accounting involved these virtual money flows, but most observers agree that UES and the Energos collected at the most 15–20 percent of receivables in cash for most of the 1990s.[63]

The lack of cash at Energos caused problems throughout the decade. Not only did it lead to unpaid wages; it also meant that the Energos

---

[58] "Чем выше доля оплаты бартером – тем больше комнат в усадьбе директора АО Энерго," *Эксперт*, No. 14, April 13, 1998, 30.

[59] "РАО – кредитор всея Руси"; Бергер and Проскурина, "Крест Чубайса," 58 (emphasis added). According to Rutland, "[UES] provided … $7–10 billion in subsidies to domestic customers through artificially low prices." Rutland, "The Business Sector in Post-Soviet Russia," 294.

[60] For a reference to barter and how debt is paid via offsets, see, for example, "Взаимовыручка познается в беде," *Утро России* April 22, 1997.

[61] Sergey I. Palamarchuk, Sergei V. Podkovalnikov, and Nikolai I. Voropai, "Getting the Electricity Sector on Track in Russia," *The Electricity Journal* 14, no. 8 (October 2001): 52–58. The regional Energo's debt was also a constant source of debate in regional newspapers. For references to Dal'energo's debt, see, for example, "Сами себя загнали в угол," *Утро России*, January 13, 1994; "Без ресурсов," *Утро России,* January 26, 1994. For reference to Krasnoiarskenergo's debt, see "Раскалять амбиции не продуктивно," *Красноярский рабочий*, March 5, 1998.

[62] Brevnov, "From Monopoly to Market Maker? Reforming Russia's Power Sector."

[63] See Бергер and Проскурина, "Крест Чубайса," 58. For example, Komienergo, the Komi Republic electricity monopoly, is said to have bartered a brand new glass-and-steel headquarters in return for offsetting unpaid electricity bills. Baker-Said, "Chubais' Shocking New Job," *Moscow Times*, June 30, 1998.

had to postpone scheduled infrastructure updates and investments.[64] The cumulative effect of regional price regulation was a price freeze in electricity from the mid- to late 1990s.[65] Regional administrations varied in the extent to which they allowed Energos to recover costs. In Primorskii Krai the governor kept prices at very low levels for a long time and customers ran up particularly large debts.[66] As a result, Dal'energo was unable to cover day-to-day costs and practically went bankrupt. The tangled web of nonpayment, debt, and offsets afflicted Dal'energo, and who owed whom and how much was very unclear.[67] One regional observer remembered the situation as follows:

The difficulties of Dal'energo began in the year 1994, when, pursuant to a decision by the regional administration and the regional energy commission, electricity prices were frozen for two years, while, at the same time, prices for fuel continued to rise. As a result, Dal'energo turned from being an economically and financially sound company, into an unprofitable operation.[68]

Dal'energos workers suffered wage arrears lasting for months they repeatedly protested the governor's policies and went on hunger strikes.[69]

[64] The problem of *износ* [wear and tear] of the aging infrastructure was a great concern; see, for example, "Раскалять амбиции не продуктивно," *Красноярский рабочий*, March 5, 1998. For another source on the concern over the obsolescence of the infrastructure in the sector, see "Энергоаудит на службе энергосбережения," *Дальневосточный капитал*, No. 8, August 2003, 54.

[65] "Тарифы на электроэнергию остаются прежними," *Восточно-Сибирская правда*, December 28, 1993. Also noted in Litwack and Thompson, *OECD Economic Survey of the Russian Federation*.

[66] For a report of a REK meeting that centered around the discussion that tariffs should remain low and on the nonpayment problem, see "Тарифы – те же!" *Утро России*, February 4, 1997.

[67] See, for example, the dispute between Dal'energo and the Vladivostok city administration: "По мнению администрации, не они должны выплатить АО 'Дальэнерго' пятьсот сорок миллиардов рублей, а наоборот – энергетики задолжали городу двадцать шесть миллиардов." ["According to the [city] administration, it was not them who owed Dal'energo 540 billion rubles; on the contrary, the *energetiki* owned the city 26 billion rubles."] In "Война энергетики?" *Утро России*, January 15, 1997. This dispute was tied to a perennial battle between the mayor of Valdivostok, Cherepkov, and the Krai administration, on which see also "Паны дерутся....," *Утро России*, January 21, 1997.

[68] "Сложности 'Дальэнерго' начались в 1994 году, когда по решению местной администрации и региональной энергетической комиссии тарифы энергосистемы были заморожены на 2 года при том, что цены на топливо продолжали расти. В результате 'Дальэнерго' превратилось из достаточно эффективной в экономическом и финансовом плане энергосистемы в убыточную." Анна Валентиновна Лобунец, "Перспективы Развития Энергетики Приморского Края с Учетом Интеграционных Процессов в Северо-Восточной Азии" (Дальневост. гос. у. Владивосток, 2004), section 2.2.

[69] See, for example, "Нет зарплаты – нет энергетики, " *Утро России*, September 17, 1997. See also several reports by *OMRI/DD*: At Primorskii power station, "300 workers have

At Irkutskenergo, salaries also went unpaid at times, but the situation was less severe, and the *energetiki* (the electricity sector professionals) decided that strikes were not an option.[70] With or without strikes, the *energetiki* suffered from unpaid wages in many Energos and were concerned about service outages that resulted from the poor condition of infrastructure. Directors of the Energos were either powerless to improve the situation or politically aligned with the governors.[71] Also, like other major industrial conglomerates of a region, the Energos were involved in a complex bargain with the regional government. Sometimes governors waived tax obligations in return for providing cheap energy to various consumers. Alternatively, Energos could pay taxes in-kind, with power deliveries to publicly owned institutions – an arrangement that placed the electricity sector at the center of Russia's barter economy.

Centralization of Regulatory Institutions

Until 1998, the regionally directed price politics described in the previous section was more or less tolerated. The liberal reformers of the Yeltsin government repeatedly tried to tackle the problems of bankrupt Energos, improve payment discipline, and raise electricity tariffs. But their efforts were mostly futile – partly because they were unable to match the influence of regional governors over the Energos, partly because they lacked allies within UES. When Chubais appointed Boris Brevnov as UES director in 1997, the latter set out to reform the electricity monopoly. One of his first steps was to order an audit by an international accounting firm, which he viewed as a prerequisite for creating payment discipline and financial stability. Symptomatic of the relationship between the liberal reformers and UES, the incumbent management of UES boycotted the audit. According to Brevnov, "UES management complained that the auditors asked too many questions."[72] Only when Chubais became head of UES in 1998 did the fight for the authority

been on hungers strike for nine days to protest a five-month delay in the payment of their wages." *OMRI/DD*, August 2, 1996, and *OMRI/DD*, September 9, 1996. The problem was not confined to the Far East, however.

[70] "Бастовать энергетики не могут. Но хотят," *Восточно-Сибирская правда*, November 23, 1995.

[71] An example is a close personal relationship between Popov and Ishaev in Khabarovsk; see also Chapter 6 on the relationship between governors and Energo directors.

[72] According to Brevnov, "they asked too many question" and were perceived to act "like the CIA"; see Brevnov, "From Monopoly to Market Maker? Reforming Russia's Power Sector," 19.

to determine electricity tariffs, to end the nonpayment crisis, to collect the Energo's outstanding bills, and to end ubiquitous creative book-keeping practices begin in earnest. The director of Krasnoiarskenergo reported in 1998 that "[w]e have to create elementary levels of order. [We have to] eliminate double book-keeping and make clear to every consumer and every energy sector employee that this is what we have decided and what we have set out to do."[73] In Chapter 3, we saw that Chubais's reforms could proceed only when UES reclaimed ownership and de facto control.

A second vital issue in the conflict between Chubais and the regional governors concerned the cash flow of the Energos and the many ways in which governors used the electricity sector to subsidies regional economies. A telling sign of Chubais' success in regularizing these issues was that the Energos did eventually manage to collect more receivables in cash. "Money flows became real" under Chubais, noted one observer.[74] After 2000, UES and the Energos were able to enforce payment discipline by cutting off nonpaying customers, something that both the federal government and regional governors had been extremely reluctant to authorize in the 1990s.[75] Also, the normalization of cash accounting made it easier for UES to supervise the financial flows of the Energos and to take measures against the use of cheap electricity as a political favor. Finally, media campaigns exhorted, cajoled, and threatened households to pay their electricity bills.[76] The enforcement of payment discipline had its cost and was accompanied by protests in a number of cities across Russia.[77] But these protests did not become widespread, and achieved little. Regional governors, who had been responsible for underwriting low

---

[73] "Приходится наводить элементарный порядок. Прекращать двойную бухгалтерию, делать для всех потребителей, да и для энергетиков, понятными наши действия и решения." In "Раскалять амбиции не продуктивно," *Красноярский рабочий*, March 5, 1998.

[74] Interview #16 with electricity sector consultant, Moscow/phone, 20061030.

[75] See "Мера жесткая, но вынужденная," *Энергия России*, No. 13/14, July 2000. Komienergo, for example, temporarily shut off the electricity supply to eighty-five organizations that were indebted to Komienergo; see "Автономное плавание," *Известия*, April 7, 2000.

[76] TV campaigns were mentioned by several people, for example, interview #39 with electrical engineer/electricity sector expert, Vladivostok, 20071004. When I was in Khabarovsk in October 2007, I saw TV commercials that urged household consumers to pay and threatened them with cutoff.

[77] Protests in response to tariff increases occurred primarily between 1999 and 2001; see Peter Rutland, "Power Struggle: Reforming the Electricity Industry," in Reddaway and Orttung, *The Dynamics of Russian Politics*, 1; Litwack and Thompson, *OECD Economic Survey of the Russian Federation*, 128.

tariffs and for tolerating nonpayment, were steadily losing their ability to influence the sector.

As Chapter 2 introduced, Chubais gained an ally in Putin, as the president's quest to curtail the authority of the regional governors dovetailed with UES directors' attempts to undercut the governor's hold on the electricity sector. Chubais wanted to de-politicize the electricity sector and create a nationwide power market. He also wanted to establish a regulatory regime that was independent from political pressures. Putin wanted a "unified legal and economic space in Russia."[78] Yet as Putin centralized federal power, at least three regulatory zones emerged, each with their own political dynamics and distinct subsidy regimes.

Nevertheless, the realignment of federal regulatory bodies proved a crucial step toward achieving both Chubais's and Putin's goals for the electricity sector. Most important was the creation of a new body, FST (*Федеральная служба по тарифам*), to replace the weak FEK. FST was to be a strong, independent institution designed to regulate price and tariff decisions.[79] In the electricity sector, the implementation of FST directives was directly supervised by the *polpredy*, presidential envoys to the region, whose offices were endowed with substantial authority. REKs were no longer accountable to regional governors, but to FST and the presidential envoys. "Everything and everybody is more closely scrutinized now,"[80] said one electricity sector engineer from Vladivostok. Indeed, the centralizing reforms seemed to work: UES price data shows that by 2005, all REKs complied with FST-recommended electricity tariffs.[81] Moreover,

---

[78] *Interfax*, March 22, 2000, also reported by *RFE/RL Newsline*, "Putin calls for new, improved federalism," March 23, 2000.

[79] Interview #15 with electricity sector analyst at financial institution, Moscow, 20061027. FST had a mandate beyond the electricity sector: "FST sets prices (tariffs) and controls issues related to determination and application of prices /tariffs/ in the electric power industry; gas industry; transmission of oil and oil derivatives through main pipelines; railroad transportation; services of cargo terminals, ports and airports; services on generally available electric and postal communications; products of nuclear fuel cycle; defense products; vodka, liquor and other alcoholic beverages. FST examines disputes between executive power bodies of the constituents of the RF in the field of the state regulation of tariffs, regulated organizations and consumers." According to the FST website, http://www.fstrf.ru/

[80] Interview #39 with electrical engineer/electricity sector expert, Vladivostok, 20071004.

[81] Unpublished UES price data, obtained through the European Bank for Reconstruction and Development (EBRD) in 2006. The way FST regulation worked was that it mandated a price band that gave REKS a minimum and maximum price levels; also referred to in interview #35 with regulator at regional electricity commission, Vladivostok, 20070924.

regulated prices increased everywhere in Russia during the 2000–2005 period (see Table 5.1 and Table A.4.1 in the Appendix), and the extent of price liberalization widened (price liberalization was phased in over a number of years; see discussion of the wholesale market later in this chapter).

Other measures aimed to increase the transparency of price regulation in the electricity sector. The period of price regulation was set to one year. Previously, governors had been able to manipulate prices quarterly, which led to much confusion and little predictability for electricity consumers.[82] Optimistically, the legislation also ruled that prices for all consumers had to be publicized and that legal proceedings for infringement of federal laws could be initiated against the REKs. A lawyer for the Primorskii Krai REK, who had little patience for my curiosity about special tariffs for industrial consumers, provided a standard answer for all my queries: "everything works according to the law" (*все по закону*).[83] Whether or not that was the case, REKs were clearly more closely supervised by the *polpred* offices and the FST, and ultimately acceded to federal regulations.

These regulatory reforms served both Chubais and Putin. They undercut the link between governors and Energos, eliminating the governors' ability to shape regional economies through targeted industrial and household subsidies. The centralization of regulatory decisions, which began with the creation of FST and the oversight of the *polpredy* continued in the years that followed. In 2008, the Market Council (*Совет Рынка*), a self-regulating power sector organization, was created to take over a number of regulatory functions. Shifting regulatory functions to the Market Council was meant to "de-politicize" and professionalize regulation, ensuring that its decisions "are shielded from short-term political pressure and intervention."[84] The Market Council's supervisory board is closely followed, as it regarded an indicator of the independence of Russian regulatory bodies. By 2011, federal officials occupied fourteen of

---

[82] Yudashkina and Pobochy, "Regulation of the Electricity Sector in Russia." Also stressed in interview #39 with electrical engineer/electricity sector expert, Vladivostok, 20071004.

[83] Interview #35 with regulator at regional electricity commission, Vladivostok, 20070924. She generally tried to evade my questions, also declaring that "конкретные цифры у нас тайна" ["concrete numbers are a secret"].

[84] Anatole Boute, "Response to IEA Consultation Paper 'Toward a More Efficient and Innovative Electricity Sector in Russia,'" *Toward a More Efficient and Innovative Electricity Sector in Russia* (2012), accessed March 14, 2014, http://papers.ssrn.com/sol3/papers.cfm?abstract_id=2078368

the twenty seats of the Market Council's board, giving federal authorities a majority of the body's voting rights.[85] Mirroring the developments that followed the creation of the FST, an institutional change meant to depoliticize regulation resulted primarily in the centralization of regulation, strengthening the authority of federal actors.

Electricity Markets Under Putin: New Zones of Regulation

The newly centralized regulatory institutions of the electricity sector reflected political dynamics introduced in Chapter 2. By 2008, electricity in Russia was increasingly traded as a commodity, and prices on the wholesale market were gradually liberalized. The Federal Tariff Service, the Federal Anti-Monopoly Service, and the Market Council regulated the sector from the center. But the new markets were subjected to a set of formal and informal rules that shaped who could buy and sell power at what price. Wholesale markets remained separated into three geographically distinct zones. Liberal reformers conceded various subsidies and price determination mechanisms to the new owners of electricity. Household consumers retained protections.

An important institutional change pertained to the prices on the wholesale market. Wholesale markets with liberalized tariffs were a key aim of reformers. Initially, though the market brought together actors in a new forum, prices for all transactions remained regulated. In 2004, a liberalized segment was introduced and a gradual shift in the balance between the regulated and liberalized portions of the transaction took place. In other words, an increasing share of long-term bilateral contracts was freed from regulated tariffs and instead subject to agreement between buyers and sellers. In 2006, the share of bilateral contracts traded at liberalized prices was still small: 15 percent in European Russia and 5 percent in Siberia. Price liberalization was scheduled to progress gradually over a five-year period, from 2006 to 2011. Starting in 2007, the liberalized segment grew annually by 5–15 percent, according to a schedule set by the government. In late 2007, a UES reformer stated confidently, "as of January 1, 2011 electric power will be sold only at free (competitive) prices."[86] By December 2010, only 15 percent of the wholesale market remained regulated, down from 95 percent in January

---

[85] Ibid.
[86] See the RAO website on reforms, http://www.rao-ees.ru/en/reforming/market/show. cgi?market.htm. Interview #63 with electricity company executive, Moscow, 20071212, statement to the same effect.

2007.[87] The number of transactions conducted on the wholesale market steadily increased over the same period. In addition to liberalized bilateral contracts, electricity was also sold freely on a day-ahead market, a mechanism that allowed consumers to buy electricity on short notice if demand exceeded amounts agreed on in the long-term contracts. Although volumes traded in this way are far smaller than the volumes traded in bilateral contracts, liberalized day-ahead markets – also called "spot-markets"– are a part of the wholesale market and a key feature of liberalized electricity systems.[88]

At the same time, at least three zones existed in the new market. The wholesale market was divided into European, Siberian, and "un-priced" (*неценовая*) zones. The Far East formed the largest part of the "un-priced" zone, which also includes Komi and Arkhangel'sk, two remote regions in the north of European Russia.[89] These markets were essentially separate. For example, almost all of Siberia's electricity was sold in the Siberian market.[90] Preceding chapters introduced a similar tripartite division, and argued that it was related to regionally patterned pacts between Moscow and different conglomerates. Toward the end of liberal reforms, an electricity sector insider predicted that the three markets were likely to remain separate, making the case that a unification of the different price zones "is not planned" for the foreseeable future.[91] The merging of markets is partly a technological issue related to the interconnectivity of high-voltage grids.[92] High-voltage transmission grids would have to

---

[87] See Alexandra Sidorenko, "Electricity in Russia: The impacts and benefits of structural reforms in transport, energy and telecommunications sectors" (APEC Policy Support Unit, January 2011), 355. The annual report of the Trading System Administrator (ATS/Администратор торговой системы) detailed the transactions conducted on the wholesale market, both at free and at regulated prices; see *Администратор торговой системы: Годовой отчет* (Moscow: ATS, 2010), p. 48, on the increase in transactions at liberalized prices, p. 40 on the decrease in transactions at regulated prices.

[88] Volumes traded on the spot-market fluctuated; in a peak month in 2007, around 14% of total electricity traded in European Russia and around 8% of that traded in Siberia was on spot-markets. See "Цены на электроэнергию в конце августа побили рекорды самых холодных дней зимы," *Interfax*, August 28, 2007.

[89] All price statistics by ATS were divided into these three zones; see ATS website, for example, http://www.np-ats.ru/. The non-priced zone includes Komi and Arkhangel'sk as well as the enclave of Kaliningrad.

[90] About 95%, according to interview #61 with employee of electricity company, Irkutsk, 20071205.

[91] "Объединение ценовых зон и неценовых не планируется," quote by ATS director, Дмитрий Пономарев, *Ведомости*, August 22, 2007.

[92] Historically, the Siberian and the European grids were connected with a high-voltage transmission link that went via Kazakhstan; interview #52 with electricity sector economist, Irkutsk, 20071117; see Chapter 3 for a discussion.

be strengthened if the Siberian market were to be linked more closely to Europe and the Far East. But it is also a policy question, one that will be resolved in the political arena.

A few observations support the projection that the three markets will remain separate. Even as power was increasingly traded on the wholesale market, the European and Siberian wholesale markets differed in a number of respects. The Siberian market had far fewer participants, and the Siberian share of the electricity traded on liberalized segments of the wholesale market was far smaller than European Russia's. In 2005, out of the total 68 billion kilowatt-hours traded on the liberalized segment wholesale market, only 3 billion kilowatt-hours were traded in Siberia. The share of electricity produced in Siberia was about a third of the electricity produced in European Russia at the time, but the volume of Siberian electricity traded on the wholesale market was less than 5 percent of European Russia's. Fewer producers participated in the Siberian wholesale market than in the European wholesale market. In 2006, out of the 249 registered participants in the wholesale market, only 33 were Siberian participants.[93] While the European share of Russia's electricity production was about 3.3 times larger than Siberia's, the share of European wholesale market participants was 7.5 times larger than Siberian participants. The low level of trading on the wholesale market was due to the fact that major Siberian electricity consumers did not switch to buying on the wholesale market, instead preferring the bilateral contracts that were not subject to competitive pricing (the section on Siberian regional arrangements later in this chapter details this trajectory).

In the Far East, the government retained full control over price levels, and power generators did not sell on the wholesale market. Remote regions in the Far East (Kamchatka, Yakutiia, Chukotka) were not physically connected to the national grid, and it was not surprising that tariffs there remained fully regulated, as little competition would be possible. The largest producers of the southern Far East (Primorskii Krai, Amur, and Khabarovsk, especially), however, were linked to Siberia and could have been integrated into a nationwide system. Preserving the Far East as a separate zone was a political decision to protect the local electricity and coal sectors.

---

[93] In 2005, there were 169 Russian European participants and 27 Siberian participants in each region's respective market; *UES Annual Reports* 2005 and 2006, available at http://www.rao-ees.ru/en/archive/

Socioeconomic Development and the Pace of Reforms

The central government retained final say over the pace of liberalization in accordance with Russia's "socioeconomic development," in the words of a bureaucrat at the Ministry of Economic Development.[94] In general, the government proceeded cautiously with price increases, weighing a possible backlash against tariff hikes and their effect on inflation. The Putin administration was keenly aware that rising household electricity prices affected a broad spectrum of the population and that they were exceedingly unpopular. In a 2006 survey, almost 60 percent of respondents stated that rising utility bills had a "significant negative effect on their life."[95] A year earlier, public demonstrations had followed social welfare reforms – the 2005 monetization of in-kind benefits, the *l'goty* (*льготы*). This provided a vivid demonstration of the pain caused by liberal reforms of basic services.[96] These protests were an important signal for electricity reforms, because special tariffs for electric power were one of the social benefits the *l'goty* reform tried to abolish.

Household tariffs increased significantly while remaining fully regulated. Unlike tariffs for industrial consumers, households were de facto excluded from price liberalization. Household consumption amounted to about 10 percent of total electricity production and it was among the most heavily subsidized segment of the sector. In a 2005 amendment to the 2003 electricity laws, the government designated so-called "guaranteeing suppliers" to sell electricity to "households and other socially important consumer groups" at prices set by the government.[97] The government thus retained an important mechanism to control electricity prices for

[94] Interview #24 with regulator/economist at the Ministry for Economic Development, Moscow, 20070214.

[95] Almost two-thirds (57%) of respondents in a 2005 survey reported that rising electricity tariffs "negatively affect their lives." Of this group, 39% reported that they will adjust spending habits as a result of rising utility prices. The 39% is divided into the following groups: 18% report that "I will save (on transport, clothing, food)," 15% report "I will look for additional income," 6% report "I will use public utilities less." Based on a survey by the Фонд Общественное мнение (FOM). The interviews were conducted nationwide, in September 2005 in 100 residencies in 44 regions, with a sample size of 1,500 respondents and additional polls of the Moscow population. Available in the archive on FOM website, in the section on *ЖКХ*; http://fom.ru/. Excerpts also published in Wengle, "Power Politics Electricity Sector Reforms in Post-Soviet Russia."

[96] Wengle and Rasell, "The Monetisation of L'goty."

[97] Interview #15 with electricity sector analyst at financial institution, Moscow, 20061027. A UES press release stated ambiguously: "The price level … should be stable enough, on the one hand, and on the other hand it should ensure a certain level of profitability for suppliers of electricity." *UES Press Release*, 2003, Moscow, May 23, available at http://www.rao-ees.ru/

household consumers. One of the key questions for the future is whether the government will rely on guaranteeing suppliers to absorb price increases on the wholesale market, or whether such increases will ultimately be passed along to retail consumers. The evidence so far is mixed. Moscow approved annual increases in the regulated tariffs for household consumers, yet each year these increases were debated. Ahead of the 2004 presidential elections, Putin increased electricity tariffs, but only as much as the general inflation level, less than reformers hoped.[98] Increases of 15 percent and 10 percent were sanctioned in 2011 and 2012, respectively; both increases outpaced inflation.[99] Cross-subsidies decreased steadily under Putin, but by the end of reforms, households were still on average charged less than cost and household prices remained below industrial prices. In 2009, prices for household consumers averaged around 1.5 times less than industrial prices.[100] Finally, the FST continued the FEK practice of approving separate price bands for each region, which delimited regional minimum and maximum tariffs for households. What this means is that central government continued to meticulously plan the marketization of Russia's regions.

While plans existed for household tariff liberalization at the time I concluded research for this project, serious obstacles will need to be addressed before this can happen.[101] One of these obstacles is technical, or material, to tie this in with the analysis in Chapter 3: retail liberalization requires cost-effective, real-time information on consumption by individual units, which in turn is predicated on apartment-level electricity meters. Such metering in Russia is notoriously difficult and costly to install, in part because the physical infrastructure was never intended to

---

[98] The Russian daily newspaper *Время* speculates that this will benefit Putin's party, United Russia, as well as Chubais's party, the Union of Rightist Forces; see "Is the Electricity Monopoly playing Politics?" *RFERL Newsline*, October 23, 2003.

[99] Increases in regulated tariffs are published by the FST: http://www.fstrf.ru/tariffs/info_tarif/electro. For a comment, see, for example, "Тарифы сошли с ума," *Независимая газета*, February 26, 2013.

[100] "Тарифы на электроэнергию для населения России в 1,5 раза ниже себестоимости," *Независимая газета*, October 12, 2009.

[101] These obstacles are detailed in an OECD/ International Energy Agency (IEA) report, Douglas Cooke, Alexander Antonyuk, and Isabel Murray, *Toward a More Efficient and Innovative Electricity Sector in Russia* (Paris: OECD Publishing, 2012), accessed March 14, 2014, http://www.iea.org/publications/insights/russian_electricity_reform-145x206.pdf. Douglass Cooke, Alexander Antonyuk, and Isabel Murray, "Toward a More Efficient and Innovative Electricity Sector in Russia," *IEA Consultation Paper*, 2012.

measure consumption at the unit dwelling level.[102] Household tariffs are thus likely to remain as much a political as an economic matter.

Regional Variation in Subsidy Regimes

That regional governors employed different types of subsidies during the 1990s is not surprising. Yet, despite the success of liberal reformers in unbundling power plants and creating a wholesale electricity market, regionally patterned differences in industrial and household subsidies persisted after 2004. Even though the Energos were dissolved into supra-regional holding companies, and the site of regulation shifted from regions to Moscow, the efforts of liberal reformers to abolish old subsidies had mixed results.

As the last chapter introduced, new owners had different interests vis-à-vis the electricity sector and their influence on sector reform varied. Table 5.2 provides an overview of the subsidy regimes in different regions of Russia.

Subsidies in European Russia

The electricity subsidy regimes in European Russia relied on subsidized gas, or more precisely on gas prices that were kept low throughout the entire post-Soviet period. Gazprom has been the essential linchpin of various energy subsidies, including electricity subsidies. During the 1990s, European Russian governors depended on Gazprom to oppose Chubais. The gas giant essentially underwrote the electricity subsidies that regional governors were handing out: regional governors and Energos could keep prices low, only because Gazprom gave them credit for gas deliveries and delivered gas at below-market prices.[103] Gazprom was generally not allowed to suspend gas deliveries to power plants in arrears, although they did often threaten to limit supplies to particularly indebted consumers.[104] Many Energos remained in constant arrears with gas payments. Around 2000, the federal government started selectively allowing Gazprom to

---

[102] The IEA report notes that this has been challenging for many countries. For Russia, the IEA also cautioned that, in practice, "benefits of extending choice to the smallest customers may be outweighed by the associated costs." For a discussion of household metering of heat, see Collier, *Post-Soviet Social*, 238.

[103] See, for example, Gustafson, *Capitalism Russian-Style*, 55.

[104] Although they did sometimes cut supplies temporarily and partially to particularly indebted consumers. In Tver, for example, "Gazprom has cut supplies to the city by 45%, until it pays its debt of 210 billion rubles [$40 million]." *OMRI/DD*, October 2, 1996.

TABLE 5.2. *Summary of cross-regional difference in subsidy regimes (2003–2008)*

Region	Subsidy Regime
European Russia	Subsidies generally decreased
Siberia	Industrial subsidies persisted in large hydroelectric regions
Far East	Cross-subsidies to households persisted or increased; subsidies in the form of direct budget transfers also persisted or increased

temporarily cut off nonpaying Energos. Gazprom and Chubais thus collaborated in some cases to get the Energo's regional customers to pay: "The natural monopolies were sometimes forced to cooperate, as they, with the help of the [federal] government, could put pressure on the regions."[105]

While Chubais did not approve of Gazprom's appetite for newly formed power companies, documented in Chapter 4, the liberal reformer's and the gas behemoth's interests coincided in the realm of price liberalization. Both wanted an end to electricity subsidies and an increase in prices. This was the case because, given that domestic prices for gas remained low, Gazprom benefited from reforms that increased electricity prices: higher prices would allow electricity companies to pay their gas bills, and they would allow Gazprom to increase profits from the electricity plants it controlled. As Chubais's reforms gained ground in European Russia, electricity prices increased across the region and subsidies generally declined. Cross-subsidies, as introduced earlier, were considered one of the main obstacles to liberal reforms, and phasing them out was a key priority. The decline of cross-subsidies in all of the large European Russian regions since 2000, then, must be seen as a major victory for the liberals, albeit one achieved due to the coincidence of interests with Gazprom. Indeed, cross-subsidies decreased more in European Russia than elsewhere. Table 5.3 shows regional variation in cross-subsidies for the three Energos at the beginning and end of the period of price liberalization, 2000 and 2005 (Table A.4.2 in the Appendix contains data for a larger set of regions).

---

[105] "Автономное плавание," *Известия*, April 7, 2000. Chapter 3 showed that Gazprom was able to swap its debt for equity in power plants in which it was interested, thereby regaining a say over who receives electricity at what price.

TABLE 5.3. *Regional differences in cross-subsidies persist*

	Mosenergo	Irkutskenergo	Dal'energo
RR/kWh			
2000	.2	No cross-subsidies	.1
2005	.05	No cross-subsidies	.66

Note: Cross-subsidies are calculated as the difference between industrial tariffs and household tariffs (urban); see Appendix. The year 1998 is the earliest one for which industrial tariffs are available. The year 2005 is the last one in the dataset on prices that I obtained from UES; I confirmed these trends with interviews and media reports.
Source: UES data set on regulated tariffs.

Industrial subsidies were harder to detect. Comparing industrial tariffs across European Russian regions suggested that this type of subsidy remained concentrated in Tatarstan, Bashkortostan, and Sverdlovsk (see Table A.4.3 in the Appendix). These three regions remained generally more independent than other regions in European Russia. Tatenergo and Bashkirenergo could count on fuel from Tatneft and Bashneft – regionally controlled energy companies. And, as we have seen previously, these populous ethnic regions negotiated special agreements with the Yeltsin government during the 1990s. They remained independent throughout the period under discussion: Tatenergo and Bashkirenergo were not integrated into the new power sector companies, the OGKs and TGKs.[106] Prices in Tatarstan, Bashkortostan, and Sverdlovsk remained lower than the regional average. With the exception of these regions, subsidies to industrial and household consumers generally declined and prices rose in European Russia.

Subsidies in Siberia

In Siberia, the sponsor of subsidies was Father Baikal and Angara the Bride, as *Irkutiane*, the residents of Irkutsk oblast', refer to the waterways that generate much of the region's hydroelectric power. A unique aspect of the Siberian subsidy regime was that prices could be kept low by separating Siberian consumers from other markets. Electricity in Siberia was cheap because it was produced by the region's huge hydroelectric power

---

[106] These two Energos control large market shares in their respective regions, which is a cause for concern for competition experts; Russell Pittman, "Chinese Railway Reform and Competition: Lessons from the Experience in Other Countries," *Journal of Transport Economics and Policy* 38, no. 2 (2004): 309–332.

plants, where the marginal cost of a kilowatt-hour was very low. If prices are low because costs are low, why refer to this as a subsidy? It is an implicit subsidy, because low prices depended on intentionally reserving Siberian electricity for the large Siberian industrial consumers, and not exporting it to European Russia, the Far East, or abroad, to China and Mongolia, where consumers would pay far more.

UES tried to equalize prices across Russia for most of the 1990s by creating a national wholesale market. A competitive nationwide wholesale market could allocate electricity to the highest bidder. This would entail moving electricity from energy-abundant regions to energy-deficient regions, generally leveling prices but increasing them for Siberians. During the 1990s, Siberian governors prevented this from happening. They believed that "there isn't enough cheap electricity for everyone."[107] Siberian governors strove to maintain a system in which Siberian consumers benefited from the region's low-cost electricity. This was the prevailing opinion of Siberian politicians, academics, and electricity sector professionals: price levels in Siberia should be kept low by reserving cheap energy for local industries.[108] Following this maxim, Siberian governors in effect created subsidies for regional industries by preventing a unified price zone and by granting regional industrial consumers privileged access to very low prices. In the 1990s, these subsidy regimes were very localized and often ad hoc. An Irkutskenergo executive described their relationship to industrial consumers: "[W]e began to reduce tariffs for select consumers in specific ways and under specific circumstances."[109] As the economic crisis of the 1990s widened, such agreements became more common across Siberia. In Krasnoiarsk, similar agreements lowered tariffs for the main consumers of Krasnoiarskenergo – the Krasnoiarsk aluminum plants. "Tariffs for them [the aluminum industry] were lowered from the get-go," said one observer about the relationship between the regional Energo and the aluminum industry.[110] In return for lowering

[107] "Дешевой энергии на всех не хватит," *Восточно-Сибирская правда*, January 6, 1997.

[108] This position is detailed in *Материалы к энергетической стратегии Сибири*, Новосибирск: Сибирское отделение РАН, July 1997, chapter 10, p. 102. This is also a recurring theme in regional newspapers, for example, "Дешевой энергии на всех не хватит," *Восточно-Сибирская правда*, January 6, 1997.

[109] "Мы начали практиковать снижение тарифов для определенных потребителей, в определенных рамках и на определенных условиях"; Сергей Куимов, *Эксперт*, No. 14, April 13, 1998, p. 35. That these agreements were supported by regional administrations was confirmed in interview #60 with energy company executive, Irkutsk, 20071203.

[110] "Тарифы для них [предприятий алюминиевой промышленности] были занижены изначально." "Красноярск пошел по приморскому пути," *Сегодня*, September 12, 1997.

electricity tariffs and taxes for the aluminum companies, the aluminum magnate Oleg Deripaska kept residents of Krasnoiarsk employed (and, it is said, at least on one occasion helped elect a governor – Aleksei Lebed).[111] The essence of these agreements was that energy-intensive industries in the region received privileged access to the low-cost power generated by Siberian rivers. Such agreements were vital for Russia's enormous and economically important metals industry, absolutely depended on cheap electricity.[112]

As prices were liberalized following Chubais's reforms of 2003, Siberian industrial subsidies did not disappear. In a number of Siberian regions, companies continued to receive electricity at low cost and did not have to rely on newly created wholesale market. This is particularly obvious for the aluminum smelters: "They [Irkutskenergo] give cheap electricity to aluminum companies."[113] As we saw previously, Rusal either controls almost all strategic hydroelectric power plants in Siberia or shares control with the government's Hydro-OGK. Eminently successful in influencing regional governors in the 1990s, Rusal continued its quest to secure electricity at low prices under Putin. In Siberia, the main producers of electricity (Rusal and the government) were at the same time the main consumers of electricity; the sale and purchase of electricity were intra-enterprise matters rather than market transactions. As long as Rusal kept ownership of power plants, the new rules of the electricity markets would not change this arrangement.

Until 2007, aluminum companies and other electricity-intensive consumers bought electricity either in bilateral contracts or at low regulated prices, enjoying substantial industrial subsidies that regional regulatory commissions set.[114] With the new rules of the wholesale market and the

---

The observer also noted that this increased prices for all the other industrial consumers. About two-thirds of Krasnoiarskenergo's electricity was produced in the Krasnoiarsk hydroelectric power plant; Krasnoiarsk Aluminum Plant used all of Krasnoiarksenergo's high-voltage output; *Вестник региональной энергокомиссии Красноярского края*, January 2005, 27.

[111] Barnes, *Owning Russia*, 138.

[112] Peter Rutland discusses the importance of the metals industry and notes the role of electricity subsidies in Rutland, "Oil and Politics in Russia," 2006, 16.

[113] Interview #52 with electricity sector economist, Irkutsk, 20071117. Statements to the same effects were also made in interview #15 with electricity sector expert at financial institution, Moscow, 20061027; in interview #53 with employee of electricity company, Irkutsk, 20071119; and in interview #54 with businessman, Irkutsk, 20071120.

[114] See, for example, *Вестник региональной энергокомиссии Красноярского края*, January 2005; this was also mentioned in interview #50 with businessman, Irkutsk, 20071115 and interview #52 with electricity sector economist, Irkutsk, 20071117.

liberalization of prices that came into effect after 2007, the electricity generators could potentially increase prices for all consumers and sell more electricity on the wholesale market. The formal institutions mandated that regulated bilateral contracts (RDD) be replaced by unregulated bilateral contracts (SDD). However, buyers and sellers were free to contract at whatever prices they saw fit under the rules that governed SDDs, and aluminum companies surely "hoped they could continue to get low prices via bilateral contracts."[115] Because of the particular ownership structures that emerged in Siberia – the vertical integration of hydroelectric dams with electricity-intensive downstream consumers – it was unlikely that electricity would be traded to achieve the highest profits. To put it differently, wholesale markets remain constrained, because more than half of the region's electricity was produced in hydroelectric plants owned by market participants who were not interested in maximizing revenues by selling to the highest bidders.[116] "Profits are made in another place; in aluminum, ... that's were profits are made," categorically stated one insider. Much of Siberia's hydroelectric power continued to be sold below market prices to the adjacent industrial plants or to government-owned consumers like the Siberian railway.[117]

Siberia sold much of its electricity at prices much lower than the average Russian tariffs and well below prices on the newly created Siberian wholesale market (see Appendix 4, Tables A.4.4 and A.4.5). Rusal, not surprisingly, was the main beneficiary because it controlled large hydroelectric power plants: "Russian aluminum companies buy electric power on average for [the equivalent of] about 1.2 U.S. cents per kilowatt-hour. Electricity is available to Rusal so cheaply because the *aliuminshchiki* had previously acquired ownership of hydroelectric plants in Siberia. In Western Europe, aluminum companies have to pay [the equivalent of] 3 cents per kilowatt-hour of electric energy."[118] Paying little for electricity lowered the cost of producing aluminum; in

---

[115] Interview #57 with electricity sector economist, Irkutsk, 20071122.

[116] The point here was explicitly that the owners of Irkutskenergo were not interested in profits from electricity generation. Interview #54 with businessman, Irkutsk, 20071120.

[117] Rail subsidies were mentioned in several interviews, for example, interview #50 with businessman, Irkutsk, 20071115, and interview #60 with energy company executive, Irkutsk, 20071203.

[118] "Российские алюминиевые компании покупают электроэнергию в среднем по $0,012 за 1 кВт/час. Однако она обходится Русалу так дешево из-за того, что алюминьщики в свое время выкупили ГЭС в Сибири в собственность. В Западной Европе электроэнергия обходится алюминиевым концернам в $0,03 за 1 кВт/час." In "Hydro-Aluminum построит завод в России; Если договорится о цене на электроэнергию," *Коммерсантъ*,

an estimate for 2002, for example, Rusal was estimated to pay around $120 for electricity per ton of aluminum, far less than that of major aluminum smelters outside of Russia.[119] A second important beneficiary of the Siberian subsidy regime was the Siberian railways. The government was the second-largest owner of power plants in Siberia, as it controlled the company Hydro-OGK. Subsidized rail tariffs allowed cargo from Siberian mineral deposits to reach domestic and international markets without paying the full price of their remoteness.

While data on how much subsidized consumers actually paid was hard to come by – "the way tariffs are determined for hydroelectric power is not very transparent"[120] – many insiders confirmed that "much of Irkutsk's hydroelectric power goes straight to aluminum companies and other big clients, which get a special rate."[121] In sum, then, unlike in European Russia, where the sponsor of energy subsidies (Gazprom) played a pivotal role in the political battles over electricity reforms, in Siberia it was the beneficiaries who mattered most. Beneficiaries such as Rusal and the Siberian railways succeeded in keeping Siberia a separate market, characterized by mutual agreement between the largest power producers and consumers to keep prices low, making it "very unlikely that there will be competition [in Siberia]."[122]

A caveat for the Siberian outcomes is that there is a sharp distinction between the large and small electricity-producing regions. Regions with little electricity production look more like European Russia in terms of their subsidies: decreasing household subsidies, no industrial subsidies, and no budget transfers. Yet, these regions shared an interest in keeping Siberia a separate price zone because they received some of the low-priced energy from their hydro-powered neighbors. Unlike in European Russia, Siberian regions did not generally have significant cross-subsidies, as the price level in Siberia was generally low. This was particularly true for the Siberian regions with large electricity production. Regions with

January 12, 2006. Deripaska's quest to secure low-cost electricity was also often reported in regional and national news; see, for example, "Русский алюминий ищет дешевую энергию," *Коммерсантъ*, November 30, 2001.

[119] One observer compares this with the costs that are typically estimated for the two U.S.-based companies, Alcoa and Kaiser: Alcoa $289 per ton, Kaiser $330; Simon Pirani, "Rusal Leaves Competitors Counting Their Costs," *Metals Bulletin*, June 9, 2002, accessed March 14, 2014, http://piraniarchive.wordpress.com/home/about/rusal-leaves-competitors-counting-their-costs/

[120] Interview #43 with electricity sector economist, Khabarovsk, 20071010.

[121] Interview #50 with businessman, Irkutsk, 20071115.

[122] Interview #16 with electricity sector consultant, Moscow/phone, 20061030.

less production did have cross-subsidies, which decreased over the five-
year period between 2001 and 2005, similar to the European regions.[123]

Subsidies in the Far East

In the Far East, subsidies took the form of direct payments to regional
governments and free or subsidized fuel deliveries to Energos. Unlike in
Siberia, where struggles over tariffs and ownership were due to abundant
cheap power, electricity in the Far East was scarce for much of the 1990s.
Power in the region was also the most expensive in all of Russia.[124] Dated
technological infrastructure resulted in large losses for the Far Eastern
power plants.[125] The Far East was also the epicenter of blackouts in the
Russian electricity sector. Coal production was privatized early and many
coalmines were closed when demand collapsed during the economic crisis and the few remaining clients were unable to pay.[126] This meant that
many of the Far Eastern Energos lacked sufficient coal supplies to get
through the winter.[127] This led to widespread electricity outages, which
remained fixed in residents' memory as the "dark times."[128]

The regional governor of Primorskii Krai was a staunch supporter of
subsidies: "I have always stressed that electricity in the Far East needs to
be subsidized."[129] The federal government consistently stepped in with
direct budget transfers to the Far Eastern regional governments and by
organizing the delivery of diesel or coal shipments to bridge fuel supply bottlenecks.[130] A 1997 presidential decree promising the "allocation

---

[123] UES price data obtained by author from UES; see Appendix Table A.4.2.

[124] UES price data obtained by author from UES; see Appendix Table A.4.4. See also various references to the cost of electricity in the Far East in local media, for example,
"Дальэнерго меняет партнеров?" *Утро России*, January 14, 1997. Also interview #32
with electricity sector economist, Vladivostok, 20070918, and interview #34 with
employee of an electricity company, Vladivostok, 20070923.

[125] Interview #39 with electrical engineer/electricity sector expert, Vladivostok, 20071004.

[126] After 2000, coal production in the Far East has recovered. Nevertheless, Far Eastern
coal was low-caloric and relatively inefficient compared to Siberian coal, which meant
that the cost of electricity production was high.

[127] For example, "Острый сигнал: прошли выборы – отключили батареи," *Утро России*,
January 15, 1994; and "Дефицит света ... " *Утро России*, March 12, 1996.

[128] Conversations with Primorskii Krai residents confirmed this point. An anthropologists
traced how the breakdown of electricity was perceived as a jolt back to premodern
times; see Platz, "The Shape of National Time: Daily Life, History and Identity During
Armenia's Transition to Independence 1991–1994."

[129] Quote by Nazdratenko in Бергер and Проскурина, "Крест Чубайса," 73.

[130] "Комиссия по чрезвычайным ситуациям предпринимает конкретные шаги по
разрешению топливного кризиса," *Утро России*, January 14, 1997. Anti-crisis measures

of financial means to be given to Primorskii Krai from the federal budget [to] normaliz[e] the situation in the heat and electricity sector of the Krai" was typical.[131] Significant sums from the federal budget were allocated to bail out Far Eastern Energos, allowing them to pay their debt to coal companies.[132] Dal'energo and Khabarovskenergo were usually at the top of the list, but most other Far Eastern Energos received help. While federal transfers were reported in local media at the time as exceptional measures for particularly dire situation, they ended up being a yearly event. Every fall, in what was called the "preparation for winter season," Primorskii Krai found itself unable to locate funds to buy fuel and needed help to keep Dal'energo afloat. Direct budget transfers were subsidies that directly benefit regional electricity companies – and they were consistently concentrated in the Far East. [133] As Table 5.4 shows, all but one region that received direct budget transfers in 2004 was located in the Russian Far East. In addition to direct budget transfers and coal deliveries, cross-subsidies were relatively high in Far Eastern regions.[134]

In theory, electricity companies were the main beneficiaries of federal budget transfers to the Far East and they were to be used as emergency relief. What actually happened with these funds ultimately depended largely on how regional administrations apportioned the funds, as Moscow was unable to oversee how funds were spent during the 1990s. The governor of Primorskii Krai, Evgeny Nazdratenko, was said to have used subsidies

and support from the central government included in-kind fuel deliveries: almost 20,000 tons of diesel fuel were allocated from the federal government's resource committee in 1997. In-kind fuel deliveries were a recurring theme in local newspapers; for an earlier reference, see "Миллиарды на топливо," *Утро России*, January 20, 1994. Also mentioned in several interviews, for example, interview #39 with electrical engineer/electricity sector expert, Vladivostok, 20071004, and interview #43 with electricity sector economist, Khabarovsk, 20071010.

[131] "УКАЗ Президента Российской Федерации: О дополнительных правах и обязанностях полномочного представителя президента Российской Федерации в Приморском крае," *Утро России*, June 10, 1997.

[132] "Energy Minister Yurii Shafranik ... said that Moscow earmarked 4.6 trillion rubles for bailing out the region's fuel and energy sector," *OMRI/DD*, August 6, 1996; and "Primoriye to receive federal funds," *OMRI/DD*, September 23, 1996.

[133] Note that Primorskii Krai and Khabarovsk were allocated the same amount, although, as Khabarovsk has a smaller population, the per capita amount is larger in Khabarovsk (306rr/capita) than in Primorskii Krai (230rr/capita).

[134] UES price data obtained by author from UES; see Appendix Table A.4.2. See also Лобунец, "Перспективы Развития Энергетики Приморского Края с Учетом Интеграционных Процессов в Северо-Восточной Азии," 108, which contains an analysis of cross-subsidies in the Far East. This was also confirmed in interview #34 with employee of an electricity company, Vladivostok, 20070923.

TABLE 5.4. *List of regions receiving direct budget transfers in 2004*

Oblast'	Million Rubles (Allocated by Federal Budget/Actually Allocated)	Supra-Region
Primorskii Krai	460/283	RFE
Khabarovsk	460/283	RFE
Amurskaia Oblast'	85/52	RFE
Kamchatka	680/418	RFE
Magadanskaia Oblast'	50/30	RFE
Chukotka	80/49	RFE
Sakhalin	225/138	RFE
Arkhangelsk	460/283	**EUR**
Yakutiia	100/61	RFE

Source: *Тарифы в электроэнергетике*, published by the Federal Tariff Service (FST), p. 46.

to leverage his influence in the region, appeasing households' demand for low *kvartplata* and selecting beneficiaries based on their loyalty to him. This meant that Primorskii Krai had the lowest electricity tariffs in all of the Far East. For the population, Nazdratenko's handling of the electricity sector was a mixed blessing, as the region also had the highest rate of blackouts (though blackouts were also due to reasons beyond his control).[135] The governor of the neighboring Khabarovsk, Viktor Ishaev, had a better reputation for his handling of the electricity sector. A Soviet-era apparatchik, Ishaev declared electricity a priority.[136] He allowed prices to be consistently higher than in neighboring Primorskii Krai, and was less generous with industrial subsidies and less lenient to nonpaying household and industrial customers. As a result, blackouts were less common than in neighboring Primorskii Krai.

In sum, as an important period of price liberalization lowered or eliminated subsidies elsewhere in Russia, they largely persist in the Russian Far East. Cross-subsidies remained relatively high (see Table A.4.2 in the Appendix).[137] An observer of the Far Eastern electricity sector argued that these cross-subsidies were considered crucial by federal authorities and

---

[135] Interview #32 with electricity sector economist, Vladivostok, 20070918. For media reports, see, for example, "В режиме отключений..." *Утро России*, September 24, 1997; for further media reports on blackouts, see Chapter 2.

[136] Interview #45 with employee of electricity company, Khabarovsk, 20071011.

[137] Interview #41 with journalist covering electricity sector, Vladivostok, 20071005. See also interview with Klimenko, in *Дальневосточный капитал*, August 2005, 8/60, p. 10.

were one of the reasons the region was not included in the liberal reform program with the rest of Russia.[138] The government also continued to pay direct subsidies to Far Eastern electricity companies in the form of direct budget transfers.[139] At the same time, as with the ownership changes, reforms did not significantly liberalize the sector, but they still served the goal of centralizing control. Although direct budget transfers continued in the Far East after the Energos were unbundled, subsidies were no longer administered via regional administrations. The federal government directly subsidized the regional electricity company, DVUEK, compensating them for the high cost of producing power in the region.[140]

Subsidies, Prices, and the Economics of the Sector

The price of power continued to differ markedly across regions even as reforms drew to a close.[141] This was true for both liberalized and regulated segments of the market. Prices in the Siberian zone were consistently lower than in the European zone, even as price liberalization progressed and the wholesale market developed (see Tables A.4.3 and A.4.4 in appendix). These price differentials resulted from different costs associated with power generation, different regulatory zones, and different subsidy regimes across the regions of Russia. Most observers agree that prices in the future will depend on how price differentials across regions, introduced at the outset, will develop. According to Chubais, the future of price differentials, in turn, depends on a variety of factors, including the "development of regions, the development of sectors; ... myriads of different interests are involved."[142]

---

[138] According to Klimenko, "Еще один фактор – значительный объем перекрестного субсидирования, которое по-прежнему сохраняется на Дальнем Востоке." ["Another reason [for why the Far East is undergoing a different reform trajectory] is the high level of cross-subsidies in the Far East."] See note 137 for the source.

[139] *Тарифы в электроэнергетике*, Федеральная служба по тарифам / Federal Tariff Service p. 46. In contrast, only one region in European Russia, Arkhangelsk, received subsidies in the form of direct federal transfers, and those subsidies were reduced to 283 million rubles in 2004 from 500 million rubles in 2003 and 2002.

[140] Industrial subsidies in the Far East are difficult to detect with the methodology I used to discern them in the other regions. Many of the electricity systems are isolated, which means the comparison of industrial tariff with supra-regional averages is not a useful proxy of industrial subsidies.

[141] That prices differ was mentioned several times in interviews, for example, interview #52 with electricity sector economist, Irkutsk, 20071117.

[142] Remark by Chubais at a conference "Энергетика: тормоз или локомотив развития экономики?" Moscow, February 13, 2007.

Different price and subsidy regimes greatly affected economic calculations in the sector. This also meant that the profitability of companies and their ability to invest in infrastructural upgrades depended to a large degree on politics. Frustration over the lack of reliable information necessary for asset valuation was a recurring theme in interviews with electricity sector analysts at Moscow's financial institutions.[143] The profitability of power companies differed widely in the 1990s, with many of the especially troubled Energos were located in the Far East.[144] After the restructuring of Energos into TGKs and OGKs, this variation in profitability persisted. The economics of the newly restructured sector – current profitability, a myriad of everyday decisions, and projections for the future – continued to depend on subsidy regimes and the politics of liberalization.[145] TGKs, for example, produced power and heat – the former under a liberalized regime that in some regions was quite profitable while the latter still operated under regulated prices.[146] The TGKs' profitability after reforms hinged as much on political decisions as did the Energos' profitability during the 1990s.

The political achievements and pacts also remained provisional. Liberal reformers, on the one hand, claimed a full political and "moral" victory in privatizing and liberalizing the Soviet-era electricity monopoly.[147] The Soviet-era monopolies, and hence the most visible and most symbolic organizations of the Russian power sector – UES and the Energos – disappeared and new, supra-regional companies took their places and were able to shape price reforms in ways that benefitted them. This meant that the dismantling of the old structures and the demolition of Soviet-era monopolies did *not* translate into a nationwide competitive market.

[143] For example, interview #7 with electricity sector analyst at financial institution, Moscow, 20061005, and interview #9 with another electricity sector analyst at financial institution, Moscow, 20061008.

[144] For much of the 1990s, a little more than half of the Energos consistently recorded losses, a group that includes most of the Far Eastern Energos. Tyumenergo, Lenenergo, and Mosenergo, by contrast, were among the most profitable; see Бергер и Проскурина, "Крест Чубайса." See also "Energos Produce Mixed Results," *Moscow Times*, October 1, 1997.

[145] OGK-4 has been profitable, while OGK-3 has incurred losses, for example.

[146] The balance sheets of TGKs hence remain the most difficult to parse: many costs could be attributable to either electricity or heat production, and much of these companies' profitability depends on how particular items are allocated.

[147] UES executive Gozman claimed the reforms were a "moral victory"; see *UES Annual Report 2007*, chapter on UES board members. Available at http://www.raoees.ru/en/invest/reporting/reports/report2007/

This chapter's focus has been the regional differences in tariff regulation that emerged along new geographical boundaries, reflected in different price levels across regions. The boundaries of regulatory zones were the outcome of political conflicts between the regions and the federal center, but they also crucially shaped market outcomes and the political arena in which prices were negotiated. These conflicts surrounding the scope of regulations then also contribute evidence to the larger claim the book that politics and markets are mutually constitutive.

6

Expertise – Engineers versus Managers

"While [the energetiki] proved to be quite knowledgeable about the industry as technical specialists, they had little desire or interest in improving the firm's position or performance. They lacked imagination and initiative."[1]

Manager, 1998

"[The problem with privatization was, that it] brought all these managers into decision-making positions within the electricity system; what is really needed ... are highly qualified and experienced leaders – namely engineers."[2]

Technical expert, 2006

Russia's Electricity Sector Experts and Their Role in Power Politics

Experts are pivotal actors situated between the regulating state and the regulated economy. Through a focus on the personnel changes at the commanding heights of one sector, this chapter suggests a third way in which the implementation of liberal reforms and the centralization of political power under Putin were mutually reinforcing processes. Both

---

[1] Brevnov, "From Monopoly to Market Maker? Reforming Russia's Power Sector," 19. Boris Brevnov was appointed general manager of Russia's electricity monopoly UES by Anatoly Chubais in 1997.

[2] "К руководству компаниями приходят менеджеры, хотя для обеспечения надежного и эффективного функционирования и развития ЕЭС нужны, в первую очередь, высококвалифицированные и опытные руководители – инженеры широкого профиля." Л. С. Беляев, "Недостатки Реализуемой Концепции Реформирования Электроэнергетики России и Необходимость Ее Корректировки," *Иркутск: Институт систем энергетики им. Л. А. Мелентьева* (2006), 20.

market making and state making relied on the displacement of a set of highly experienced and well-connected experts.[3] Specifically, the chapter documents the changing roles of two groups of experts in Russia's electricity sector: the engineers/technical experts (*energetiki – энергетики*) and the managerially trained experts (*menedzhery – менеджеры*). I argue that a shift in their relative power positions was a constitutive element of the liberalization of the electricity sector. With the victory of the *menedzhery* and the marginalization of the *energetiki*, electricity assets were standardized and disentangled from inherited social and technological contexts. The *menedzhery* introduced norms and practices that transformed organizations inherited from the Soviet Ministry of Energy into companies that were legible in emerging capitalist systems of asset valuation. This in turn allowed for the influx of domestic and international private capital, a key component in the marketization and liberalization of the electricity sector.

At the same time, the *menedzhery*'s rise and the *energetiki*'s ouster was also highly political. The Russian government was interested in promoting the *menedzhery* because it promised to increase the value of state-owned assets slated to be privatized, but also because it served a political goal. State capacity in post-Soviet Russia reached its nadir in the late 1990s.[4] As we have seen in Chapter 2, Putin eliminated challengers to the federal government's authority to regulate economic activity. The replacement of the *energetiki* was congruent with political centralization: it undercut the autonomy of regional governors, among the most powerful challengers to Moscow's authority during the nineties. The promotion of the *menedzhery*, a key step in the process of market making, helped disempower regional governors. It thus contributed as much to state building as it did to market making.

Existing studies on the challenges of asset valuation tend to focus on the lack of appropriate institutions.[5] Here the emphasis shifts to an understudied group of actors and their role in the creation of institutions,

---

[3] Timothy Mitchell has been interested in how politics is premised on shifting bodies of expertise. My research draws on Mitchell's work in the sense that I see expertise as an ideological framework mobilized as a political justification for economic policy. Mitchell, *Rule of Experts*, 41.

[4] It is well established that many of the liberal reforms of the 1990s contributed to undermining state capacity. For a discussion of several aspects of state capacity, see Laszlo Bruszt, "Market Making as State Making: Constitutions and Economic Development in Post-Communist Eastern Europe," *Constitutional Political Economy* 13, no. 1 (2002): 13.

[5] See, for example, Gustafson, *Capitalism Russian-Style*. A fuller discussion of this debate appears later in this chapter.

bridging the gap between studies of market creation (economic sociology) and of state-market relations (political economy). Economic sociology has long recognized the importance of processes of valuation for the creation of markets.[6] The chapter draws on this literature's focus on standardization and decontextualization as prerequisites for asset valuation and for marketization more generally, but adds to these debates by explicitly addressing the *political* dimension of these processes, which tend to be an afterthought in economic sociology.[7] To be precise, I show how asset valuation compatible with the influx of private capital hinged on displacing a set of well-established and politically connected experts.

The process of assigning values and prices to material things is a core function of a market economy. While economists rely on abstract models of supply and demand to explain how prices are made, sociologists understand asset valuation as a complex interplay between people, institutions, and material entities. Callon and Calışkan recently called for more attention on the dynamic relationships involved in the valuation of things, "how complex and hybrid social configurations are perpetually being constructed through the conjoined contributions of circulating material entities, as well as competent agents engaged in valuation practices."[8] Russia's new electricity markets were precisely such "hybrid social configurations." By documenting how valuation practices changed during the post-Soviet transformation of the power sector, this chapter ties into debates on their construction in general, and the construction of value in particular.

The chapter proceeds as follows: after establishing the identities of the two groups of experts, I outline a shift in their ability to influence the sector during the 2000–2004 period. The next section demonstrates the key role this shift played in the marketization of the Russian electricity sector. The third part of the chapter shows how experts were implicated in power politics, the politics of electricity sector liberalization.

---

[6] Michel Callon and Koray Calışkan provide a summary of recent studies that examine valuation as a key aspect of marketization; see Çalışkan and Callon, "Economization, Part 1"; Çalışkan and Callon, "Economization, Part 2." Callon and other sociological studies of expertise were particularly interested in the conflict between experts and non-experts, rather than in the conflict between different sets of experts.

[7] Donald MacKenzie's fascinating account of the construction of emissions markets is attentive to the political forces shaping the architecture of emissions markets; political influence is conceptualized as industry lobbying. MacKenzie, *Material Markets How Economic Agents Are Constructed*, 159. See Chapter 1, note 81 for a discussion.

[8] Çalışkan and Callon, "Economization, Part 1," 390. Note that their emphasis on material entities gives credence to the relevance of physical ties discussed in Chapter 3.

The *Energetiki* and the *Menedzhery*

Two groups of experts, the *menedzhery* and the *energetiki*, played a crucial role in the sector's transformation. The *menedzhery* were the new executives in the electricity sector. *Menedzhery* were self-described business leaders, operating in the world of markets. Often they worked as "businessmen" (*бизнесмен*), post-Soviet self-made entrepreneurs, before transitioning to the electricity sector.[9] The *menedzhery* stressed the skills and knowledge gained as entrepreneurs, and because of these skills liberal reformers regarded them as the right cadre to run new electricity companies. One observer noted that the *menedzhery* "come straight from Moscow's business schools ... or even from the US."[10] Anatoly Chubais typifies the managers in that he was, in many ways, a true believer in market forces. The sector's new managers shared his vision of markets as the most efficient allocation mechanism of scarce resources. Like Chubais, the *menedzhery* saw themselves as "agents of change;" their mission was to turn a Soviet-era ministry into profitable enterprises, increasing efficiency and attracting investment to the sector.[11] Chubais and the *menedzhery* described their task as a crusade to introduce markets, private property, and free prices.[12] They contrasted themselves with "old cadres," who, as one manager put it, "could not adjust to the new conditions of a market economy."[13]

---

[9] A manager interviewed for a Russian magazine, Viktor Minakov, stresses that he is *not* an *energetik* ("Я по образованию не энергетик"). It is said about him that he had been a businessman for ten years ("10 лет занимался бизнесом"). He himself emphasizes that the experience as a businessman was useful for his current job ("Для моей сегодняшней должности эти знания и опыт оказались очень полезны.") Interview in *Дальневосточный капитал*, October 2003, No.10/38, p. 48–49. In Russian, the term "businessman" has a very particular connotation; see Alexei Yurchak, "Russian Neoliberal: The Entrepreneurial Ethic and the Spirit of 'true Careerism,'" *The Russian Review* 62, no. 1 (2003): 72–90; Alexei Yurchak, "Entrepreneurial Governmentality in Post-Socialist Russia: A Cultural Investigation of Business Practices," in *The New Entrepreneurs of Europe and Asia. Patterns of Business Development in Russia, Eastern Europe and China* (Wiley, 2002).

[10] This remark was made about the new management at Irkutskenergo. Interview #48 with academic, Irkutsk, 20071113.

[11] Interview #63 with electricity company executive, Moscow, 20071212.

[12] Chubais, interview in Mellow, "Is This a Way to Create Capitalism?"

[13] Viktor Minakov describes himself in the following terms: "He [Chubais] needed managers and businessmen in the electricity sector, because the old cadres, it turned out, could not adjust to the new conditions of a market economy/Ему нужны были энергетики-управленцы и коммерсанты, потому что старые кадры, выросшие в закрытой технической системе, оказались не приспособлены к новым рыночным условиям." Interview in *Дальневосточный капитал*, October 2003, No. 10/38, pp. 48–49.

The term *energetiki* dates to the Soviet era and refers to the work collective of electricity sector professionals. The *energetiki* were widely held to be "one of the oldest and best organized professional collectives."[14] Many *energetiki* could look back on long years of professional experience, often dating to the expansion of the electricity sector in the late 1960s and 1970s. As electricity was a priority sector in the Soviet Union, the *energetiki* were closely connected to party nomenklatura. Perspectives and values of the *energetiki* were shaped by the ethos of their work collective, which emphasized technological expertise and a commitment to reliability.[15] As engineers, their concerns centered on technological challenges, technological achievements, and technological requirements for secure provision.[16] They often stressed their role in building the Soviet Union's electricity system, considered the backbone of Soviet social order. Their personal biographies were intertwined with the Soviet modernization project. For example, one *energetik*, the director of Bratsk hydroelectric station, included his own story in a history of Bratsk station: he dreamt of building the dam as a schoolboy, ended up marrying the daughter of the station's general director, and finally ascended to that post himself.[17] While the *energetiki* self-identified as part of a tightly knit community everywhere, the collective identity of Siberian *energetiki* was particularly strong: the construction of Siberian hydroelectric dams brought together young engineers and volunteers to "build socialism" in remote and uninhabited areas of Siberia.[18] Many of the most prominent *energetiki* hailed from Siberia.

The *energetiki* and *menedzhery* had different conceptions of the electricity system's value.[19] For the *energetiki*, the electricity sector was

---

[14] "Энергетики – одна из самых старых и хорошо организованных профессиональных каст." Бергер and Проскурина, "Крест Чубайса," 29.

[15] Reliability as the main concern of the "technical point of view" of the *energetiki* was mentioned in interview #57 with electricity sector expert, Irkutsk, 20071122.

[16] Security of provision is a high priority for *energetiki*; see, for example, *Основные проблемы и направления обеспечения энергетической безопасности* (Irkutsk: Siberian Section of the Russian Academy of Sciences, 2001).

[17] Interview with Viktor Rudykh in *Свет негасимый: энергетике Приангарья 50 лет.* (Иркутск: Восточно-Сибирская издательская компания, 2004,) 50.

[18] Вениамин Васильевич Алексеев, *Электрификация Сибири: Историческое Исследование..... 1885–1950.* I (Наука, 1973), 186. *Energetiki* later often lived and worked in the mono-industrial towns that were built around these dams, where their vocational ethic was part of their everyday lives.

[19] The *energetiki*'s and the *menedzhery*'s value systems are derived here from their statements in interviews. An interesting theoretical angle could be gained from comparing

valuable as a highly sophisticated technological system. Its value was both intrinsic (it turns night into day) and derives from its supportive role for other industries and activities (it functions as the "material-technological" basis of the economy).[20] Like the *menedzhery*, the *energetiki* were interested in efficiency, but technical efficiency (preventing energy losses) rather than economic efficiency (maximizing profits). The *menedzhery*, by contrast, assessed the value of the electricity sector by its bottom line, and saw little value in a company that provides services but is unable to collect bills, for example. In theory, technical efficiency and economic efficiency should eventually overlap. In practice, however, the different sets of values and different fields of expertise led to immense conflict and frustration. This surfaced in *energetiki*'s complaints about the *menedzhery* who "don't understand the technological side."[21] Chubais was reportedly unschooled in the basic laws of physics. The *energetiki* were outraged when he – "a person with no knowledge of Ohm's law and [other] basic formulas"[22] – was appointed to head UES.

This stylized opposition of the *menedzhery* and *energetiki* does not mean to suggest that impermeable boundaries isolated the groups from each other. Some *energetiki* became successful *menedzhery*, and some *menedzhery* were also trained as electric engineers. The first UES chairman, Boris Brevov, trained as an engineer in the 1990s before he became an entrepreneur and later a banker. Moreover, as different as the *energetiki* and the *menedzhery* were, interesting parallels between the two groups emerged. Both relied on references to economic development to justify their positions. Both drew on the symbolic capital imbued in Soviet-era imagery – turbines, grids, and wires – which originated in

them to Boltanski and Thévenot's categories or logics of justification in Luc Boltanski and Laurent Thévenot, *On Justification: Economies of Worth* (Princeton, NJ: Princeton University Press, 2006).

[20] Belyaev uses this term in Беляев, "Недостатки Реализуемой Концепции Реформирования Электроэнергетики России."

[21] Interview #57 with electricity sector economist (*energetik*), Irkutsk, 20071122. *Energetiki* also thought that reforms were rushed, without due consultation of technical experts, for example, interview #60 with energy company executive (former *energetik*), Irkutsk, 20071203.

[22] "Крупнейшую энергокомпанию страны возглавляет человек, не знающий даже закона Ома и простейших формул." This is a quote by Zhores Alferov, a well-known Russian physicist who became member of the Communist Party and opposed Chubais's plans for electricity reforms. "Физика большой политики," *Ведомости*, February 9, 2007. Another source, by contrast, claims that Chubais did know Ohm's law; Бергер and Проскурина, "Крест Чубайса," 29.

Lenin's era and still resonates widely. The *energetiki* often used Soviet-era language to stress the importance of the electricity sector for social and economic life. It is perhaps more surprising that the liberal reformers and the *menedzhery* also sought to capitalize on Soviet-era symbolism. Like the *energetiki*, the *menedzhery* used Soviet-era language and symbols to refer to the sector's vital function for the economy. For example, Chubais's investment plan to upgrade ailing Soviet-era infrastructure was named "*GOELRO-2*," after the original *GOELRO*, Lenin's 1920 initiative to bring electricity to the newly created Soviet Union. Liberal reformers and the *menedzhery* mobilized Lenin's vision to gain support for their plan to *privatize* the country's power plants.[23] Nevertheless, the *menedzhery* and the *energetiki* explicitly distinguished themselves – each generally regarded the views, values, and priorities of the other to be incompatible with their own.[24]

The clash between economic and technical experts during electricity sector reforms is not unique to Russia. Technical experts in other countries where electricity provision was radically restructured along market lines clamored about the detrimental long-term effects of operating complex technical systems on the basis of cost rather than technical specifications.[25] They also emphasized uncertainty about how specific technical aspects of the system would function (load management, for example) after implementation of reforms based on economic logic. Differences between managerial and technical experts have a long history – they have been examined at least as far back as Thorsten Veblen's account of business enterprises in the industrial age. In Veblen's account, however, engineers and businessmen were not at odds with each other. For Veblen, businessmen gave "general direction" to industry, but it was engineers

---

[23] Valentin San'ko was one of the *menedzhery* who used references to GOELRO; interview in *Красный Север*, May 17, 2007.

[24] In many ways these practices of distinguishing one group from another reflect rhetorical practices that distinguish between "ours / not ours" (*наши / не наши*), resonant in Russian culture.

[25] Alexandra von Meier traces how operators and engineers in U.S. and German utilities relate differently to technological innovation in Alexandra Von Meier, "Occupational Cultures as a Challenge to Technological Innovation," *IEEE Transactions on Engineering Management* 46, no. 1 (1999): 101–114. For concerns by technical experts about the effects of economic reforms on technical aspects of electricity provision, see Deepak Sharma, "The Multidimensionality of Electricity Reform – an Australian Perspective," *Energy Policy* 31, no. 11 (2003): 1093–1102; Edward Vine et al., "Public Policy Analysis of Energy Efficiency and Load Management in Changing Electricity Businesses," *Energy Policy* 31, no. 5 (April 2003): 405–430, a study by a group of U.S., UK, and Australian electricity sector.

and experts that created the conditions for profitability through the "standardization of industrial processes, products, services," which then "permit[ted] a uniform routine in accounting, invoices, contracts, etc., and so admit[ted] a large central accounting system."[26] Further, Veblen argued, it is the engineers who make opportunities "visible" to businessmen, and "create the mechanical possibility of ... new and more efficient methods."[27] Why were the two sets of experts in the Russian electricity sector pitted against each other in an apparently zero-sum competition, and why did the *menedzhery* ultimately win?

Post-Soviet literature on elites would have predicted that the *energetiki's* odds were pretty good. Studies of Russian elites generally stress the continuity between Soviet-era cadres and post-Soviet elites. Relationships and connections acquired under socialism were often enormous assets for building post-Soviet careers.[28] David Lane observed that many post-Soviet oil sector elites had a background in the Soviet Ministry of Energy.[29] In politics, likewise, Soviet-era ties often proved useful for post-Soviet careers. Kryshtanovskaya and White show that many of the security system's old guard (*силовые структуры*) were appointed to leading positions within the executive under Putin.[30] In the case of the *energetiki*, however, Soviet-era ties proved to be a liability. Why was this the case?

Shifting Positions of the *Energetiki* and *Menedzhery* – and the Managers' Victory

The position of the two groups of experts in terms of power and influence and their position within the political and administrative structures changed dramatically over the two decades under discussion. The *energetiki* lost control of the commanding heights of the electricity sector. This process was variously described as a "purge" or a "wave" that ended with "an almost wholesale replacement of management," the

---

[26] Thorstein Veblen, *The Theory of Business Enterprise* (Scribner, 1904), 36. Thanks to Gary Herrigel for bringing Veblen to this discussion.

[27] Ibid., 47.

[28] For discussion of this theme in the post-Soviet literature, see Verdery, *The Vanishing Hectare*, 311. Verdery observes this trend for agricultural elites in Romania. See also Olga Kryshtanovskaya and Stephen White, "From Soviet Nomenklatura to Russian Élite," *Europe-Asia Studies* 48, no. 5 (1996): 711–733.

[29] David Stuart Lane, *The Political Economy of Russian Oil* (Lanham, MD: Rowman & Littlefield, 1999), 79.

[30] Kryshtanovskaya and White call this the "FSB-isation" of politics; see Kryshtanovskaya and White, "Putin's Militocracy," 291.

"managers' victory."[31] As director of UES, Chubais actively pursued the replacement of *energetiki* with *menedzhery*: "[W]hen Anatoly Chubais ascended to the leadership of [UES], the formation of a new leadership team began," said one manager.[32] The replacement of old Soviet-era cadres with younger, "unspoiled" minds had already been one of his priorities when he was head of the State Privatization Commission under Yeltsin. Once director of UES, he moved decisively to replace older personnel in the electricity sector and remove high-profile *energetiki* from their posts.

Orchestrated from UES headquarters in Moscow, the turnover of experts replaced Energo leadership across Russia. According to one source, four out of five Energo directors were replaced between 1998 and 2002/3.[33] Media sources give an account of the most high-profile leadership changes during these years, although many probably went unreported. An early leadership change happened at Tyumenenergo, the country's second-largest Energo, where the director lost his seat both at the head of the Energo and on UES's board of directors.[34] Once a director changed, so did most of the other executives within an Energo. Another prominent *menedzher*, Viktor Miasnik at Chitaenergo, is said to have fired most of the executives at the Energo during his "clean sweep" of the company: "[A]fter a year, not one of the old bosses who had worked there before Miasnik was left at the company."[35] This policy clearly had its intended effects. UES's 2001 annual report notes that "the policy of decreasing the average age of personnel is ... a consistent priority,"[36] and

---

[31] A leadership change at Krasnoiarskenergo is referred to as a purge (чистка), in "Красноярск пошел по приморскому пути," *Сегодня*, September 12, 1977. For the characterisation of events as a wave (волна), see Надежда Воронцова, *Дальневосточный капитал*, October 2003, No. 10/38, 48. Also in this article is the notion of wholesale replacement of management (*почти полностью сменил менеджмент*), which was said to be Chubais's achievement. The term "managers' victory" was used in Interview #57 with electricity sector economist, Irkutsk, 20071122.

[32] "Когда к руководству единой российской энергосистемы РАО ЕЭС России пришел Анатолий Чубайс, началось формирование новой команды управленцев энергетическими предприятиями." *Дальневосточный капитал*, October 2003, No. 10/38, 48.

[33] Алексеев, *Электрификация Сибири*.

[34] "Энергетиков выбирают первыми," *Сегодня*, October 2, 1999. The directors at Mosenergo, Irkutskenergo, and Dal'energo were all fired within a few years.

[35] "За год ... не осталось ни одного из начальников, которые работали там до прихода Мясника." In "Новые менеджеры АО Энерго исполнительны до и после передела?" *Правда*, June 28, 2001.

[36] UES 2001 Annual Report, section 5.4.5. "Personnel management." Report available online at http://www.rao-ees.ru/en/business/report2001/

that the average age of the Energos' general directors decreased by three years between 1999 and 2001.[37]

While extensive, the *menedzhery*'s victory was not complete. Not even Chubais could replace all *energetiki*, nor would he have wanted to lose their knowledge, experience, and expertise entirely. Nevertheless, the *energetiki* portrayed a wholesale purge: "All *energetiki* left UES, there is nobody left. There are only the managers left at UES," said one veteran *energetik*.[38] This perception was created by the turnover of high-profile decision makers and the fact that the *energetiki* were demoted and subordinated to the new managers. Also, when battles over high-profile positions came to a standoff, the incumbent *energetik* tended to lose.[39] Viktor Kudriavyi, for example, trained as electrical engineer in Ivanovo, and had been an *energetik* since the 1960s. By the 1990s, he had become Mosenergo's head of engineering. In 1996, Boris Yeltsin appointed Kudriavyi Deputy Minister of Energy where he was an outspoken, high-profile critic of liberal reforms who consistently voted against Chubais' reforms.[40] He was dismissed from his post in 2003, after refusing to authorize a number of key elements of the proposed reform plans.[41] Most *menedzhery*, on the other hand, were able to retain their positions when confronted with political maneuverings to oust them from power. The most high-profile UES manager was, of course, Chubais. The Russian parliament (the Duma) repeatedly passed motions to replace him as the director of UES.[42] Victor Kress, governor of a wealthy Siberian region, Tomsk, and a prominent political leader of the *energetiki*, was in 2001 widely rumored to be Chubais's replacement.[43] This never happened.

[37] From fifty-three years in 1999 to fifty years in 2001, according to the UES 2001 Annual Report. As the average age of existing directors should have increased by three years during this time, the decrease can only mean that a number of younger directors were appointed during this time.
[38] Interview #39 with electrical engineer/electricity sector expert, Vladivostok, 20071004.
[39] Kudriavyi was dismissed in August 2003 for blocking presidential directives on the formation of the Federal Network Company and the System Operator. "Энергетика," *Журнал Власть*, No. 23, June 14, 2004.
[40] Бергер and Проскурина, "Крест Чубайса," 224.
[41] Рыбалченко, "Электроэнергия 1991–2000," *Коммерсантъ*, November 13, 2001. See also *Журнал Власть*, No. 23, June 14, 2004.
[42] The Duma was repeatedly trying to replace him as the head of UES; Petrosyan, *What Is the Current Status of Russian Electricity Sector in the Light of Restructuring Laws and RAO UES Breakup Strategy*.
[43] "Как Виктор Кресс предложил уволить Анатолия Чубайса," *Коммерсантъ*, May 18, 2001; also "Кресс вместо Чубайса?" *Век*, July 27, 2001.

Finally, it is worth asking why liberal reformers thought it necessary to replace old experts. Why not rely on *energetiki*'s long-standing experience and technical expertise for critical decisions during the
period of modernization? An answer might be found in an intellectual
current among post-Soviet Russian liberals, and earlier among dissi-
dents, considered the *homo Sovieticus* to be fundamentally corrupted
and unable to adapt to a new world order.[44] A liberal Soviet intellectual phrased this as follows: "[A] Soviet man is a product of invisible changes, degradation and progressive deformation. Breaking the
chain of those changes is hard. Perhaps they are irreversible."[45] Many
Russian liberals thought that members of the old cadres, "spoiled" in
this way, were unable to adapt to the requirements of a market economy.
Chubais once noted that among the Soviet-era factory directors "there
remain the same instincts, habits, connections and the same bend in the
spine."[46]

The training of Soviet engineers helps explain the gulf separating the
menedzhery and the *energetiki*. Loren Graham shows that Stalin's purges
of "bourgeois specialists" in the late 1920s targeted particularly those
engineers who saw themselves as active, independent, and outspoken
economic planners and advocated for broad training in economic, social,
and political matters. Fearful of sharing the fate of arrested colleagues,
engineers increasingly focused on narrow technical tasks and remained
silent about the human and social cost that the era's gigantic engineering projects entailed. Graham also documents that in the decades after
the purges, engineers' training narrowed over time, becoming ever more
restricted to purely technical problems and subdivided into highly specific specializations.[47] In the post-Soviet period, this meant that *energetiki*'s expertise was particularly narrow; reformers deemed their expertise

---

[44] *Homo Sovieticus* is a term initially coined by Aleksandr Zinovyev. The debate on how
Soviet citizen or the Soviet subject could adapt to the post-Soviet context is large and
diverse both in Russia and among Western academic circles. For a discussion, see Alexei
Yurchak, *Everything Was Forever, until It Was No More: The Last Soviet Generation*
(Princeton, NJ: Princeton University Press, 2013), 5.

[45] Quote by Merab Mamardashvili, a Georgian public intellectual; quoted in "Georgia's
mental revolution," *The Economist*, August 19, 2010.

[46] Chubais, quoted in Gustafson, *Capitalism Russian-Style*, 37. Chubais's assessments continues as follows: "It is a rare director that does not rush off to the government, that
doesn't seek connections with high-placed officials, that doesn't beg for subsidized credits, tax breaks, quotas and privileges."

[47] Loren R. Graham, *The Ghost of the Executed Engineer: Technology and the Fall of the
Soviet Union* (Cambridge, MA: Harvard University Press, 1993), 87.

overly technical and too specialized to warrant leadership positions in a new market order. In a study of Soviet and post-Soviet modernization projects in Chukotka, Niobe Thompson points out that expert and elite turnovers were a part of past Russian and Soviet modernization projects, and that modernity was often interpreted "as an embodied quality," which meant that the "old vessels of Soviet modernity" could not be "recycled to carry forward a new wave of center-led change."[48] Purges swept old cadres aside, paving the way for the new "bodies" needed to execute modernization plans.

Expertise and the Marketization of the Russian Electricity Sector

The replacement of the *energetiki* with managers was constitutive to the creation of markets in the electricity sector. The *menedzhery* restructured the Soviet-era electricity sector into companies that were recognizable to domestic and foreign investors (as well as to intermediaries such as analysts and credit rating agencies). Electricity companies became legible and "value-able" units through a set of reforms that standardized accounting practices, shed employees and non-core assets, and introduced a new, post-Soviet culture of professionalism. This process also largely erased the sector's historical, social, and technological exceptionalism, long nurtured by the *energetiki*. "It's just a business," said one manager[49] – a statement that epitomizes how the *menedzhery* sought to decontextualize the sector from its Soviet past.

The importance of standardization for valuation and price setting is well accepted. William Cronon's study on the standardization of wheat as a prerequisite for its commodification and marketization by the Chicago Board of Trade impressively demonstrated this intuitive argument.[50] Here I am particularly concerned with the valuation of companies, although, of course, this is related to the valuation of turbines, grids, and dams, as well as of electricity, of expected future profits, and so forth.[51] As we have seen in Chapter 4, during the early years of Russia's market transition, incredibly valuable state-owned assets sold for trivial sums. Processes of asset

---

[48] Thompson, *Settlers on the Edge*, 186.

[49] Interview #37 with electricity sector executive, Vladivostok, 20071002.

[50] William Cronon, *Nature's Metropolis: Chicago and the Great West* (W. W. Norton & Company, 1992).

[51] In Callon and Calışkan's formulation, these materialities are all a relevant in the construction of value. Çalışkan and Callon, "Economization, Part 1"; Çalışkan and Callon, "Economization, Part 2."

valuation clearly did not work properly. Many observers have suggested that this happened because important institutions that value assets, such as security exchanges, and institutions that secure property rights, such as contract law, were largely absent during the initial reform period.[52] The lack of institutions necessary to value assets was most visible during the early years of the privatization auctions. Auctions and sales were also corrupt: buyers with political and personal connections to decision makers rigged transactions in their favor. Assets changed hands for what were essentially arbitrary prices that had far more to do with who was allowed to bid than some intrinsic value of the asset.[53]

Studies focusing on institutional weakness and corruption fail to account for arbitrary asset valuations that occurred well after the establishment of security exchanges. The transformation of electricity sector expertise suggests another explanation: assets and companies *could not* be valued by market participants until new managers *made* them legible. In other words, the creation of standardized units and their disentanglement from Soviet-era social, economic, and technological contexts hinged upon large-scale expert turnover. Once the *menedzhery* were made executives of regional electricity companies throughout Russia, they were instrumental in bringing about at least three important changes in the electricity sector: (1) they turned organizational structures inherited from Soviet branch ministries into "real" companies; (2) they introduced a set of values and standardized mechanisms to value electricity assets; and (3) they introduced a novel professional culture rooted in the principles of a market economy.

What then were the processes of standardization and decontextualization that the *menedzhery* undertook? What were the practices and norms they introduced? A first set of tasks the *menedzhery* tackled involved turning regional electricity monopolies into "real" companies, ready to be restructured and privatized. In the 1990s, Russia's electricity system consisted of seventy-one regional vertically integrated monopolies, the Energos, a structure inherited from the Soviet era. Two 1992 presidential decrees turned the Energos into *акционерное общество*, the Russian version of a joint stock company. In reality, many continued to resemble

---

[52] See, for example, Gustafson, *Capitalism Russian-Style*; Hoffman, *The Oligarchs*. For an account of the emergence of equity markets, see also chapter 5 in Timothy Frye, *Brokers and Bureaucrats: Building Market Institutions in Russia* (Ann Arbor: University of Michigan Press, 2000).
[53] See the discussion of privatization and relevant debates in Chapter 4.

government agencies.[54] Electricity companies owned and operated a host of assets that provided services for employees, but which had little to do with power production. Companies continued to own "atypical" assets: apartments that housed employees, recreation and vacation facilities, and, in one case, even a chicken farm.[55] Energos also employed large numbers of staff relative to electricity companies in other countries. The *energetiki* and *menedzhery* differed in their position toward redundancies and staff reductions. One *menedzher* noted, "of course, many people at work today [in the electricity sector] are not needed; all this amounts to is an unnecessary expense."[56] The *energetiki*, on the other hand, regarded the people who built and maintained the electricity system as central to its value. One *energetik*, the director of Bratsk hydroelectric plant mentioned earlier, recounted the history of the plant by equating it with its employees – "most of all, Bratsk hydroelectric power plant *is its remarkable people*, its devoted workers and its highly qualified specialists."[57] Once in charge of Energos, managers moved swiftly to reduce staff numbers and to rid balance sheets of atypical assets.[58] Their goal was to increase the "net power output per employee," their indicator of plant efficiency.[59] *Energetiki* bemoaned the loss of the many "highly qualified and experienced leaders,"[60] but were not in a position to halt or reverse this process.

Another important change executed by the *menedzhery* was the implementation of a crucial reform step referred to as unbundling. As introduced in Chapter 2, unbundling broke vertically integrated monopolies

[54] A similar statement was made to describe Dal'energo, the regional electricity company in Primorskii Krai – "it looked more like a government agency than a company for most of the 1990s." Interview #33 with journalist covering electricity sector, Vladivostok, 20070921.

[55] In Russian these are called *непрофильные активы*; see also Chapter 4.

[56] "Понятно, что столько людей, сколько сегодня в ней занято, не нужно, это все лишние затраты." Viktor Minakov, a manager of a Far Eastern electricity company. Interview with Minakov in *Дальневосточный капитал*, October 2003, No. 10/38, 49.

[57] "Прежде всего Братская ГЭС – это замечательные люди, преданные труженики, специалисты высочайшей квалификации," quote by Viktor Rudykh in *Свет негасимый: энергетике Приангарья 50 лет* (Иркутск: Восточно-Сибирская издательская компания, 2004), 46.

[58] Successive UES Annual Reports provide updates on the reduction of staff numbers.

[59] Interview #37 with electricity sector executive (*menedzher*), Vladivostok, 20071002. See also UES 2001 Annual Report, section 5.4.5, available at http://www.rao-ees.ru/en/archive/

[60] See chapter epigraph, by Беляев, "Недостатки Реализуемой Концепции Реформирования Электроэнергетики России."

into separate companies, a process central to the introduction of markets and competition.[61] Unbundling required a host of organizational and legal steps, such as corporate and management restructuring and the incorporation of the new businesses. The *menedzhery* were selected and placed in executive positions in regional electricity companies to manage this process. *Energetiki* were generally not in favor of unbundling. They considered it detrimental to the goal of guaranteeing the security of provision. One *energetik* thought of it as "separating limbs from a body." With no single entity responsible for planning and management of output and investment decisions for the electricity system as a whole, there would be no "brain," and system failures were bound to happen, he worried.[62] The detrimental impact of corporate restructuring on the career paths of the *energetiki* also likely played a role in their opposition to unbundling. Despite the opposition of the *energetiki*, the process of unbundling the regional Energos was complete by 2005.

The most important set of tasks tackled by the *menedzhery* was the introduction of a set of values and standardized accounting practices. Before reforms, Russian electricity companies' accounting practices were often highly opaque. Although Russian and Western observers have tended to highlight corruption as the root cause of this problem, nontransparent accounting was also related to the widespread use of barter and surrogate currencies during the 1990s.[63] As Chapter 5 addressed, a central problem for Russia's electricity companies for much of the 1990s was their inability to collect payments from customers. In turn, they fell behind in wage, pension, and tax payments, while also running up large debts with fuel providers and repair companies.[64] In the late 1990s, this led to a situation so severe that most transactions were noncash, settled instead by barter, promissory notes, or mutual

[61] Vertical monopolies are broken up as a way to separate the competitive from the noncompetitive elements in the sector. Potentially competitive are the generation and retail subsectors; the network sectors, transmission and distribution, have inherent natural monopoly character. For a discussion of unbundling in post-Soviet economic reforms, see Collier, *Post-Soviet Social*, pp. 205 and 234.

[62] Interview #39 with electrical engineer/electricity sector expert (*energetik*), Vladivostok, 20071004. Another *energetik* expressed concerns about who was to have the ultimate responsibility for the functioning of the system. The same person also stressed that because "electricity has many difficult and interconnected technological aspect, [it is] very questionable what will happen to the system after unbundling." Interview #57 with electricity sector economist (*energetik*), Irkutsk, 20071122.

[63] For a full discussion of the barter crisis, see Woodruff, *Money Unmade*.

[64] See UES 1997 Annual Report for a statement of the centrality of the nonpayment problem, available at http://www.rao-ees.ru/en/invest/reporting/reports/report97/

settlements. The cash flow and balance sheets of electricity companies were accordingly incomplete and difficult, if not impossible, to interpret.[65] The *energetiki*, and their lack of experience in business matters, were frequently blamed for failing to collect bills and neglecting to regularize cash flow.

For much of the 1990s, domestic and international investors were at a loss to interpret the value of electricity companies. Initially, this was a boon for various local intermediaries, who possessed specialized knowledge of the strengths and weaknesses of particular electricity companies. International investors either sought to enlist the help of these intermediaries or relied on a very rough shorthand measure of whether or not a company was undervalued: current asset price/kilowatt of installed capacity, a measure that was then compared to power plants in other emerging markets. Both practices were inherently limited and imprecise and, together with the nonpayment, inhibited private investment sought by liberal reformers. The *menedzhery* were thus charged with establishing payment discipline and getting company books in order. Boris Brevnov was briefly UES chairman and arguably its first *menedzher*. In 1997, Brevnov initiated a reform of the Energo accounting system to make their accounts more transparent to UES and to potential outside investors. He ordered a comprehensive audit by an international accounting firm. As we have seen in previous chapters, these early attempts failed. Incumbent leadership at UES, mostly *energetiki*, who still exercised significant control, boycotted the accounting reforms and succeeded in ousting Brevnov within months.[66]

After several years, the accounting systems of Russian electricity companies were brought in line with Western standards. UES annual reports reflected the ongoing struggle to improve financial transparency and increase the effectiveness of its accounting and budgeting mechanisms.[67] The 1998 Annual Report vaguely mentioned adopting "modern management structures" and "standard economic criteria for assessing

---

[65] For example, the section on "Finances and Accounting" in UES's 1998 Annual Report that notes the "high level of uncollectable receivables." Available at http://www.rao-ees. ru/en/invest/reporting/reports/report98/

[66] According to Brevnov, "From Monopoly to Market Maker? Reforming Russia's Power Sector," 19.

[67] See, for example, the section on "financial management" in the 2002 Annual Report, which describes a series of rules that were introduced to "increase responsiveness of financial management and improve quality of budget planning." Available at http://www. rao-ees.ru/en/invest/reporting/reports/report2002/

operational results."[68] The 1999 Annual Report noted that UES was trying to get its subsidiary companies to comply with two recent governmental directives on accounting practices, the "Federal Law on Financial Accounting" and the "Decree on Bookkeeping and Accounting."[69] The 2002 report described concrete improvements in "financial management technologies" and outlined measures to "increase responsiveness of financial management."[70] Newly appointed *menedzhery* were indispensable for realizing the goals set forth in annual reports, implementing changes at the regional electricity companies, and improving their legibility to domestic and foreign investors. A prominent head of a Far Eastern electricity company noted that his primary goal was to "increase the attractiveness of the company for investors."[71]

Beyond enhancing accounting standards and improving systems, the *menedzhery* ushered in a broader set of values. A set of practices modeled on Western-style "corporate governance codes" replaced the *energetiki*'s emphasis on technological standards and security of provision. UES claimed to be one of the first Russian companies to introduce an explicit corporate governance code, maintaining that it set up an "efficient system of [monitoring] corporate governance."[72] Enhancing UES and new electricity company's shareholder value was a core aspect of this agenda, as noted by a prominent manager of a Far Eastern electricity company: "[T]he market capitalization of [our] company is the most important indicator of its general condition ..... It's precisely the market capitalization that is the only objective and adequate indicator of the value of a company."[73] This is a long way from the *energetiki*'s emphasis on technological sophistication and service to other sectors.

---

[68] See UES's 1998 Annual Report, section 7 "Asset Management." Available at http://www.rao-ees.ru/en/invest/reporting/reports/report98/

[69] The first one is Federal Law No. 129-FZ of November 21, 1996, the second one is a Decree on Bookkeeping and Accounting, Decree No. 34, confirmed by the Ministry of Finance of the Russian Federation on July 29, 1998. Available at http://www.rao-ees.ru/en/invest/reporting/reports/report99/, section on "Financial Management," subsection on "Improving the System of Financial Management"

[70] See UES's 2002 Annual Report, section on "Management System," subsection "Financial Management." Available at http://www.rao-ees.ru/en/invest/reporting/reports/report2002/

[71] "Повышение инвестиционной привлекательности," interview with Miasnik in *Дальневосточный капитал*, February 2006, No. 2/66, 23.

[72] 2002 UES Annual Report, section on "Corporate Governance." Available at http://www.rao-ees.ru/en/invest/reporting/reports/report2002/

[73] "Капитализация компании – это важнейший показатель ее самочувствия, естественно ..... Именно капитализация является единственно объективной и адекватной оценкой

Finally, at an even more general level, the *menedzhery* sought to introduce a new professional culture congruent with market principles. Shortly after joining UES, Chubais announced a new system of performance indicators to evaluate executives at both UES and the Energos.[74] One of the sector's new *menedzhery* noted in 2003 that "today, electricity company leadership understands that a director is a hired manager, somebody with a plan and a budget to execute; they understand that everything has to be paid for, and that one needs to live according to market principles. And as a result, we now ride on the rails toward the market."[75] Such statements implicitly contrast *menedzhery*'s professionalism with imputed failings of the *energetiki*, whose norms and practices prevented them from collecting electricity bills in cash, from cutting off nonpaying customers, from prioritizing profitability, or from firing personnel. The *energetiki*, in short, were thought to be a fundamental obstacle to the system's trajectory on the "rails toward the market."

The *menedzhery*'s efforts at UES and at regional energy companies created the basis for an influx of domestic and international investment in the Russian electricity sector after about 2003. Corporate restructuring and the influx of private capital were not the only elements of marketization and liberalization. Equally important were the new legal and regulatory frameworks that were introduced contemporaneously. As we saw previously, a set of new regulatory bodies was created – most importantly in this context, the Federal Tariff Service (*Федеральная служба по тарифам*/FST). Liberal reformers, however, never believed that the creation of regulatory institutions alone would be sufficient to restore the federal government's ability to regulate economic activity and to implement reforms. The displacement of a well-established, well-reputed, and well-connected group of incumbent political actors by the *menedzhery* was considered critical for the effective functioning of the new institutions.

стоимости компании." Interview with Miasnik, in *Дальневосточный капитал*, February 2006, No. 2/66, 23.

[74] Бергер and Проскурина, "Крест Чубайса," 63.

[75] "... стоим на рыночных рельсах." Full quote: "Сейчас руководство энергокомпаний понимает, что ... директор – это нанятый менеджер, который должен планировать и исполнять бюджет, что со всеми надо расплачиваться деньгами, т.е. надо жить рыночной экономикой.... И сегодня стоим на рыночных рельсах." Viktor Minakov, interview in *Дальневосточный капитал*, October 2003, No. 10/38, 48. While managers indeed contributed to increasing payment discipline at the Energos, the recovery of the Russian economy and the gradual end of the barter crisis after 1998 were also important factors.

Experts and Power Politics

The political dynamics that propelled liberal reforms in the electricity sector are key to understanding the shifting positions of the two groups of experts, and the concomitant changes in the sector's value systems. While marketization would not have been possible without the victory of the *menedzhery*, this victory hinged on the Putin government's support of Chubais and his agenda. The ascendancy of the *menedzhery* owed much to Putin's ability to centralize political power. With Moscow's increasing control over the economy came an increased emphasis on corporate legibility and the further integration of Russian companies into international markets. I argued above that legibility was necessary for marketization; James Scott has noted more broadly that "[l]egibility is [also] a condition of manipulation."[76] In what follows I show that legibility and the promotion of the *menedzhery* were more than a tactic of liberal reformers. They served *political* goals; beyond the goal of sector liberalization, they contributed to the centralization of political authority.

Sketching the "power positions" of the *menedzhery* and the *energetiki* helps us understand the politics of expert turnover. The chief proponents of electricity sector reforms, the "young reformers" under Yeltsin and the liberal faction of Putin's government, supported the *menedzhery*. High-level UES *menedzhery*, in particular, had close ties to the liberal faction of the Putin government. This is not surprising; Chubais, who had himself been a key member of Yeltsin's young reformers, remained closely connected to the liberal faction of Putin's government when he became director of UES. Following Putin's rise to the presidency in 2000, a turnover in Russian power elites swept in his loyalists who formed the security apparatus and displaced Yeltsin-era liberals. A few high-profile liberals found a position, or a refuge, in "Chubais's empire," as UES was sometimes called.[77] The *energetiki* had well-established ties

---

[76] James C. Scott, *Seeing Like a State: How Certain Schemes to Improve the Human Condition Have Failed* (New Haven, CT: Yale University Press, 1998).

[77] Aleksander Voloshin, UES board member, was Yeltsin's Chief of Staff in the late 1990s. Yakov Urinson, another high-ranking UES executive, was Economics Minister under Yeltsin in the late 1990s. The biographies of these UES executives are described in Берер and Проскурина, "Крест Чубайса." For another reference to this connection between the Yeltsin-era government and UES executives, see *Дальневосточный капитал*, June 2005, No. 6/58, 10.

to regional governors, who were not only the main opponents of electricity sector reforms but also one of the two main challengers to the sovereignty of the central government. *Menedzhery*, by contrast, were typically *not* rooted in regional politics. They were intentionally transplanted from other regions, where they had proven loyal to the reformist agenda.

As previous chapters document in detail, governors opposed liberal reforms because they threatened to undermine regional control of the electricity sector as well as the governors' ability to influence regional economies. The *energetiki* were also firmly opposed to unbundling, which they regarded as a recipe for system failure, and favored maintaining the "integrity" of the unified electricity system. While *energetiki* often suffered the consequences of regional policies – Energos were hopelessly cash-starved – they nevertheless usually sided with governors and against liberal reformers. *Energetiki*'s ties to regional administrations dated to the Soviet era. "During Soviet times, the electricity general [leading *energetiki*] always came from regional elites and always belonged to the same circle as the regional governors (formerly the party elites)."[78] As a vital infrastructure, the electricity sector had been the responsibility of the deputy secretary of the regional assembly (the "second крайком secretary.")[79] This meant that during the first post-Soviet decade, the *energetiki* at the head of the Energos were part of the old Soviet regional party nomenklatura.[80] They remained in charge for most of the 1990s, which facilitated tight personal connections between regional administrations and the Energos. Examples of this close relationship can be found in many regions. In Khabarovsk, for example, the Energo director Vladimir Popov was said to be a close friend of Governor Ishaev.[81] In Novosibirsk, the head of Novosibirskenergo,

---

[78] "Энергетические генералы еще и при советской власти всегда входили в состав региональных элит и всегда вращались в одном кругу с местными губернаторами (раньше – партийными боссами)." *Дальневосточный капитал*, June 2005, No. 6/58, 29.

[79] Interview #39 with electrical engineer and electricity sector expert (*energetik*), Vladivostok, 20071004.

[80] Бергер and Проскурина, "Крест Чубайса," 29.

[81] In fact, Popov became vice-governor. Popov is an *energetik*, having worked for Kahabarovskenergo since 1984. He was removed from Khabarovskenergo in 2001, during the Chubais-led reforms, but then became first deputy chairman of the Khabarovsk Krai administration and given the portfolio of overseeing the fuel and energy complex. Popov's biography is available on the Khabarovsk Krai government site, http://www.adm.khv.ru. Also interview #45 with employee of electricity company, and #46 with academic and journalist, both in Khabarovsk, 20071011.

Vitalii Tomilov, was a loyalist of Governor Tolokonskii, who supported Tomilov in a fierce, albeit ultimately vain, attempt to resist Chubais's efforts to replace him.[82]

The struggle between liberal reformers and regional governors over the future of the electricity sector played out in conflicts between the *menedzhery* and the *energetiki* in policy bodies and consulting committees. At the federal level, two committees were particularly influential in the formulation of liberalization plans around 2001 and 2002: the Kress committee and the Gref team.[83] The Kress committee was a working group of the State Council (*Госсовет*). It was staffed with *energetiki* and backed by powerful regional governors, including, for example, Leonid Roketskii, the governor of Tyumen, one of Russia's richest regions.[84] Viktor Kress, the head of the committee, was the independent-minded governor of Tomsk, another Siberian region with a strong agenda in the electricity sector. The Kress commission proposed to modernize the electricity system while leaving intact the vertically integrated Energos.[85] It also suggested that states retain substantial ownership of electricity companies and opposed privatization of generation companies, arguing that unbundling would decrease reliability.[86] The plan also recommended that only a small amount of wholesale electricity should be freely traded, while the state continued regulating the bulk of wholesale and all retail prices.[87] The Kress plan drew on a modernization proposal created by the Institute for Electric Energy Systems at the Siberian Branch of the Russian Academy of Sciences, a prominent institutional home of the academics among the *energetiki*.[88]

---

[82] The struggle between the regional government and UES over the director of Novosibirskenergo stretched over a few months; "Запрет не подействовал," *Ведомости*, April 26, 2001; "РАО ЕЭС готовит силовые акции в Новосибирске," *Коммерсантъ*, May 11, 2001; "Новосибирскэнерго без боя не сдается," *Коммерсантъ*, May 16, 2001; "РАО ЕЭС России решило конфликт в Новосибирскэнерго," *Известия*, July 13, 2001.

[83] See, for example, "Кресс добавит энергетики," *Российская газета*, April 20, 2001.

[84] Interview #39 with electrical engineer/electricity sector expert, Vladivostok, 20071004, interview #57 with electricity sector economist, Irkutsk, 20071122 and interview #52 with electricity sector economist, Irkutsk, 20071117.

[85] Interview #52 with electricity sector economist, Irkutsk, 20071117.

[86] The Kress committee's concern with reliability was stressed in interview #57 with electricity sector economist, Irkutsk, 20071122.

[87] In Хлебников, *Рынок Электроэнергии в России*. Also, interview with high-level administrator of the Melentiev institute, who confirmed the involvement of his team, interview #52 with electricity sector economist, Irkutsk, 20071117.

[88] Energy Systems Institute, named after L. A. Melentiev at the Siberian Branch of Russian Academy of Sciences (Институт систем энергетики им. Л. А. Мелентьева Сибирского

The Gref team was the reform committee of the Ministry of Economic Development and Trade, whose head was German Gref.[89] Made up of the *menedzhery*, the Gref team by and large recommended the liberalization plan favored by Chubais. The Gref team supported the unbundling of the Energos into the supra-regional wholesale and territorial companies (the *OGKs* and *TGKs*). It also favored full price liberalization and the creation of competitive markets for the exchange of all electricity, both long-term contracts as well as the day-ahead and balancing markets. The *menedzhery* also supported Chubais's policy to cut off nonpaying customers.[90]

While experts played an important role in federal reform commissions, their influence on the day-to-day activities of oblast-level administrative bodies, the Regional Energy Commissions (REKs) in particular, was more significant.[91] REKs administered widespread subsidies to maintain low prices for various consumers, and were considered by liberals to be key obstacles to reform (Chapter 5). For most of the 1990s, REKs were staffed by the *energetiki*, representatives of both the Energos and of regional administrations.

Shifting Power Positions and the Federal Government's Modernization Agenda

The Putin government believed that promoting a new class of managers would enhance the sector's value during privatization and increase returns on sector assets retained by the government. But a political logic was also at play. Replacing the *energetiki* with the *menedzhery* helped sever the link between governors and the electricity sector, and weakened the ability of governors to shape regional economies through targeted

---

отделения РАН). Much of their work is published on their website, http://www.sei.irk. ru/. Their involvement is also mentioned by Khlebnikov (see source in the previous note). The opposition of the institute to Chubais's plan was mentioned in an interview with two prominent members of the Melentiev Institute, interview #52 with electricity sector economist, Irkutsk, 20071117, and interview #57 with electricity sector economist, Irkutsk, 20071122.

[89] The working groups were active in 2001 and 2002. For an overview of the position of the two committees, see "Последняя схватка за РАО ЕЭС," *Ведомости*, May 15, 2001. For details on the different proposals, see Хлебников, *Рынок Электроэнергии в России*. See also Rutland, "Power Struggle: Reforming the Electricity Industry." The remainder of this discussion of the Gref team's plan is based on these sources.

[90] Miasnik is said to have been very strict about nonpayments; "Новые менеджеры АО Энерго исполнительны до и после передела?" *Правда*, June 28, 2001.

[91] Interview #39 with electrical engineer/electricity sector expert, Vladivostok, 20071004.

electricity subsidies. *Menedzhery*'s ascendancy between 2000 and 2004 was simultaneously a defeat of regional governors. Expert turnover ended regional influence and effectively shifted the site of sector regulation from the regional to the federal level. A few events are symptomatic of these trends: at the federal level, the advice of the Kress team (the voice of regional governors) was largely ignored in favor of a plan that unbundled Energos and privatized power plants. As mentioned earlier in the chapter, Viktor Kudriavyi, a high-profile *energetik* and outspoken critic of reform, was removed from office as Deputy Energy Minister.[92] We see a similar pattern at the regional level: the *energetiki* lost their positions as directors of power plants and seats in the REKs.

A government that encourages liberal reformers to install the *menedzhery* is largely incompatible with the predictions of capture and rent-seeking theories. If illegitimate rents and corrupt side payments were the government's main goal, established insiders presumably were more reliable partners than were new managers charged with improving transparency and boosting shareholder value. The empirical question to what extent Putin supported Chubais, then, is of some theoretical significance. From a purely legal perspective, the wholesale replacement of management in the electricity sector required at least a tacit approval of the federal government. As Chapter 4 outlined, the federal government held majority stakes in most electricity companies, and on the whole, the large-scale replacement of the incumbent *energetiki* with the *menedzhery* would not have been possible without the consent of dominant political factions in Moscow. The fact that the federal government legally controlled Energos did not necessarily make the process clear-cut, however; de jure ownership in post-Soviet Russia by no means guaranteed de facto control. Two developments suggest that the federal government actively supported Chubais's agenda of promoting the *menedzhery*. First, in regions where Putin replaced rebellious regional governors, unprotected *energetiki* soon lost their positions too. In Primorskii Krai, for example, the old Energo management was thrown out as soon as the rebellious regional governor Evgeny Nazdratenko was removed from his post in 2001.[93] The new manager of the restructured electricity company in the Far East had few established ties to regional governors. This

[92] Interview with Kudriavyi in Экcперт, No. 14, April 13, 1998. About his removal, see "Энергетика," Журнал Власть, No. 23, June 14, 2004.
[93] Ibid.; see also discussion in Chapter 3.

was true of the *menedzhery* in general, some of who were said to spend as much time in Moscow as they did in the regions.

A reorganization of the regulatory institutions in the sector was a second development that revealed Moscow's intentions concerning the *menedzhery*. As previous chapters outlined, the creation of FST was meant to tame the disobedient regional regulators – the REKs. The implementation of FST directives was supervised by the *polpredy*, presidential envoys to the region, whose offices were endowed with substantial authority. The transition to this regime (FST/*polpredy*) from the regional arrangements (REK/governors) was greatly facilitated by the arrival of the new managers. Initially, in regions were the *menedzhery* arrived prior to the taming of the governor, managers and regional governors clashed: "[T]he new *menedzhery* constantly conflicted with [the governor], a conflict that was carried out in the REK," noted one observer.[94] Where old REK delegates and the *energetiki* retained their seats, they were increasingly monitored by the *polpredy* and the FST and eventually had little choice but to go along with Moscow's liberalization agenda. As governors were replaced or weakened by Putin's reforms, the *menedzhery* cooperated with the FST and the *polpredy*.

In sum, the centralization of political power and the implementation of liberal reforms were mutually reinforcing processes. The *menedzhery's* promotion undercut the influence of the regional governors in the sector and contributed to the centralization of sector regulation. At the same time, the centralization of political power enabled Chubais and the liberal reformers to promote the managers, who then proceeded to collect bills from regional businesses, standardize accounts, shed employees, and sell off atypical assets.[95]

Scott argues that legibility enables rent extraction by private capital and the state: "[T]he more legible ... form can be more readily converted into a source of rent – either as private property or as monopoly rent of the state."[96] I argued earlier, the *menedzhery's* reforms created the prerequisite for rent extraction by private investors. It would be plausible to

---

[94] Interview #39 with electrical engineer/electricity sector expert, Vladivostok, 20071004.

[95] Two types of state power are at play: one based on formal, rational accounting procedures, the other based on more informal, personal, and patronage relations. While I do make the point that the centralization of power allowed the dispersion of expertise that values the former type of rationality, I do not want to imply that the latter no longer played a role in the government from the center. Centralized governance under Putin is certainly not devoid of paternalistic, personalized power structures.

[96] Scott, *Seeing like a State*, 220.

argue that the *menedzhery*'s success in collecting outstanding bills, as well as the standardization of electricity sector companies, also enabled the state to extract fiscal revenues from the sector. While this may have been the case, the state's ability to tax private owners is a difficult endeavor that also depends on many other factors.[97] The argument here is more modest: the *menedzhery*'s transformation of the electricity sector enabled a concomitant shift in the site of authority from the regional to the federal level, which allowed the central government to govern and regulate the sector and to implement a liberal reform agenda.

Finally, it is worth noting an interesting feedback effect at play between the promotion of the *menedzhery* and the success of liberal reforms. While the victory of the *menedzhery* would not have been possible without the political support of the Putin government, the new managers also legitimized liberal reforms. Today "modernization" of the sector is generally equated with privatization and liberalization. According to one observer, "many people believe that there is no other way."[98] Approval of the modernization=liberalization equation varied in different political circles. Kremlin insiders subscribed to it for the electricity sector, but it also had broader support among electricity sector professionals. Even the *energetiki* among my interviewees resigned themselves to the inevitability of liberalization. The *energetiki* I interviewed frequently resigned themselves to the inevitability of liberalization, conceding that liberal ideas were unstoppable, though still refusing to relinquish their opposition to "economistic ideas," preferring other ownership structures and other ways of organizing production.[99] Almost everybody involved in the electricity sector believed that "there [was] no way back,"[100] a notion shared by observers of electricity sector privatizations in other countries.[101] Government support of the expert turnover thus legitimized the values, ideas, and methods of the new expert regime.

---

[97] See Chaudhry, "The Myths of the Market and the Common History of Late Developers." For a discussion of the Russian state's efforts to strengthen its fiscal capacity, see Luong and Weinthal, "Contra Coercion."

[98] Interview #8 with electricity sector expert at financial institution, Moscow, 20061006. Ironically, the blackouts and the threat of blackouts helped the liberal reformers, serving as proof for their argument that there was no other way.

[99] Interview #39 with electrical engineer/electricity sector expert, Vladivostok, 20071004. He also noted that he prefers municipal ownership of power plants, for example, but that this never seemed to be a politically viable option.

[100] Interview #57 with electricity sector economist (*energetik*), Irkutsk, 20071122.

[101] Sally Hunt, *Making Competition Work in Electricity* (New York: John Wiley & Sons, 2002).

To sum up, this chapter documented how a shift in the relative power positions of the *energetiki* and the *menedzhery* was constitutive to liberalization of the electricity sector. I stressed that establishing the prerequisites for asset valuation compatible with internationally recognized standards and methodologies required not only changing rules on paper but replacing "bodies" in electricity companies, regulatory agencies, and policy committees. Precisely because it involved displacing a well-established, well-connected group of incumbent actors, the promotion of managerial experts was a deeply political transformation. The victory of the *menedzhery* and the legibility of the electricity sector owed much to the federal efforts to centralize political power. Putin's goal to undercut the governors' control of regional economies was congruent with the marginalization of the *energetiki*, whose regional political networks, norms, and practices left them unsuited for center-led modernization efforts.

The introduction of new systems of valuation is an inherently political project. This point is worth making because governments often have a stake in "de-politicizing" modernization projects, rooting them in technocratic governance rather than representative government. The legitimacy of the Putin government was buttressed by claims to implement the "right solutions" rather than politically negotiated ones. The Russian government tried to de-politicize the nature of the disputes surrounding the electricity sector and de-emphasized the political nature of the conflict between the *energetiki* and the *menedzhery*. "This meeting [of the Kress and Gref commissions] will not be political, but purely technical,"[102] commented the deputy minister for economic development on a controversial meeting between the opposing commissions.[103] De-emphasizing the political aspects of governance is also a core tenet of technocratic governance, which favors policy making by scientific experts uniquely capable of determining "right solutions" to political conflicts. Science replaces politics – a political version of Frederick Taylor's maxim that "scientific management will mean the elimination of almost all causes for dispute and disagreement."[104] Yet clearly the victory of the *menedzhery* and the *energetiki*'s marginalization were eminently political.

---

[102] A comment by Andrei Sharonov, deputy minister for economic development. "Великое стояние," *Ведомости*, May 18, 2001.

[103] Other commentators dismissed the conflict between *energetiki* and *menedzhery* as personal squabbles between loyalists and enemies of Chubais. Interview #8 with electricity sector analyst at financial institution, Moscow, 20061006.

[104] Frederick Winslow Taylor, *The Principles of Scientific Management* (Harper, 1914), 142. Technocratic idea became popular in the early twentieth century both in the United

This chapter concludes Part II of the book, which examined how three important elements of the electricity sector's institutional underpinnings were reshaped during the implementation of Chubais's liberal reforms: ownership structures, tariff regulation and subsidies, and finally regimes of expertise. Each chapter traced changes over time, stressing the affinities of the liberal reform project with President Putin's reassertion of federal sovereignty. The chapters also compared processes and outcomes across Russia, demonstrating that variation in the way markets evolved maps on to differences in the developmental strategies devised by regional and federal authorities. Taken together, these over-time and cross-regional comparisons demonstrate that the liberal reform agenda and the state's attempts to govern were intertwined in Russia's post-Soviet developmental agenda.

States and the Soviet Union, as a corollary of industrialization and a few decades later, as the solution to the Great Depression; see William E. Akin, *Technocracy and the American Dream: The Technocrat Movement, 1900–1941* (Berkeley: University of California Press, 1977). The legitimization of political authority via claims to technocratic governance is an interesting aspect of post-Soviet governance that has received relatively little attention. This kind of legitimization is a hallmark of technocratic governance, as is the rejection of legitimization through political representation. Technocratic governments claim to rely on the advice of experts to "govern well," rather than by seeking consensus and compromise. See, for example, Kramer, A., "Dmitri A. Medvedev: Young Technocrat of the Post-Communist Era," *New York Times*, December 11, 2007. See Chapter 2 for a discussion of legitimation of authority in post-Soviet Russia.

Conclusion: Development as Contingent Transformations

From Ministry to Market: The Red Threads

The transformation of the Russian electricity sector from ministry to market was forged by regional and federal officials trying to achieve multiple goals: regulate regional economies at a time when authority structures were being challenged, promote economic development when deindustrialization loomed large, and, finally, legitimize governance when the government was unable to provide many essential public goods. Rather than focusing on the rent-seeking and power-maximizing motives of corrupt bureaucrats, my narrative stresses the developmental motives that crucially shaped political battles over power plants and subsidies. During the 1990s, regional governors sought control of electricity sector assets and prices to prevent deindustrialization and cushion the impact of hyperinflation on household incomes. Governors kept prices low for regional industrialists and determined who would benefit from early privatization and ownership changes. With the centralization of political power under Putin, the site of property battles and of tariff regulation shifted to the federal government. Developmental pacts continued to matter: the federal government under Putin enlisted conglomerates for its developmental goals, selectively accommodating demands by large conglomerates during the second phase of the sector's transformation. Energy and industrial conglomerates had different interests vis-à-vis the electricity sector. These developmental pacts protected or promoted particular industries, thereby preserving different inherited economic structures across regions. For the electricity sector this meant that diverse regional human and economic geographies shaped the ownership and subsidy regimes that emerged during the sector's marketization.[1]

A second key argument this book advances concerns the dynamic two-way relationship that existed between market reforms and political authority. Chapters 4, 5, and 6 demonstrated that the centralization of political authority under President Putin made liberal reforms possible, but that market reforms at the same time solidified the centralization by sidelining actors that had critically undermined the sovereign authority of the federal government. Electricity sector reforms intentionally and effectively redefined the *political* arena in which the future of electricity markets was negotiated. I highlight three dynamics: first, the unbundling and privatization of regional vertical monopolies centralized control of power plants in the hands of Russia's largest conglomerates; second, new supra-regional regulatory institutions undercut regional governor's influence over subsidies and ownership transfers; and finally, the marginalization of Soviet-era technical experts severed personal ties between electricity companies and regional governments. This argument travels beyond Russia in that it suggests that market arrangements are premised upon certain political conditions, but that actors' political and social status is also produced by the markets they created. Pacts between economic and political actors evolve and are renegotiated as economies develop; or in even more general terms, markets and political authority co-evolve and continuously redefine each other. This dynamic evolution of markets and authority structures eludes approaches to political economy that conceptualize the market as a set of fixed mechanisms and regard its link with politics as a well-defined, unidirectional relationship.

While interests loom large in this account of the making of Russian capitalism, they alone do not help us understand the complex combination of liberal and illiberal elements that characterized the sector's transformation. Oligarchic conglomerates influenced emerging markets

---

[1] The protection of existing industrial structures is a common phenomenon even if they seem incompatible with a liberal rhetoric of free markets and even if it is not politicized as the protection of national champions; see Block, "Swimming Against the Current"; Robert Wade, "The Mystery of US Industrial Policy: The Developmental State in Disguise," *Transforming Economies: Making industrial policy work for growth, jobs and development.* Jose M. Salazar-Xirinachs, Irmgard Nübler, Richard Kozul-Wright eds. Geneva: International Labor Organization (2014): 379–400. Which structures are protected and which ones are allowed to decay is an interesting question not only in Russia, as industrialization trajectories left behind uneven maps with regions that are more or less vulnerable to pressures of globalization or deindustrialization everywhere.

institutions, when and where their interests in electricity sector reforms were legitimized via politically resonant developmental strategies. Many accounts of the post-Soviet transition stress the role of oligarchs as powerful new economic actors. While oligarchic conglomerates were indeed crucial, this book stresses that they were not autonomous. In contingent political struggles, the oligarchs and the strongest political factions – liberals and statists – were forced to compromise at each step of the reforms. These contingent compromises were precisely what shaped the institutional underpinnings of the electricity sector. The adaptation of the liberal reform plans meant that no single ideology, no lasting consensus, and no single coherent set of policies shaped post-Soviet markets. These observations draw attention to adaptations of liberal reform programs – how reforms are forged in contingent domestic political battles – and, more broadly, to the force of evolving, contested and unmoored ideational frameworks for explanations of complex market arrangements.

Post-Soviet histories of the largest electricity-producing regions in European Russia, Siberia, and the Far East strongly support these interpretations of state-market relations. The political dynamics of reform in smaller regions, which receive less attention in the preceding discussion, sometimes differed from those of their larger neighbors, in particular during the 1990s. Smaller regions typically imported electricity and generally followed federal government directives. The Energos in remote regions were not subject to ownership struggles by large conglomerates. In Siberia and the Far East, smaller Energos relied on coal, were expensive to run, and hence were less valuable. However, under Chubais's aegis, smaller regional electricity companies were at first de facto and later de jure merged with the electricity assets of their larger neighbors as they were bundled into the one of the fourteen territorial generation companies (*TGKs*). Such consolidations ensured that smaller, more remote regions followed a reform trajectory similar to their more important neighbors during this later period. There were also a number of anomalous cases among large regions where trajectories and outcomes did not fit neatly into the triptych narrative of the book. I have introduced Tatarstan and Bashkortostan in passing; they are two subnational regions with the status of ethnic republics. As they enjoyed far more autonomy from the federal government than other regions did, their electricity companies were excluded from the UES-led reform plans from the start. For different reasons, the North Caucasian regions affected by the Chechen wars (Chechnya, Ingushetiya, Kabardino Balkariya, North Osetiya, and Karachaevo-Cherkessiya) were also not included in the liberalization plan; regional Energos in these regions were unbundled, but the federal government retained a majority stake in their power assets.[2]

Developmentalism Beyond the Electricity Sector

The Russian state's developmental ambitions shaped the transformation of the electricity sector. A particularly close connection exists between this sector and economic development, but post-Soviet developmentalism was not confined to utilities reform. The type of pacts that I describe between Russian authorities and oligarchic conglomerates – pacts with long-term time horizons that respond to the need to legitimize emerging authority structures – characterize state-market relations more broadly. Gazprom's role in sector transformation, detailed in Chapters 3, 4, and 5, highlighted developmental aspects of the gas sector's transformation. The basic rationale of the intricate pact between the Russian state and Gazprom is to keep domestic gas prices low to fuel industrial production and employment, and to retain the gas sector as a central channel for domestic energy subsidies. The Russian railways was another networked infrastructure sector whose post-Soviet transformation was driven by developmental considerations. Russell Pittman found that the government introduced some competition among private actors while retaining control of key aspects of the sector and subsidizing both rail cargo and passengers in various ways. As in the electricity sector, complex subsidy regimes shaped the market transition of the rail system, including both freight-to-passenger and within-freight subsidies.[3] Transport subsidies for coal provide clear evidence for this: Siberian coal was transported at very low cost to European and Far Eastern consumers, as well as to the booming Asian economies. Rail subsidies also benefited other export-oriented sectors located in remote territories.[4] While the logic of

---

[2] The four regions of Ingushetiya, Kabardino Balkariya, North Osetiya, and Karachaevo-Cherkessiya were merged into the North Caucasus Energy Management Company; see Rutland, "Power Struggle: Reforming the Electricity Industry." Neighboring Dagestan is the home to a number of small, though valuable, hydroelectric plants that were integrated into the federal government–owned Hydro-OGK.

[3] Russell Pittman, "Railway and Electricity Restructuring in Russia: On the Road To... Where?" (n.d.): 5, accessed March 13, 2014, http://uisrussia.srcc.msu.ru/docs/nov/leontief/2007/papers/russel.doc. Pittman's research on the Russian railways reform is also informative; see Russell Pittman, "Russian Railways Reform and the Problem of Non-Discriminatory Access to Infrastructure," *Annals of Public and Cooperative Economics* 75, no. 2 (2004): 167–192.

[4] See European Conference of Ministers of Transport, *Regulatory Reform of Railways in Russia* (Paris: OECD Publishing, 2004).

subsidies is multilayered, developmental considerations were clearly at play. And as in the electricity sector, attempts to liberalize the railway system (although far less radical than in the electricity sector) had "territorial" aspects – patterns of rail sector transformation were shaped by economic geography.

Rather than simply retreating from ownership, regional and federal administrations played an active role in the post-Soviet transformation of many sectors beyond networked infrastructure, from metals to machine building, from agriculture to financial services. Each of these sectors was in its own way the backbone of a particular regional economy, in part because Soviet planners favored mono-industrial towns. More research is needed to examine how regional and federal authorities shaped institutional structures in each of these sectors. Rather than branding subsidies and ownership transfers as illegitimate outgrowths of a corrupt system, attention to developmental strategies opens the possibility of regarding them as part of ongoing negotiations based on mutual dependence, and ultimately as evolving social agreements that profoundly shape markets.

Liberalization and Developmentalism Beyond Russia

In many ways the marketization described here is historically unique. At the same time, *Post-Soviet Power* does not jettison theorization in favor of thick description, and I want to restate its theoretical intervention. The book does not offer a theory of how development works, but an analytical lens to study economic development as a political process. What I propose is a view of economic development and political transformations as mutually constitutive. This, together with the contingency of the political compromises that shape economic institutions, in essence also suggests that the relationship between politics and markets is better understood as a dynamic, reflexive, and evolving process, and not a causal and unidirectional one. At its broadest this book argues for economies and markets as constructed and contingent entities, and for a dynamic constructivist research program that grasps their evolution as ongoing, political construction projects.[5]

This view has at least two important consequences for how we study economic development and developmental states beyond Russia. First, it

---

[5] Chapter 1 discusses in more detail how this book draws on and develops frameworks by others who take a constructivist starting point, including Gary Herrigel, Kiren Chaudhry, David Woodruff, Timothy Mitchell, and Michel Callon.

suggests that contrasting forms of state intervention along the spectrum of legitimate market governance versus distorting dirigisme is ultimately flawed. Such a dichotomy always relies on assumptions of what development should look like that are ultimately not warranted and not useful. They are not warranted, because significant evidence suggests that a wide a variety of state-market relationships can underpin economic growth.[6] They are not useful because they limit analysis of this multiplicity of governance arrangements and the variety of economies that shape everyday lives. Similarly, assessments whether a particular state is a successful developmental state that fosters competitive markets then also always remain "deficit" models that can obscure or overshadow important changes and trajectories that are taking place.[7] Departing from the notion that one set of market relationships are the ultimate goal of development allows us to shed the normative baggage that color the terms statism and cronyism and to be more appreciative of a diversity of state-market relations. Post-Soviet Russia is by no means a coherent developmental state that has fostered free market competition; yet this book has argued that the Russian authorities' developmental and modernization strategies are nevertheless critical to understanding post-Soviet political economies and the tremendous structural changes that have occurred.

A second, related reason why an approach to development that takes construction and contingency seriously is promising has to do with the types of comparisons of market governance that this allows. If all markets are constructed, there is no reason why state-led development projects cannot be compared with transformations in mature capitalist economies, and why state-oligarch bargains in Russia should not be compared to state-market pacts elsewhere.[8] I refer to the post-Soviet transition as a state-led development and modernization project in this book because there is clear evidence that Russian authorities perceived it in this way, but it could just as well be placed in a comparison with the reform

---

[6] Charles F. Sabel, "Self-Discovery as a Coordination Problem," in *Export Pioneers in Latin America*, ed. Charles F. Sabel et al. (Washington, DC: Inter-American Development Bank, 2012), 1–46; Dani Rodrik, *One Economics, Many Recipes: Globalization, Institutions, and Economic Growth* (Princeton, NJ: Princeton University Press, 2007).

[7] Collier and Way, "Beyond the Deficit Model."

[8] As some scholars have indeed done; see Block, "Swimming Against the Current"; Wade, "The Mystery of US Industrial Policy." Similarly, this move also makes clear that studies of interconnections between developing, transition, and industrialized economies are interesting and understudied; see Gary Herrigel, Volker Wittke, and Ulrich Voskamp, "Governance Architectures for Learning and Self-Recomposition in Chinese Industrial Upgrading" in Berk, Galvan, and Hattam, *Political Creativity*.

strategies by mature capitalist economies. In 2004, Andrei Shleifer and Daniel Treisman argued that Russia had become a "normal country," by which they meant "a typical middle-income capitalist democracy."[9] In many ways, this book makes a similar effort to "normalize" Russia, albeit in a different way. In Shleifer and Treisman's framework, normality is a very particular outcome, a "typical" type and the endpoint of a presumed transition. In *Post-Soviet Power*, Russia is a normal country, because just like other countries, its economy is constructed and contingent. The point is then not to argue for convergence, but for an analytical framework that takes constructivism seriously, and for an understanding of development and market governance that is not premised on a distinction between developing/emerging, transitioning, and advanced economies and on the implicit teleology that accompanies these terms.

The implications of this normalization for comparative political economy is that we can compare market governance across various economies as ongoing construction projects, rather than having to classify outcomes as particular types, or as particular stages of development. Thinking of markets as construction sites also opens opportunities to look for politics in new places. Political questions surrounding the provision of infrastructure is one such site. Modalities of infrastructure provision and regulation have been at the core of both state-led development and liberalization projects across the world. For most of the twentieth century, a solid consensus held that governments should provide infrastructure as the basis for economic growth. More recently, governments confronted the challenge of decaying roads, electricity grids, and ports, although the acuteness of such problems varied.[10] At the same time, contra convergence, there is now *less* agreement about the role of the state in infrastructure provision, and *more* diversity in public-private arrangements than ever before. The liberal paradigm that emerged in the 1980s equated infrastructure modernization with increased private ownership and decreased

---

[9] Andrei Shleifer and Daniel Treisman, "A Normal Country," *Foreign Affairs* (April 2004).

[10] One key challenge is that governments generally want to ensure a minimum level of service provision in places, or times, when doing so is not profitable for private companies. These challenges are not confined to developing countries. Owing to the increasing focus on the vulnerability of critical infrastructure (be that because of ageing capital stock, as terrorist targets, or as environmental hazards), debates how private ownership can be reconciled with public interests, and how regulators can contribute to this, have been rekindled in the United States and elsewhere. See, for example, Emery Roe and Paul R. Schulman, *High Reliability Management: Operating on the Edge*, High Reliability and Crisis Management (Stanford, CA: Stanford Business Books, 2008).

state regulation of tariffs. After a series of crises and increased political resistance to infrastructure liberalization, however, the type of state involvement in infrastructure and the methods by which governments and polities reach decisions were again subject to intense debates. A better understanding of a government's responses to infrastructural challenges hinges on a mode of analysis that compares market regulations as politically contested arrangements, and is not helped by studies that seek to assess their relative distance from stylized best-practice institutions.

Political battles over the geographical scope of infrastructure liberalization are an interesting case for such a comparison of governance arrangements as ongoing construction processes rather than as desirable/undesirable outcomes. Liberal reformers have tried to generalize and standardize market regulations to scale up markets in various sites, including the United States, the EU and Russia. In Russia, we saw that new zones of governance emerged during the process of marketization and re-regulation over the two post-Soviet decades. Regional (oblast') governance was effectively supplanted by regulation at the federal and supra-regional levels. Russia's liberal reformers redrew zones of regulation while making concessions to conglomerates and the government's developmental agenda along the way. The struggle that confronted Russian reformers attempting to institute a unified regulatory regime across an enormous geographical region mirrors the efforts of European and North American reformers to liberalize and reorganize electricity sector regulation from national to supranational and from state to national levels, respectively.

The EU's liberalization project had two main goals: to create a common liberalization agenda and to unify adjacent electricity zones to create larger markets. EU member states did indeed liberalize many aspects of domestic electricity provision in the decade following the first EU liberalization directive passed in 1996. Yet, despite significant liberalization of electricity markets, by 2007 the EU concluded that markets remained *national* in scope and that tariffs remained regulated in many countries. For example, liberal reformers had tried to unite Spanish and French electricity markets since the late 1990s, arguing that the two countries have complimentary generation capacity. But political opposition prevented the strengthening of high-voltage connections between the two countries for years, even as the liberalization agenda gained increasing support in Brussels. Attempts to coordinate liberalization and market design across Europe have also met with resistance.[11] As in Russia, many European

---

[11] "Energy Liberalisation in Europe," *The Economist*, December 6, 2007.

countries viewed their autonomy in infrastructure sectors as tools to influence national (and regional) development; utilities in particular were seen as "important vehicles for the realizing *national* energy planning and related policy objectives."[12] Opposition to liberal reform in the European electricity sector was deeply rooted in the central role this sector played in national energy and development strategies, rather than merely reflecting the efforts of rent seeking utility companies.

In the United States, the federal efforts to align states behind a liberal reform agenda also encountered difficulties. The regulatory regime that governs utilities in the United States has historically left most of the jurisdiction over sector regulation to states. Since the mid-1990s, the Federal Energy Regulatory Commission (FERC) has been trying to create a set of unified institutions to regulate utility markets.[13] Many states and a majority of congress have rejected FERC's plans to create a "standard market design" (SMD).[14] States in the Southeast (Arkansas, Georgia, Louisiana, Mississippi, and North Carolina) have traditionally been a stronghold of opposition to the SMD proposal. Comprised of large and relatively low-density rural areas, these states have opposed marketization because of concerns about reduced service provision and higher prices.[15] States in the Pacific Northwest have also opposed FERC's attempts to impose the SMD because of the higher prices and increasing price volatility that it would imply. Many of these utilities feared that the SMD would end their ability to enter into long-term agreements with large consumers, requiring them to expose transactions to market prices.[16]

[12] Quote by Leigh Hancher, "Slow and Not so Sure: Europe's Long March to Electricity Market Liberalization," *The Electricity Journal* 10, no. 9 (November 1997): 93. See also Jacint Jordana, David Levi-Faur, and Imma Puig, "The Limits of Europeanization: Regulatory Reforms in the Spanish and Portuguese Telecommunications and Electricity Sectors," *Governance* 19, no. 3 (2006): 437–464.

[13] See Joskow, "Markets for Power in the United States."

[14] Attempts to introduce SMD started in 2001. See Hunt, *Making Competition Work in Electricity*, 286.

[15] Mathew J. Morey and Christina C. Forbes, "How Can FERC Find Its Way out of the SMD Cul-de-Sac? Stimulate the Transmission Sector!" *The Electricity Journal* 16, no. 7 (2003): 74–85.

[16] One representatives of a Northwestern utility argued that SMD proposals would "eviscerat[e] our long-term firm transmission contract rights by exposing these transactions to market prices in real-time." Aleka Scott, "FERC Needs to Listen to the Regions before Racing to Its Standard Market Design," *The Electricity Journal* 15, no. 9 (2002): 91. This low-cost region reluctant to sign on to FERC SMD is also mentioned by Hunt, *Making Competition Work in Electricity*, 39.

Agreements between states, utilities, and consumers made Congress unwilling to allow FERC to implement reforms based on SMD. Large electricity consumers in Oregon, for example, rely on cheap power from regional hydroelectric power plants, and the state has a long history of guaranteeing low-cost energy to industrial consumers. Traditionally, aluminum smelters located near hydroelectric power plants scattered along Oregon's Columbia River were the state's largest electricity consumers. More recently they have been joined by server farms (owned by Microsoft and Google), also looking to locate close to hydroelectric dams and reliably cheap power.[17] Political struggles to prevent nationwide markets and preserving special price zone, essential to understand the Pacific Northwest's position on electricity reforms, are remarkably reminiscent of the public-private pacts I found in Siberia. California and Texas, on the other hand, were early and ardent supporters of liberalization in the electricity sector.[18] In both states, the energy company Enron pushed for reforms and price liberalization while it sought novel ways to profit from electricity sector liberalization. While Enron's political clout in DC was legendary, it might fall shy of Gazprom's stature in Moscow. It appears, then, that both in Russia and the United States, conglomerates located either upstream or downstream of the electricity sector formed different pacts with political authorities and thereby shaped electricity markets. The point is not that we can predict a liberalization outcome by measuring the political connectedness of conglomerates, but that if we view these political struggles as integral to the construction of markets, we gain a new analytical lens of the types of economic and political actors and their influence on the evolution of markets appears in a new light.

In all three cases – Russia, the EU and the United States – the resistance to giving up regulatory authority at a lower level of governance was significant. The liberal project to create enlarged and unified electricity markets, with one set of market regulations, was opposed (and shaped) by economic and political actors who sought more place-specific, national, or regionalist arrangements. What is interesting here is that with a constructivist lens, we see that the creation of supra-regional, deterritorialized ownership and regulatory arrangements in Russia appears to have

---

[17] According to the *Economist*, "the largest data centers now rival aluminum smelters in the energy they consume.... As a result, finding a site for a large data center is now, above all, about securing a cheap and reliable source of power." "Down on the Server Farm: The Real-World Implications of the Rise of Internet Computing."

[18] In 1994, California was the first state to liberalize retail access; see Hunt, *Making Competition Work in Electricity*, p. 386 for a timeline of California's reforms.

gone further than the European and North American reforms. Putin's project to create supra-regional market governance was in fact remarkably successful. This was the case because an unlikely political alliance of liberals and statists in Moscow united to undercut the influence of regional governors, which then led to a shift in public-private pacts to the center. The centralization of governance is not surprising in light of the story this book emphasizes, but it confounds theoretical approaches that place economies on a spectrum of liberal leaders and reform laggards, of developing, transitioning and advanced economies.

Russian Electricity Beyond 2008

Given that Russia is the main site of this book's narrative, I want to end it with a note on how the developments since 2008 challenged the framework proposed here. By 2008, a few big things have changed in the Russian electricity sector: UES and the Energos, the vertically integrated monopolies erected during the Soviet Union, were dismantled, and power plants now have new owners. Both processes fundamentally transformed the organization of power provision as well as the political dynamics of the sector – and neither is likely to be reversed. Electricity markets in European Russia, Siberia, and the Far East are separate from each other, with different price, subsidy, and ownership regimes. In the years since 2008, the agreements between liberal reformers, the government, and new owners of electricity assets agreed in the period under discussion here – from the early 1990s through to 2008 – remained in place in broad terms. Dmitry Medvedev, who took over the presidency of the Russian Federation for four years between 2008 and 2012, launched a "modernization" program that essentially continued much of the development agenda that I described under Vladimir Putin. Medvedev handed the presidency back to Putin in 2012, whose present, third term in office was shortly thereafter extended from four to six years.

While the broad contours of the power sector's restructuring are unlikely to be reversed, some aspects of the pacts between the state and Russia's oligarchs were ultimately provisional. Since 2008, two major events have shifted the terrain of power politics: the global economic crisis of 2008 and popular resistance to the Putin/Medvedev government at its height in 2011 and 2012. The negotiations and pacts in the years between 2003 and 2008 that form the basis for the analyses in this book were in large measure premised on rapidly *growing* demand for electricity and hence the need for technological updates. When the global economic crisis of 2008 hit Russia, electricity demand and prices fell. In the last quarter of 2008, the price of electricity on the liberalized segment of the wholesale market fell by some 40 percent compared to the previous quarter, and electricity demand in January 2009 fell by more than 7 percent compared to the previous year.[19] Investment in new infrastructure was a significant part of the privatization bargains described here. Against the background of this economic slowdown, however, various parties to the bargains surrounding privatization and liberalization sought to revise their commitments. New owners partially reneged on promises to invest in technology upgrades, arguing that the magnitude of investments was untenable given the changed economic environment. In 2010, Putin, by then prime minister, though just as influential as he had been as president, repeatedly criticized new owners of electricity companies for failing to invest as much as they had promised.[20] New owners, on the other hand, criticized Chubais and liberal reforms for using exaggerated projected growth rates to calculate investment contributions: "Chubais tricked not just the energy companies, but the government itself. He based the sector's official report on winter 2006 consumption when there were freak frosts, and record GDP growth. Needing another 750 billion kilowatt hours by 2020 is twice the best-case and 3.5 times the likely scenario," opined one observer.[21] What I tried to show in this book, however, is precisely that liberals did not have to "trick" or deceive the government, as the economic agenda of creating markets went hand in hand with the political agenda of centralization. At the same time, the balance in the political alliance between the liberals and statists faction was unstable and has, after the second term of Putin's presidency, increasingly tipped in favor of the latter.

Challenges to agreements made during the period of reforms confirm that bargains between different factions of the state and Russia's

[19] "Russian electricity consumption declines 9.3% in second week of June," *Interfax Russia & CIS Business and Financial Newswire*, June 15, 2009.
[20] "Putin Threatens to Fine Four Tycoons," *Moscow Times*, February 25, 2010.
[21] The upshot of this argument is that Chubais's calculations of the need for investments was based on political rather than economic calculations to "trick" the government of President Putin – a curious assessment, as the *siloviki*, with their KGB background, are not usually known to be a gullible lot. Portraying Chubais as a trickster echoed a very common sentiment among Russians, who regarded him as a charlatan, responsible for the betrayal of every citizen who was promised much and received little during privatization. "E.On warns on electricity investment," *Russia Today/Ria Novosti*, March 25, 2009.

oligarchs are ongoing negotiations, and that an analytical framework that can account for the evolving nature of developmental pacts is useful. Liberal reformers continued to push for one national market and for an end to various price-distorting subsidies after 2008. Only if this happens, they argued, will service quality improve and prices fall. For the moment, it is unlikely that liberals have enough support to convince other political factions and the Russian population. Development strategies that rely on the current subsidy and ownership regimes enjoy both political support and legitimacy. The benefits of the negotiated bargains for both the government and for Russia's conglomerates are likely to outweigh the promises of full liberalization for some time to come.

At the same time, Russian discontent with the Putin/Medvedev government has risen steadily since 2008. In the fall and winter of 2011 and again in spring of 2012, demonstrators and activists mobilized in response to pervasive corruption and the government's lack of accountability. That the focus of criticism was President Putin and his circle of loyalists in many ways confirmed how successful he had been in centralizing authority. It also demonstrated that a critical, though perhaps not large, segment of the Russian population saw it as an illegitimate amassing of power.[22] Given just how tenuous, even fragile authorities' claim to legitimacy remained, the argument that the state and Russia's oligarchs relied heavily on development as legitimizing strategies makes sense. It is not clear at this point whether these protests will continue in the near future and whether unrest will significantly challenge the dynamics of Russian politics. What is clear is that protests were a critical response to Putin's post-Soviet strategy, and that the future of this strategy will at least to some extent depend on Russian authorities' ability to deliver on its promises. Since the government controls media outlets, the appearance of delivery might suffice for a while. But electricity might well be a test case for the legitimacy of the government, the type of developmentalism it is pursuing and the state-oligarch bargains it relies on. For Russian citizens, tariffs have been the most tangible result of electricity sector reforms. Most Russians make ends meet on small household incomes, and future price increases will not go unnoticed.[23] Russians also care about reliable electricity provision, as everybody is wired into its tangible

---

[22] Many activists voiced more targeted critique, such as Pussy Riot's sophisticated criticism of the Putin government's alliance with the Orthodox Church.

[23] Increasing electricity bills following liberalization were the immediate trigger for the popular rebellion in Kyrgyzstan in April 2010; see Reeves, "The Latest Revolution."

networks and relies on light and warmth; power is more than a mere commodity as this book argued. Whether or not Russians will ultimately hold the state accountable for the promises that post-Soviet developmentalism makes, electric power will likely remain a fascinating prism that refracts the political battles surrounding Russia's marketization.

Appendixes

Appendix 1: Major Russian Newspaper Sources Used for This Research; Full Citations in the Footnotes

Vedomosti	*Ведомости*	National/business
Kommersant"	*Коммерсантъ*	National/business
Ekspert	*Експерт*	National/business
Gazeta	*Газета*	National/general
Izvestiya	*Известия*	National/general
Segonia	*Сегодня*	National/general
Vostochno Sibirskaia Pravda	*Восточно Сибирская Правда*	Irkutsk
Utro Rossii	*Утро России*	Vladivostok
Krasnoiarskii Rabochii	*Красноярский рабочий*	Krasnoiarsk

Appendix 2: Interviews, Location, and Dates

Interviews conducted 2006/2007

Position	Place	Date	No.
Electricity sector expert at international financial institution	Moscow	20060721	1
Journalist covering electricity sector	Moscow	20060806	2
Employee of electricity company	Moscow/phone	20060904	3
Journalist	Moscow/phone	20060912	4
Electricity sector expert at international financial institution	London	20060920	5
Academic	London	20060920	6
Electricity sector analyst at financial institution	Moscow	20061005	7
Economist at financial institution	Moscow	20061006	8
Electricity sector analyst at financial institution	Moscow	20061008	9
Journalist covering electricity sector	Moscow/phone	20061009	10
Electricity sector expert	Moscow	20061018	11
Academic	Petersburg	20061023	12
Academic	Petersburg	20061023	13
Electricity sector expert	Moscow	20061026	14
Electricity sector analyst at financial institution	Moscow	20061027	15
Electricity sector expert/ consultant	Moscow	20061030	16

Interviews conducted 2006/2007

Position	Place	Date	No.
Electricity sector expert	Moscow	20061101	17
Journalist covering electricity sector	Moscow	20061109	18
Academic/policy analyst	Moscow	20061122	19
Electricity sector analyst at financial institution	Moscow	20061126	20
Electricity sector economist/ consultant	Moscow	20061214	21
Electricity sector expert at financial institution	Moscow	20070210	22
Electricity sector expert at international financial institution	Moscow	20070210	23
Regulator/Ministry for Economic Development	Moscow	20070214	24
Journalist	Moscow	20070217	25
Energy sector expert/policy analyst	Berkeley	20070613	26
Energy sector expert/policy analyst	Berkeley	20070613	27
Academic	Vladivostok	20070912	28
Academic	Vladivostok	20070913	29
Policy analyst	Vladivostok	20070914	30
Journalist covering electricity sector	Vladivostok	20070915	31
Electricity sector economist	Vladivostok	20070918 and 0925	32
Journalist covering electricity sector	Vladivostok	20070921	33
Academic/Employee of electricity company	Vladivostok	20070923	34
Regulator	Vladivostok	20070924	35
Program officer at international organization	Vladivostok	20070924	36
Electricity sector executive	Vladivostok	20071002	37
Academic	Vladivostok	20071003	38
Electrical engineer/electricity sector expert	Vladivostok	20071004	39
Pensioner	Vladivostok	20071004	40
Journalist covering electricity sector	Vladivostok	20071005	41
Academic	Vladivostok	20071005	42
Electricity sector economist	Khabarovsk	20071010	43

(*continued*)

Interviews conducted 2006/2007

Position	Place	Date	No.
Electricity sector economist	Khabarovsk	20071010	44
Employee of electricity company	Khabarovsk	20071011	45
Academic	Khabarovsk	20071011	46
Businessman	Vladivostok	20071017	47
Academic	Irkutsk	20071113	48
Academic	Irkutsk	20071114	49
Businessman	Irkutsk	20071115	50
Academic	Irkutsk	20071115	51
Electricity sector economist	Irkutsk	20071117	52
Employee of electricity company	Irkutsk	20071119	53
Businessman	Irkutsk	20071120	54
Employee of electricity company	Irkutsk	20071120	55
Journalist	Irkutsk	20071120	56
Electricity sector economist	Irkutsk	20071122	57
Academic	Irkutsk	20071124	58
Politician/former executive at electricity company	Irkutsk	20071130	59
Energy company executive	Irkutsk	20071203	60
Employee of electricity company	Irkutsk	20071205	61
Electricity sector expert	Moscow	20071210	62
Executive of electricity company	Moscow	20071212	63
Electricity sector expert at international financial institution	Moscow	20071212	64
Electricity sector expert at financial institution	Moscow	20071213	65
Journalist covering electricity sector	Moscow	20071213	66
Electricity sector expert/economist	Berkeley	20080414	67
Academic/Employee of electricity company	Berkeley	20080417	68
Electricity sector expert at international organization	Paris/email	20070212	69
Regulator/electricity sector	Washington, DC/email	20090317	70

Note: Interviewees were identified through the "snowball method": I relied on interviewees to identify other persons. Interviews were semi-structured conversations, typically lasting between 45 and 90 minutes. Interviews were conducted in person, with the exception of three cases in which the conversations happened by phone (3, 4 and 10). Two extensive and ongoing e-mail conversations are listed separately at the end (69 and 70). Repeat interviews are listed separately only if substantially new information was obtained and significant time had passed between interviews; this happened in three cases (interviews 1, 23, and 64; interviews 17 and 62; and interviews 18 and 66, respectively, are with the same person)

Appendix 3: Ownership Calculations in Chapter 4

TABLE A.3.1. *European power plants and new owners (2008)*

Power Plant	Company Name	Installed Capacity	New Owner*
Permskaia GES	OGK-1	2,400	InterRAO
Nizhnevartovskaia GRES	OGK-1	1,600	InterRAO
Iriklinskaia GRES and GES	OGK-1	2,130	InterRAO
Urengoiskaia GRES	OGK-1	24	InterRAO
Kashirskaia GRES-4	OGK-1	1,580	InterRAO
Verkhnetagil'skaia GRES	OGK-1	1,497	InterRAO
Pskovskaia GRES	OGK-2	430	Gazprom
Stavropol'skaia GRES	OGK-2	2,400	Gazprom
Serovskaia GRES	OGK-2	526	Gazprom
Surgutskaia GRES-1	OGK-2	3,280	Gazprom
Troitskaia GRES	OGK-2	2,059	Gazprom
Iuzhnoural'skaia GRES	OGK-3	882	NorNickel
Kostromskaia GRES	OGK-3	3,600	NorNickel
Cherepetskaia GRES	OGK-3	1,425	NorNickel
Yavinskaia GRES	OGK-4	600	EON
Surgutskaia GRES-2	OGK-4	4,800	EON
Shaturskaia GRES-5	OGK-4	1,100	EON
Smolenskaia GRES	OGK-4	630	EON
Nevinnomysskaia GRES	OGK-5	1,290	Enel
Sredneural'skaia GRES	OGK-5	1,182	Enel
Reftinskaia GRES	OGK-5	3,800	Enel
Konakovskaia GRES	OGK-5	2,400	Enel
Cherepovetskaia GRES	OGK-6	630	Gazprom
Riazanskaia GRES	OGK-6	2,650	Gazprom
GRES-24	OGK-6	310	Gazprom

(continued)

TABLE A.3.1. (*continued*)

Power Plant	Company Name	Installed Capacity	New Owner*
Kirishskaia GRES	OGK-6	2,100	Gazprom
Novocherkasskaia GRES	OGK-6	2,112	Gazprom
Volzhskaia GES	HydroOGK	2,541	HydroOGK
Zhigulevskaia GES	HydroOGK	2,300	HydroOGK
Kaskad Kubanskikh GES	HydroOGK	463	HydroOGK
Nizhegorodskaia GES	HydroOGK	520	HydroOGK
Saratovskaia GES	HydroOGK	1,360	HydroOGK
Kaskad Verkhnevolzhskikh GES	HydroOGK	456	HydroOGK
Zelenchukskie GES	HydroOGK	160	HydroOGK
Sualenergo	HydroOGK	400	HydroOGK
Zagorskaia GAES	HydroOGK	1,200	HydroOGK
Votinskaia GES	HydroOGK	1,020	HydroOGK
Kamskaia GES	HydroOGK	501	HydroOGK
Cheboksarskaia GES	HydroOGK	1,370	HydroOGK
Gergebil'skaia GES	HydroOGK	18	HydroOGK
Chiriurtskie GES	HydroOGK	81	HydroOGK
Miatlinskaia GES	HydroOGK	220	HydroOGK
Chirkeiskaia GES	HydroOGK	1,000	HydroOGK
TGK-1	TGK-1	6,162	Gazprom
TGK-2	TGK-2	1,393	RWE
Mosenergo	Mosenergo	10,611	Gazprom
TGK-4	TGK-4	3,284	Czech and Korean company
TGK-5	TGK-5	2,467	KES
TGK-6	TGK-6	2,919	KES
TGK-7	TGK-7	6,880	KES/Gazprom
TGK-8	TGK-8	3,312	Lukoil
TGK-9	TGK-9	2,590	KES
TGK-10	TGK-10	3,253	E-On/GdF
Tatenergo	Tatenergo	6,986	Republic of Tatarstan
Bashkirenergo	Bashkirenergo	2,796	Republic of Bashkortostan
Severo-Zapadnaia TETs	Severo-Zapadnaia TETs	900	InterRAO

TABLE A.3.2. *Siberian power plants and new owners (2008)*

Power Plant	Company Name	Installed Capacity	New Owner
Gusinoozerskaia GRES	OGK-3	1,100	NorNickel
Kharanorskaia GRES	OGK-3	430	NorNickel
Berezovskaia GRES	OGK-4	1,500	EON
Krasnoiarskaia GRES	OGK-6	1,250	Gazprom
Saiano-Shushenskaia GRES	HydroOGK	6,721	HydroOGK
Zeiskaia GES	HydroOGK	1,330	HydroOGK
Novosibirskaia GES	HydroOGK	455	HydroOGK
Bureiskaia GES	HydroOGK	670	HydroOGK
TGK-11	TGK-11	2,051	SUEK
TGK-12	TGK-12	4,392	SUEK
Iuzhnokuzbasskaia GRES	Iuzhnokuzbasskaia GRES	554	Mechel
Zapadno-Sibirskaia TETs	Zapadno-Sibirskaia TETs	600	EvRaz
TGK-13	TGK-13	2,458	SUEK
TGK-14	TGK-14	643	NorNickel
Novosibirskenergo	Novosibirskenergo	2,522	Novosib. energo
Irkutskenergo	Irkutskenergo	12,925	Rusal
Krasnoiarskaia GES	Krasnoiarskaia GES	6,000	Rusal

Sources: The first three columns of the Appendix 3 tables were compiled based on *"Тепловые генерирующие компании РАО ЕЭС России"* a publication by RAO/UES (2006) as well as information about Hydro-OGK from Hydro-OGK website and websites of the various independent power plants. The column on "New Owner" is based on press reports of take-overs and on self-reporting by these power plants, as indicated in footnotes in text above. The tables were initially compiled with the help of Tatiana Gavrilova.

Appendix 4: Price and Subsidy Calculations in Chapter 5

TABLE A.4.1. *Price increases between 2000 and 2005*

European Russia	%	Siberia	%	Russian Far East	%
Moscow	164	Tyumen	78	Primorskii Krai	67
Sverdlovsk	82	Irkutsk	216	Amurskaia oblast'	136
Saratov	160	Krasnoiarsk	123	Khabarovsk	174
Leningrad Oblast'	90	Kemerovo	165	Yakutiia	106
Kursk	152	Khakassiia	156	Sakhalin	192
Perm	110	Novosibirsk	167	Magadan	130
Tver'	179	Omsk	182	Kamchatka	29
Samara	189	Chita	136	Chukotka	274
Rep. of Bashkortostan	65	Tomsk	97		
Tatarstan	109	Altaiskii Krai	267		
Moscow Region	187	Buriatiia	142		
Smolensk	123				

Note: These are average of all price increases (i.e., household, urban, rural and industrial).
Source: Calculated based on UES tariff data.

TABLE A.4.2. *Cross-subsidies as percentage of industrial tariffs between 2000 and 2005*

European Russia		%	*Change*	Siberia		%	*Change*
Moscow	2000	35.8		Irkutsk	2000	7.5	
	2005	4.7	−31.1		2005	3.6	−3.9
Sverdlovsk	2000	10.5		Krasnoiarsk	2000	39.4	
	2004	−5.3	−15.8		2005	15.8	−23.6
Saratov	2000	50.9		Kuzbass	2000		
	2005	12.1	−38.8		2005	no cross subs	
Leningrad	2000	47.1		Khakassiia	2000		
Oblast'	2005	21.9	−25.2		2005	no cross subs	
Kursk	2000	29.1		Novosibirsk	2000	29.1	
	2004	23.2	−5.9		2005	24.2	−4.9
Perm	2000	29.5		Omsk	2000	50.1	
	2005	27.5	−2		2005	31.9	−18.2
Tver	2000	55.7		Chita	2000	30.8	
	2005	52.1	−3.6		2005	9.2	−21.6
Samara	2000	40.7		Tomsk	2000	30.2	
	2005	−5.2	−45.9		2005	21.8	−8.4
Rep. of	2000	35.5		Altaiskii	2000		
Bashkortostan	2005	29.8	−5.7	Krai	2005	no cross subs	
Tatarstan	2000	20.3		Buriatiia	2000		
	2005	11.1	−9.2		2005	no cross subs	
Moscow	2000	48.5					
Region	2005	15.2	−33.3	**Far East**			
Smolensk	2000	35.5		Primorskii	2000	30.2	
	2005	31.8	−2.6	Krai	2005	44	13.8
				Amurskaia	2000	17.5	
				oblast'	2004	23	5.5
				Khabarovsk	2000	44.5	
					2005	40.1	−4.4
				Yakutiia	2000	45.1	
					2005	52.9	7.8
				Sakhalin	2000	15.1	
					2005	27.9	12.8
				Magadan	2000	13.3	
					2002	12.6	−0.7
				Kamchatka	2000	68.3	
					2003	no cross subs	
				Chukotka	2000	3	
					2005	47.6	44.6

Note: I look at whether the difference between household and industrial tariffs as a percentage of industrial tariffs has increased or decreased over the 2000–2005 period (if 2005 is not available, I use the most recent available year).
Source: Calculated based on UES tariff data.

TABLE A.4.3. *Industrial subsidies, 2005*

European Russia			Evidence of ind. subs	Siberia			Evidence of ind. subs
Supra-reg. Average 107.6				*Supra-reg. Average 85.2*			
Moscow	Ind. Tariff	113.4		Irkutsk	IT	28.2	
	difference	5.8			difference	−57	Yes
Sverdlovsk	IT	77.5		Krasnoiarsk	IT	54.7	
	difference	−30.1	Yes		difference	−30.5	Yes
Saratov	IT	106.4		Kuzbass	IT	63.5	
	difference	−1.2			difference	−21.7	Yes
Len. Oblast'	Ind. Tariff	105		Khakassiia	IT	28.6	
	difference	−2.6			difference	−56.6	Yes
Kursk	IT	114.1		Novosibirsk	IT	110.2	
	difference	6.5			difference	25	
Perm	IT	95.1		Omsk	IT	120.35	
	difference	−12.5			difference	35.15	
Tver	IT	154.6		Chita	IT	104	
	difference	47			difference	18.8	
Samara	IT	92.7		Tomsk	IT	89.5	
	difference	−14.9			difference	4.3	
Rep. of	IT	82.6		Altaiskii Krai	IT	137.3	
Bashkortostan	difference	−25	Yes		difference	52.1	
Tatarstan	IT	83.3		Buriatiia	IT	115.8	
	difference	−24.3	Yes		difference	30.6	
Moscow Reg.	IT	113.1					
	difference	5.55		**Far East**			
Smolensk	IT	112.9		*Supra-reg. average of Primorskii Krai,*			
	difference	5.3		*Amurskaia oblast' and Khabarovskii Krai:*			
				138.9			
				Primorskii	IT	150	
				Krai	difference	11.1	
				Amurskaia	IT	100.7	Yes
				oblast'	difference	−38.2	
				Khabarovsk	IT	166	
					difference	27.1	

Note: As discussed in Chapter 5, I calculate industrial subsidies as the difference between a region's industrial tariffs and the supra-regional average. Price differentials across regions can serve as a proxy indicator for industrial subsidies. While data on industrial subsidies would be preferable, I doubt that such data exists. They have always been based on informal negotiations, and special deals for select industrial enterprises are concealed in the average industrial tariff data that is publicly available.
Source: Calculated based on UES tariff data.

TABLE A.4.4. *Levels and differentials for regulated prices, 2005*

Average price for all consumers	RR/kwH
European Russia*	0.93
Large Siberian Hydro Regions	0.37
Russian Far East	1.48

* For European Russia, I excluded Tatarstan and Bashkortostan; a discussion of their exceptional status can be found in Chapters 4 and 5.
Note: Based on averages of the largest producing regions in each of these supra-regions, see Tables A.4.1, A.4.2, and A.4.3.
Source: Calculated based on UES tariff data.

TABLE A.4.5. *Price differentials in the liberalized segment of the wholesale market, 2009*

Average price wholesale market, July 2009	RR/kwH
European Russia	0.69
Siberia	0.30
Russian Far East	*prices not liberalized*

Source: ATS, "Итоги работы оптового рынка электроэнергии и мощности за 24.07.2009–30.07.2009," *ATS Moscow*, July 31, 2009.

Bibliography

Abdelal, Rawi. *National Purpose in the World Economy: Post-Soviet States in Comparative Perspective*. Cornell Studies in Political Economy. Ithaca, NY: Cornell University Press, 2001.

Abdelal, Rawi, Mark Blyth, and Craig Parsons, eds. *Constructing the International Economy*. Ithaca, NY: Cornell University Press, 2010.

Abrami, Regine, and David Woodruff. "Toward a Manifesto: Interpretive Materialist Political Economy." Paper presented at the American Political Science Association Annual Conference, August 24, 2004.

Adachi, Yuko. *Building Big Business in Russia: The Impact of Informal Corporate Governance Practices*. London; New York: Routledge, 2010.

Ahrend, Rudiger, and William Tompson. "Unnatural Monopoly: The Endless Wait for Gas Sector Reform in Russia." *Europe-Asia Studies* 57, no. 6 (2005): 801–821.

Akin, William E. *Technocracy and the American Dream: The Technocrat Movement, 1900–1941*. Berkeley: University of California Press, 1977.

Allina-Pisano, Jessica. *The Post-Soviet Potemkin Village: Politics and Property Rights in the Black Earth*. Cambridge: Cambridge University Press, 2008.

Amsden, Alice H. *The Rise of "the Rest": Challenges to the West from Late-Industrialization Economies*. Oxford: Oxford University Press, 2001.

Anderson, Perry. "Russia's Managed Democracy." *London Review of Books*, January 25, 2007.

Andrusz, Gregory D., Michael Harloe, and Iván Szelényi, eds. *Cities after Socialism: Urban and Regional Change and Conflict in Post-Socialist Societies*. Cambridge, MA: Bleckwell, 1996.

Appel, Hilary. "The Ideological Determinants of Liberal Economic Reform: The Case of Privatization." *World Politics* 52, no. 4 (2000): 520–549.

Aron, Leon. "Privatizing Russia's Electricity." *American Enterptise Institutue Russian Outlook* (Summer 2003). Online at http://www.aei.org/article/foreign-and-defense-policy/regional/europe/privatizing-russias-electricity/

"The Merger of Power and Property." *Journal of Democracy* 20, no. 2 (2009): 66–68.

Åslund, Anders. *Building Capitalism: The Transformation of the Former Soviet Bloc.* Cambridge: Cambridge University Press, 2002.

——— *How Capitalism Was Built: The Transformation of Central and Eastern Europe, Russia, and Central Asia.* Cambridge: Cambridge University Press, 2007.

Balzer, Harley. "The Putin Thesis and Russian Energy Policy." *Post-Soviet Affairs* 21, no. 3 (2005): 210–225.

——— "Vladimir Putin's Academic Writings and Russian Natural Resource Policy." *Problems of Post-Communism* 53, no. 1 (2006): 48–49.

Barnes, Andrew Scott. *Owning Russia: The Struggle over Factories, Farms, and Power.* Ithaca, NY: Cornell University Press, 2006.

Bennett, Jane. *Vibrant Matter: A Political Ecology of Things.* Durham, NC: Duke University Press, 2010.

Berk, Gerald, Dennis C. Galvan, and Victoria C. Hattam, eds. *Political Creativity: Reconfiguring Institutional Order and Change.* 1st ed. Philadelphia: University of Pennsylvania Press, 2013.

Blanchard, Olivier, and Michael Kremer. "Disorganization." *The Quarterly Journal of Economics* 112, no. 4 (1997): 1091–1126.

Block, Fred. "Swimming Against the Current: The Rise of a Hidden Developmental State in the United States." *Politics & Society* 36, no. 2 (2008): 169–206.

Block, Fred, and Peter Evans. "The State and the Economy." In *The Handbook of Economic Sociology*, 2nd ed. edited by Neil J. Smelser and Richard Swedberg, 505–526. Princeton, NJ: Princeton University Press, 2005.

Boltanski, Luc, and Laurent Thévenot. *On Justification: Economies of Worth.* Princeton, NJ: Princeton University Press, 2006.

Boute, Anatole. "Response to IEA Consultation Paper 'Toward a More Efficient and Innovative Electricity Sector in Russia.'" *Toward a More Efficient and Innovative Electricity Sector in Russia* (2012). Online at http://papers.ssrn.com/sol3/papers.cfm?abstract_id=2078368.

Boycko, Maxim, Andrei Shleifer, and Robert W. Vishny. "A Theory of Privatisation." *The Economic Journal* 106, no. 435 (March 1996): 309–319.

Boym, Svetlana. *The Future of Nostalgia.* New York: Basic Books, 2001.

Bradshaw, Michael, and Peter Kirkow. "The Energy Crisis in the Russian Far East: Origins and Possible Solutions." *Europe Asia Studies* 50, no. 6 (1998): 1043–1063.

Bremmer, Ian, and Samuel Charap. "The Siloviki in Putin's Russia: Who They Are and What They Want." *The Washington Quarterly* 30, no. 1 (2007): 83–92.

Breslauer, George W. *Gorbachev and Yeltsin as Leaders.* Cambridge: Cambridge University Press, 2002.

Brevnov, Boris. "From Monopoly to Market Maker? Reforming Russia's Power Sector." Belfer Center Programs or Projects: Strengthening Democratic Institutions Project, 2000.

Brie, Michael. "The Moscow Political Regime: The Emergence of a New Urban Political Machine." In *The Politics of Local Government in Russia*, edited by Alfred B. Evans and Vladimir Gel'man, 203–234. Lanham, MD: Rowman & Littlefield, 2004.

Brown, J. David, John S. Earle, and Scott Gehlbach. "Privitization." In *The Oxford Handbook of the Russian Economy*, edited by Michael V. Alexeev and Shlomo Weber, 161–188. Oxford: Oxford University Press, 2013.

Bruszt, Laszlo. "Market Making as State Making: Constitutions and Economic Development in Post-Communist Eastern Europe." *Constitutional Political Economy* 13, no. 1 (2002): 53–72.

Burawoy, Michael, and Katherine Verdery, eds. *Uncertain Transition: Ethnographies of Change in the Postsocialist World*. Lanham, MD: Rowman & Littlefield, 1999.

Burganskij, Alexander, and Irina Elinevskaya. *Hydro Power: Super-Profits or Super-Regulation?* Moscow: Renaissance Capital, 2005.

Çalışkan, Koray. *Market Threads: How Cotton Farmers and Traders Create a Global Commodity*. Princeton, NJ: Princeton University Press, 2010.

Çalışkan, Koray, and Michel Callon. "Economization, Part 1: Shifting Attention from the Economy towards Processes of Economization." *Economy and Society* 38, no. 3 (2009): 369–398.

"Economization, Part 2: A Research Programme for the Study of Markets." *Economy and Society* 39, no. 1 (2010): 1–32.

Callon, Michel, ed. *The Laws of the Markets*. Sociological review monograph series. Oxford: Blackwell Publishers, 1998.

"Careful What You Wish for." *The Economist*, July 14, 2012. Online at http://www.economist.com/node/21558433.

Chaudhry, K. A. "The Myths of the Market and the Common History of Late Developers." *Politics & Society Politics & Society* 21, no. 3 (1993): 245–274.

Colas, Dominique, and Oleg Kharkhordin. *The Materiality of Res Publica: How to Do Things with Public?* Newcastle: Cambridge Scholars, 2009.

Collier, Stephen J. "Pipes." In *Patterned Ground: Entanglements of Nature and Culture*, edited by Stephan Harrison, Steve Pile, and N. J. Thrift, 50–51. London: Reaktion, 2004.

Post-Soviet Social: Neoliberalism, Social Modernity, Biopolitics. Princeton, NJ: Princeton University Press, 2011.

Collier, Stephen J., and Lucan Way. "Beyond the Deficit Model: Social Welfare in Post-Soviet Georgia." *Post-Soviet Affairs* 20, no. 3 (2004): 258–284.

Cooke, Douglas, Alexander Antonyuk, and Isabel Murray. *Toward a More Efficient and Innovative Electricity Sector in Russia*. Paris: OECD Publishing, 2012. Online at http://www.iea.org/publications/insights/russian_electricity_reform-145x206.pdf.

Coopersmith, Jonathan. *The Electrification of Russia, 1880–1926*. Ithaca, NY: Cornell University Press, 1992.

Cornillie, Jan, and Samuel Fankhauser. *The Energy Intensity of Transition Countries*. Working paper series. London: European Bank for Reconstruction and Development, June 2002. http://www.ebrd.com/downloads/research/economics/workingpapers/wp0072.pdf.

"The Energy Intensity of Transition Countries." *Energy Economics* 26, no. 3 (May 2004): 283–295.

Coronil, Fernando. *The Magical State: Nature, Money, and Modernity in Venezuela*. Chicago: University of Chicago Press, 1997.

Crang, Mike, and N. J. Thrift, eds. *Thinking Space*. Critical geographies 9. London; New York: Routledge, 2000.

Cronon, William. *Nature's Metropolis: Chicago and the Great West*. New York: W. W. Norton & Company, 1992.

Derluguian, Georgi M. *Bourdieu's Secret Admirer in the Caucasus: A World-System Biography*. Chicago: University of Chicago Press, 2005.

Doner, Richard F., Bryan K. Ritchie, and Dan Slater. "Systemic Vulnerability and the Origins of Developmental States: Northeast and Southeast Asia in Comparative Perspective." *International Organization* 59, no. 2 (2005): 327–361.

"Dubna's Tale." *The Economist*, July 31, 2008. Online at http://www.economist.com/node/11849278.

Easter, Gerald M. "Revenue Imperatives: States over Markets in Postcommunist Russia." In *The Political Economy of Russia*, edited by Neil Robinson, 51–68. Lanham, MD: Rowman & Littlefield, 2013.

Emirbayer, Mustafa. "Manifesto for a Relational Sociology." *American Journal of Sociology* 103, no. 2 (September 1, 1997): 281–317.

Emirbayer, Mustafa, and Ann Mische. "What Is Agency?" *American Journal of Sociology* 103, no. 4 (January 1, 1998): 962–1023.

Ericson, Richard E. "Does Russia Have a 'Market Economy'?" *East European Politics & Societies* 15, no. 2 (March 1, 2001): 291–319.

European Conference of Ministers of Transport. *Regulatory Reform of Railways in Russia*. Paris: OECD Publishing, 2004.

Evans, Peter B. *Embedded Autonomy: States and Industrial Transformation*. Princeton, NJ: Princeton University Press, 1995.

Fairbanks, Charles H. "The Feudal Analogy." *Journal of Democracy* 11, no. 3 (2000): 34–36.

Feklyunina, Valentina, and Stephen White. "Discourses of 'Krizis': Economic Crisis in Russia and Regime Legitimacy." *Journal of Communist Studies and Transition Politics* 27, no. 3–4 (2011): 385–406.

Fish, M. Steven. *Democracy Derailed in Russia: The Failure of Open Politics*. Cambridge Studies in Comparative Politics. Cambridge: Cambridge University Press, 2005.

Florio, Massimo. "Economists, Privatization in Russia and the Waning of the 'Washington Consensus.'" *Review of International Political Economy* 9, no. 2 (2002): 374–415.

Fortescue, Stephen. *Russia's Oil Barons and Metal Magnates: Oligarchs and the State in Transistion*. Basingstoke, Hampshire; New York: Palgrave Macmillan, 2006.

Fourcade, Marion. *Economists and Societies: Discipline and Profession in the United States, Britain, and France, 1890s to 1990s*. Princeton Studies in Cultural Sociology. Princeton, NJ: Princeton University Press, 2009.

Freeland, Chrystia. *Sale of the Century: Russia's Wild Ride from Communism to Capitalism*. 1st ed. New York: Crown Business, 2000.

Frye, Timothy. *Brokers and Bureaucrats: Building Market Institutions in Russia*. Ann Arbor: University of Michigan Press, 2000.

Building States and Markets after Communism: The Perils of Polarized Democracy. Cambridge University Press, 2010.

"Original Sin, Good Works, and Property Rights in Russia." *World Politics* 58, no. 4 (2006): 479–504.

Frye, Timothy, and Andrei Shleifer. *The Invisible Hand and the Grabbing Hand*. Working Paper. National Bureau of Economic Research, December 1996. Online at http://www.nber.org/papers/w5856.

Gaddy, Clifford G. *The Price of the Past: Russia's Struggle with the Legacy of a Militarized Economy*. Washington, DC: Brookings Institution Press, 1996.

Gans-Morse, Jordan. "Threats to Property Rights in Russia: From Private Coercion to State Aggression." *Post-Soviet Affairs* 28, no. 3 (2012): 263–295.

Gereffi, Gary. "Shifting Governance Structures in Global Commodity Chains, With Special Reference to the Internet." *American Behavioral Scientist* 44, no. 10 (June 1, 2001): 1616–1637.

Gerschenkron, Alexander. *Economic Backwardness in Historical Perspective, a Book of Essays*. Cambridge, MA: Belknap Press, 1962.

Gessen, Keith. "Cell Block Four." *London Review of Books*, February 25, 2010.

Geesen, Masha. *The Man Without a Face: The Unlikely Rise of Vladimir Putin*. New York: Riverhead Books, 2012.

Gingrich, Jane R. *Making Markets in the Welfare State: The Politics of Varying Market Reforms*. Cambridge: Cambridge University Press, 2011.

Goldgeier, James M., and Michael McFaul. "What to Do about Russia?" *Policy Review* 133 (2005): 45–62.

Goldman, Marshall I. *Petrostate: Putin, Power, and the New Russia*. Oxford: Oxford University Press, 2008.

Götz, Roland. "Nach dem Gaskonflikt: Wirtschaftliche Konsequenzen für Russland, die Ukraine und die EU." *Stiftung Wissenschaft und Politik: SWP-Aktuell no.3* (2006): 1–4.

Graham, Loren R. *Lonely Ideas: Can Russia Compete?* Cambridge, MA: MIT Press, 2013.

The Ghost of the Executed Engineer: Technology and the Fall of the Soviet Union. Cambridge, MA: Harvard University Press, 1993.

Granberg, Alexander, Alexander Pelyasov, and Ul Vavilova. "Programs of Regional Development Revisited: Case of the Russian Federation." In *ERSA Conference Papers*. Vrije Universitet Amsterdam: European Regional Science Association, 2005. Online at http://www-sre.wu.ac.at/ersa/ersaconfs/ersa05/papers/101.pdf.

Granovetter, Mark, and Patrick McGuire. "The Making of an Industry: Electricity in the United States." In *The Law of Markets*, edited by Michel Callon, 147–173. Oxford: Blackwell, 1998.

Guriev, Sergei, and Andrei Rachinsky. "Ownership Concentration in Russian Industry." *Background paper for Country Economic Memorandum for Russia, World Bank*, 2004. Online at http://www.cefir.ru/papers/WP45_OwnershipConcentration.pdf.

"The Role of Oligarchs in Russian Capitalism." *The Journal of Economic Perspectives* 19, no. 1 (2005): 131–150.

Gustafson, Thane. *Capitalism Russian-Style*. Cambridge; New York: Cambridge University Press, 1999.

Haggard, Stephan. *The Political Economy of Democratic Transitions*. Princeton, NJ: Princeton University Press, 1995.

Hancher, Leigh. "Slow and Not so Sure: Europe's Long March to Electricity Market Liberalization." *The Electricity Journal* 10, no. 9 (November 1997): 92–101.

Hanson, Philip. "The Center versus the Periphery in Russian Economic Policy." *RFE/RL Research Report* 3, no. 17 (1994): 23–28.

"The Russian Economic Recovery: Do Four Years of Growth Tell Us That the Fundamentals Have Changed?" *Europe-Asia Studies* 55, no. 3 (2003): 365–382.

Hausmann, Ricardo, and Dani Rodrik. "Economic Development as Self-Discovery." *Journal of Development Economics* 72, no. 2 (December 2003): 603–633.

Hellman, Joel S. "Winners Take All: The Politics of Partial Reform in Postcommunist Transitions." *World Politics* 50, no. 2 (1998): 203–234.

Hellman, Joel S, Geraint Jones, and Daniel Kaufmann. "Seize the State, Seize the Day: State Capture and Influence in Transition Economies." *Journal of Comparative Economics* 31, no. 4 (December 2003): 751–773.

Henry, Laura A., Soili Nysten-Haarala, Svetlana Tulaeva, and Maria Tysiachniouk, "Corporate Social Responsibility and the Oil Industry in the Russian Arctic: Global Norms and Neo-Paternalism." Unpublished manuscript under review.

Herrera, Yoshiko M. *Imagined Economies: The Sources of Russian Regionalism*. Cambridge Studies in Comparative Politics. Cambridge: Cambridge University Press, 2005.

Herrigel, Gary. *Industrial Constructions: The Sources of German Industrial Power*. Cambridge: Cambridge University Press, 2000.

Manufacturing Possibilities: Creative Action and Industrial Recomposition in the United States, Germany, and Japan. Oxford: Oxford University Press, 2010.

Hill, Fiona, and Clifford G. Gaddy. *The Siberian Curse: How Communist Planners Left Russia out in the Cold*. Washington, DC: Brookings Institution Press, 2003.

Hoff, Karla, and Joseph E. Stiglitz. "After the Big Bang? Obstacles to the Emergence of the Rule of Law in Post-Communist Societies." *American Economic Review* 94, no. 3 (2004): 753–763.

"Exiting a Lawless State." *The Economic Journal* 118, no. 531 (2008): 1474–1497.

Hoffman, David E. *The Oligarchs: Wealth and Power in the New Russia*. New York: Public Affairs, 2003.

Hughes, Thomas Parke. *Networks of Power: Electrification in Western Society, 1880–1930*. Baltimore, MD: Johns Hopkins University Press, 1983.

Hunt, Sally. *Making Competition Work in Electricity*. New York: John Wiley & Sons, 2002.

International Energy Agency. *Coal Mine Methane in Russia: Capturing the Safety and Environmental Benefits.* Paris: OECD/IEA, 2010. Online at http://www.iea.org/publications/freepublications/publication/Coal_Mine_Methane_Russian.pdf.

  Russia Energy Survey 2002. Paris: OECD/IEA, 2002. Online at http://www.iea.org/publications/freepublications/publication/russia_energy_survey.pdf.

Jabko, Nicolas. *Playing the Market: A Political Strategy for Uniting Europe, 1985–2005.* Ithaca, NY: Cornell University Press, 2006.

Janos, Andrew C. *The Politics of Backwardness in Hungary, 1825–1945.* Princeton, NJ: Princeton University Press, 2012.

Johnson, Chalmers. *MITI and the Japanese Miracle: The Growth of Industrial Policy, 1925–1975.* Stanford, CA: Stanford University Press, 1982.

Johnson, Juliet. *A Fistful of Rubles: The Rise and Fall of the Russian Banking System.* Ithaca, NY: Cornell University Press, 2000.

Jordana, Jacint, David Levi-Faur, and Imma Puig. "The Limits of Europeanization: Regulatory Reforms in the Spanish and Portuguese Telecommunications and Electricity Sectors." *Governance* 19, no. 3 (2006): 437–464.

Joskow, Paul L. "Markets for Power in the United States: An Interim Assessment." *Energy Journal* 27, no. 1 (2006): 1–36.

Kharkhordin, Oleg. *Main Concepts of Russian Politics.* Lanham, MD: University Press of America, 2005.

Kirkow, Peter. "Regional Warlordism in Russia: The Case of Primorskii Krai." *Europe-Asia Studies* 47, no. 6 (1995): 923–947.

Kohli, Atul. *State-Directed Development: Political Power and Industrialization in the Global Periphery.* Cambridge: Cambridge University Press, 2004.

Kornai, János. *The Socialist System: The Political Economy of Communism.* Princeton, NJ: Princeton University Press, 1992.

Kotkin, Stephen. *Magnetic Mountain: Stalinism as a Civilization.* Berkeley: University of California Press, 1995.

Kryshtanovskaya, Olga, and Stephen White. "From Soviet Nomenklatura to Russian Élite." *Europe-Asia Studies* 48, no. 5 (1996): 711–733.

  "Putin's Militocracy." *Post-Soviet Affairs* 19, no. 4 (2003): 289–306.

Kuchins, Andrew, ed. *Russia after the Fall.* Washington, DC: Brookings Institution Press, 2002.

Lane, David Stuart. *The Political Economy of Russian Oil.* Lanham, MD: Rowman & Littlefield, 1999.

Lapidus, Gail W. "Asymmetrical Federalism and State Breakdown in Russia." *Post-Soviet Affairs* 15, no. 1 (1999): 74–82.

LaPorte, Jody, and Danielle N. Lussier. "Revisiting the Leninist Legacy: Conceptualization and Measurement for Meaningful Comparison". Paper presented at the Annual Conference of the American Political Science Association, August 28–31, Boston, MA, 2008.

  "What Is the Leninist Legacy? Assessing Twenty Years of Scholarship." *Slavic Review* 70, no. 3 (October 1, 2011): 637–654.

Latour, Bruno, and Peter Weibel. *Making Things Public: Atmospheres of Democracy.* Cambridge, MA: MIT Press, 2005.

Lie, John. "Sociology of Markets." *Annual Review of Sociology* 23 (January 1, 1997): 341–360.

Linz, Susan J., and Gary Krueger. "Enterprise Restructuring in Russia's Transition Economy: Formal and Informal Mechanisms." *Comparative Economic Studies* 40, no. 2 (1998): 5–52.

Litwack, J., and W. Thompson. *OECD Economic Survey of the Russian Federation.* Paris: OECD, 2002.

Luong, Pauline Jones, and Erika Weinthal. "Contra Coercion: Russian Tax Reform, Exogenous Shocks, and Negotiated Institutional Change." *American Political Science Review* 98, no. 1 (2004): 139–152.

MacKenzie, Donald A. *Material Markets How Economic Agents Are Constructed.* Oxford: Oxford University Press, 2009.

Markus, Stanislav. "Capitalists of All Russia, Unite! Business Mobilization Under Debilitated Dirigisme." *Polity* 39, no. 3 (2007): 277–304.

"Corporate Governance as Political Insurance: Firm-Level Institutional Creation in Emerging Markets and beyond." *Socio-Economic Review* 6, no. 1 (January 1, 2008): 69–98.

Marx, Karl, and Friedrich Engels. "The Future Results of British Rule in India." In *The Marx-Engels Reader*, 2nd ed., edited by Robert C. Tucker, 659. New York: Norton, 1978.

McFaul, Michael, and Tova Perlmutter, eds. *Privatization, Conversion, and Enterprise Reform in Russia.* Boulder, CO: Westview Press, 1994.

McFaul, Michael, and Kathryn Stoner-Weiss. "The Myth of the Authoritarian Model: How Putin's Crackdown Holds Russia Back." *Foreign Affairs* 87, no. 1 (2008): 68–84.

Mellow, Craig. "Is This a Way to Create Capitalism? Maybe So." *Institutional Investor*, June 1, 2003.

Minakir, P. A. *Economic Cooperation between the Russian Far East and Asia-Pacific Countries.* Khabarovsk: RIOTIP, 2007.

Mitchell, Timothy. *Rule of Experts: Egypt, Techno-Politics, Modernity.* Berkeley: University of California Press, 2002.

Morey, Mathew J., and Christina C. Forbes. "How Can FERC Find Its Way out of the SMD Cul-de-Sac? Stimulate the Transmission Sector!" *The Electricity Journal* 16, no. 7 (2003): 74–85.

Murillo, María Victoria. "Political Bias in Policy Convergence: Privatization Choices in Latin America." *World Politics* 54, no. 4 (2002): 462–493.

Political Competition, Partisanship, and Policymaking in Latin American Public Utilities. Cambridge: Cambridge University Press, 2009.

Nelson, Lynn D. *Property to the People: The Struggle for Radical Economic Reform in Russia.* Armonk, NY: M.E. Sharpe, 1994.

Radical Reform in Yeltsin's Russia: Political, Economic, and Social Dimensions. Armonk, NY: M.E. Sharpe, 1995.

O Riain, Sean. "The Flexible Developmental State: Globalization, Information Technology and the 'Celtic Tiger.'" *Politics and Society* 28, no. 2 (June 2000): 157–193.

Orttung, Robert W. "Business and Politics in the Russian Regions." *Problems of Post-Communism* 51, no. 2 (2004): 48–60.

Padgett, John Frederick, and Walter W Powell. *The Emergence of Organizations and Markets.* Princeton, NJ: Princeton University Press, 2012.

Palamarchuk, Sergey I., Sergei V. Podkovalnikov, and Nikolai I. Voropai. "Getting the Electricity Sector on Track in Russia." *The Electricity Journal* 14, no. 8 (October 2001): 52–58.

Petrosyan, Kristine. *What Is the Current Status of Russian Electricity Sector in the Light of Restructuring Laws and RAO UES Breakup Strategy.* University of Dundee, UK: Centre for Energy, Petroleum and Mineral Law and Policy, 2004.

Petrov, Nikolay. "How Have the Presidential Envoys Changed the Administrative-Political Balance of Putin's Regime?" In *The Dynamics of Russian Politics: Putin's Reform of Federal-Regional Relations,* Vol. 2, edited by Peter Reddaway and Robert W. Orttung, 33–64. Lanham, MD: Rowman & Littlefield, 2005.

Pierson, Paul. *Politics in Time: History, Institutions, and Social Analysis.* Princeton, NJ: Princeton University Press, 2004.

Pirani, Simon. "Rusal Leaves Competitors Counting Their Costs." *Metals Bulletin,* June 9, 2002. Online at http://piraniarchive.wordpress.com/home/about/rusal-leaves-competitors-counting-their-costs/.

Pittman, Russell. "Chinese Railway Reform and Competition: Lessons from the Experience in Other Countries." *Journal of Transport Economics and Policy (JTEP)* 38, no. 2 (2004): 309–332.

"Railway and Electricity Restructuring in Russia: On the Road To... Where?" Online at http://uisrussia.srcc.msu.ru/docs/nov/leontief/2007/papers/russel.doc.

"Russian Railways Reform and the Problem of Non-Discriminatory Access to Infrastructure." *Annals of Public and Cooperative Economics* 75, no. 2 (2004): 167–192.

Platz, Stephanie. "The Shape of National Time: Daily Life, History and Identity During Armenia's Transition to Independence 1991–1994." In *Altering States: Ethnographies of Transition in Eastern Europe and the Former Soviet Union,* edited by Daphne Berdahl, Matti Bunzl, and Martha Lampland, 114–138. Ann Arbor: University of Michigan Press, 2000.

Polanyi, Karl. *The Great Transformation: The Political and Economic Origins of Our Time.* Boston, MA: Beacon Press, 1944.

Pop-Eleches, Grigore. "Historical Legacies and Post-Communist Regime Change." *Journal of Politics* 69, no. 4 (2007): 908–926.

Post, Alison E. "Pathways for Redistribution: Privatisation, Regulation and Incentives for pro-Poor Investment in the Argentine Water Sector." *International Journal of Public Policy* 4, no. 1 (January 1, 2009): 51–75.

Prasad, Monica. *The Land of Too Much: American Abundance and the Paradox of Poverty.* Cambridge, MA: Harvard University Press, 2013.

Przeworski, Adam. *Democracy and the Market: Political and Economic Reforms in Eastern Europe and Latin America.* Studies in Rationality and Social Change. Cambridge: Cambridge University Press, 1991.

Rasell, Michael. "Neoliberalism in the North: The Transformation of Social Policy in Russia's Northern Periphery." *Polar Geography* 32, no. 3–4 (2009): 91–109.

Reddaway, Peter, and Robert W. Orttung, eds. *The Dynamics of Russian Politics: Putin's Reform of Federal-Regional Relations*. Vol. 1. 2 vols. Lanham, MD: Rowman & Littlefield, 2004.

——— eds. *The Dynamics of Russian Politics: Putin's Reform of Federal-Regional Relations*. Vol. 2. 2 vols. Lanham, MD: Rowman & Littlefield, 2005.

Reeves, Madeleine. "The Latest Revolution." *London Review of Books*, May 13, 2010.

Robinson, Neil. "Introduction: The Political Problems of Russian Capitalism." In *The Political Economy of Russia*, edited by Neil Robinson, 1–15. Lanham, MD: Rowman & Littlefield, 2013.

Rodrik, Dani. *One Economics, Many Recipes: Globalization, Institutions, and Economic Growth*. Princeton, NJ: Princeton University Press, 2007.

Roe, Emery, and Paul R. Schulman. *High Reliability Management: Operating on the Edge*. High Reliability and Crisis Management. Stanford, CA: Stanford Business Books, 2008.

Rogers, Douglas. "The Materiality of the Corporation: Oil, Gas, and Corporate Social Technologies in the Remaking of a Russian Region." *American Ethnologist* 39, no. 2 (2012): 284–296.

Rutland, Peter. "Business-State Relations in Russia". Berlin, 2005. Online at http://prutland.web.wesleyan.edu/Documents/berlin1.pdf.

——— "Oil and Politics in Russia." Paper prepared for the American Political Science Association Annual Convention, Philadelphia, PA, September 2, 2006.

——— "Power Struggle: Reforming the Electricity Industry." In *The Dynamics of Russian Politics: Putin's Reform of Federal-Regional Relations*, Vol. 2, edited by Peter Reddaway and Robert W. Orttung, 267–294. Lanham, MD: Rowman & Littlefield, 2005.

——— "The Business Sector in Post-Soviet Russia." In *Routledge Handbook of Russian Politics and Society*, edited by Graeme J. Gill and James Young, 288–304. London: Routledge, 2012.

——— "The Oligarchs and Economic Development." In *After Putin's Russia: Past Imperfect, Future Uncertain*, edited by Stephen K. Wegren and Dale Herspring, 159–182. Lanham, MD: Rowman & Littlefield, 2010.

Sabel, Charles F. "Self-Discovery as a Coordination Problem." In *Export Pioneers in Latin America*, edited by Charles F. Sabel, Eduardo Fernández-Arias, Ricardo Hausmann, Andrés Rodríguez-Clare, and Ernesto Stein, 1–46. Washington, DC: Inter-American Development Bank, 2012.

Sabonis-Helf, Theresa. "The Unified Energy Systems of Russia (RAO-UES) in Central Asia and the Caucasus: Nets of Interdependence." *Demoraktizatsiya* 15, no. 4 (2007): 429–444.

Sakwa, Richard. *Russian Politics and Society*. 4th ed., London; New York: Routledge, 2008.

——— "Systemic Stalemate: *Reiderstvo* and the Dual State." In *The Political Economy of Russia*, edited by Neil Robinson, 69–96. Lanham, MD: Rowman & Littlefield, 2013.

The Quality of Freedom: Khodorkovsky, Putin, and the Yukos Affair. Oxford: Oxford University Press, 2009.

Sargsyan, Gevorg, Ali Balabanyan, and Denzel Hankinson. *From Crisis to Stability in the Armenian Power Sector: Lessons Learned from Armenia's Energy Reform Experience.* World Bank working paper no. 74. Washington, DC: World Bank, 2006.

Scott, Aleka. "FERC Needs to Listen to the Regions before Racing to Its Standard Market Design." *The Electricity Journal* 15, no. 9 (2002): 91–98.

Scott, James C. *Seeing Like a State: How Certain Schemes to Improve the Human Condition Have Failed.* New Haven, CT: Yale University Press, 1998.

Shandarov, Maksim. "Siberian Federal Okrug." In *The Dynamics of Russian Politics: Putin's Reform of Federal-Regional Relations*, Vol. 1, edited by Peter Reddaway and Robert W. Orttung, 211–242. Lanham, MD: Rowman & Littlefield, 2004.

Sharma, Deepak. "The Multidimensionality of Electricity Reform – an Australian Perspective." *Energy Policy* 31, no. 11 (2003): 1093–1102.

Shevtsova, Lilia Fedorovna. *Yeltsin's Russia: Myths and Reality.* Washington, DC: Carnegie Endowment for International Peace, 1999.

Shlapentokh, Vladimir. *Contemporary Russia as a Feudal Society: A New Perspective on the Post-Soviet Era.* 1st ed. New York: Palgrave Macmillan, 2007.

Shleifer, Andrei, and Daniel Treisman. "A Normal Country." *Foreign Affairs* (April 2004), online at http://www.foreignaffairs.com/articles/59707/andrei-shleifer-and-daniel-treisman/a-normal-country.

Without a Map: Political Tactics and Economic Reform in Russia. Cambridge, MA: MIT Press, 2000.

Shleifer, Andrei, and Robert W. Vishny. *The Grabbing Hand: Government Pathologies and Their Cures.* Cambridge, MA: Harvard University Press, 1998.

Sidorenko, Alexandra. *Electricity in Russia: The impacts and benefits of structural reforms in transport, energy and telecommunications sectors.* APEC Policy Support Unit, January 2011.

Sikkink, Kathryn. *Ideas and Institutions: Developmentalism in Brazil and Argentina.* Cornell Studies in Political Economy. Ithaca, NY: Cornell University Press, 1991.

Sil, Rudra and Calvin Chen, "Communist Legacies, Postcommunist Transformations, and the Fate of Organized Labor in Russia and China," *Studies in Comparative International Development* 41, no. 2 (2006): 62–87.

Sim, Li-Chen. *The Rise and Fall of Privatization in the Russian Oil Industry.* New York: Palgrave Macmillan, 2008.

Smelser, Neil J., and Richard Swedberg, eds. *The Handbook of Economic Sociology.* 2nd ed. Princeton, NJ: Princeton University Press, 2005.

Snyder, Richard. *Politics after Neoliberalism: Reregulation in Mexico.* Cambridge Studies in Comparative Politics. Cambridge: Cambridge University Press, 2001.

Solanko, Laura. *The Policy of National Champions and Russian Competitiveness.* Expert Position. Institute for Economies in Transition at the Bank of Finland, June 2007. Online at http://www.bof.fi/.

Solnick, Steven. "The New Federal Structure: More Centralized, or More of the Same?" *Policy Memo* 161 (2000).

Solnick, Steven Lee. *Stealing the State: Control and Collapse in Soviet Institutions.* Russian Research Center Studies 89. Cambridge, MA: Harvard University Press, 1998.

Spanjer, Aldo. "Russian Gas Price Reform and the EU–Russia Gas Relationship: Incentives, Consequences and European Security of Supply." *Energy Policy* 35, no. 5 (May 2007): 2889–2898.

Stammler-Grossmann, Anna. "Reshaping the North of Russia: Towards a Conception of Space." In *Northern Research Forum*, 24–27, 2007. Online at http://www.rha.is/static/files/NRF/OpenAssemblies/Anchorage2008/stammlergrossman_5thnrf_position_paper_session4.pdf.

Stark, David Charles. *Postsocialist Pathways: Transforming Politics and Property in East Central Europe.* Cambridge Studies in Comparative Politics. Cambridge: Cambridge University Press, 1998.

Starr, Paul. "The Meaning of Privatization." *Yale Law & Policy Review* 6 (1988): 6–41.

Stern, Jon, and John Cubbin. *Regulatory Effectiveness: The Impact of Regulation and Regulatory Governance Arrangements on Electricity Industry Outcomes.* Washington, DC: World Bank Publications, 2005.

Stern, Jonathan P. *The Future of Russian Gas and Gazprom.* Oxford: Oxford University Press, 2005.

Stiglitz, Joseph E. "Who Lost Russia?" In *Globalization and Its Discontents*, 133–165. New York: W. W. Norton & Company, 2002.

Stoner, Kathryn. *Local Heroes: The Political Economy of Russian Regional Governance.* Princeton, NJ: Princeton University Press, 1997.

Tarr, David G., and Peter D. Thomson. "The Merits of Dual Pricing of Russian Natural Gas." *World Economy* 27, no. 8 (2004): 1173–1194.

Taylor, Frederick Winslow. *The Principles of Scientific Management.* New York: Harper, 1914.

Thelen, Kathleen Ann. *How Institutions Evolve: The Political Economy of Skills in Germany, Britain, the United States, and Japan.* Cambridge Studies in Comparative Politics. Cambridge: Cambridge University Press, 2004.

Thompson, Niobe. *Settlers on the Edge: Identity and Modernization on Russia's Arctic Frontier.* Vancouver: University of British Columbia Press, 2009.

Settlers on the Edge: Identity and Modernization on Russia's Arctic Frontier. Vancouver: University of British Columbia Press, 2009.

Tompson, William. "Electricity Legislation Passes Second Reading." In *Prospects for the Russian Federation Project.* London: Royal Institute of International Affairs: Russia and Eurasia Programme, 2003: 1–5.

Treisman, Daniel. *After the Deluge: Regional Crises and Political Consolidation in Russia.* Ann Arbor: University of Michigan Press, 1999.

"Deciphering Russia's Federal Finance: Fiscal Appeasement in 1995 and 1996." *Europe-Asia Studies* 50, no. 5 (1998): 893–906.

Trenin, Dmitri. "Russia Redefines Itself and Its Relations with the West." *The Washington Quarterly* 30, no. 2 (2007): 95–105.

Trumbull, Gunnar. *Strength in Numbers the Political Power of Weak Interests.* Cambridge, MA: Harvard University Press, 2012.

Tsygankova, Marina. "An Evaluation of Alternative Scenarios for the Gazprom Monopoly of Russian Gas Exports." *Energy Economics* 34, no. 1 (January 2012): 153–161.

"When Is a Break-up of Gazprom Good for Russia?" *Energy Economics* 32, no. 4 (July 2010): 908–917.

Van de Walle, Nicolas. "Privatization in Developing Countries: A Review of the Issues." *World Development* 17, no. 5 (May 1989): 601–615.

Vasiliev, Sergei, A. B. Chubais, and Andrei Illarionov. *Ten Years of Russian Economic Reform : A Collection of Papers.* London: Centre for Research into Post-Communist Economics, 1999.

Veblen, Thorstein. *The Theory of Business Enterprise.* New York: Scribner, 1904.

Verdery, Katherine. *The Vanishing Hectare: Property and Value in Postsocialist Transylvania.* Ithaca, NY: Cornell University Press, 2003.

What Was Socialism, and What Comes Next? Princeton, NJ: Princeton University Press, 1996.

Vine, Edward, Jan Hamrin, Nick Eyre, David Crossley, Michelle Maloney, and Greg Watt. "Public Policy Analysis of Energy Efficiency and Load Management in Changing Electricity Businesses." *Energy Policy* 31, no. 5 (April 2003): 405–430.

Vogel, Steven. *Freer Markets, More Rules: Regulatory Reform in Advanced Industrial Countries.* Ithaca, NY: Cornell University Press, 1996.

Volkov, Vadim. "Hostile Enterprise Takeovers: Russia's Economy in 1998–2002." *Review of Central and East European Law* 29, no. 4 (2004): 527–548.

"Standard Oil and Yukos in the Context of Early Capitalism in the United States and Russia." *Demokratizatsyia* 16, no. 3 (2008): 240–264.

Von Meier, Alexandra. "Occupational Cultures as a Challenge to Technological Innovation." *IEEE Transactions on Engineering Management* 46, no. 1 (1999): 101–114.

Wade, Robert. "After the Crisis: Industrial Policy and the Developmental State in Low-Income Countries." *Global Policy* 1, no. 2 (2010): 150–161.

Governing the Market: Economic Theory and the Role of Government in East Asian Industrialization. Princeton, NJ: Princeton University Press, 1990.

"The Mystery of US Industrial Policy: The Developmental State in Disguise." *Transforming Economies: Making industrial policy work for growth, jobs and development.* Jose M. Salazar-Xirinachs, Irmgard Nübler, Richard Kozul-Wright eds. Geneva: International Labor Organization (2014): 379–400..

"What Strategies Are Viable for Developing Countries Today? The World Trade Organization and the Shrinking of 'Development Space.'" *Review of International Political Economy* 10, no. 4 (2003): 621–644.

Weaver, Catherine. "The Meaning of Development: Constructing the World Bank's Good Governance Agenda." In *Constructing the International Economy,* edited by Rawi Abdelal, Mark Blyth, and Craig Parsons, 47–67. Ithaca, NY: Cornell University Press, 2010.

Wegren, Stephen K., and Dale Herspring, eds. *After Putin's Russia: Past Imperfect, Future Uncertain.* Lanham, MD: Rowman & Littlefield, 2010.

Weingast, Barry, and Rui De Figueiredo. "Pathologies of Federalism, Russian Style: Political Institutions and Economic Transition", April 2002. Online at http://faculty.haas.berkeley.edu/rui/mpfrussia.pdf.

"Russian Federalism: A Contradiction in Terms." *Hoover Digest*, no. 4 (2001), available online: http://www.hoover.org/research/russian-federalism-contradiction-terms.

Wengle, Susanne. "Power Politics Electricity Sector Reforms in Post-Soviet Russia." *Russian Analytical Digest*, no. 27. Center for Security Studies ETH Zurich (2007): 6–10..

"Engineers versus Managers; experts, market-making and state-building in Putin's Russia." *Economy and Society*, 41, no. 3 (2012): 435–467.

"Post-Soviet Developmentalism and the Political Economy of Russia's Electricity Sector Liberalization." *Studies in Comparative International Development* 47, no. 1 (2012): 75–114.

Wengle, Susanne, and Michael Rasell. "The Monetisation of L'goty: Changing Patterns of Welfare Politics and Provision in Russia." *Europe-Asia Studies* 60, no. 5 (2008): 739–756.

Woodruff, David. *Money Unmade: Barter and the Fate of Russian Capitalism.* Ithaca, NY: Cornell University Press, 1999.

Woodruff, David M. "Property Rights in Context: Privatization's Legacy for Corporate Legality in Poland and Russia." *Studies in Comparative International Development* 38, no. 4 (2004): 82–108.

Yakovlev, Andrei. "The Evolution of Business – State Interaction in Russia: From State Capture to Business Capture?" *Europe-Asia Studies* 58, no. 7 (2006): 1033–1056.

Yudashkina, Galina, and Sergey Pobochy. "Regulation of the Electricity Sector in Russia: Regional Aspects." *Quantile*, no. 2 (2007): 107–130.

Yurchak, Alexei. "Entrepreneurial Governmentality in Post-Socialist Russia: A Cultural Investigation of Business Practices." In *The New Entrepreneurs of Europe and Asia. Patterns of Business Development in Russia, Eastern Europe and China.* New York: Wiley, 2002.

Everything Was Forever, until It Was No More: The Last Soviet Generation. Princeton, NJ: Princeton University Press, 2013.

"Russian Neoliberal: The Entrepreneurial Ethic and the Spirit of 'True Careerism.'" *The Russian Review* 62, no. 1 (2003): 72–90.

Zhuravskaya, Ekaterina, and Sergei Guriev. "Why Russia Is Not South Korea." *Journal of International Affairs* 63, no. 2 (2010): 125–139.

Zysman, John, and Abraham Newman, eds. *How Revolutionary Was the Digital Revolution? National Responses, Market Transitions, and Global Technology.* Innovation and Technology in the World Economy. Stanford, CA: Stanford Business Books, 2006.

Russian-Language Sources
(Note: newspaper articles are fully cited in footnotes and not repeated here)

Администрация Приморского края. *Стратегия социально-экономического развития Приморского края на 2004–2010 гг., под общей редакцией С.М. Дарькина,* Владивосток: Издательство ТЦСП, 2004.

Актуальные вопросы государственного регулирования регионального развития. Байкальский Государственный Университет Экономики и Права, Иркутск, 2002.

Алексеев, Вениамин Васильевич. *Электрификация Сибири: Историческое Исследование. 1885–1950. I.* Наука, 1973.

Беляев, Л. С. "Недостатки Реализуемой Концепции Реформирования Электроэнергетики России и Необходимость Ее Корректировки." *Иркутск: Институт систем энергетики им. Л.А. Мелентьева* (2006).

Бергер, М., и О. Проскурина. "Крест Чубайса." *Москва: Колибри* (2008).

Бриль, Р. Я., и И. М. Хейстер. *Экономика Социалистической Энергетики: Допущено в Качестве Учебника для Инженерно-Экономических Вузов и Факультетов.* Высшая школа, 1966.

Вестник региональной энергокомиссии Красноярского края. Январь 2005.

Федеральная служба по тарифам (ФСТ). *Информационно-аналитический бюллетень: тарифы в электроэнергетике.* Москва: ФСТ/Академией народного хозяйства, Сентябрь 2004.

Губогло, М. Н. "Федерализм Власти и Власть Федерализма." *Москва: ИнтелТех* 1997.

Гурвич, Е. "Оценка Эффекта Удешевления Энергетических Ресурсов." *Энергетическая политика* 1997, no. 3.

Калашников, В. Д., и Гулидов, Р. В. "Основные предпосылки в анализе развития ТЭК Дальнего Востока." *Стратегия развития Дальнего Востока: возможности и перспективы, Том I.* Хабаровск, 2003.

Колесников, А. В. *Неизвестный Чубайс: Страницы из Биографии.* Москва: Захаров, 2003.

Ленин, В. И. *О Развитии Тяжелой Промышленности и Электрификации Страны.* Москва: Государственное издательство политической литературы, 1956.

Лобунец, Анна Валентиновна. "Перспективы Развития Энергетики Приморского Края с Учетом Интеграционных Процессов в Северо-Восточной Азии." Дальневост. гос. у. Владивосток, 2004.

Логинов Е. Л. и др. "Либерализация национального рынка газа: проблемы реформирования российской экономики," *Экономика региона,* 8/23, 2005.

Материалы к энергетической стратегии Сибири. Новосибирск, Сибирское отделение РАН, 1997.

Мелентьев, Лев Александрович. *Очерки Истории Отечественной Энергетики: Развитие Научно-Технической Мысли.* Наука, 1987.

Министерство регионального развития Российской Федерации. Several documents related to regional development are available on the Minregio website; documents published before 2013 are now archived at http://old.minregion.ru/

Концепция совершенствования региональной политики в Российской Федерации (2008).

Концепция Стратегии социально-экономического развития регионов Российской Федерации (2005).

Программа Экономического и социального развития Дальнего Востока и Забайкалья на период до 2013 года.

Требования/технический стандарт к стратегии социально-экономического развития субъекта РФ.

Ножиков, Ю. А. *Я Это Видел, или Жизнь Российского Губернатора, Рассказанная Им Самим.* Иркутская областная типография №1, Иркутск, 1998.

Свет негасимый: энергетике Приангарья 50 лет. Восточно-Сибирская издательская компания, Иркутск, 2004.

Сожинов, В. А. "Регулирование экономического развития на уровне субъекта федерации," *Эко*, 3, 2006.

Тепловые генерирующе компании РАО ЕЭС РОССИИ. Москва: ЮЭС, 2006.

Хлебников, Владимир Викторович. *Рынок Электроэнергии в России.* Москва: ВЛАДОС, 2005.

Энергетическая стратегия России на период до 2020 года. Online at http://minenergo.gov.ru/aboutminen/energostrategy/.

Index

Lightning Source UK Ltd.
Milton Keynes UK
UKHW022144250719
346845UK00020B/427/P